Rome's Most Faithful Daughter

Ohio University Press Polish and Polish-American Studies Series

Series Editor: John J. Bukowczyk

Framing the Polish Home: Postwar Cultural Constructions of Hearth, Nation, and Self, edited by Bożena Shallcross

Traitors and True Poles: Narrating a Polish-American Identity, 1880–1939, by Karen Majewski

Auschwitz, Poland, and the Politics of Commemoration, 1945–1979, by Jonathan Huener

The Exile Mission: The Polish Political Diaspora and Polish Americans, 1939–1956, by Anna D. Jaroszyńska-Kirchmann

The Grasinski Girls: The Choices They Had and the Choices They Made, by Mary Patrice Erdmans

Testaments: Two Novellas of Emigration and Exile, by Danuta Mostwin

The Clash of Moral Nations: Cultural Politics in Piłsudski's Poland, 1926–1935, by Eva Plach

Holy Week: A Novel of the Warsaw Ghetto Uprising, by Jerzy Andrzejewski

The Law of the Looking Glass: Cinema in Poland, 1896–1939, by Sheila Skaff

Rome's Most Faithful Daughter: The Catholic Church and Independent Poland, 1914–1939, by Neal Pease

SERIES ADVISORY BOARD

M. B. B. Biskupski, Central Connecticut State University
Robert E. Blobaum, West Virginia University
Anthony Bukoski, University of Wisconsin-Superior
Bogdana Carpenter, University of Michigan
Mary Patrice Erdmans, Central Connecticut State University
Thomas S. Gladsky, Central Missouri State University (ret.)
Padraic Kenney, Indiana University
John J. Kulczycki, University of Illinois at Chicago (ret.)
Ewa Morawska, University of Essex
Antony Polonsky, Brandeis University
Brian Porter-Szûcs, University of Michigan
James S. Pula, Purdue University North Central
Thaddeus C. Radzilowski, Piast Institute
Daniel Stone, University of Winnipeg
Adam Walaszek, Jagiellonian University
Theodore R. Weeks, Southern Illinois University

Rome's Most Faithful Daughter

The Catholic Church and Independent Poland, 1914–1939

Neal Pease

OHIO UNIVERSITY PRESS
ATHENS

Ohio University Press, Athens, Ohio 45701
www.ohioswallow.com
© 2009 by Ohio University Press
All rights reserved

To obtain permission to quote, reprint, or otherwise reproduce or distribute material from Ohio University Press publications, please contact our rights and permissions department at (740) 593-1154 or (740) 593-4536 (fax).

Printed in the United States of America
Ohio University Press books are printed on acid-free paper ∞ ™

17 16 15 14 12 11 10 09 5 4 3 2 1

Library of Congress Cataloging-in-Publication Data

Pease, Neal.
Rome's most faithful daughter : the Catholic Church and independent Poland, 1914–1939 / Neal Pease.
p. cm. — (Ohio University Press Polish and Polish-American studies series)
Includes bibliographical references and index.
ISBN 978-0-8214-1855-0 (cloth : alk. paper) — ISBN 978-0-8214-1856-7 (paper : alk. paper)
1. Catholic Church—Foreign relations—Poland. 2. Poland—Foreign relations—Catholic Church. 3. Poland—Church history—20th century. 4. Catholic Church—Poland—History—20th century. 5. Catholic Church—Bishops—Poland—History—20th century. 6. Piłsudski, Józef, 1867–1935. 7. Church and state—Poland—History—20th century. 8. Secularism—Poland—History—20th century. 9. Poland—Politics and government, 1918–1945. I. Title.
BX1566.P39 2009
327.456'3404380904—dc22

2009019643

Publication of books in the Polish and Polish-American Studies Series has been made possible in part by the generous support of the following organizations:

Polish American Historical Association,
New Britain, Connecticut

Stanislaus A. Blejwas Endowed Chair in Polish and Polish American Studies,
Central Connecticut State University,
New Britain, Connecticut

The Polish Institute of Arts and Sciences of America, Inc.,
New York, New York

The Piast Institute: An Institute for Polish and Polish American Affairs,
Detroit, Michigan

For Ewa, Andrzej, Krystyna . . . and

this time, Alex and Betsy.

Contents

Illustrations

PLATES
Following page 100

MAPS

TABLE

Series Editor's Preface

Although the topic of *Rome's Most Faithful Daughter: The Catholic Church and Independent Poland, 1914–1939,* might seem to some readers fairly specialized and even arcane, Professor Neal Pease's study of church-state affairs in interwar Poland is an original, engaging, and important examination of this central dimension of political and social affairs. Pease unfolds the narrative of a society and polity in the throes of a difficult transition, one abruptly cut short on September 1, 1939. Poland was a fulcrum for forces that moved the politics and foreign policy of both the European Great Powers and the United States at a critical moment in the twentieth century and shaped the contours of the postwar world order for the next fifty years.

Gracefully written and meticulously researched, *Rome's Most Faithful Daughter* charts the intricate relationship among Poland's bishops, the Vatican, and the secular and anticlerical Piłsudski regime, even as international politics lurched toward crisis. The Church reached a tenuous arrangement with the Polish strongman, Marshal Józef Piłsudski, based on limited shared interests—the most important of which was halting the westward march of Bolshevism—but also, in large measure, on the personal friendship and mutual respect shared by the Polish general and Monsignor Achille Ratti, the apostolic nuncio to Poland (and future Pope Pius XI). Throughout the period, the Church pursued its own bureaucratic and ideological interests, but as Pease masterfully demonstrates, the former was no monolith, and the latter were far from unitary. The Polish episcopate, itself internally divided, frequently pulled and tugged in different directions from the Vatican over religious (and political) issues like Church-state relations, the evangelization of the Orthodox east, and the future of Poland. Pease portrays Poland's bishops as complex men of contrasting styles, dispositions, subjectivities, and politics. Through the lens of Church policy, Pease sheds light on Polish-Ukrainian relations, the connection between religion and nationalism in modern Poland, and, of course, a central leitmotif in nineteenth- and twentieth-century Polish affairs, the "Jewish Question."

Rome's Most Faithful Daughter is the tenth volume in the Ohio University Press Polish and Polish-American Studies Series. The series revisits the historical and contemporary experience of one of America's largest European ethnic groups and the history of a European homeland that has played a disproportionately important role in twentieth-century world affairs. The series publishes innovative monographs and more general works that investigate under- and unexplored topics or offer new, critical, revisionist, or comparative perspectives in the area of Polish and Polish-American Studies. The series seeks manuscripts of interdisciplinary or multidisciplinary profile on Polish immigration and ethnic communities, the country of origin, and its various peoples in history, anthropology, cultural studies, political economy, current politics, and related fields.

Publication of the Ohio University Press Polish and Polish-American Studies Series marks a milestone in the maturation of the Polish studies field and stands as a fitting tribute to the scholars and organizations whose efforts have brought it to fruition. Supported by a series advisory board of accomplished Polonists and Polish-Americanists, the Polish and Polish-American Studies Series has been made possible through generous financial assistance from the Polish American Historical Association, the Polish Institute of Arts and Sciences of America, the Stanislaus A. Blejwas Endowed Chair in Polish and Polish American Studies at Central Connecticut State University, and the Piast Institute and through institutional support from Wayne State University and Ohio University Press. The series meanwhile has benefited from the warm encouragement of a number of other persons, including Gillian Berchowitz, M. B. B. Biskupski, the late Stanislaus A. Blejwas, Mary Erdmans, Thaddeus Gromada, James S. Pula, Thaddeus Radzilowski, and David Sanders. The moral and material support from all of these institutions and individuals is gratefully acknowledged.

John J. Bukowczyk

Preface

My wife Ewa and I happened to be living temporarily in Warsaw in June 1979, when the newly elected Pope John Paul II made his epochal first pilgrimage to his homeland. That experience, unforgettable on many levels, instilled in me an abiding interest in the role of the Catholic Church in the history of Poland. As time went on, I became struck by the scarcity of scholarly work on Catholicism in Poland during the period of my specialization, the phase of the independent Second Republic whose free existence began in 1918 and ended in 1939. This was outwardly an interval of "normal" church-state relations that lacked both drama and the noble theme of the Church as the defender of Polish culture and national identity against foreign oppressors, which is considered its chief historical merit. I guessed that there must be more to the story, and decided to try to find out.

The resulting book you are reading is not intended to be a comprehensive history of the Catholic Church in Poland between the wars. Its more modest two goals are to describe and explain the significance of Catholicism in Polish politics from 1914 to 1939, and of Poland in the politics of the wider Catholic world. I hope it will be considered a worthwhile contribution to the fields of the history of Poland and the Catholic Church in general. It attempts to explore the issue of Catholicism in the public life of the interwar Second Republic in greater depth than has been done before. Along the way, maybe it will help to shed light on the important but somewhat overlooked pontificate of Pius XI, the first "Polish pope," according to one way of looking at it, and add some useful words to the lively controversy over the conduct of Pope Pius XII during the Second World War.

If the book manages to do these things, it is not due to any insight of mine, but to the advantage of having been able to carry out extensive original archival research in a variety of locations in four different countries. In particular, I have had the good fortune to examine collections of documents from the rich holdings of the Vatican Secret Archives only recently opened to scholars. While I owe a great deal to the earlier work of accomplished predecessors in the study of interwar Polish Church history, as the notes and bibliography will demonstrate, it may be fair to claim that mine is the first monograph on the subject to have the benefit of such a wealth of primary sources.

Readers may deserve a brief explanation of my chosen usage of placenames, a tricky business in writing about a region of mixed populations, many languages, shifting frontiers, and long memories, where the adoption of one form or another may confuse, or be construed as taking sides in old disputes. In general, if an accepted term for a place exists in English, I have used it; if not, I have employed the variant corresponding to the interwar boundary lines: hence, for example, Warsaw, Upper Silesia, and Danzig, but Poznań, Breslau, and Kaunas. The closest calls involve the two metropolises of what was then eastern Poland, but now are parts of successor states to the former Soviet Union. The city called Wilno in Polish, now Vilnius, the capital of Lithuania, was usually referred to as Vilna in English parlance of the time, so Vilna it will be here. On the other hand, having discerned no comparable Anglophone consensus regarding the city known as L'viv in contemporary Ukraine, I have settled on the Polish Lwów. Along the same lines, I am aware that Polish opinion objected to the expression "Corridor," which implied the injustice and artificiality of one notoriously contested sector of the boundary between Poland and Germany, but it remains the most recognizable shorthand name for the international dispute it stood for, so I have not tried to avoid it. Of course, none of these choices has the slightest intention of hinting at any covert authorial opinion on the merits of these arguments. While widely accepted, the term "Uniate" can offend Eastern-rite Catholics, who rightly note its origins as a label of opprobrium; my occasional resort to it here is meant to lessen repetitiveness of language, and intends no disrespect. There are fewer such hazards in Italy: while there are subtle shades of difference among the terms "Holy See," "Apostolic See," and "Vatican," I have used them interchangeably as pertaining to the papacy, its policy, or its authority.

It is a pleasure to acknowledge the generous help that has come to me along the way. My labors have been aided in large part by research grants from the American Council of Learned Societies, the American Philosophical Society, the International Research and Exchanges Board (IREX), the National Endowment for the Humanities, and the Center for International Education at my own University of Wisconsin–Milwaukee. A research fellowship from the Pew Evangelical Scholars Program provided a year's leave of absence from other duties at UWM to devote to the project. I am indebted as well to many individuals, who deserve much credit for the worth of the book, such as it is, and no blame for its shortcomings, which are my responsibility alone. The list is long, and only a few can be mentioned by name. I have benefited greatly from the advice and example of my mentors, Professor Piotr S. Wandycz and Professor Anna M. Cienciała, and my predecessor and colleague at UWM, the late Professor M. K. Dziewanowski. A dear friend of long standing, Dr. Thomas S. Dyman, looked over the manuscript with expert eyes at various stages of preparation, offering encouragement and valuable suggestions for improvement. A former colleague, Professor Kathleen Wellman, and her family acted as gracious hosts during a research stay in Rome, and a family friend, Teresa Korzeniowski, arranged accommodations in Warsaw for similar purposes. For their efforts toward the production of this book, my sincere thanks go to Professor John J. Bukowczyk, editor of the Polish and Polish-American Studies Series, and to the team at Ohio University Press: Nancy Basmajian, managing editor; Gillian Berchowitz, assistant director and senior editor; Ricky S. Huard, project editor; Beth Pratt, production manager; John Morris, copyeditor; and Chiquita Babb, designer and typesetter. Donna G. Genzmer, director of the Cartography and GIS Center, University of Wisconsin–Milwaukee, prepared the maps. Krystyna K. Matusiak, senior academic librarian at the UWM Libraries, assisted in reproduction of photographs.

A select few people have meant more to me than I am able to convey in words and have contributed to the making of the book in ways indirect but profound. My parents, Wanda Adkins and H. W. Pease, inspired a youthful interest in history that I never outgrew. My parents-in-law, Wiktor and Zofia Barczyk, have touched me with their appreciation for their son-in-law's professional focus on the land of their birth. Above all, I have been blessed by the love, support, and patient forbearance of my cherished wife, Ewa Barczyk, director of the University of Wisconsin–Milwaukee Libraries, and our children; and it is to them, as before, that this book is dedicated.

Abbreviations

AAN	Archiwum Akt Nowych, Warsaw
AAN-MSZ	Ministerstwo Spraw Zagranicznych, AAN
AAN-MWRiOP	Ministerstwo Wyznań Religijnych i Oświecenia Publicznych, AAN
ADSS	*Actes et documents du Saint Siège relatifs à la seconde guerre mondiale,* ed. Pierre Blet, Angelo Martini, and Burkhart Schneider (Vatican City: Libreria Editrice Vaticana, 1965)
AGND	Archiwum Adiutantury Generalnej Naczelnego Dowództwa (Archiwum Belwederskie) (microfilm), Yale University Library
ANP	*Achilles Ratti (1918–1921),* ed. Stanisław Wilk, Acta Nuntiaturae Polonae 57 (Rome: Institutum Historicum Polonicum Romae, 1995–96)
APIP	*Archiwum polityczne Ignacego Paderewskiego,* ed. Halina Janowska (Wrocław: Zakład Narodowy im. Ossolińskich, 1973–74)
APP	Archiwum Prymasów Polskich, Archiwum Archidiecezjalne w Gnieźnie, Gniezno
ASV	Archivio Segreto Vaticano, Vatican City
BPPP	*Bulletin périodique de la presse polonaise,* France, Ministère des Affaires Étrangères
DBFP	*Documents on British Foreign Policy,* Great Britain, Foreign Office
HIA	Hoover Institution Archives, Stanford, Calif.
IDDI	*I documenti diplomatici italiani,* Italy, Ministero degli Affari Esteri

IHGS	Instytut Historyczny im. Generała Sikorskiego, London
NKUPMJP	Naczelny Komitet Uczczenia Pamięci Marszałka Józefa Piłsudskiego, AAN
PIA	Joseph Pilsudski Institute of America, New York
RDHS	*Records and Documents of the Holy See Relating to the Second World War*, ed. Pierre Blet, Angelo Martini, and Burkhart Schneider (Washington, D.C.: Corpus Books, 1968)
SDNA	State Department Decimal File, National Archives, Washington, D.C.
Szembek	*Diariusz i teki Jana Szembeka (1935–1945)*, ed. Tytus Komarnicki and Józef Zarański (London: Polish Research Centre, 1964)

Guide to Pronunciation

The following key provides a guide to the pronunciation of Polish words and names.

a is pronounced as in *father*
c as ts, as in *cats*
ch as guttural h, as in German *Bach*
cz as hard ch, as in *church*
g (always hard), as in *get*
i as ee, as in *meet*
j as y, as in *yellow*
rz as hard zh, as in French *jardin*
sz as hard sh, as in *ship*
szcz as hard shch, as in *fresh cheese*
u as oo, as in *boot*
w as v, as in *vat*
ć as soft ch, as in *cheap*
ś as soft sh, as in *sheep*
ż as hard zh, as in French *jardin*
ź as soft zh, as in *seizure*
ó as oo, as in *boot*
ą as a nasal, as in French *on*
ę as a nasal, as in French *en*
ł as w, as in *way*
ń as ny, as in *canyon*

The accent in Polish words almost always falls on the penultimate syllable.

Rome's Most Faithful Daughter

1 ׀ Polonia Restituta

The Catholic Church and the Revival of Poland

THE FORMAL RESUMPTION OF POLISH STATEHOOD in modern times began in church. On February 9, 1919, not quite three months after its inception, the government of the fledgling Second Polish Republic marked the convocation of its first parliament, or Sejm, in Warsaw with an inaugural Roman Catholic high mass, reviving the custom of the bygone commonwealth of Poland-Lithuania before its partition and subjection to foreign rule for a century and a quarter. In its form and dramatis personae, this ceremony vividly asserted the prominence of the Roman confession in national life and tradition, as well as its intimate association with the temporal power. At the hour of eleven that Sunday morning, Chief of State Józef Piłsudski entered the crowded nave of St. John Cathedral, thus sparing himself the sight of the incongruous nineteenth-century facade that defaced the Gothic antiquity of this oldest church of the capital. He began a procession down the aisle toward the altar, followed in turn by the prime minister, Ignacy Jan Paderewski, and his cabinet; the papal emissary to the country, Monsignor Achille Ratti, who would become pope himself three years later almost to the day; the assembled Catholic hierarchs of restored Poland; and finally the celebrant, the archbishop of Warsaw, Aleksander Kakowski. The solemnities reached their emotional peak when the lawmakers heard a patriotic sermon from one of their own, the Armenian-rite archbishop of Lwów Józef Teodorowicz, the most senior of thirty-two deputies who wore the collar, one-twelfth of the membership of the body. A noted homilist of the hellfire school and never a man given to understatement, to put it delicately, Teodorowicz reminded his audience of their duty to God and country with characteristic vehemence, his words laden with gravity and drama. On this momentous occasion, the speaker surpassed even his own impressive standards of fiery rhetoric, and sympathetic listeners afterwards described the prelate's oratory as magnificent, divinely inspired. Even some political foes paid grudging tribute to his eloquence, barbed with not altogether complimentary comparisons with Piotr Skarga, the legendary Jesuit royal preacher who had harangued a previous Sejm in the heyday of Poland-Lithuania. As a final flourish, at the close of his exhortation Teodorowicz administered to the legislators their oaths of office in unison. When the liturgy ended, the congregation sang the national hymn "Boże coś Polskę"—"God, protector of Poland"—and then the freshly minted deputies emptied out of the cathedral to walk the length of Krakowskie Przedmieście and New World streets, amid cheering throngs, to the parliament building off of Three Crosses Square. There, later in the day, the primate of Poland, Archbishop Edmund Dalbor of Gniezno-Poznań, consecrated the chamber in the presence of the same collection of ranking worldly dignitaries.[1]

In its symbolic union of church and state, this set piece of official pageantry neatly echoed the litany of historical axioms that commentators habitually cited—and cite to this day, for that matter—to prove the indomitable Catholicity of the Poles throughout the ages and the natural affinity of Catholicism with Polish patriotism: the conventional dating of the origins of Poland from its baptism in 966, the status of the Catholic primate as *interrex* in Poland-Lithuania, the miracles of the icon of the Black Madonna of Częstochowa, the veneration of the Blessed Virgin as perpetual queen and patroness of Poland, the reputation of the old republic as the easternmost rampart of western Christendom against Turk, Tatar, and schismatic. Indeed, the famous Roman religiosity of Poland was the main thing—in not a few cases, practically the only thing—that many foreigners knew of the country or its people, and so they tended not to subject the time-honored legend of *Polonia semper fidelis* to rigorous examination. In reporting his initial impression from Warsaw to his superiors at the Vatican Secretariat of State, even the scholarly and matter-of-fact Monsignor Ratti intoned the truism "Dire polacco è dire cattolico"—to say Polish is to say Catholic—and plainly meant it, and only closer acquaintance with the subtleties of his new assignment would teach him not to accept the formula at face value.[2] Small wonder, then, that observers more distant assumed the truth of the stereotype and took for granted the Catholic nature of the Second Republic and its readiness to serve the aims of the Church at home and abroad, whether they welcomed or rued the prospect. In the same year

1919, for instance, a French Catholic journalist rejoiced at the revival of Poland as "a political miracle," stressing that in that land of fabled piety "the interests of Church and State not only coincide, but are actually dependent upon each other."[3] Surveying the perils facing Europe in the wake of a ruinous world war, others called on the newly emancipated Poles to take up once more their historic mission as guardians of religion and civilization. Still three years from full reception into the Church, but already Roman at heart, the English literary eminence G. K. Chesterton warned—accurately, after a fashion, if twenty years too soon—that "a flood threatens the West from the meeting of two streams, the revenge of Germany and the anarchy of Russia" and concluded that Europe had "only one possible dyke against such a flood, which is . . . the might and majesty of Poland," the "Christian and chivalric shield" of the Occident.[4] On the other hand, Polish diplomats arriving in Rome encountered brusque greetings from the government of Italy, which suspected them of being little more than agents of its papal rival across the Tiber. While concerned above all with the unresolved Roman question, Italian officials might have spoken for disapproving liberals and anticlericals everywhere when they complained to the Poles that "you are papists, the only ones in Europe nowadays; on you the Vatican pins all its hopes; you are to be a branch of the church-state and a base for the reborn temporal power of the papacy."[5] "The new born Polish republic," an American newspaper correspondent told his readers in 1932, not reporting news so much as reinforcing an adage, "is Rome's most faithful daughter."[6]

Proclamations of this sort, celebratory and alarmist alike, proceeded from a common impression of Poland as a Catholic monolith and ultramontane bastion, the idea symbolically expressed and reinforced in the parliamentary mass in St. John's Cathedral. Yet closer scrutiny of the participants in that ritual might have suggested a more guarded estimate of the influence of Catholicism in the councils of state in the Second Republic. Prime Minister Paderewski was rumored to be a Freemason, an affiliation forbidden by the Church. Chief of State Piłsudski, acclaimed by millions as the hero of the struggle for independence and destined to become the dominant figure of interwar Polish history, was at best a wandering and idiosyncratic Catholic openly despised by more than a few of the prelates in attendance that morning, and his retinue of cronies and devoted associates—the main pool of recruitment for high governmental position in the years to come—was notorious as a hotbed of unbelief and Freemasonry. For his part, within two years Achille Ratti would be hounded from his nunciature in Poland amid a din of furious protests and cries for a rupture of Polish relations with the Holy See; subsequently, as occupant of the throne of St. Peter under the name of Pius XI for the better part of the Second Republic's free existence, he saw his cherished projects for a historic expansion of Catholicism eastward into the territories of the former Russian empire bitterly opposed and frustrated by the very government in Warsaw that many regarded as the cat's-paw of the Vatican. To judge from the tenor of their sermons and public statements, the Catholic bishops and clergy of the country saw no grounds for confidence in the future of their Church, but instead saw it as embattled and under siege, even in Poland, beset by inner frailties and vulnerable to powerful foes, including scores of the very men who filled the pews of the cathedral that day. Most of the political parties represented in that first parliament could have been described fairly as anticlerical by instinct or heritage, even without the presence of deputies from the regions largely neither Polish nor Catholic that would be joined to the Second Republic only after prolonged and frequently military dispute. Once the dust settled and boundaries became more or less fixed, if not universally accepted, roughly three-quarters of Poland's population of twenty-seven million professed themselves Catholics—a lesser percentage than in neighboring Lithuania or Czechoslovakia, and far fewer in number than in Germany, the birthplace of the Reformation and the Kulturkampf—and of those, some three million were Ukrainian Eastern-rite Catholics estranged from their nominal Polish coreligionists by barriers of mutual suspicion and national rivalries. One might well have wondered if this was the same country so often glibly described by supposedly knowledgeable contemporaries as a modern version of the confessional state, republican in form but Catholic in essence.[7]

In many ways, it was not: the pluralist, polyglot Poland of reality differed from the Poland of pious myth, but the confusion between the two sprang precisely from the fact that the myth held enough truth in it to persuade beholders that it was so. Outsiders were especially prone to this simplifying tendency. Most Poles knew better, but by the same token a great many of them believed that the myth could and should be made so, and thought and acted accordingly, while a great many others feared that attempts might be made to make it so and resolved to take care that it should not, and still others cared little one way or the other but gave the myth lip service to suit their purposes. The potent legend of "Poland ever faithful," then, operated simultaneously as illusion, as ideal to be approached and possibly realized, as threatening prospect to be averted, and as handy polemical weapon. Owing to the conflicting reactions it inevitably evoked, the vision of a Catholic Poland could not serve as the unifying principle of the Second Republic, as widely assumed; on the contrary, perhaps no other theme held such power to polarize the country or set its various peoples and constituencies at odds.

Even so, the reflexive predisposition to equate Poland with the Roman church was not a mistaken judgment, but merely one that meant less in political terms than met the eye. It often proceeded from, or led to, an exaggerated appraisal of the collaboration of throne and altar throughout the history of Poland as well as a lack of understanding that, in fact, Catholicism occupied a somewhat ambiguous place in Polish political culture. True, the vast majority of Poles proclaimed themselves Catholics of the Latin rite, and the link between Catholicism and Polish identity was manifestly real, hallowed by time, accentuated by adjacency to peoples of other creeds, and starkly defined by the recent dominion of Protestant and Orthodox sovereigns over most of the Polish lands. Adherence to the Roman faith resoundingly supported the Polish ethos, then, and in Poland Catholicism bore no taint of association with foreign rule or of conflict with patriotic ideals, as in the Czech lands or in Hungary. However, these facts had exerted less influence on the behavior or inclinations of the former Polish Respublica than might have been expected, and less still on the creators of its interwar reincarnation. To put it mildly, old Poland had scarcely qualified as a crusader or inquisitorial realm, a Spain of the east. Indeed, its tradition had been to approach religion in moderate and latitudinarian fashion. More often than not, the commonwealth preferred to apply a cautious pragmatism in managing its multiconfessional populace, and Poland-Lithuania's lack of zeal in enforcing religious uniformity had earned it occasional reproaches as a paradise for heretics and Jews. In other words, Catholicism acted as a salient indicator of Polish identity, but not as an element of great political significance or priority in statecraft. The pattern held during the era of partition, when the Church and its representatives played at most a secondary role in the struggle for independence, and the Polish political and intellectual elites that would later emerge into leadership of the interwar republic came to cultivate attitudes of indifference or outright hostility to Catholicism as a dubious force in national affairs.[8]

So as Poland entered a new phase of statehood in 1918, its Church occupied a formidable but awkward and undefined position in the country, looming as an imposing presence but by no means an uncontested or irresistible civic colossus. In truth, perhaps no other institution could lay so plausible a claim to the right and duty to speak for Poles on matters of governmental as well as private conduct; certainly the Church thought so, and did not shrink from attempting to exercise that prerogative. Too much a fixture in national life to be content with less than a commanding voice in public concerns and official recognition of its moral authority, and far too big to be ignored or underestimated as a political factor even by its most determined antagonists, it nevertheless fell short of the ability to translate its will into law or policy by persuading or overawing the combination of factions and constituencies that regarded the Church as an agent of clericalism, reaction, and bigotry and saw the shadow of black dictatorship lurking behind its every move. Nor did the dispute over the proper role of Polish Catholicism confine itself within the boundaries of the republic, for the Church of Poland did not exist as an isolated or fully autonomous entity, after all, but as an integral part of an avowedly universal religious body with sweeping worldly—and, literally, otherworldly—interests and aspirations. The popes of the day and their ministers in the Roman Curia considered the twentieth century a time of both frightful dangers and extraordinary opportunities, requiring prudence and daring alike, and the course on which they chose to steer the bark of Peter and its implications for Poland brought them into repeated disagreement with not only the secular rulers of that country, but also with the leaders of the Polish Church and the faithful. Such questions resisted easy solution because sooner or later debates over the proper place of the Church within Poland, and of Poland within the Catholic world, became emotive arguments over the fundamental character of the Second Republic and contrasting visions of Polish history. The argument went on unabated and unresolved right up to the day in October 1939 when Pope Pius XII called on Catholics around the world to mourn the martyrdom of Poland by invasion and conquest yet once more.

The argument had begun in earnest roughly a century earlier, during the decades of tripartite Russian, German, and Austrian sway over the lands of the once and future Poland. The conditions of captivity produced the paradoxical dual result of transforming the Church into a far more visible and powerful symbol of Polish identity, on the one hand, while on the other steadily alienating it from those elements within society who saw themselves as the true keepers of the national flame and formed the vanguard of the independence movement. Although during this time a "Polish Church" existed in none but the sentimental sense, having been apportioned among the ecclesiastical jurisdictions of the partitioners, the bond of Catholicity helped to maintain an indelible consciousness of nationhood that transcended the boundary lines of the moment. Apart from the example of the Habsburg Empire, where a common religion contributed to generally milder and more tolerable terms of confinement for Poles in Austrian Galicia, Catholicism and the Church also functioned as an obvious focus of Polish differentiation from their foreign masters and a national rallying point of solidarity and refuge. Especially during the latter half of the century, official anti-Catholic campaigns in Protestant Germany and Orthodox Russia had magnified the burdens of Poles in those domains. For all the famous rigor of Bismarck's Kulturkampf, the repression of the Church in the Russian zone typically surpassed it in harshness by far, magnified by reprisal against ecclesiastical sympathy or support for the Polish rebellions of 1830–31 and 1863–64. Hundreds of Polish clergy, and even some hierarchs, suffered execution, banishment, or *katorga* (penal servitude) at the hands of Petersburg for real or suspected transgressions of this sort. By 1870, all but one Catholic bishopric in Russian Poland stood vacant, and the archbishop of Warsaw was consigned to an internal exile that would last twenty years. Even so unoffending a holy man as Fr. Honorat Koźmiński, the founder of twenty-six religious congregations, spent much of his life confined to a monastery at Russian behest. In such circumstances, the natural struggles of the Polish Church to withstand these assaults and shelter its faithful from religious persecution inevitably strengthened the tie between the Roman confession and Polishness. The apparent merging of faith and ethnicity that occurred in these times gave rise to the doctrine of *polak-katolik*—the conviction that to be Polish was to be Catholic, and, just as important, not to be Catholic was not to be genuinely Polish—a formula that would leave a deep and enduring impression on the mentality of subsequent generations of Poles. In short, the patriotic devout would not have hesitated to accord their Church much credit for having kept alive the Polish spirit throughout the ordeal of statelessness: Catholicism had sustained Poles in adversity and enabled them to preserve their cultural integrity, while the Church had shared and helped to shoulder the misfortunes of its flock and acted as a comforting and uniquely authentic Polish institution, an irreplaceable example and moral guide to the nation under siege.

All the same, the Church in the Polish lands found itself in an uncomfortably equivocal position, as suggested in the aphorism that it functioned much like a prison chaplain—a solace to the inmate, to be sure, but also an accessory to the jailer.[9] While reluctant to endorse the dismemberment of Poland, Rome consistently preferred to swallow it as a necessary evil rather than incur the risks of disturbing the status quo. Nineteenth-century popes sympathized with the Poles in bondage but condemned their occasional resort to insurrection and advised them to accept their lot and obey their foreign monarchs. This guarded Vatican policy stemmed from doctrinal abhorrence of violence, mistrust of nationalism, ingrained aversion to political and social disorder, and, not least, the larger worldly imperatives of the Holy See. Pope Gregory XVI first made this bluntly plain in 1832, when his encyclical *Cum primum* upbraided the bishops of Russian Poland for their support of the recently suppressed "November Revolt" in their precincts. *Cum primum* came as a shock to Poles, and the document inflicted lasting damage to the prestige of the papacy in the eyes of Polish patriots. Never one to mince words, his successor Pius IX sought to redress the balance by tending more to speak up for the Poles and chide their masters, but the diplomatic Leo XIII paid little heed to the Polish issue throughout his long pontificate. For one thing, the Vatican saw little choice but to maintain at least correct relations with the partitioning empires in the era of the Roman question, the Kulturkampf, and harsh repression of Poles in the tsarist domain. Craving international support for its disputed sovereignty after the liquidation of the Papal State by Italy in 1870, and beset by recurrent waves of governmental attacks against the Church throughout Europe, Rome took care to keep its customary rapport with the Habsburg kingdom in good repair and attempted to restrain German and Russian hostility toward Catholic interests by conciliation, and part of the price was to mute its complaints about the oppression of Poland. Furthermore, the Vatican feared that pressing the Polish matter might only make a bad situation worse, especially in Russia, provoking the standardbearer of Orthodoxy to impose still harsher measures on Ukrainian or Polish Catholics, or even to mandate a schism. As a result, the pontiffs of the day confined themselves to offering comfort to the Poles in affliction and urging their rulers to show magnanimity, persuaded that any more assertive course would only invite retribution and endanger higher priorities to no purpose.

For their part, the Polish bishops as a body gradually fell into line with this strategy over the decades, both out of duty and inclination. Following the lead of Rome, the predominantly aristocratic and conservative hierarchs of the later nineteenth century by and large kept their distance from the national movement, having been systematically vetted for caution and acceptability to Vienna, Berlin, or Petersburg. Drawn from lower social strata, more attuned to the mood of their parishioners, and less burdened by visibility, the weight of responsibility, and pressure to conform, lesser clergy participated in political action far more frequently, but often in opposition to the recommendations of their superiors. It was both characteristic and ironic that the most celebrated Polish clerical martyr of the day, Archbishop Mieczysław Halka Ledóchowski of Gniezno-Poznań, had been a loyal subject of the German Kaiser who had discouraged his priests against identification with the Polish cause only to run afoul of the persecutions of the Kulturkampf.

While shying away from dabbling overtly in politics or endorsing separatist aspirations, the Polish Church in no way meant to default its obligation to the nation, according to its lights. Indeed, ecclesiastical life in the former Poland was so saturated in the Polish question in all its various forms that it scarcely had any capacity to absorb the debates over modernism and the social issue that gripped the Church elsewhere in Europe. In many ways, the approach of the Polish Church matched that of the advocates of "Organic Work": to better the lot of Poles by quotidian, legal efforts within the given political framework, assigning greater value to the defense of culture than the dream of liberation. At bottom, the Church best contributed to resistance against the foreign yoke not by any bold or conscious action, but simply by being itself, its very existence underscoring and reinforcing the traits of Polish identity that the German and Russian assimilationists had tried to obliterate. In so doing, the Church indeed donated vital service to the eventual restoration of an independent Poland, but did so almost by accident and even in spite of the counsel of its most prominent and authoritative spokesmen to the contrary, so that it might be extolled as a national paragon or censured as a collaborationist element with equal ease, according to taste.

At any rate, the rising generation of Polish political activists that came to the fore at the turn of the century, espousing novel doctrines and bolder agendas, came to regard the Church with attitudes ranging from reserve to outright disdain. The Polish intelligentsia, the traditional custodians of national values who supplied the ideas and leaders of the new movements, had drunk deeply from the same wells of skepticism and anticlericalism then fashionable among their counterparts in other Catholic lands. To the Left, the Roman Church signified reaction, obscurantism, and bigotry, the synthesis of all they despised and wished to change, although the moderate socialists who sought self-rule as well as social transformation tempered their hostility toward the cloth out of respect for the centrality of Catholicism in Polish life. While the peasantry constituted the bedrock of the Catholic following among Poles, the chieftains of the budding agrarian parties had learned their catechisms instead from the age-old undercurrent of rustic grumbling about the village priest as the freeloading martinet of the countryside.

Of the modern orientations, the National Democracy, the standard bearer of the patriotic right, maintained the most complex and ambivalent relationship with the Church. Taking its cue from its preeminent theorist and spokesman, Roman Dmowski, the Endecja offered a program of integral nationalism, social conservatism, and lack of sympathy for Jews and other minorities residing in Polish territories. Much of the National Democratic platform appealed to Catholic sentiment. The party recognized the Church as a pillar of the social order and by its nature tended to advocate the supremacy of Catholic Poles over peoples of other faiths, and its opposition to socialism nicely coincided with the views of the clergy and many of the faithful. However, much about the philosophical underpinnings of National Democracy contradicted Church teaching, and neither the movement nor its champion made a comfortable fit with Roman belief and ethos. As a disciple of positivist materialism, Dmowski denied the supernatural essence of the Church and remained outside its fold until late in life. Above all, his enshrinement of the nation as the highest good and paramount object of devotion, and his insistence that national issues lay "outside the realm of Christian ethics," baldly flouted fundamental tenets of Catholic dogma.[10] Although Endecja had gradually toned down the blatant anticlericalism of its formative days, it still took a purely instrumental approach to Catholicism, embracing it as a useful political ally rather than for any intrinsic value. In the eyes of the Church, then, National Democracy posed a dilemma: it was often right, but for all the wrong reasons, a virtual Polish twin of the Action Française of Charles Maurras, which for decades walked a thin line between papal applause and condemnation. Despite these ambiguities, many clergy and laymen joined or promoted National Democracy as the most promising political haven for Polish Catholics, and more than a few hierarchs looked upon Endecja with a kindly eye.

When the First World War erupted in Europe in 1914, splitting the ranks of the partitioning emperors, the separate branches of the Polish Church responded according to established form, attempting to carry off the difficult trick of balancing respect for the existing political order with the call of duty to the divided nation. As the guns commenced firing, few Poles foresaw independence as an outcome of the fighting, and of those, fewer wore the collar. In addition, at the time the situation of the Church in all three zones of former Poland seemed more satisfactory than ever in long memory: Austria was Austria, Catholic and unexacting; the severity of German administration had eased perceptibly of late; and even in Russia the ukase of toleration of 1905 had permitted the resumption of something resembling normal ecclesiastical operation. Just as clerics in all lands rallied to the flag at the opening of hostilities, Polish Catholic leaders warily followed suit, issuing proclamations of loyalty to respective king and country in exchange for the vague promises of their rulers that the Poles would share the fruits of victory. Loyalism appeared most plausible in Austria-Hungary, where Polish ecclesiastics could embrace it with honest conviction; in August 1914 the archbishop of Lwów, and future saint, Józef Bilczewski, pronounced a blessing on the arms of the Dual Monarchy, a Catholic realm that had "allowed us to be Poles."[11] Already in the opening phase of the conflict, some Galician clergy thought in terms of an Austrian triumph that might reunify the Polish lands under the mild Habsburg scepter. In the German and Russian districts, on the other hand, unhappy experience had taught Polish churchmen to expect little from their monarchs and to lie low, and for the most part they restricted their commentaries on the war at this early date to safe, bromidic prayers for its speedy and successful conclusion.

In reacting to the outbreak of the European conflict in a tentative and equivocal manner, the Polish clergy matched the example set by their superiors at the seat of Church government. Few topics in the modern history of the papacy have generated so much heat as the wartime policy of Benedict XV, the former cardinal-archbishop Giacomo Della Chiesa of Bologna who took the tiara in September 1914, on the same day Russian troops captured Galician Lwów and three days before the Battle of the Marne. Throughout the next four years the pope issued urgent appeals for an immediate end to the fighting as a savage and pointless folly—a "horrible butchery," he called it, the "suicide of civilized Europe"—and assured the world of the fatherly disinterest of the vicar of Christ. This stance made worldly as well as moral sense for a church that preached nonviolence, claimed universal jurisdiction, and harbored profoundly cautious political instincts; content with the antebellum European balance, the Vatican feared the consequences of its overthrow by the decisive victory of either coalition.[12] Still, suspicion prevailed at the time, and lingers to this day, that Benedict's statements of evenhandedness thinly masked his true preference for Germany and Austria. The case for papal partiality is often crudely put, and evidence to the contrary may be adduced. Striving to act as mediator, Benedict scrupulously avoided endorsement of either side or its aims, to the dissatisfaction of all parties: Germans complained of him as the *Franzosenpapst* just as the French maligned him as the "Boche pope." Nevertheless, the Central Powers cardinals had voted as a bloc for his election at the conclave of 1914, backing him as the candidate most likely to show sympathy for the cause of their governments in the great struggle just begun.[13] For that matter, any pope would have had ample reason to look askance at an alliance consisting of Orthodox Russia, anticlerical France, and Protestant England, the dominator of Ireland, with the subsequent addition of usurpatory Italy to boot. Moreover, the Vatican regarded Austria-Hungary as the only reliably Catholic power in Europe and lost little sleep over Germany with the "war for culture" long over. All in all, the Apostolic See had stronger grounds on principle to favor one side over the other than nearly all the combatants themselves, and most observers of the time simply took for granted that the neutrality of Pope Della Chiesa amounted to a neutrality for Vienna and Berlin.

Because in the end Poland regained independence under the banner of the Allies, the pope's presumed tilt toward their opponents, and particularly his barely disguised protectiveness toward Austria-Hungary, are sometimes assumed to explain his supposed tardiness to back the restoration of Polish statehood. At best this qualifies as an ahistorical half truth that obscures the fact that many contemporaries could consider the Central Powers as the more likely liberators of Poland with good reason, and regard the welfare of the Poles and the Habsburgs as not only compatible but inextricably linked. If nothing else, the Holy See could not have deemed the westward expansion of the Russian sphere of influence—the natural outcome of the victory of the Entente in its original constellation—as anything but a catastrophe for the Poles and other central European Catholics. In fact, one of the founding premises of Vatican wartime diplomacy concerning the region was precisely the calculation that what was good for Russia was bad for Poland.[14]

At any rate, the powers paid little attention to the fate of Poland in the early stages of the war, nor did the Curia force the matter, but by the time the conflict entered its first spring, Benedict decided to drop a none-too-subtle hint that the peace to come should alter the status of the Polish lands. After the bishop of Kraków, Prince Adam Stefan Sapieha, organized a campaign to carry out charitable and relief work in all three zones of partition, the Vatican bestowed official blessings on his initiative in April 1915; what is more, the letter employed the occasion to convey papal greetings to "*Polonia tutta intera*," Poland as a whole. Furthermore, from that point Rome began to address messages and instructions to the Polish episcopate as a united, separate entity. Later that November, Catholics throughout the world issued prayers for Poland at Sunday mass at papal behest. While these small gestures hardly resembled a clarion call for the reconstitution of the quondam republic, they still plainly implied the artificiality of its division and suggested the readiness of the pope to see the topic of Poland placed more prominently on the international agenda.[15]

The pope got his way, for although belligerents of all stripes routinely ignored the recommendations of the Vatican after making a show of a respectful hearing, as the war protracted and intensified, the Polish question inevitably returned to center stage. The ultimate, improbable result was the restoration of Polish independence for two decades, and much of what occupies the pages to come stems from the striking fact that of the two figures who emerged during the war years to become the great rival protagonists of the history of the proverbially Catholic nation of Poland in the first half of the twentieth century, neither could have been described as a Catholic in particularly good standing, and neither bothered much to pretend otherwise. In most respects, Roman Dmowski (b. 1864), the standardbearer of National Democracy, and his counterpart, the erstwhile socialist Józef Piłsudski (b. 1867), were as opposite as north and south, unlike in personality as well as program. Icy and theoretical, Dmowski envisaged a national Poland that excluded, assimilated, or disfranchised minority peoples to the extent possible, while the more colorful Piłsudski upheld the old "Jagiellonian" ideal of the polyglot and tolerant Respublica. Regarding Germany as the primary enemy of Poles, Dmowski waged a diplomatic campaign from abroad to link Polish fortunes with the Entente, viewing the unification of Poland under Russian protection as a decisive step toward selfrule. On the other hand, Piłsudski led his own Polish legions into battle against Russia in conjunction with the Central Powers, apparently in prophetic anticipation of an eventual debacle of all three partitioners that would permit the creation of a fully independent Poland. However, these two present and future antagonists agreed in their secular conception of politics: neither appealed to religious conviction or tradition to win adherents to his cause, or promised any special role for the Church in the Poland he sought to fashion.[16]

Had the guardians of Polish catholicity known that no one would exert so much influence on the politics of reborn Poland as Józef Piłsudski, or more affect the relationship of church and state, few would have relished the prospect. A mixture of equal parts genius, magnetism, and eccentricity, Piłsudski maintained an affiliation with Catholicism that was inconstant and peculiar, to say the least. Raised in the faith, he converted superficially to the Evangelical Augsburg confession in 1899 to circumvent Russian restrictions against political activity by Catholics and, incidentally, to wed a divorcée; by the time he returned to Rome in 1916, he had formed another liaison that produced a child well before its legitimation by marriage upon the death of his estranged spouse. Aside from Piłsudski's personal meanderings from the straight and narrow, many Catholics mistrusted him for the company he kept. His socialist pedigree and growing stature as the main hope of the Polish Left made him the natural favorite of those elements in society most inclined to anticlericalism and skepticism, a fact underscored by the conspicuous irreligiosity of his inner circle of fiercely loyal associates, veteran comrades of his conspiratorial and legionary days who made careers as retainers of the man they revered as their commandant. Yet despite his nonchalance, the scandal of his private life, and the indevotion of his entourage, Piłsudski never shook off a lifelong sentimental attachment to the traditional Marian piety of his native Lithuania. "I, an old socialist," he confided to a colleague in 1912, "when I have an important decision to make, I pray first to the Holy Mother of Ostrabrama," and on journeys he carried a medallion of this famous Virgin of Vilna.[17] More than once Piłsudski inspired witticisms along the lines of the timeworn tale of the man who professes that there is no God, and that Our Lady is surely His mother.[18]

While most Polish churchmen, true to established form, continued to shy away from identification with either of the two strategies for independence, those who did plainly regarded Dmowski and his line as the more palatable alternative. Very few ecclesiastics expressed solidarity with Piłsudski and his legions; many more rejected him as a radical who consorted with forces inimical to the Church. Sermons reviled Piłsudski as a common bandit, and the combative Bishop Sapieha of Kraków, linking two staple priestly bugbears, accused him of wishing to construct "a socialist and Jewish Poland."[19] On the other hand, Dmowski and his nationalist party attracted considerable clerical support. The two most prominent Polish hierarchs of Austrian Galicia, Sapieha and Archbishop Teodorowicz, were both staunch proponents of the Endecja, although they stopped short of backing its wager on the Entente, the enemy of the Habsburg kingdom.

The crucial weakness of the National Democratic plan lay in its reliance on a Russian victory on the eastern front, where the Central Powers seized the initiative in short order. By 1915, nearly all the Polish territories had fallen into German and Austrian hands, and the Vatican showed no signs of unease at this development or its implications for the destiny of the Poles. In June 1916 the British Catholic writer Hilaire Belloc obtained an audience with Benedict XV and used the occasion to deliver an impassioned plea for the reconstruction of Poland—"that is the key after the war." The English pilgrim based his argument on the patriotic assumption that the Allies would prevail; the pope parried, "But do you think they will, Mr. Belloc?"[20] In fact, by that time the Vatican had settled on the advantages of an "Austro-Polish" approach, foreseeing the creation of a Polish kingdom connected to the Habsburg monarchy by personal rule, much in the manner of dualist Hungary. Such notions appealed especially to Fr. Włodzimierz Ledóchowski, the Polish Galician aristocrat who became general superior of the Society of Jesus in 1915. Routinely described as the last of the formidable Jesuit commanders of the old school, Ledóchowski had a knack for gaining the ear of his pontiffs, and he acted as the leader of a small but active "Polish lobby" within the Vatican during the war and thereafter exerted no little influence on the shaping of curial policy toward his native land over the next quarter century.[21] A Poland under Habsburg tutelage also seemed the best solution to Pope Della Chiesa and his secretary of state, Pietro Cardinal Gasparri, a bluff canon lawyer who impressed many as a living confirmation of the stereotype of slippery Italian diplomacy.[22] Making the rounds of the Vatican in February 1916 to sound out Benedict and his lieutenants, Dmowski found no takers for his Allied strategy. While the pope confined himself to vague assurances of his paternal solicitude, Gasparri was blunt, asking the Pole the scolding, incredulous question "Why are you going with Russia?. . . You truly believe that a united Poland will be contented under the scepter of the Russian monarch?" When Dmowski spoke of full Polish independence, Gasparri broke into laughter and protested that the idea was no more than "a dream, an impossible goal! . . . Your future is with Austria."[23]

Although Gasparri had failed to take into account the steady relegation of Austria-Hungary to the status of a satellite of Germany, his prediction appeared borne out the following November when Berlin and Vienna announced the creation of a nebulous Polish kingdom carved out of districts captured from Russia. Fanfare notwithstanding, the enterprise amounted to scarcely more than a glorified garrison of the Central Powers, and it drew a skeptical initial response from Rome and the Polish hierarchy. The scheme failed to satisfy Gasparri on the grounds that it granted the Hohenzollerns, not the Habsburgs, a de facto trusteeship over a still-partitioned Poland, and even though many of the Polish clergy of the new "kingdom" inwardly welcomed the Germans and Austrians as liberators of the devout from the more onerous yoke of Petersburg, they thought better of saying so, hedging their bets against a possible Russian recovery.[24] Furthermore, this rump state fell far short of the ideal of national reunification. For his part, Bishop Sapieha pointedly refused requests to have the Te Deum sung in honor of the creation of a "Poland" that implausibly excluded his Diocese of Kraków, the queen of Polish cities.[25] Nor had the Polish Church forgotten its decades of persecution at the hands of Germany, the primary sponsor of the initiative. To overcome this legacy of ill will, German policy during wartime had made a calculated appeal to Polish Catholics in hopes of securing their loyalty. In the opening weeks of the conflict Berlin hurriedly had withdrawn its objections to the nomination of Edward Likowski to fill the long-vacant archbishopric of Gniezno-Poznań, the traditional primatial see of Poland, and then followed this opening concession with a consistent pattern of scrupulous treatment of the Church in its own Polish provinces and those wrested from Russia. Despite these encouraging signs, Likowski's successor, Archbishop Edmund Dalbor, did no more than to extend public but pro forma gratitude to the German Kaiser upon the creation of his puppet Poland.

In the oracular custom of its diplomacy, the Vatican never made an unequivocal statement of its Polish policy during the war, despite all manner of hints of the pope's kind regard for that loyally Catholic nation. Even so, by its own reckoning Rome thought it had made its stance clear enough and in later years showed little patience with Polish critics who contended otherwise. In 1921, stung by one too many accusations of his wartime indifference to the Polish cause, Benedict hotly objected that "only the Apostolic See" had declared plainly "that Poland needed full and complete freedom, that is to say independence."[26] Strictly speaking, this was an exaggeration born of pique; still, he legitimately might have claimed credit as the first head of state to call publicly for an authentic, if ill-defined, Polish self-rule that went beyond the tentative proposals of belligerents that would have tethered the Poles fast to Russia or the Germanic powers. Benedict's definitive statement on the war, his famous "Peace Note" of August 1, 1917, among other points urged the world to apply the principles of "equity and justice" to the resolution of the Polish question. On its face, this pontification could mean anything, or nothing, but those attuned to the delphic ways of Rome construed it to suggest the fashioning of a fully united Poland with at least autonomous standing. The pope received little recognition or applause for his recommendation. Although his initiative preceded Wilson's corresponding reference to Poland in his Fourteen Points by several months, it was more vaguely framed and gingerly worded than the American document and evoked no more than a tepid reaction from Polish opinion. It made such a poor impression on the Poles of Galicia that the bishops of the region quietly undertook efforts in damage control to persuade their flock that the pope had not turned his back on them.[27]

Meanwhile, the Church gradually shed many of its hesitations regarding the kingdom of Poland the Central Powers had patched together. For all its limitations, the protectorate of the Germanic emperors seemed an irrevocable step toward eventual Polish sovereignty, and at any rate it plainly surpassed any offer the Allies had made the Poles so far. More to the point, as Sapieha noted, so long as London and Paris counted on Russia, the Entente would not dare to raise the bid on the Polish card.[28] Even so, a full year elapsed before the Polish Church and the Vatican decided to put their money on the German-Austrian horse, not without misgivings, and only after the firm nudge given them in that direction by the onset of revolution in Russia. In autumn of 1917, Berlin got around to forming a government for its satellite Poland, and invited the archbishop of Warsaw, Aleksander Kakowski, to lend the authority of the Church by serving as one of three members of the Regency Council it established as the nominal ruling authority of its fiefdom. The gesture inspired mutual distaste, for Kakowski bore no love for the Germans, and they knew it. Still, the collapse of the tsardom the previous March and the subsequent advent of Bolshevism had sufficed to convince even the invincibly circumspect Kakowski that the perils of inaction outweighed those of decision: Russia looked finished, and the promised kingdom under German sponsorship appeared to him and the predominantly conservative and monarchist Polish clergy as the only possible shelter against Russian disorder, social upheaval, and the rise of republican sentiment among their own people. Shortly before the Bolshevik coup in Russia, having first obtained permission from the pope, Kakowski agreed to enter the Regency Council—against his will, so he privately insisted, and out of a sense of sacrificial duty to his nation and Church.[29] Once in office, Kakowski quickly showed that he had not erred in choosing a priestly vocation instead of politics, and his earnest but inept struggles to manage his new civic chores drove his Vatican superiors to distraction.[30]

Once having made up its mind, the Church at home and abroad showed an increasing commitment to the Polish kingdom cobbled up by the German and Austrian emperors. In January 1918 the pope pronounced a blessing on the Regency Council, whose composition and policies reflected a strongly clerical streak. Polish clergymen made up a substantial share of the administrative apparatus of the protectorate, and its foreign ministry urged the speedy conclusion of a concordat.[31] Responding to the appeal of the Polish bishops, Benedict also dispatched to the embryonic state an apostolic visitor, his house librarian, who would become the next pope within months of returning to Italy.

In any case, the dynamic course of the last year of the war nullified all previous calculations regarding Poland, as the collapse of the Central Powers coupled with the widening revolution in Russia produced Polish independence under the banner of the victorious Allies. The addition of the United States to its ranks permitted the Entente to gain a decisive advantage, while the subtraction of Bolshevist Petrograd released the invigorated coalition from the need to cater to Russian sensibilities concerning Poland and enabled it to outbid Berlin and Vienna for the allegiance of the subject peoples of the heart of Europe. Given their innate caution, both Rome and the Polish Church struggled to keep up with the dizzying rush of events, and neither saw the Allied triumph coming until it was practically upon them. Some Polish hierarchs remained loyal to the old regime virtually to its last gasp, while on the other extreme, Archbishop Teodorowicz addressed the Austrian parliament as early as October 1917 to demand the liberation of Poland.[32] Until very late in the game, however, the Vatican and most of the Polish bishops continued to pin their hopes on the Austro-Polish conception of a reconstituted Poland under nominal sovereignty of the Habsburgs, and Gasparri was still defending the merits of the project well into the autumn of 1918.[33] By October, however, as the imminent breakdown of the Central Powers approached, Catholic spokesmen at last sensed the drift of things and took up the cry for the unconditional restoration of the

Rzeczpospolita. As the unthinkable became the inevitable, and a renewed Poland emerged from the ruins of the shattered empires, the Church lent its institutional imprimatur to full Polish independence. The bishops of Russian Poland went on record in favor of ecclesiastical and political reunification with the more westerly Polish provinces. In mid-month, Pope Benedict announced to the Polish faithful his joy that "at last the dawn of the resurrection of Poland has broken," adding his "most ardent prayer" that the emancipated country might soon "resume her career as a civilizing and Christian force."[34] On November 1, on the feast of All Saints, which was dear to Polish Catholic culture, the bishops of Galicia called on all churches to celebrate the national rebirth by singing the Te Deum followed by "Boże coś Polskę."[35]

The implosion of the Central Powers also brought down their satellite Poland with them and put the faltering and now abruptly vestigial Regency Council out of its misery. Over the preceding weeks, mounting enthusiasm for liberation had turned Polish opinion decisively against the occupation regime as well as the harried regent, Archbishop Kakowski, its most prominent figurehead. Only too glad to be rid of his unwanted political burdens, the exhausted prelate made haste to dissolve what remained of his government. In the anarchic last days of the war, Kakowski coaxed the Regency Council into abdication and acquiescence in the transfer of power as interim dictator to none other than Józef Piłsudski, the bane of the clergy, persuaded that the renegade socialist might best supply the strong leadership that would shield the infant state from the greater dangers of chaos.[36]

With independence an accomplished fact, the Polish Church promptly struck a newly assertive and confident note, hurrying to identify itself with the revived republic and fill the void of leadership left by the German debacle while the new government in Warsaw attempted to gain its footing. This increased ecclesiastical visibility during the first heady weeks of statehood had various motives: genuine enthusiasm for the national deliverance; the need of the Church to burnish its patriotic credentials and dispel the impression that it had cast its lot with the Central Powers; above all the natural prestige of the cloth, which introduced an element of familiarity and stability into the prevalent atmosphere of civic confusion. No doubt aware of their vulnerability to criticism as compromised holdovers from the partition era, Archbishops Dalbor and Kakowski hastened to scold Berlin for having dealt with the Poles in bad faith, demanding the speedy evacuation of the remaining German occupation forces.[37] As they withdrew, hundreds of priests assisted in the reorganization of former German Poland, most conspicuously the young Fr. Stanisław Adamski, who would become one of the more notable cleric-politicians of the Second Republic and survive to endure the persecutions of the Polish People's Republic. In Galicia, many Poles looked to the imperious figure of Bishop Sapieha of Kraków as the sole figure of recognizable authority amid the shambles of the defunct Habsburg monarchy.[38]

For its part, the papal state welcomed the reappearance of Poland on the map of Europe with unfeigned satisfaction as one of the few redeeming features of an otherwise deplorable postwar continental order. From its own distinctive vantage point, the Vatican would have preferred to see the fighting end with Russia defeated and the Central Powers intact; instead, in Roman eyes the war had raged on to the death, demolished the crucial elements of European stability, and purchased the downfall of the Orthodox colossus—in itself an agreeable development—at the high cost of unleashing Bolshevism, opening the gates to atheistic revolution. As for the victorious Allies, so the analysis continued, their triumph cemented the hegemony of a liberal and anticlerical worldview inherently hostile to the Church, a conviction hardened by the unceremonious exclusion of the Holy See from the peace councils of Paris. Within this unpromising constellation of powers, Warsaw appeared as likely a friend as the popes were going to find, the natural successor to the Habsburg Empire as the mainstay of Catholicism in Central Europe. In fact, the Curia had accepted the demise of the Dual Monarchy with a brisk absence of fuss or sentimentality. Even before Austria-Hungary had breathed its last, Benedict ordered his nuncio in Vienna to leave the deathbed and shift his attention to cultivating good contacts with the insurgent nationalities of the dying kingdom, "which, at the present hour, are reconstituting themselves as independent states."[39] Of these, the Poles seemed the most suitable candidates to inherit the mantle of the Habsburgs. Aside from his genuine personal warmth for a people so axiomatically devout, Pope Della Chiesa trusted that the erection of a Catholic Poland on the western flank of Russia might advance the interests of the faith and serve as a partial remedy for the deranged condition of Europe. The Apostolic See bestowed formal recognition upon the country in March 1919, lauding it in terms calculated to suggest parental affection for a favored child.

More than most newborns, Poland went through considerable growing pains before attaining its final dimensions. Over the course of three turbulent years, a combination of uprising, plebiscite, and Allied diplomatic

TABLE 1.1.
Population of Poland by religion and nationality, 1921

Religion			*Nationality*		
	Population (in millions)	Percent		Population (in millions)	Percent
Roman Catholic	17.4	63.8	Polish	18.8	69.2
Greek Catholic	3.0	11.2	Ukrainian	3.9	14.3
Orthodox	2.8	10.5	Jewish	2.1	7.8
Jewish	2.8	10.5	Belorussian	1.1	3.9
Protestant	1.0	3.8	German	1.1	3.9
Other	0.1	0.2	Other	0.2	0.9

Source: Figures from official Polish census of 1921.

fiat had drawn frontiers with Germany and Czechoslovakia that only partially fulfilled Polish objectives and left Berlin immovably unreconciled. Toward the east, Polish arms secured a broad swath of the Lithuanian, Belorussian, and Ukrainian *kresy,* the marchlands historically linked with the Rzeczpospolita where Poles made up a minority clustered within such ancient citadels of Polish culture as Vilna and Lwów, standing amid a hinterland of different ethnic complexion. By 1921, these exertions had defined the extent of the population and territory of the Second Republic and left it a country of medium size with most of its boundaries in dispute, ominously squeezed between Germany and the Soviet Union, hostile and irredentist great powers in sulky temporary eclipse. The new Poland emerged as a hybrid polity, recognizably Polish and Roman Catholic at its core yet not quite an incontestably national state of compact religious makeup. The government reported this fact with reasonable frankness in its first census, issued in 1921 (see table 1.1).

While the official figures must be taken with a dose of salt—no doubt the ethnicity count was fudged somewhat to Polish advantage, and the confessional table misleads by omitting unbelievers—they correspond roughly with the estimates of other contemporary surveys[40] and may be trusted sufficiently to yield several general conclusions of importance to the interplay of religion and politics in the Second Republic.

In the first place, three of every four Polish subjects proclaimed themselves in communion with Rome in some fashion, the main body of Latin Catholics—the "real" Catholics, in the minds of many—supplemented by some three million adherents of two Eastern rites. Of these, the handful of Armenian Catholics, the fold of Archbishop Teodorowicz, scarcely dented the statistical ledgers. A vestige of the polyglot Respublica of old, these five thousand souls clustered in the Lwów region had become thoroughly polonized over time and felt strong kinship with their Latin brethren. In almost every respect, the Ukrainian Greek Catholics of formerly Austrian eastern Galicia, the second-largest religious congregation in the land, represented a different case altogether. Founded by the Union of Brest in 1596 as a means to convert the Orthodox of the kresy, the "Uniate" Church incorporated much of the trappings and tradition of the east, including its Church Slavonic liturgy and married parish clergy, while acknowledging the supremacy of the pope. Despised as apostates by the Orthodox and subjected to tsarist repression over the centuries, commonly patronized as religious inferiors and mistrusted as Ukrainian separatists by the Latin Poles, the Greek Catholics retained a proud sense of their unique ecumenical mission and regarded their Polish counterparts with a prickly wariness amply repaid by their western half brothers in Christ.

Moreover, confessional affiliation in reconstituted Poland closely followed lines of ethnicity, and dissent from the Roman Catholic religious norm qualified as one of the most reliable indicators of national minority status. So, then, Germans were mainly Protestants of Lutheran persuasion, and vice versa; Belorussians were Orthodox; Ukrainians were solidly Greek Catholic in Galicia and heavily Orthodox in the provinces once Russian, where official pressure had forced them to renounce Uniatism; and Jews were Jews, the largest Jewry in the world and the only significant body of non-Christians in the country, for the most part not assimilated into Polish culture and destined to pose a singularly delicate and difficult challenge of coexistence both for the secular and sacred authorities of interwar Poland. As a corollary, religious identity prompted inevitable and sometimes accurate inferences concerning political loyalty to the Polish state, or its lack. Protestant Poles labored mightily to combat the impression that their membership in a denomination so closely associated with Germanic persecution was somehow outlandish and unpatriotic. In the east, Orthodoxy inescapably carried the taint of Russophilia, while the Greek Catholic sect functioned virtually as a national church of west Ukraine.

Looked at from the other angle, the demographic arithmetic also demonstrated that, for practical purposes, the old saw was true, after all: that in Poland, indeed, the Poles were Catholic, and the Catholics—at any rate, the Roman Catholics—were Poles. Exceptions to both generalizations could be found easily enough. Measurable fragments of the Polish nation adhered to Protestant groups or to Orthodoxy or, more often, to Judaism as "Poles of Mosaic faith." By the same token, national minorities accounted for about two hundred thousand of the western Catholics of the country, Germans making up a little more than half the total, with the remnant filled out by the small but overwhelmingly Roman contingent of Lithuanians plus odds and ends of the Ukrainian, Belorussian, and Czech populace. These were the anomalies that proved the rule. None of this changed the blunt facts that all but 2 percent of the 17.4 million Latin Catholics resident in Poland were Poles, and that 91 percent of Poles declared themselves Catholics. In other words, like many stereotypes, the doctrine of polak-katolik and the related idea of Catholicism as the Polish national religion contained a semblance of validity, quite enough to satisfy those inclined to defend such propositions.

Rooted in the soil of a historically agrarian society, Polish Catholicism exhibited many of the attributes of its rural origins and upbringing. The peasant masses supplied the base of its constituency and gave their church its definitive earthy qualities: sturdy if unlettered piety, an emphasis on outward devotion, a conspicuous Marian streak, and—so said its critics—a blinkered, bigoted, and stultifying provinciality. Aside from filling the pews of the churches, the folk of the countryside peopled its sanctuaries as well, furnishing the bulk of the more than ten thousand clergy and religious. Hewing to timeworn patterns, nearly half of the episcopate sprang from the nobility or landed gentry, while parishes found their priests among the sons of the peasantry. With greater advantages of birth, and usually the possessors of higher education, the bishops as a group reflected the values and abilities of the elite. Whether well born or plebeian, the typical Polish cleric did not enjoy a high reputation. He and his colleagues were frequently described as wanting in aptitude and formation, seldom rising above the prejudices and narrow horizons of their rustic background; collectively, they remained "in knowledge mediocre: in literary and scholarly accomplishment worse than mediocre," according to Ermenegildo Pellegrinetti, Nuncio Ratti's chargé d'affaires, betraying the wearied air of one accustomed to dealing with them.[41] What Polish churchmen lacked in education and polish, they made up in zeal and readiness to mix in politics, a trait carried over from the partition era, when the priest acted as the grassroots spokesman for Poles against the alien regime. Emerging into the changed conditions of independence, the Catholic clergy retained its instinct for excitable, sometimes crude nationalism and took for granted its right and duty to enter the civic fray in word and deed, rarely subtly, usually on behalf of the parties of the Right, and by no means always in line with the wishes of the Vatican. Such habits, reported Monsignor Pellegrinetti at the end of the Ratti mission in 1921, had caused the Warsaw nunciature no little anxiety and trouble, a diplomatic way of saying that they had cost his chief his job.[42]

At the pinnacle of its hierarchy, the reassembled Polish Church had inherited a generation of leadership that has inspired few superlatives. Neither of the two archbishops from the German and Russian zones, Edmund Dalbor (b. 1869) and Aleksander Kakowski (b. 1862), owned a strong personality, and both bore the tarnish of unpopularity as relics from the days of national servitude, widely suspected of having kowtowed to foreign masters. Dalbor and Kakowski paid a dear price in public esteem for their grudging wartime bows toward Berlin, for in the light of the changed perspective that prevailed in Poland after 1918, they never entirely shed an undeserved reputation as lukewarm patriots, onetime lapdogs of the Germans insufficiently devoted to the ideal of complete independence. Although few Poles could match these prelates for patriotic convictions, in the glare of hindsight their cautious wartime approach to the Polish question was seen as halfhearted and unduly deferential toward the occupier. Indeed, when Pope Benedict promptly announced his intention to confer a cardinalate on the archbishop of Warsaw in recognition of the renewed sovereignty of his country, the Polish government grumbled mildly on the grounds that the honor might be construed as a reward for Kakowski's unhappy service in the German Regency Council, which in fact was precisely the idea; the pontiff relented only to the extent of simultaneously elevating Dalbor and Kakowski to the purple in 1919.[43] Dalbor assumed the status of primate, the president of the national episcopate, which historically accompanied his see of Gniezno-Poznań, but the post almost might have remained vacant for all the difference it made. Retiring and passive by nature, Dalbor had no taste or gift for politics, and his public demeanor was subdued to the point of invisibility. He ranks as one of the least memorable and least remembered of Polish primates. For his part, Kakowski also shunned the spotlight, but as the ordinary of the capital he could not evade notice so easily as the all-but-faceless Dalbor. By and large, observers were unimpressed by what they saw. Contemporaries tended to describe Kakowski as a good-hearted mediocrity, bright enough, perhaps, but clumsy and erratic, distinguished above all by an invincible capacity for discretion and fencesitting. Kakowski was not cut out for politics, and knew it. His lackluster performance as wartime regent had won him nothing but trouble and opprobrium, and it is scarcely surprising that afterward he reverted to his habit of keeping his cards close to his vestments. No one knew for certain his inner partisan sympathies, but throughout his career he showed himself reliably able to get along with the authority of the day. Despite his reputation as a bumbler, the Holy See appreciated his loyalty to Rome and viewed him as its man within the hierarchy of Poland, but he carried no great influence in the country and seemed content to maintain an unobtrusive profile.[44]

The reticence of the two cardinals magnified the importance of the Galician bishops, Sapieha of Kraków (b. 1867) and Teodorowicz of Lwów (b. 1864), who possessed in abundance the energy and decisiveness their nominal superiors so obviously lacked. Fast friends and allies of long standing, they shared an enthusiasm for the Dmowski Endecja and diligently worked in tandem to galvanize the Catholic episcopate in support of the nationalist Right. Although not yet an archbishop—he would not receive that designation until 1925—Sapieha stood out as the most naturally impressive figure within the Latin hierarchy, his innate talents enhanced by the prestige of his family name, one of the most illustrious in the rolls of Polish nobility. His lengthy custody of the historic royal cathedral on Kraków's Wawel Hill began before the First World War and did not end until after the Second, and in his later years he numbered among his protégés the young priest Karol Wojtyła. Fearless, headstrong, and irascible, imbued with aristocratic pride and arrogance, he commanded respect even from his numerous enemies. Teodorowicz was, to borrow the phrase of Evelyn Waugh, Sapieha carved by an Aztec, reproducing in coarser, exaggerated form the features of his patrician colleague. Sapieha was resolute, impatient, and combustible; Teodorowicz obstinate, rash, and combustion itself, a human volcano in constant eruption. He also exerted a strong sway over the bishop of Kraków, his junior in age and rank. Teodorowicz lived and breathed politics and intrigue, and his light load of pastoral duties as curate of Poland's few Armenian Catholics afforded him ample time to engage in his favorite pastimes, to the despair of the many who conceded his undeniable abilities but thought of him mainly as a reckless troublemaker who also brought out the cantankerous worst in Sapieha.[45] As time went on, the Vatican would make a point of warning newly appointed papal nuncios to Warsaw to watch their step around Teodorowicz, based on the unhappy experiences of their predecessors.[46]

Apart from Sapieha, only one member of the Catholic hierarchy of reborn Poland bore the stamp of true greatness, and as fate would have it he was an outsider generally regarded by Poles as a national and religious enemy. If Andrei Sheptyts'kyi, the Greek Catholic metropolitan of Halicz-Lwów, was not "the most remarkable of living Slavs," as some contended, then he was at the least one of the most striking and fascinating figures of modern Christendom.[47] Born Roman Aleksander Maria Count Szeptycki in 1865, the son of Polish nobility of the Galician kresy and the grandson of the famed playwright Aleksander Fredro, he adopted Ukrainian identity and the Greek Catholic rite in adulthood, reversing the adage "*gente Ruthenus, natione Polonus.*" Since 1900 the "Bishop of St. George," the head of the Uniates of Galicia, he tirelessly presented his church as a foundation for the reconciliation of western and eastern Christianity and did not discourage the opinion that his own personal metamorphosis incarnated the ecumenical spirit: "I am like St. Paul, who became . . . all things to all men so as to save all."[48] Physically imposing and full-bearded, Sheptyts'kyi possessed the visage and thundering moral certitude of an Old Testament prophet, and he fiercely guarded his Ukrainian and Greek Catholic flock against the pretensions of the Latin Poles. He had championed the cause of west Ukrainian independence at the end of the world war, and after Poland captured eastern Galicia by force of arms in 1919 he held himself aloof from the Polish episcopate and frequently challenged the government in Warsaw, acting virtually as the chaplain of a church and a people under foreign occupation. A complex blend of sweeping vision, iron will, and inexhaustible self-righteousness, Sheptyts'kyi had a genius for exasperating all the various rulers of his metropolitanate from the Habsburgs to Stalin and Hitler, and the Polish Second Republic would prove no exception.

Aside from the shortage of brilliance at its top, the Polish Church faced the same daunting task that challenged Poland in every facet of its existence: that of welding itself into a coherent whole out of the disjointed fragments of the partitioning empires. Superimposed upon the intersection of three national episcopates, the rebuilt country was bequeathed a hodgepodge of ecclesiastical structures and laws that had been designed to meet the requirements of the obliterated prewar world and now made no sense. Diocesan boundaries no longer agreed with the radically altered state frontiers, stranding millions of Catholics on both sides of the Polish borders under the unwanted jurisdiction of suddenly "foreign" bishops, and leaving absurd disparities of territory and population in the residual organization of the Church on Polish soil. The confusion extended even to the residence of the primacy, claimed alike by Gniezno-Poznań on the grounds of tradition and by Warsaw by virtue of the status of its incumbent as primate of antebellum Russian Poland. This argument dragged on until 1925, debated by canon lawyers and historians, until the Vatican settled the matter by splitting the difference: both archbishops kept their primatial dignity, and Dalbor of Gniezno-Poznań retained his honorific title as primate of Poland, but without any real authority over Kakowski of Warsaw. However, no curial decree could so easily undo the legacy of twelve decades of tripartite separation that had produced significant disparities of ecclesiastical circumstances and culture in the various sectors of the Polish lands. Catholicism and the clergy enjoyed high prestige and influence in the former German and Russian zones for their role in the nationality wars of the previous century, but Berlin had not plundered the wealth or landholdings of the Church, while tsarist repression and expropriations had depleted the eastern dioceses. In political terms, western Poland was the heart of Endecja country, known as home to legions of rightist Catholic laymen and pugnacious priests like Fr. Adamski, battle-hardened in the forge of the Kulturkampf and the resistance against Germanification. Spared the lash of persecution, the Church in the Austrian south had changed the least since the partitions, its noble, conservative hierarchs reigning over an intact collection of extensive, though hardscrabble, Galician lands. Not even the passage of the twenty coming years of independence would suffice to complete the integration of the reunited branches of the Polish Church, or to efface entirely its acquired regional differences of custom and psychology.[49]

The political transformation also thrust Polish Catholicism into legal limbo. In the absence of a concordat, what rules defined the relationship of Poland with the Holy See, or guaranteed the rights of the Church within the republic? Until Warsaw crafted its own constitution and laws, did the religious legislation of the old regimes remain in force in their respective jurisdictions, including the German and Russian statutes Catholics regarded as inimical and discriminatory? Or did the Church simply stand *extra legem*, hostage to the goodwill and arbitrary whim of each rotating cabinet and

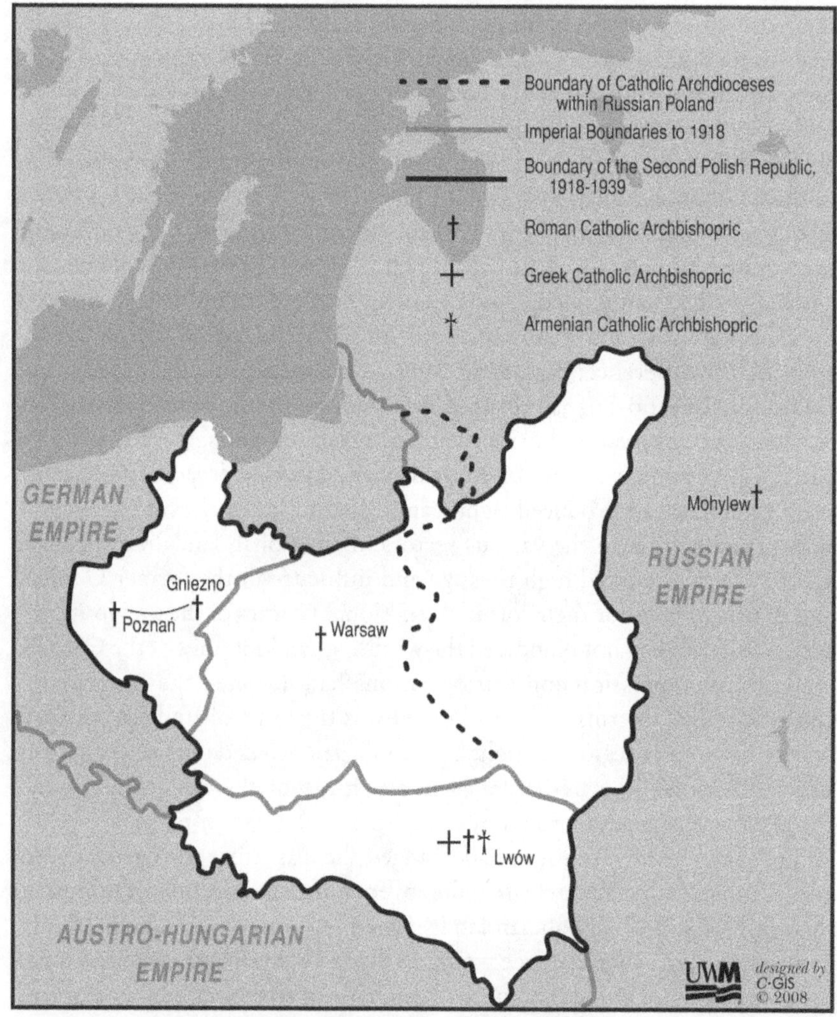

MAP 1. Diocesan organization of Poland, 1918–25. Map by Donna G. Genzmer, University of Wisconsin–Milwaukee. Copyright © 2009 Board of Regents of University of Wisconsin System

every petty local functionary? Such uncertainties nagged at Catholic opinion, especially in light of the prominence of Piłsudskiites and the Left in the initial interwar governments.

While Poland might be *semper fidelis,* its Catholics saw reasons for worry on all sides. Already damaged by nineteenth-century confiscations, the material condition of the Church had suffered further buffeting by wholesale wartime destruction of its buildings and properties. Perhaps most of the faithful and their clergy believed, with varying degrees of urgency and intonation, in the mounting threat posed by Communism, Freemasonry, and the Jews, possibly joined in unholy alliance. Others focused on corrosive shortcomings found within their own ranks. Thinkers fretted over a growing religious indifference among males and the embarrassing intellectual poverty of Polish Catholicism; from the pulpits, priests chastised their parishioners for a host of moral failings attributed to the degrading influence of foreign rule and the iniquities of modern life: drunkenness, petty dishonesty, impiety.[50] Some went so far as to dismiss the famed Polish devotion as little more than a national tic, a communal display of obligatory sanctimoniousness. When a Pole removed his hat when passing a church, sniffed one of the pope's men at the Warsaw nunciature, "it is not a sign of respect for the house of the Lord, but a way of saying: see, I am Polish."[51]

Still, the formidable list of troubles and burdens did not overshadow the greater sense of satisfaction that the deliverance of Poland, the unexpected prize of a terrible war, had fulfilled one of the fondest longings of the Catholic world, offering hope for an anxious age and proof of the workings of Providence in human history. As the new year 1920 dawned, Benedict XV fulfilled a promise made by his predecessor twice removed, sending to Warsaw a candle once set aside by Pius IX to await the return of a free Poland.[52] To those who believed, faith and perseverance had won their reward, and God had redeemed his people out of bondage once again.

2 ı|ı Il Papa Polacco

The Making of Pius XI, 1918–1922

As the First World War entered its last months in 1918, the Vatican knew only two things for certain regarding the future of the Catholic Church in central and eastern Europe: that the antebellum order would be transformed beyond recognition, and that some sort of sovereign Poland would return to the map after its lengthy absence. Indeed, thanks to the initiative of the German and Habsburg emperors, a Polish kingdom already existed on paper, even if its independence was largely a fiction. Even at that late date, everything else concerning the prospects for the Roman mission in that zone of the continent remained shrouded in confusion. Above all, the widening revolution in Russia and the incipient breakup of the farflung realm of the tsars both freed and threatened several Catholic peoples while holding out the dazzling promise of a historic expansion of the Church into the Orthodox east. Unsure of its best approach to this combination of danger and opportunity, the papal state counted on the new Poland as its natural base of activity in that turbulent region. So when the Polish bishops requested the posting of an apostolic visitor to their theoretically restored country after the Treaty of Brest-Litovsk certified the Russian surrender, the Holy See happily obliged: not only was the suggestion a useful idea on its own merits, but the new man could also serve as the eyes and ears of the pope in the European borderlands. The Vatican functionaries took the appointment seriously as an important decision bearing on the development of the Church in Poland and other formerly Russian territories, although few could have suspected just how important it would turn out to be; surely none divined that the choice would identify the eventual successor to Benedict XV and forcefully alter the destiny of Catholicism in the twentieth century.

Because the nominee for the Polish errand reached such exalted and surprising heights, the tale of his selection became the stuff of minor legend, often retold in ecclesiastical circles. According to the story, either Cardinal Gasparri, more likely his *sostituto* within the Secretariat of State, or even a transient Polish cleric suggested the name of the little-known prefect of the Vatican Library as a suitable candidate. This unconventional recommendation intrigued Pope Benedict, who had occasionally consulted his resident scholar on the historical background of the war and its related issues and had formed a good opinion of his judgment and abilities. In April 1918, the pontiff offered the librarian the embassy to Poland. Startled, the designee asked for time to consider, hesitant to accept an assignment so remote from his experience and expertise. The very next day, Benedict summoned the reluctant bibliophile for a second audience. Well, now you have had a chance to think it over, the pope is supposed to have said—"When do you leave for Poland?"[1] Thus, according to lore, did Monsignor Achille Ambrogio Damiano Ratti, the bookish sixty-year-old son of a Lombard silk factory manager, take the first tentative step down a remarkable path that led him through an eventful three-year Polish nunciature to the see of St. Peter.

Before its unlikely climax, his career had prospered in obscurity, far removed from the fast track toward the upper reaches of Church government. Following ordination, Ratti had settled into the leisurely routine of academics, making methodical advancement until arriving at the prefecture of the Vatican Library in 1914, seemingly having attained the limit of his ambitions. His learned demeanor and duties masked a steely and imperious temperament, qualities that came to the fore only after the subsequent and ultimate promotion that released him forever from the obligation to play the loyal subordinate. That lay in the future; for the time being, the posting to Poland involved more than enough difficulty and complexity to challenge even the most seasoned papal diplomat, let alone a neophyte. At bottom, the Vatican had no idea what to make of the chaotic picture in the European east, or how best to pursue its own interests. Contending factions within and around the Curia advocated a variety of incompatible policies, ranging from open reliance on the Poles as the flagbearers of the Catholic cause in their vicinity to warnings that precisely this was the surest way to hamper the work of the Church in Russia and the kresy by aggravating old antagonisms and resentments toward Poland. In its initial conception, the Ratti mission had no clearer or more urgent mandate than the vague instruction simply to take stock of the situation and sort through the bewildering alternatives.[2] The mediation of Archbishop Eugenio Pacelli, the nuncio in Munich, procured the imprimatur of the German authorities, who still held sway in that theater for the moment, and by the summer of 1918 Ratti had been installed as apostolic visitor to Poland and Lithuania, resident in Warsaw but responsible for all the lands of the crumbling Russian imperium.[3]

The Ratti sojourn was originally devised as a reconnoitering expedition of a zone in flux possibly lasting only a few months, and the pope had told him to plan on returning home by Christmas.[4] His task took on a different, less improvisatory character once the war ended, sweeping away the German sphere of conquest and replacing the puppet Poland with the Second Republic—genuinely independent and presumably there to stay—but answering little else Rome wanted to know. To reflect the changed circumstances, after the official papal recognition of the new Polish state in 1919 Ratti assumed the title of full nuncio to Poland, the first since 1796, and an accompanying elevation to the rank of archbishop. In corresponding fashion, he began to focus the bulk of his attention on Polish affairs while yet keeping a watchful eye on developments in the east. This somewhat narrower definition of his job hardly left Ratti with time on his hands, for the task of rehabilitating the Polish Church and placing its relationship with the Warsaw government on acceptable footing more than sufficed to keep him busy. In the eyes of the Vatican, achievement of these goals required a satisfactory concordat above all, and the Secretariat of State instructed Ratti to regard preparing the groundwork for such a treaty as his top priority. At the same time, he was asked to pull off a tricky political balancing act, on the one hand coaxing the Polish bishops to sacrifice some Church properties to the popular demand for land reform, on the other doing all in his power to protect the economic standing of a Church that had been bled of much of its wealth during the past century of persecution and war.[5]

After decades spent keeping company with books, Nuncio Ratti eagerly tackled the challenge of his new responsibilities in stimulating and exotic foreign surroundings. His official dispatches and private letters to friends and family mixed matters official with chatty observations on Polish customs and conditions and a touristic delight in sights and the odd detail. He found the country endearing and maddening at the same time. He never ceased to laud the simple piety of Poles, although he worried that a national weakness for ostentatious public religiosity did the Church there no credit. At first astonished and made uneasy by the multitudes of Jews he encountered in Polish cities, he adjusted soon enough and in later years drew on the experiences of his nunciature to undergird his relatively enlightened views on the Jewish question. Impatient by nature, he fumed regularly over the proverbial Polish inefficiency that combined with the messy aftermath of war to hamper his communications with Rome and multiply the already considerable frustrations of dealing with the curial bureaucracy. However, from first to last the Polish episcopate itself caused the nuncio his worst headaches. Despite his declarations to the Polish bishops that he thought of himself as one of them, holding the interests of their country close to his heart, the fractious and intensely political inclinations of the Catholic hierarchy of Poland took him by unpleasant surprise, complicated his work until the day he returned to Italy, and smoldered in his memory as long as he lived.[6]

The nub of the problem Ratti faced was that a solid majority of the Polish episcopate backed the National Democratic brand of rightist politics, putting them at odds with much of the governing establishment of the country and the preference of the Vatican itself. Shortly after the armistice Benedict XV had urged bishops in the new states of Europe to avoid embroiling the Church in partisan controversies, and to see that their priests followed suit;[7] undeterred, the Polish clergy had wasted little time confirming the impression that it meant to act as a virtual auxiliary of Endecja. During the parliamentary elections of 1919, much of the Catholic press and priesthood had endorsed the Dmowski party, sometimes directly from the pulpit, and eleven ecclesiastics sat among the Endek delegation in the Sejm, swelling its plurality in the legislature. While technically nonpartisan, the leader of this bloc of rightist cleric-deputies, as well as the loudest, was the fiery Archbishop Teodorowicz, who described politics as a sort of holy war against those he suspected of wishing to turn the Second Republic into a "pagan state."[8] He and his close friend Bishop Sapieha pressed these ideas upon Cardinal Dalbor, the likeminded but less forceful primate. Together this trio exercised what the nunciature disapprovingly called a *dittatura* over the episcopate, converting their own sympathy for National Democracy into all-but-declared policy of the Polish Church—although, to be sure, the "dictatorship" largely amounted to herding the bishops in the direction most of them already wanted to go.[9] This left Cardinal Kakowski as the odd man out among the ranking hierarchs of Poland, in more ways than one. The archbishop of Warsaw declined invitations to stand for election on the

Endecja ticket, and before long observers began to note his tendency to hold the Right at arm's length and to maintain some distance from the politics of the Teodorowicz-Sapieha-Dalbor triumvirate. In fact, the isolation of Kakowski within the episcopate resulted from more than mere differences in partisan allegiance. During the protracted dispute over the primacy of Poland, most of the clergy sided with Dalbor and Gniezno against Warsaw and closed ranks against the bishop of the capital. Given a cold shoulder by his colleagues, Kakowski still retained the confidence of the Vatican, which clearly preferred him to Dalbor and treated him as the first dignitary of the Polish Church in all but name.[10]

The rightward leanings of the clergy went hand in hand with its collective distaste for the charismatic Józef Piłsudski, both the most popular and the most reviled public figure in the country, who had assumed the rank of chief of state in the provisional government of the young republic. The dignity of high office failed to persuade Polish churchmen that the man they had grown accustomed to condemn as a leftist highwayman of low morals had suddenly become any more acceptable or respectable. When Cardinal Dalbor, speaking for the Church, addressed Piłsudski directly from the pulpit at a ceremonial mass in 1919, stressing that "we entrust to you the heritage we have safeguarded," few could have missed the cautionary hint that the national fate had passed into unreliable hands.[11] In fact, the whole country knew that most of the clergy turned up their noses at Piłsudski, sometimes on grounds of policy, more often on a more visceral level as the embodiment, so they imagined, of all they found intolerable. In keeping with his status as foremost episcopal irreconcilable, Archbishop Teodorowicz above all flaunted his loathing for Piłsudski, who repaid the sentiment with interest and made sure that army intelligence kept the Armenian-rite pastor under close watch.[12] On this count too, Cardinal Kakowski stood out as the exception among Polish archprelates for his ability to find redeeming qualities in the chief of state that remained well hidden from most of his colleagues in holy orders.[13]

For his part, once he got his bearings Nuncio Ratti had little difficulty deciding that he much preferred Piłsudski to Teodorowicz and his Endek coterie among the bishops. In the first place, the papal envoy concluded, somewhat to his surprise, that the Polish strongman did not deserve his reputation for irreligiosity. Piłsudski kept to himself his spiritual and philosophical convictions, such as they were, inviting all manner of speculation, and his grasp of theology and Catholic doctrine lacked sophistication, to put it gently. Once asked by a priest about the persistent rumor that he was a Freemason, he emphatically avowed his refusal on principle to have anything to do with the secret brotherhood, not for the reasons a catechist would have approved, but on the less-than-categorical grounds that he could not belong in good conscience to an international fraternity that might expose the interests of Poland to foreign manipulation—a description that, after all, might just as easily have applied to the Church.[14] Still, some spied within Piłsudski, beneath his wayward and lax exterior, a sort of noble savage of untutored piety. The battle-hardened chief of state had a soft spot for Church spectacle and lore that touched on national themes or his Lithuanian boyhood, and Ratti and his lieutenants took careful note when Piłsudski shed tears at the shrine of Ostrabrama in Vilna, or received the nuncio's blessing "with a lovely, even devout demeanor," or attributed the revival of Poland to the intervention of the saints.[15] All in all, the Warsaw nunciature reported to Rome, despite his notoriety, Piłsudski at heart was a religious man whose heterodoxy had been exaggerated by his enemies and magnified by the reflected real sins of his entourage, written off as an unsavory crew of flunkies, atheists, Freemasons, anticlericals, and apostates, for the most part rogues of easy virtue.[16] However, they took an indulgent view of Piłsudski's own marital peccadilloes, treating them as the indiscretions of an errant but well-meaning soul. Upon the death of his estranged uncanonical wife in 1921, the nunciature did no more than whisper to the Vatican the hope that the chief of state might use the occasion to "mend the condition of his private life," as Chargé Pellegrinetti delicately phrased it, and when Piłsudski wed his mistress two months later, Cardinal Kakowski was on hand to assist in the nuptials.[17]

In addition, Piłsudski satisfied Ratti that he meant no harm to the Church. By this time he had already turned his back on the Left, having ridden the red streetcar of socialism only as far as the independence stop, in the trenchant image attributed to him. Furthermore, he served notice that he lacked enthusiasm for the agenda of the anticlerical wing of his constituency. In March 1919, speaking with an interviewer in his chambers, a reproduction of a Raphael Madonna hanging on the wall, Piłsudski dwelt on the need to respect the power and prestige of Catholicism in his country and declared that "we cannot think in Poland, as yet, of a separation of the State and Church—as in France."[18] Taking the cue, the Piłsudskiite press echoed the call for good relations with the Vatican and peace with the Church at home. No matter that this policy was largely motivated by a pragmatic concern not to drive the Catholic faithful into the arms of the National Democrats, the practical effect remained the same: Piłsudski wanted a modus vivendi with the Roman confession, and would restrain the militant anti-clericals within his camp.[19] Indeed, in certain crucial respects his politics suited Rome far better than those of Endecja and its ecclesiastical claque, above all his more expansive notion of the nature of the Polish state and its mission in the kresy of Belorussia and Ukraine.

Not least, Ratti and Piłsudski simply liked each other. According to Ratti, the improbable friendship between the future pope and the man the Polish clergy loved to hate dated from an official reception in 1919, when he deftly rescued Piłsudski from an awkward interlude prompted by the tactless remark of a foreign diplomat. Touched by the gesture, Piłsudski took the Italian monsignor into his confidence, and over time the cordiality ripened into a lifelong mutual esteem.[20] This was a case of like attracting like, for each recognized in the other a kindred spirit, a similar mix of temper, bullheadedness, and autocratic spirit. "*Ha un carattere difficile, come il mio,*" Ratti said of the Polish strongman, and Piłsudski is supposed to have returned the wry compliment in almost the same words.[21] When Ratti and his lieutenants looked at Piłsudski, they saw a Polish Garibaldi, a flawed but charismatic man of qualities, capable of broad vision and great deeds.[22]

Out of this tangled knot of clashing politics and personalities emerged two distinct factions that vied for control over the direction of the interwar Polish Church in its formative years. On one side stood Ratti and, by extension, Benedict XV, determined to press the agenda of the Holy See. Usually they could count on the support of Cardinal Kakowski, deferential to the papacy, well disposed toward the nuncio and not at all offended by his bet on Piłsudski, and somewhat at odds with the prevailing rightward sentiment within the national episcopate. At every step this alliance ran into stubborn opposition from the circle of Endecja partisans who dominated their fellow bishops, especially the Galician duo of Teodorowicz and Sapieha, who held sway over the primate, Cardinal Dalbor. These balky prelates resisted Ratti as the agent of an unwanted degree of Roman influence over their Church. Apart from a natural concern for turf, they possessed a certain skepticism of the intentions of the Vatican, magnified by lingering suspicions that the Curia nursed a special solicitude for Germany, the most dangerous enemy of Poland in National Democratic eyes. The evident willingness of the nuncio to make common cause with Piłsudski only confirmed their worries that he was up to no good.[23] The fact that this struggle between the Vatican and the nationalist leadership of the Polish hierarchy took place under the obligatory cover of discretion and courtesy—at least until its very public final stages—did not reduce the intensity of the contest that defined and ultimately undid the Ratti mission to Poland.

Among other points, the two contending ecclesiastical parties disagreed on the need for a Polish concordat, the centerpiece of papal policy in the country. Following his instructions from Rome, Ratti lost no time in attempting to prepare the ground for a treaty between Warsaw and the Holy See, prodding the preoccupied ministers of the Second Republic to pay attention to the project and move it higher up their crowded list of priorities. Cardinal Kakowski dutifully went along.[24] However, Teodorowicz and Sapieha flatly rejected the line of the nunciature, arguing that any concordat would entail burdensome concessions to the civil power, that the Church stood a good chance of having its essential desiderata written into the forthcoming state constitution free of cost, and that—in so many words—the Vatican should leave these matters to the Polish bishops and mind its own business. In 1919 they prevailed on a number of their episcopal brethren to draft a letter to Pope Benedict in this very spirit, forcing the nuncio to squelch the initiative as directly contrary to the will of the pontiff. This combination of governmental distraction and dissent within the ranks of the hierarchy itself prevented any meaningful progress. By 1920 the pope had accepted the bishops' advice to await passage of the constitution, and Ratti departed Poland with the concordat still in embryo.[25]

The nuncio also parted company with the Polish bishops on matters of foreign policy relating to differing visions of the proper role of Poland in the eastern marches. Because Ratti continued to function as the Vatican's man in all reaches of the former Russia, not just Poland, he retained the Roman tendency to regard the Second Republic as certainly the foundation of east European Catholicism, but by no means the whole edifice. He took seriously his responsibilities as papal legate to the emerging polities of the area, although Lithuania kept him at arm's length out of fear that he might harbor a bias toward rival Warsaw, while the unfolding revolution in Russia —the most cherished target of Vatican missionary ambition—thwarted his aim of visiting that country and forced him to grapple at long distance with the myriad trials of a church in Bolshevist hands. At the same time, he took care to maintain scrupulous neutrality in the inevitable territorial disputes that erupted between the Poles and the other peoples of the kresy, favoring neither Poland nor Lithuania in their quarrel over Vilna and urging restraint in the Polish-Ukrainian war for title to eastern Galicia. Despite these poor auguries of concord in the borderlands—indeed, more likely in part on their account—and in keeping with his inclination to think of Poland within its broader regional setting, Ratti saw much to recommend in Piłsudski's vision of a reconstituted Polish republic as a confederation embracing the lands of old Lithuania, a latter-day incarnation of the Jagiellonian Respublica that would shove the Russian frontiers far away from central Europe. While Piłsudski embraced the project for historic and strategic reasons, the papal ambassador hoped that the collection of these expanses under the presumably benign rule of Catholic Poland might facilitate the conversion of Belorussia and Ukraine, quarantine the fever of revolution, and contract the political reach of Orthodoxy once the Bolshevik moment had passed.[26] This put him, as usual, on the wrong side of the Teodorowicz wing of the Polish episcopate, which preferred the National Democratic ideal of a more compact, westerly, and homogeneous Poland.[27]

In the meantime, just as Ratti found himself on unexpectedly tricky political terrain in Warsaw, so did his Polish counterparts in the Eternal City get off to a rocky start in their work at the hub of Church government. First, the habitual prickly insistence of the popes that their diplomatic friends should accord them precedence over the upstart Italian kingdom on the other bank of the Tiber made the task of staying on good terms with both the Vatican and the Quirinale a trying exercise in hairsplitting protocol. Moreover, the appointment of an obscure academic, Józef Wierusz-Kowalski, as the first minister of free Poland to the Holy See disappointed Benedict XV, who had expected the Poles to do him the honor of choosing a nobleman of distinguished pedigree. "What professor are they sending to Us?" snapped the pontiff upon hearing the news. Besides lacking the respect of his hosts, Wierusz-Kowalski won few plaudits for competence or professionalism. Behind his back his legation staff grumbled that their chief tiptoed into the chambers of the Curia as a penitent entered a confessional, overcome with awe, piety, and reverence for the cloth. Worse, they complained, he grossly underestimated the potential for discord between Poland and the Vatican, blandly assuming that religious solidarity guaranteed that nothing could disturb the relationship despite a gathering of warning signs to the contrary.[28]

In truth, apart from the obvious bond of Catholicism—and even that impressed Polish officialdom less than the pope and his men thought it should—Poland and the Holy See shared little in common in matters of international politics. Before long, grasping for explanations of a growing papal impatience with Polish foreign policies, Wierusz-Kowalski trotted out the theory that the Vatican bureaucracy sheltered a pro-German cabal that had managed to corrode the goodwill of the Holy Father toward the Polish cause.[29] The remarkable aspect of this argument was not the thesis itself—just a new twist on a well-worn theme of wartime gossip—but that its adherents should have felt the need to seek answers in shadowy intrigues when more compelling reasons were plain to see. Although the process of peace-making had not entirely satisfied its territorial and security goals, the Second Republic naturally regarded the European order established by the world war and symbolized by the Treaty of Versailles as the charter and sine qua non of its existence, to be defended at all costs. On the other hand, Rome held the jaundiced conviction that—as a French publicist of the day put it—"the peace of Versailles is not the peace of the Vatican, but rather an Anglosaxon [*sic*], puritan, and secularist peace," reflecting the values and interests of a dubious collection of regimes and worldviews. More to the point, in the hardheaded and freely advertised opinion of Cardinal Secretary of State Gasparri, the postwar settlement was simply unworkable and stupidly vengeful, bound to result "not in one but in ten wars."[30] Benedict XV made his disapproval of the Versailles order sharply explicit in his encyclical *Pacem Dei munus,* issued on May 23, 1920. Trying to soften the blow, the pope went out of his way that same day to assure Warsaw that he was "completely satisfied" with their mutual relations, but in fact the Curia found little to like in Polish foreign policy.[31] In particular, Gasparri belonged emphatically to the large camp of diplomats who thought freedom had intoxicated the Poles and that they should curb their appetite for territory, particularly in the west, before they got themselves, and Europe, in trouble; Poland could not afford to make enemies of both Russia and Germany, and should not burn its bridges to Berlin by pressing excessive claims against its German neighbor in the vicinity of Danzig and Silesia. Sooner or later, he warned, Warsaw would "pay dearly" for its land greed, and might even bring on its own ruin by provoking a disastrous German-Soviet alliance.[32]

Before the year was out, crises erupted on each of Poland's contested flanks that brought these tensions into the open and led first to the triumph, then rapidly to the inglorious end of the nunciature of Achille Ratti. In the east, where Polish and Soviet military forces had been jockeying for position in the no-man's-land of the kresy, Piłsudski threw the hostilities into higher gear in spring 1920 by launching an offensive intended to fulfill his goal of securing the borderlands and tilting the regional balance of power decisively toward Poland. The initial success of the drive brought Kiev into Polish hands by May and sparked an outburst of national euphoria. The Polish Church joined in the enthusiasm by celebrating masses to honor these feats of arms, although some prelates could not bear the fact that the accomplishment had made Piłsudski the hero of the hour. When the conquering general received a thunderous welcome in the parliament upon returning to Warsaw, his sworn enemy Archbishop Teodorowicz stood in the hall speechless and visibly agitated, his patriotic pride wrestling with his hatred of Piłsudski.[33] For its part, the Vatican also found itself torn, but for different reasons, pleased by every inch gained by the Poles at Russian expense, but convinced that the Polish advance was a rash venture that was bound to end badly.[34]

As if to confirm Cardinal Gasparri's fears of Polish overreach, the tide of battle shifted quickly in the summer, and a Red Army counteroffensive threatened to engulf Poland and, perhaps, to spill out into war-weary central Europe as well. The swift reversal of Polish fortunes that now jeopardized the existence of the state spurred the local Church into action. Rightist clerical foes of Piłsudski who had bitten their tongues while he was winning now turned their fury on him as the instigator of disaster: at one tempestuous meeting, Father Adamski publicly and loudly branded him a traitor to his face.[35] On a more dignified level, as the emergency grew more grave, the Catholic leadership of Poland concentrated on rallying the religious sentiments of their people in defense of nation and faith. In July the episcopate called on Poles to maintain unity and brace themselves to resist the invaders, and simultaneously appealed for the prayers and assistance of believers throughout the world to help them shield Europe against the Bolsheviks, "the living negation of Christianity." At the end of the month the bishops symbolically underscored their petition by asking the pope to canonize Andrzej Bobola, a seventeenth-century Polish Jesuit missionary who had suffered martyrdom by Cossacks while evangelizing the kresy.[36]

While the Catholic friends of Poland abroad had little aid of their own to give, they freely abetted the cause by invoking the greater powers of the Almighty and lending words of encouragement sometimes chilled with the cold comfort of reproachful advice. Churches throughout Europe raised prayers for the Poles. In Rome, the Jesuit chieftain Ledóchowski ordered hundreds of masses said for his endangered countrymen, and in early August Benedict XV urged moral and material help for Poland, once again the rampart of Christianity.[37] Even so, on August 14, as the Reds bore down on Warsaw to deal a possibly mortal blow, the Vatican chided the Poles for having brought misfortune upon themselves in a remarkable commentary in *L'Osservatore romano.* The article had the fingerprints of Cardinal Gasparri all over it. After making the obligatory tributes to the "noble, devoutly Catholic, chivalrous and brave Polish nation," it went on to say, in effect, we told you so. Declaring the Russian war a "risky adventure," it took pains to point out that "the Holy See . . . has never ceased to exhort [Poland] to moderation in seeking or even accepting territories inhabited by majorities of other nationalities. These warnings were repeated several times." The tone of the piece was grim and valedictory, and readers might well have taken it as an editorial bestowal of last rites upon the Second Republic as a favored but errant son of the Church.

On the front line in Warsaw, Nuncio Ratti also suspected that his host government was doomed, but refused to evacuate his post even as other diplomats fled westward in anticipation of a climactic battle at the gates of the city. In part, he remained out of a sense of pastoral duty, just as Archbishop Kakowski ordered the priests of his diocese not to abandon their flocks, and Rome may too have wanted him on the spot to begin the distasteful but necessary job of making contact with the Bolsheviks in the event of their victory. As the moment of truth neared, the Vatican changed its mind and recommended that Ratti depart, and the Polish foreign ministry made last-minute contingency plans to whisk him to safety, but he chose to stay. On the night of August 14, the eve of the clash, the last train carrying foreign officials pulled out of Warsaw, leaving behind only Ratti and a handful of ministers from other legations. According to his own later account, during these tense hours he conferred with General Maxime Weygand, the French military adviser, and the two conversed about the importance of the coming day for the future of civilization.[38]

When the battle joined, the Poles unexpectedly prevailed as Piłsudski stopped the Red Army in its tracks and sent it reeling in retreat. The war ended some months later with Poland not only intact, but even having got the better of the fighting. The good news from the east struck a chord throughout the Catholic world, and enhanced the venerable Polish reputation as the shield of Christendom against the barbarian. The episcopates of western Europe raised hosannas of thanksgiving for the delivery of Poland, and the pope spoke for many by congratulating the country for having saved not only itself, but perhaps the whole continent.[39] Instantly hailed as an epochal historic event, the decisive clash at Warsaw became known as the "Miracle on the Vistula," and reports circulated of divine or Marian intervention on behalf of the God-fearing winners. Within Poland these claims took on a partisan edge. Detractors of Piłsudski fostered the accounts of supernatural assistance as a means of denying credit for the triumph to their political foe, much to the displeasure of his admirers.[40] Among other things, although at the time no one could foretell its full import, the showdown with Communism before the Polish capital made the reputation of Achille Ratti. His decision to stand by Poland in its desperate hour, recalling the defiance of Pope Leo I in the face of Attila, became the signature of his nunciature and, in retrospect, his crucial stepping-stone toward the throne of Peter. For the moment, at least, it also won him the gratitude of Poles and allayed their nagging suspicions that the papacy could not be trusted to uphold the interests of their nation.

Ratti did not have long to bask in Polish affections, however, for within months he landed square in the middle of another frontier dispute to the west that turned him virtually overnight from a friend in the eyes of Warsaw into persona non grata. The peace conference had determined that the disposition of the coveted mining and industrial district of Upper Silesia, formerly part of Germany but plausibly demanded on ethnic and historical grounds by Poland as well, would be settled by plebiscite, which, in the event, did not take place until March 1921. The run-up to the vote was fractious and occasionally violent, with both sides contending for advantage and seeking ways to create a favorable environment for the balloting. Good reason existed to believe that Roman and local Church authorities inclined to the German position in the controversy. In the first place, Silesia was just the sort of nationally ambiguous claim that Cardinal Gasparri had urged Poland to avoid. Furthermore, many took it as axiomatic that the arithmetic of religious realpolitik gave the Vatican a powerful incentive to wish that the heavily Catholic region should remain German: a few Catholics more or fewer in Poland would make no difference, but the same numbers on the other side of the frontier could tilt the confessional balance in the Weimar Republic by cutting into the Protestant majority and bolstering the strength of the Center Party. The Curia also may well have calculated that with Poland menaced by Soviet Russia, Silesian Catholics might be safer in Germany. The Vatican regularly heard, and heeded, such arguments from the German ordinary of Silesia, Adolf Cardinal Bertram, the patriotic archbishop of Breslau, who spared little effort to prevent the loss of this vital slice of his diocese to Poland. As preparation for the plebiscite began in earnest, Poland harbored no illusions concerning the preferences of the Holy See on the matter, but expected to manage to agree to disagree, taking comfort from the fact that the papacy would have little say in the outcome.[41]

Cardinal Bertram may have been the first to suggest the appointment of Ratti as ecclesiastical commissioner for the plebiscite to lend the appearance of clerical decorum and integrity to the rowdy contest in Silesia. Ratti did not welcome his nomination to this largely honorific title that combined high visibility with a minimum of true authority. Indeed, the proposal was a bad idea for so many reasons that at first neither Cardinal Gasparri nor the Allied overseers of the vote saw much merit in it, but in the end the Vatican could not resist accepting even so modest an opportunity to escape its galling diplomatic isolation, and so sought and eventually procured the post for its reluctant emissary in March 1920.[42]

From the start, the Silesian duty caused Ratti nothing but trouble. In the first place, he entered office under the general suspicion that he could not help but be partial to Poland, the country of his nunciature. Warsaw surely hoped so, and lobbied eagerly to see that he got the job, with some clout to go with it. Once he was installed, Poland looked to him as an advocate, while German opinion regarded him as an enemy. Both sides misread their man: in fact, Ratti shared Gasparri's preference for minimizing German losses in Silesia.[43] He observed careful neutrality, and urged even-handed restraint and civility in his public statements. These policies provoked grumblings of disappointed expectations from the Polish quarter, which he took as a good sign. "When only the Germans were against me, I did not know whether I was on the right track," he later recalled, "but when also the Poles expressed their feelings against me, I was certain that I was doing the right thing."[44]

Nuncio Ratti also found himself caught in the middle of a sharp partisan divide among the Catholic churchmen of the plebiscite region with no power to enforce a disinterested *via media.* The predominantly Polish lesser clergy of Upper Silesia comprised the most articulate, nationally conscious, and influential segment of the Poles of the province. With more or less open encouragement from Warsaw, many of these priests threw themselves into the political arena on behalf of Polish interests, while other itinerant clergy filtered in from Poland proper to lend support to the cause.[45] This agitation annoyed the German archbishop, Cardinal Bertram, on two counts: not only did he oppose the pretensions of Poland to Silesia, as he often reminded

Ratti, but he also resented the widespread electioneering of his own Polish priests as well as the unregulated comings and goings of the carpetbaggers in collars as a challenge to his right to maintain ecclesiastical order within his diocese. In the summer and fall of 1920, as German complaints mounted that the Poles were exploiting Silesian pulpits as nationalist soapboxes, Bertram gradually resolved to put a stop to it. Ratti was helpless to ward off the looming collision. Despite his symbolic stature as commissioner, he possessed no mandate to curb the freelance Polish clerics, and even less to override the legitimate pastoral and disciplinary authority of an angered ordinary much his senior. His only option was to apply moral suasion, but this was hampered by his frequent absence from the scene. After all, his residence and primary responsibilities remained in Warsaw, not Silesia, and the considerable distraction of the Polish-Soviet war also preoccupied his time and attention as the pressure mounted in the plebiscite zone.[46]

Cardinal Bertram dropped the other shoe on November 21, 1920, by issuing a decree pronouncing a ban on various types of politicking by clergy within Upper Silesia. Although it applied equally to both nationalities, Poles and Germans alike instantly grasped that the practical effect of the order, and doubtless its intent, was to damage the Polish chances to prevail in the vote. No ecclesiastics from other jurisdictions would be allowed to enter Upper Silesia for the purpose of influencing the outcome of the plebiscite. As for the mainly Polish priests of the archdiocese, they could comment or take part in political controversies only with permission of their parish pastors, seventy percent of whom happened to be German. To enraged Poles, the Church had cast its ballot for Germany by hamstringing the patriotic Polish clergy, thus arbitrarily nullifying their strongest asset in an uphill struggle to overcome the inherent advantages of the wealthier and better placed Germans in Silesia.

At the time and for years afterward, many wondered whether Ratti and the Vatican knew and approved of the Bertram decree in advance. The answer is both yes and no. The announcement apparently came as a complete and unwelcome surprise to Nuncio-Commissioner Ratti, who politely but firmly remonstrated with the cardinal for having handed down his edict without consultation or warning, as did Gasparri.[47] On the other hand, Bertram had sent a number of signals to the Secretariat of State that he meant to assert his prerogatives as ordinary to pacify the turmoil in his churches, and Rome had voiced no objection, not realizing that he would act in such high-handed and one-sided fashion. Although Bertram had done the Curia no favor by exposing it to this unexpected embarrassment, the Vatican chose to put the best face on the matter, loath to undercut the archbishop of Breslau in the normal exercise of his valid authority. While privately conveying his reservations to the German prelate, Gasparri defended his right to enact the edict and allowed it to stand, doggedly insisting that Bertram had conducted himself as the "Priest-Pastor of all."[48]

The Bertram decree stirred a hornet's nest of protest in Poland, directed above all at the offending German archbishop, but also against Ratti and the Holy See as having been either complicit in the outrage or negligent in failing to prevent it. The incident swiftly reawakened all of the old Polish grievances against the Vatican, and even the pillars of Catholicism in the country gave way to expressions of shock and dismay. The press of all parties raised such a furor that the foreign minister made apologies to Benedict XV.[49] However, the Warsaw government could barely contain its own wrath and sense of betrayal. Poland implored the pope to countermand Bertram, while official circles buzzed in private with rumors of spies, collusion, payoffs, and Germanophilia in Rome.[50] The liveliest and most ominous reaction arose in the Sejm, where nationalists and anticlericals joined in denouncing the deed. The chamber echoed with calls to expel Ratti or break off relations with the Holy See before settling for demanding the separation of Upper Silesia from the Archdiocese of Breslau. The temper of the body was such that the highest ranking deputy-cleric, Archbishop Teodorowicz, stood not to defend the Vatican, but to pin the blame for the injustice squarely on Ratti, and to announce that the Polish episcopate had called on Pope Benedict to undo the offending order.[51]

From the midst of the storm, Ratti alerted Rome to the urgent need "to calm the Poles and restore their trust in the Holy See and the nuncio," but already he had lost the ability to do any of those things.[52] He no longer enjoyed the confidence of the Second Republic or of Polish public opinion, despite his celebrated valor at the Battle of Warsaw only three months earlier. Crowds staged hostile demonstrations outside his residence in the capital, where he went into virtual hiding. Among the prelates of the Polish Church the balance now swung in favor of the nationalist bishops, who, like Teodorowicz, never had much use for Ratti, his policies, or his alignment with Piłsudski. Rome stood by its beleaguered emissary, insisting that he had acted properly, but soon began a diplomatic retreat to extricate him from an impossible situation. Assuring Ratti that he had done no wrong, Gasparri relieved him of his Silesian assignment and quickly sent a substitute, Fr. Giovanni Ogno Serra, to take his place.[53] These reverses stunned and wounded the nuncio, who felt illused and misunderstood. The pope tried to console him with words that revealed his own exasperation with Ratti's newly inhospitable hosts: the Poles, he wrote, were "fickle" and "suspicious to excess," guilty of ingratitude to the Holy See, "which has done so much for them." Approached at the time by a Polish spokesman about Silesia, Benedict fixed him with a wintry smile and sighed, "Yes, I know, you want the coal."[54]

Scrambling to salvage something from the wreckage, Cardinal Gasparri and the Polish minister to the Vatican, Wierusz-Kowalski, tried to repair the damage, but their efforts managed only to compound the predicament. The cardinal secretary of state agreed that Bertram had stepped out of line and that his decree should be tactfully annulled, and suggested a compromise: all Silesian clergy were to refrain from participating in the plebiscite campaign, and churches were to be off limits to political activity of any sort. Out of his depth, Wierusz-Kowalski somehow convinced himself that the deal served his country's interest.[55] Accordingly, in late December Fr. Ogno Serra, Ratti's freshly installed replacement in Silesia, issued the new formula. Of course, from the Polish standpoint, this simply made a bad situation worse. As evidently every Pole besides Wierusz-Kowalski readily grasped, they needed fewer restrictions on priestly political agitation, not more, so the hasty revision merely deepened their dissatisfaction with the Vatican.

Meanwhile, Prime Minister Wincenty Witos asked the Polish Church to intercede with the pope, and in early December the bishops dispatched their colleagues Sapieha and Teodorowicz as a delegation to the Vatican to vent the displeasure of the episcopate and, apparently, to seek the recall of Nuncio Ratti. Sapieha was a logical choice, well connected in Rome and seasoned in its ways dating from his youthful service as chamberlain to Pius X. However, sending Teodorowicz on a delicate diplomatic errand was like sending gasoline to put out a fire. His blood up, the Armenian-rite pastor barged through the Vatican like a maddened bull, leaving a trail of disarray and hard feelings that hurt the standing of Poland with the Curia more than helped it.[56] Granted an audience with Benedict shortly after the new year, the Polish bishops explained their country's objection to the Ogno-Serra declaration, much to the surprise of the pontiff, who informed his equally startled visitors that Minister Wierusz-Kowalski had happily assented to that very plan. After the confusion was sorted out, the pope relented to the extent of permitting Silesian clergy to take part in public political meetings not on church grounds. Sapieha and Teodorowicz returned to Poland believing they had attained at least some of the goals of their mission, but unsettled by the prevalent mood of sympathy for Germany and skepticism toward Poland they had encountered in Rome. Their qualms deepened a few days later when Cardinal Gasparri, after consulting with Ratti's replacement in Silesia, instructed them that the new policy would go into effect only insofar as it was consistent with the original Ogno-Serra design, which was to say not at all.[57] The Sapieha-Teodorowicz embassy had come to nothing, the latest casualty of a series of snafus within the Curia or, as the latter feared, of a deliberate attempt to help Germany win the Silesian plebiscite.

Both bishops shot off letters of protest to Benedict XV, and Teodorowicz's epistle trespassed outside the bounds of expected courtesy. Furious, he flatly accused Gasparri of dealing in deception and bad faith on the Silesian question, citing as evidence fragments of internal Polish foreign ministry correspondence shown him by Wierusz-Kowalski while in Rome. These charges scarcely endeared Teodorowicz or his case for Silesia to the Vatican, and especially the cardinal secretary of state. After pointed delay, Gasparri delivered a cold response to Sapieha, tersely defending the conduct and good intentions of the Holy See and adding that he would not deign to reply to the Armenian archbishop who had impugned his integrity.[58]

As it happened, fortune or judicious leak provided Gasparri with a measure of revenge that embarrassed Teodorowicz and ended the Roman tenure of Wierusz-Kowalski. Within weeks, the news got out that the Polish envoy to the Vatican had divulged confidential state documents to a private citizen, the archbishop, who in turn had passed on the contents to a foreign power, according to one way of looking at it. These revelations touched off yet another uproar in the Sejm, where both men came under fire for their indiscretions. As a consequence, the hapless Wierusz-Kowalski got the sack and a ticket to a less demanding post, while deputy Teodorowicz had to endure a very public hazing from the benches of the anticlerical Left, a sport encouraged by the Piłsudski camp, which saw a chance to score points at the expense of their adversary. In retort, the excitable Fr. Adamski asked how anyone could expect the Vatican to want to see Upper Silesia "toss[ed] . . . into the jaws of the Jewish-socialist Polish government." This farcical affair was, as one of Ratti's staff noted, a tempest in a teapot, for neither Wierusz-Kowalski nor Teodorowicz had meant or done real harm to Polish interests; still, he admitted, he did not grieve unduly to see the turbulent archbishop get a taste of comeuppance, deserved in this instance or not.[59]

When Poland lost the Upper Silesian plebiscite in March 1921, as prelude to a distasteful eventual partition of the province, Ratti made a handy scapegoat for the disappointment, and public opinion and officialdom alike called for his head. Convinced that his scholar-turned-diplomat had performed well in a difficult and sensitive assignment, Pope Benedict at first resisted the demands for his ouster, warning the Poles that if they forced him to bring the embattled nuncio home, he would refuse to appoint a successor. However, the death of the archbishop of Milan, the see of Ratti's native region, afforded the pontiff the chance to solve his problem and reward his protégé simultaneously. In short order, Ratti received both Milan and a cardinalate, and by June he had exchanged the rigors of Poland for the relative serenity of Lombardy.[60]

Not content with merely sending Ratti packing back to Italy, Poland pelted him with indignities on his way out to make sure nobody missed the message. Plans to award him an honorary degree from the University of Warsaw were scrapped, and the government took the even more drastic step of refusing to present him with the medal of the Order of the White Eagle, normally given to departing diplomats, despite the warnings of Wierusz-Kowalski that the snub would give great offense to the Vatican. By the time Cardinal Gasparri lodged a complaint with the Polish legation about the ferocity of the vindictive campaign against Ratti, Wierusz-Kowalski was gone, and his replacement gave no ground, coolly answering that the attacks were but an accurate gauge of "the disquiet of the majority of Polish society."[61]

The Silesian fiasco took a heavy toll in acrimony and ill will and subjected the relationship between Poland and the papacy to severe, if temporary, strain. On the governmental level, the bruises healed within a few months, with both sides chalking it up to normal diplomatic rough-and-tumble: although they clearly did not see eye to eye on Silesia, other common interests bound them together, and neither could afford to let the partnership dissolve. The Vatican held much keener resentment toward the Polish Church for its behavior in the quarrel. For his part, Achille Ratti never forgot his unhappy last months in Poland and nursed a grudge against his tormentors among the Polish bishops, especially Sapieha and Teodorowicz, until his dying day. In July 1921, in one of his last communications with the Church of Poland, Benedict XV sent the bishops an acerbic, scolding letter that upbraided them for allowing their patriotic sentiments concerning Upper Silesia to lead to words and actions "ill intentioned or . . . disrespectful of the Holy See." Reminding them of his need to remain impartial, he advised them to show charity toward Catholics of other nationalities and bluntly told them to stay out of politics. Merely bringing up the subject of Poland could make Cardinal Gasparri see red in those days. "Can this be a Catholic episcopate," he would exclaim, "can this be a Catholic press!"[62]

A decade later, Cardinal Kakowski wrote that in spite of the bitter unpleasantness of the Silesian affair, the passage of time had shown it to be an act of Providence, for without it the Church would not have gained its "Polish Pope."[63] In January 1922 Benedict XV died in the ninth year of his reign, and the combination of suitable age and prestigious see made plain that the select number of *papabili* included none other than the freshly minted Cardinal Ratti, not a favorite but a well-positioned dark horse. The prospect of a Ratti papacy unnerved many of the clergy of Poland, but gladdened one of the electors, Kakowski, who had been the main backer of the former nuncio among the Polish episcopate. Much to his agreeable surprise, before his departure for the conclave the new Polish government of Antoni Ponikowski, letting bygones be bygones, informed him that Ratti was its preferred candidate, and upon arriving in Rome he learned that the archbishop of Milan also stood high on the list of France, the principal ally of Warsaw. As the cardinals assembled in the Eternal City and parleyed while awaiting the vote, Kakowski set about lobbying them regarding the sterling qualities of his choice. Countering descriptions of Ratti in the Italian press as a liberal, a term they would have taken as a black mark against him, the Pole assured his colleagues, "*Si*, he has a liberal heart, but a Catholic head and a holy life."[64]

The rise of Ratti's star prompted Poland to offer some quick amends. Sensing that he stood a decent chance of election as the next pope, the Polish legation to the Vatican recalled one slight he had suffered and put in a rush order for belated conferral of the White Eagle decoration denied him at the end of his nunciature out of pique. Warsaw complied, but as a final comic touch to this complicated story that had begun four years earlier when Benedict XV sent his librarian off to the east, the courier bearing the award to Italy stopped off in Vienna for an unauthorized holiday until almost too late. Once the cargo finally arrived, the Polish minister just managed to dash off and make the hurried presentation to Ratti at literally the last minute before he entered his car to be taken to the conclave.[65]

Once the voting began, Ratti emerged as a compromise victor in classic fashion. The two leading contenders, Cardinals Gasparri and Merry del Val, representing differing orientations within the Sacred College, canceled each other out in the early balloting while the Polish and French electors worked discreetly to position the archbishop of Milan as a suitable fallback candidate. The deadlock ended when Gasparri threw his votes to the eventual winner, and on February 6, 1922, Achille Ratti became the 256th Vicar of Christ, taking the name Pius out of respect for two recent predecessors.[66]

The selection of the little-known Ratti as pope startled the world outside the Vatican walls, and much was made of his ties to Poland as observers tried to take his measure. As his identifying feature, they seized on his Polish exposure, exotic by the insular standards of the "captive" papacy of those days, and the Italian press nicknamed him *il papa polacco* when Karol Wojtyła was but a boy.[67] Beaming, his sponsor Cardinal Kakowski declared his nation "delighted" at the news from the Sistine Chapel, and much of it was indeed.[68] By and large, Polish opinion turned in favor of the new Pope Ratti just as quickly as it had turned against him over the Silesian question, taking reflected pride in his election and trusting that the country would benefit from it. Most of the press rejoiced that, at last, the Church had a pope who knew Poland, understood its importance to the Catholic world, and would put an end to hostile intrigues in the Vatican.[69]

Amid the cheers, others were not so sure, and wondered if they were getting more than they bargained for. When a Roman cleric congratulated a Polish colleague on the familiarity of the new pontiff with his country, the Pole answered, "We fear he knows it too well."[70] Along the same lines, no doubt many within the national episcopate worried that they had made an unfortunate choice of enemies by their rough treatment of the former nuncio who now wore the papal ring. The socialist paper *Naprzód* gloated, "the election of Cardinal Ratti is a disaster for our bishops."[71] As if to ease their fears, two months after his accession to Peter's throne Pius XI received several Polish hierarchs and demonstratively kissed Archbishop Teodorowicz as a gesture of *perdono* for the buffets he had suffered at their hands.[72] Still, time gave clear evidence that if the pope had forgiven, he had not forgotten, and his two chief Polish clerical antagonists paid a price in thwarted ambitions. Teodorowicz never gained the cardinalate he coveted, and Sapieha had to outlive Ratti to win the red hat that normally accompanied the see of Kraków, and no one had to wonder why.[73]

Biographers of Pius XI routinely assert that his dramatic experiences as nuncio to Poland impressed him profoundly, set the tone for his subsequent pontificate, and may have persuaded the Sacred College that he was the right man to lead the Church at that moment in history.[74] Certainly all of these claims are true to some degree. After all, Poland was Achille Ratti's introduction to the world outside the cloistered confines of ecclesiastical scholarship, and to the issues that gripped Europe in the years between the wars. At the same time, Pius never strayed far from the agenda of the papacy that had been carved out by his immediate predecessors, and the Polish influence served to emphasize or confirm particular aspects of his policy, not to inspire or originate new departures. For example, commentators never fail to point out his fascination with the possible conversion of the Orthodox east, or his unyielding conviction of the danger posed by Communism, and to chalk these up to his adventures in Poland. In fact, Ratti was scarcely the first pope to feel the strong tug of Russia, and had been sent to Warsaw in the first place largely owing to the lively interest of Benedict XV in opening the Orient to Rome. As for Communism, any pope during the era of Lenin and Stalin would have decried it as satanic anathema, but it is readily understandable that the menace of Bolshevism would have seemed more viscerally urgent to one who had spent August 1920 in the Polish capital awaiting the onslaught of the Red Army. By the same token, popes before Pius XI had urged bishops and clergy to keep their hands out of politics as not in keeping with the priestly office, but he had seen and felt the consequences of clerical partisanship firsthand in Poland, giving him extra incentive to squelch it during his custody over the Church.[75]

On other counts, the historians seem to have misread the lessons Poland taught Ratti, or to have overlooked them. One common, disapproving claim is that the pope's admiration and fondness for Józef Piłsudski made him an easy mark for charismatic strongmen, blinded him to the true nature of the Fascist regime, and contributed to his willingness to strike a deal with the Duce to settle the Roman question. The argument, in essence, is that when Ratti looked at Piłsudski, he saw Garibaldi, and that when he looked at Mussolini, he saw Piłsudski. There is less in this proposition than meets the eye. Superficial comparisons of Piłsudski and Mussolini were a staple of European journalism in the 1920s, but beneath their swaggering, uniformed exteriors they had little in common, and there is no good reason to suppose that Pius XI, who knew them both, was not smart enough to tell the difference.

For what it is worth, the pope paid countless tributes to Piłsudski, public and private, and comparisons of his Polish friend with Mussolini are notable for their absence. In the end, the decision of Pius to establish a wary working relationship with the Fascisti was the result of hardheaded calculation with a certain logical basis in Italian politics, not the fault of the fatal charm of Józef Piłsudski. At the same time, the standard lives of Ratti tend to ignore the influence of his Polish sojourn on the gradual evolution of Catholic teaching on the Jewish question in the twentieth century. In the course of his papacy, Pius XI made a number of comments expressing sympathy for Jews and acknowledging a spiritual debt owed by Christians to the people of Abraham and Moses. While grudging and incomplete by later standards, in their time these small gestures played a measurable part in nudging the Church away from its traditional condemnation of Jews as deicides and along the path toward *Nostra aetate.* The pope himself credited his time in Poland with having given a human face to his stereotyped and abstract image of Jewry, and we may safely take him at his word.

To the surprise of those who had not paid attention during the Silesian plebiscite, the Polish credentials of Pius XI did not prevent him from continuing his predecessor's criticism of the Versailles order and related keenness to shield Germany from excessive loss of land on its eastern frontier. Not for the first time, many presumed that he would favor Poland in any such dispute, but before long he gave notice that his Polish education had bred in him a strong dash of skepticism toward the territorial ambitions of Warsaw. As secretary of state, he retained Cardinal Gasparri, whose low opinion of Polish foreign policy was well known. Speaking to a Polish diplomat about Upper Silesia, the pope warned, as had Benedict before him, "Believe me, you will absorb too many Germans." The Vatican counted as merely a cipher in the equation of European international power, and could do little more than irk the Poles, but Pius faithfully hewed to the line of Gasparri and Benedict XV that the greater good for Poland was to cooperate with Germany for protection against Soviet Russia, and if need be, pay the price of making concessions to its aggrieved western neighbor.[76]

Pius XI encouraged his reputation as the "Polish pope," and sincerely cherished the reminiscences of his nunciature that did not cause him pain. Shortly after his election, he sent to his favorite Pole, Józef Piłsudski, a signed portrait inscribed with personal greetings to his friend and his nation.[77] Settling into his job, he had his summer residence at Castel Gandolfo decorated with scenes from the history of Poland and an icon of the Holy

Mother of Częstochowa.[78] He could be grateful even for his Polish tribulations, he claimed, which had prepared him to be a better pope. "I did not know how to be patient," he told Cardinal Kakowski, "I learned patience in Poland. . . . I love Poland, as always."[79] He meant these words, after his fashion, but his was the stern, paternalistic love of a father convinced he knew what was best for an immature child even though, and especially when, the child might disagree. Two months into his pontificate, he gave an audience to the Polish minister to the Vatican, assuring the diplomat that on matters touching the welfare of his second homeland he thought "not as a foreigner, but as the best Pole." The envoy reported to his superiors that Pius was obviously fond of Poland, but added the uneasy note that "he has returned . . . with settled ideas concerning . . . [it], and as an expert on that country he is prepared eventually to take very fundamental actions that undoubtedly will be animated by a spirit of good intentions toward us but more than once might present us with an unwelcome surprise."[80] For the next seventeen years, the great majority of its free existence as the Second Republic, Catholic Poland would enjoy the benefits and bear the trials of living with a pope who carried intense memories, good and bad, of the days he had spent in the lands of the Vistula.

3 ılı From Constitution to Concordat, 1921–1925

THE BEGINNINGS OF NORMAL POLITICAL CONDITIONS in interwar Poland, or at least their approximation, had to await the end of the chaotic formative phase of independence, and so it was with the relationship of the Second Republic with the Roman Catholic Church at home and abroad. Not until the restored Rzeczpospolita had ensured its survival and more or less fixed its boundaries could it afford the luxury of attempting to decide the chief issues of church and state: the status of Catholicism within Poland, and of Poland within the Catholic world. Resolution of the first question required a constitution, while the second implied a concordat. These projects were separate but linked to a considerable degree. The constitution would fix the place of the Church in the country, define the state as confessional or secular or something in between, and provide the basis for subsequent legislation. While the constitution was, in theory, solely a Polish domestic matter, the concordat would consist of a treaty between the Holy See and the civil government of Poland devoted to religious affairs and policies of mutual concern.[1] Strictly speaking, the concordat was dispensable, but the Vatican coveted such agreements in that era. For one thing, signing a concordat amounted to a de facto recognition of the sovereignty of the papacy—no small matter in those days before the Lateran Accords—and Rome much preferred the bond of an international compact as a guarantee of Catholic interests in a given land to the unilateral laws of a government that might be changed on a whim. Upon the conclusion of these two documents, the constitution in 1921 and the concordat in 1925, the legal and diplomatic foundations of the relations of church and state in the Second Republic came into being.

Tentative, previous efforts had been made to speed the process or settle the debate at a stroke, but these had failed. In the dawn of independence, the Polish episcopate called for the establishment of the Church as the official national religion in keeping with the precedent of the Constitution of 1791, but this proposal elicited such spirited opposition from the Left and the sizable non-Catholic minority that Nuncio Ratti predicted that the famous motto *Polonia semper fidelis* soon might become "merely a historical memory."[2] Feelers for a Polish concordat had gone out as early as 1918, but had come to nothing owing to the resistance of an unlikely tacit coalition of anticlerical politicians and a faction among the bishops of Poland. Both camps disliked the idea on principle out of hostility toward each other, fearing that any deal would mean intolerable concessions to their foes. The unfinished business of the constitution also contributed to the postponement of a concordat. The dissident bishops hoped that a favorable constitution could take the place of the concordat, granting the Church benefits without strings attached. In any event, no matter what one thought of a concordat on its own merits, common sense suggested that it should follow, not precede, a constitution that would determine the nature of the state and its fundamental stance toward Catholicism, and before long the Vatican and the Polish episcopate agreed to that order of priority.

The regulation of the ties of church and state in interwar Poland depended on the interplay of three entities: the Holy See, the country's Roman Catholic hierarchy, and the government of the Second Republic. This was largely a dialogue of elites, as only the Warsaw regime was answerable to public opinion in any meaningful way. None of these parties saw the other members of the trio as enemies. To the contrary, all of them understood that Polish tradition and religious sentiment, and pragmatic calculations of shared interests, dictated that they maintain at least a decent working relationship. Still, each partner wanted different things out of the association, and these variations of outlook and goals made their collaboration bumpy and tense, perhaps all the more so since none could afford to let it break down. The Vatican expected the new Poland to serve the mission of Catholicism in central and eastern Europe, and expected the sometimes refractory Polish episcopate to fall into line with the agenda of the papacy. For their part, to the extent that they had a unified policy, the bishops demanded that their reborn republic grant honored status to the Church and enshrine its precepts in law, while hoping that Rome would leave management of Polish affairs to those who knew what they were doing, namely themselves. Meanwhile, the government, as governments will, sought to stay on good terms with the Church without paying too high a price in obligations or inconvenience, trying to strike the balance of mollifying the faithful without alienating the various constituencies that saw clericalism as a menace.

In fact, the Polish political order contained a surprisingly abundant number of adversaries of the Church, and the highly segmented multiparty system adopted by the republic accentuated their importance by giving them representation and making them eligible for membership in a series of shaky, revolving-door ruling coalitions. Broadly speaking, the Left and the national minorities combated the country's predominant religious body, and the Center and Right supported it in roughly equal proportions, with the peasant clubs occupying the middle and acting as makeweights. If, as the saying went, the government of Poland in those days was less Catholic than the Polish nation as a whole, the explanations were that the Polish political class was less pious than other Poles, and that Poland consisted of more than just the Poles. The third of the population made up of peoples not Polish and, for the most part, not Catholic had their own parties that normally voted against the interests of the Church, although for reasons of discretion they tended to let the Polish anticlericals take the lead in such debates. The hostility of the Polish Left toward Catholicism was neither unanimous nor unrestrained. All but the most extreme factions included at least nominal Catholics within their ranks and leadership, or felt the need to mute their attacks on the Church to some degree out of deference to a national institution and reluctance to offend potential Catholic supporters. The main home of political anticlericalism was the benches of the Polish Socialist Party and its breakaway wing that rallied around Józef Piłsudski. Generally suspicious of the Church, these groups favored its separation from the state and the reduction of its influence in society and education, in accord with the standard European Left and liberal agenda. A goodly share of peasant legislators ended up on the same side of the argument as the socialists, usually for different reasons. Subdivided along ideological lines, the peasants gave top priority to land reform and looked hungrily at the ecclesiastical domains. Many of them saw the Church as a villain in this litmus-test issue, and the radical Wyzwolenie (Emancipation) faction produced much of the shrillest clergybaiting of the era. The larger and more moderate Piast Party, the customary bellwether of Polish politics, furnished the key swing votes in disputes over church and state. This scarcely comforted Catholics, for the Piast outlook contained a strong streak of mistrust of the clergy as potential manipulators of the common folk. It favored lay control over education and marriage law, and many of its leading personalities qualified as unbelievers or disgruntled Catholics. Even the devout Wincenty Witos, the Piast chieftain, drew his share of attacks from Church spokesmen over the course of his career.

This left a near-majority Center-Right bloc of reliable political allies of Catholicism in Poland, anchored by the National Democrats. A declared confessional party, the Christian Democracy (Chadecja), which drew inspiration from the landmark encyclical *Rerum novarum,* never amounted to much in size or mass appeal. Founded only in 1919, the Chadecja struggled to pry adherents away from their habitual affiliation with more established rivals. Furthermore, the Christian Democrats encountered the same obstacles that frustrated their Italian counterparts, the Popolari. In a country where Catholicism was the norm and had at least a foothold in most political camps, the point of an avowedly Catholic party was unclear. Partly for that reason, the Church in Poland, as in Italy, saw no reason to put its eggs in one partisan basket and gave no special blessing to the Chadeks, who were relegated to the status of junior partners of the National Democrats, already identified in the public mind as the main defenders of the Polish faith.[3] By default, then, the rightist Endecja of Dmowski assumed the role of standardbearer of the Catholic cause in the early years of the Second Republic despite its heritage of dubious attachment to Christian beliefs and principle. Whatever their other differences, this assortment of conservatives, nationalists, and social Catholics agreed that the Church played an essential role in Polish life and deserved a privileged place within the state.

Just as the Center and Right backed the Church, so the Church backed the Center and Right, out of both philosophical sympathy and the realistic understanding that it would find political friends in those quarters or not at all. Simultaneously flushed by liberation and unnerved by the complexion of a provisional government dominated by Piłsudskiites and socialist anticlericals, the Polish bishops urged voters in the first parliamentary elections of 1919 to elect candidates committed to defense of Christian values, a recommendation that needed no spelling out. The results were only partly successful: the Right gained a plurality, but not sufficient to form a stable cabinet. After that episode, the episcopate reverted to a stance of official nonpartisanship, but there was no mistaking the political leanings of the Church and its clergy. The unicameral Constituent Assembly included thirty-two clerics, headed by Archbishop Teodorowicz, nearly all of them dependable supporters of the Right. Outside the confines of the legislature, Bishop Sapieha and Cardinal Dalbor, among other hierarchs, were well known for their inclinations toward the National Democrats, while parish priests tended, if anything, to exceed their superiors in outspoken fealty to the Dmowski party.

The belligerently rightist posture of the interwar Polish Church in the early stages of independence stemmed from a deep sense of embattled vulnerability, in sharp contrast to the imposing national reputation for Catholicity. In part, this reflected the defensiveness in the face of an increasingly secular modern culture that was common to European political Catholicism in those days, but it was also a response to conditions specific to the newly reassembled Poland. From the vantage point of the Church, its legal standing in the country at the dawn of statehood presented a dilemma of unpalatable alternatives. If the laws left over from the partitioning empires remained in force, then they preserved a network of statutes and regulations largely inimical to Catholic teachings and interests. For example, the districts of Poland formerly ruled by Protestant Germany had permitted civil marriage and divorce, and as late as 1922 the Polish bishops felt compelled to issue a pastoral letter condemning the admission of these practices in a Catholic land. On the other hand, if the law of the ancien régime did not apply, then there was no law at all, and the Church forced to depend on the goodwill of the government of the moment. At best, this meant a lack of continuity in official policy toward the Church, as each successive short-lived coalition reinvented the wheel and improvised its own ad hoc approach, in practice leaving much authority in the hands of lackluster, capricious, or corruptible local bureaucrats. At worst, the precariousness of the political balance in Poland lent credence to the fear that the anticlerical Left might gain the upper hand and that its loose talk of a secular state and confiscation of ecclesiastical lands might become reality. The Church was naturally eager to settle the fundamental questions regarding its status on the best terms possible, and as quickly as possible, before the window of opportunity afforded by a Center-Right parliament might close. These anxieties were magnified by a prevalent mentality of persecution, a habit of mistrust of state power carried over from the days of foreign rule. As a result, the political voice of Polish Catholicism and its sympathizers in this interlude was noisy, impatient, unyielding in defense of the rights and prerogatives of the Church, and caustic toward its enemies.[4]

The first serious test of strength and will concerning the Catholic Church in the civic affairs of the Second Republic arose out of the contentious agrarian question, in the course of horse trading and voting that produced a modest land reform in 1920, during the tenure of a Piast ministry. The peasant deputies who sponsored the measure naturally sought access to a fraction of Church properties for parceling out by the state, but when they pleaded their case to their colleague Archbishop Teodorowicz, they went away empty-handed. Responding for the clerical delegation, Teodorowicz expressed approval of reform in principle, but reminded his petitioners that Church holdings had been diminished sharply over the past century through expropriation and war damage and now made up less than 1 percent of the total area of the country. These professions of poverty failed to impress the peasant politicians, but they reflected the genuine concerns of an institution responsible for the support of forty thousand clergy and lay employees and sensitive to its own economic straits. So far as the Church was concerned, it was entitled to recover a share of the properties and wealth lost during the era of captivity, not to have them depleted further now that the day of liberation had dawned. In the end, the parliament put off the issue to a later day: no ecclesiastical lands would be made available for reform until an international agreement had been reached with the Holy See as part of a comprehensive settlement of church-state matters, a concordat, in so many words. In effect, round one had gone to the Church, as most of the rounds would.[5]

In the meantime, the Constituent Assembly spent two years carrying out its primary responsibility, the drafting and approving of a republican constitution, which was passed in March 1921. By its nature, the debate over the religious clauses to be written into the document opened the parliamentary floor to expression of the most fundamental and emotional opinions, pro and con, regarding the role and legacy of Catholicism in Poland. For all the spirited give-and-take of the exchanges, the outcome was predictable. The Center-Right bloc in the chamber was sufficient to have its way and fend off the impassioned calls of the anticlerical Left for the separation of church and state. In an era when separation smacked of irreligion and war against the Church, such a prospect struck the majority as contrary to national tradition and unthinkable.[6] With the option of the secular state removed from the table, the meaningful discussion focused on working out the nuances of the inevitable official recognition of the Roman confession. The Church opened the bidding with hopes for establishment or, barring that, for acknowledgment as the "predominant religion" of Poland, but ended by having to settle for a compromise formula borrowed from the Napoleonic concordat of 1801.[7] In its final wording, the key Article 114 declared that the Catholic faith, "being the religion of the overwhelming majority of the nation, occupies in the state a leading position among religions endowed with equal rights." This first-among-equals language disappointed some within the clerical camp, but the fine print of the measure secured several crucial privileges for the Church that made plain that if all religions in Poland were equal, then one was more equal than the others. In the first place, by singling out Catholicism for specific mention, the document automatically set it apart from other creeds. Second, the state conceded that the Church, and the Church alone, "govern[ed] itself by its own laws" (*własnymi prawami*), whereas all other churches would be subject to the dictates of civil law. This provision was meant to safeguard the autonomy of the Church and to limit the scope of governmental interference in its activity. Finally, the constitution obliged the republic to reach a concordat with the Holy See to provide the basis of the coexistence of church and state. While the concordat might well have turned out much as it did in any event, by thus committing itself in advance to conclude a treaty, Warsaw yielded a certain edge in the haggling of negotiation to the Vatican, which could afford to drive a hard bargain in the knowledge that at some point Poland would have to make a deal.[8] In sum, although the Church had not gained all it sought from the "March constitution," it still had done well for itself. While necessarily vague, the basic law of the Second Republic treated the Church with dignity and respect, did nothing to foreclose or impede any of its aspirations to prominence in the country, and encouraged it to press forward to put flesh on the constitutional bones by completing the legal and political agenda that had been successfully begun.

Since the constitution had been regarded as the necessary precondition of a concordat, its adoption temporarily revived the topic of the treaty that would represent the next, and presumably final, stage of the normalization of church-state relations. Out of different motives, both Warsaw and the Vatican were impatient for the speedy and definitive resolution of these matters that only a concordat could provide. So far as the republic was concerned, the constitution had raised more questions than it had answered by continuing a pattern that had emerged of putting off hard decisions on ecclesiastical issues until a concordat settled them for good, and the time had come to pin down the Church on its rights and obligations. For its part, Rome would stay nervous so long as Poland stayed theoretically free to deal with the Church as it pleased, so the bond of a treaty could come none too soon for its liking. In 1921 the Polish Ministry of Religious Confessions and Public Education began a series of meetings and consultations aimed at resuming talks toward a concordat, but the project made little progress over the next three years, stalled by frequent cabinet changes and, perhaps, intermittent pique with this or that element of Vatican policy.[9] The delays and snags made both the Polish bishops and the government testy. On several occasions in 1922, Primate Dalbor and the episcopate peppered Warsaw with sharp protests against its handling of the Church, accusing it of dragging its feet in undoing the inherited discriminatory legislation that left the status of Catholicism the "worst of all confessions" in the land.[10] Cardinal Dalbor went so far as to complain improbably that so long as these statutes remained on the books, the legal standing of the Church in Poland was worse than in any other country save Soviet Russia. These hyperbolic tactics tried the patience of the Polish Foreign Ministry, which laid blame for the lack of headway toward a concordat on the demanding and contrary stance of the episcopate itself.[11]

The growing friction between the government and Church of Poland enhanced the intermediary importance of the third partner in the triangular dialogue, the Vatican, whose new sovereign considered himself fully qualified to manage Polish issues, to say the least. Pope Pius XI retained a lifelong soft spot for the country of his nunciature, but observers agreed that he did not allow sentiment to affect his judgment of the proper policy of the Holy See in the postwar era, or of the proper place of Poland within that strategy. At a time when Europe was constructing a new political order complicated by the emergence of a drastically changed state system, the papacy was presented with the need and opportunity to redefine its status in the political realm, affording the chance to begin recovery from the historic setback of 1870. As the pope saw it, the answer was to sign as many concordats as possible, protecting the see of Peter with a fortress of parchment that would simultaneously provide recognition of its independence from Italy and escape from the isolation in which it had languished for five decades.[12] As for Poland, not only was it a significant country in its own right, but as a famously devout land with venerable ties to Rome, it was an excellent candidate to arrive at a concordat in short order that might serve as a favorable model for similar compacts with other powers. Having learned the hard way that the religious politics of Poland were more complicated than most outsiders fathomed, Pius was confident of his own ability to deal effectively and knowingly with Warsaw.

For nearly the entirety of the eighteen-year pontificate of Pius XI, the career diplomat Władysław Skrzyński headed the Polish mission to the Apostolic See. Skrzyński took the place of his hapless predecessor

Wierusz-Kowalski in 1921 and served first as minister, then from 1924 as ambassador to the Vatican until his death in harness in 1937, the longest posting of any interwar Polish envoy. A languid, easygoing sort who relished the Italian *dolce far niente,* he preferred the charms of Roman society to the humdrum toil of the embassy and delegated most everyday duties to his underlings while bestirring himself as necessary to cultivate friendly relations with the pope, Secretary of State Gasparri, and the other major players in the Curia.[13] He believed at heart that Poland and the Vatican needed each other and that no momentary difficulty between them could not be worked out, and his natural indolence and imperturbability aided him in smoothing over disagreements as they popped up. Warsaw nursed a touchy, easily awakened sense of being taken for granted by the papacy, and occasionally vented displeasure by firing off orders to Skrzyński to demand the ouster of an objectionable bishop or obtain an audience for an antagonistic airing of grievances. His instinctive reaction was to sit on the directive and wait for the problem to go away by itself, as it usually did.[14] On the other side, Skrzyński grumbled about the annoyances of navigating the cumbersome and inefficient curial bureaucracy, but the main test of his patience was the legendary volcanic temper of the pope himself, who did not take kindly to being crossed. The story goes that on one occasion Skrzyński delivered an unpleasant message from his foreign minister to Pius, who leaped from his throne, shouting, "On ne dit pas celà à un pape!" Skrzyński said nothing and just waited. After a long pause, the pope repeated his rebuke, at somewhat lesser volume. Skrzyński waited. Presently the pope sat down, calmly spoke the same words in a measured voice, and the interview resumed as if the outburst had never happened.[15]

By way of contrast, leadership of the nunciature in Warsaw turned over three times during the interwar period, beginning with the departure of Achille Ratti. For one thing, apparently none of the trio of elderly Italians who followed him as nuncio could endure more than a few years of the rawer climate of the north. His successor, Lorenzo Lauri, was liked well enough by the Poles, but his conversation tended to dwell on his infirmities and the impressive array of medicines he had brought from home to ease his aches and pains.[16] Despite its reputation as a hardship post, Warsaw in those days developed a track record as a tour of duty on the résumés of rising curial stars on their way to bigger things. In 1923, when the former Nuncio Ratti already wore the papal tiara, a young Vatican diplomat was briefly assigned to Poland before his delicate constitution required his return to the warmth of Italy. Supposedly, at the time Skrzyński said, "Watch him, he might be pope someday."[17] If so, he was right: Giovanni Battista Montini took the name Paul VI forty years later. His immediate predecessor, John XXIII, born Angelo Roncalli, was offered the Polish nunciature in 1936 but turned it down to remain nuncio in Turkey, Moslem but sunny.[18] In other words, three of the four popes over a span of fifty-six years starting in 1922 were graduates, in a sense, of Warsaw, or could have been, before a genuine Pole took the job in 1978.

Aside from the terrors of the Polish weather, the Warsaw nuncios had to live in fear of the wrath of Pius XI, who took them to task regularly for their shortcomings and did not try to hide his conviction that he could do without them. The pope trusted and sought the advice of Father Ledóchowski, his Polish superior general of the Jesuits, but for the most part he chose to act as his own secretary of state on questions regarding Poland. He would listen to the arguments of Cardinal Gasparri and brush them aside, saying, "Does Your Eminence know Poland? I know her! . . . I am still the better expert in Polish affairs." Then he would do things his way, always reserving the final decision for himself.[19]

His first decrees pleased the Poles by extending an olive branch on the dispute that had brought about the unhappy end of his nunciature, their dissatisfaction with the administration of the Church in territories they claimed from Germany. Having first won the confidence of German opinion by initial word and gesture that he would not blindly side with Poland against their nation, he named the Polish archbishop of Riga as apostolic delegate to the contested Free City of Danzig in April 1922, the third month of his reign.[20] Next, the pope quietly turned to allay the persistent complaints of Poles, including his friend Marshal Piłsudski, that their old nemesis Cardinal Bertram was continuing to discriminate against their countrymen in his Archdiocese of Breslau. In November Pius appointed the young Polish Salesian priest August Hlond, the son of a railway lineman, as apostolic administrator of his native Upper Silesia, effectively removing the districts belonging to Poland from Bertram's jurisdiction. Warsaw officials were delighted by the selection of Fr. Hlond, who assured them that the Polish clergy and faithful would receive more sympathetic treatment under his authority, and the government welcomed his eventual nomination as the first bishop of Katowice in 1925.[21]

To mollify Polish Catholics by freeing them from the dominion of Cardinal Bertram, all the pope had to do was say the word; the harder challenge, and his higher priority, was to disentangle the Polish Church from the endemic political warfare in the country and sever its alliance with the factions of the right. Throughout his pontificate, Pius XI consistently discouraged associating the Church with partisan causes, whether confessional parties, as in Italy or Germany, or independent secular movements of self-proclaimed Catholic character, such as Action Française. The legitimate political work of the Church, he insisted, should be carried out in strictly nonpartisan fashion by the bishops themselves or by lay organizations under their direction, especially Catholic Action, his pet cause. While none of this departed from standard Vatican practice, Pope Ratti stressed the policy with a special vigor derived from his own experiences as nuncio in Poland, where—he was convinced—the Church had developed an unwholesome absorption in politics and had fallen in with a bad lot of friends of the National Democratic ilk.

The chronic infighting between the forces of the Polish Left and Right, personified to a large extent by the rivalry of Piłsudski and Dmowski, reached a venomous height in the elections of November 1922, the first conducted under the new constitution. Members of the cloth figured prominently in a nasty campaign. As before, the episcopate made no specific endorsements but exhorted voters to select friends of the faith, and many rural priests made less subtle pitches for the rightist Christian National, or Chjena list, a common front of National Democrats, Christian Democrats, and like-minded splinter groups claiming a Catholic orientation. In reply, the socialists predictably attacked the clergy as the handmaids of reaction.[22]

In the run-up to the vote, the pope ran into trouble from two familiar sources. Bishops Sapieha and Teodorowicz, his old antagonists from his days as nuncio, decided to stand for election to the Senate on the Chjena ticket. The idea appalled the pontiff, and displeased Cardinal Dalbor as well, as out of keeping with the priestly office, but the candidates received encouragement from other episcopal colleagues with Endek leanings and concluded that in the absence of an outright prohibition from Rome, they were free to do as they liked. Instead, the pope played a waiting game that furnished an inelegant solution, but one that allowed him to make his point with all the greater emphasis by dint of its very awkwardness. He permitted Sapieha and Teodorowicz to be elected, and then forced them to resign their seats. The discipline gained wide notice and was taken as a precedent with general applicability beyond Poland, as was intended. No doubt Pius would have done the same if the clerics involved had not been the pair who had been his crosses to bear as nuncio, but one gets the impression from the episode that he did not entirely regret the chance to even an old score.[23]

As before, the election returned a parliament with a rightist plurality, but a leftist and national minority coalition of deputies combined to choose a candidate of its liking as the first president of the republic. Against expectations, the incumbent chief of state, Marshal Piłsudski, refused to contend for the feeble presidency that had been constitutionally crafted by the National Democrats precisely to curb his influence, opting to withdraw from public life for the time being. In his place, the legislature tapped Gabriel Narutowicz, the sitting foreign minister. The selection of Narutowicz inflamed the Right and much of Catholic opinion. The new president was a nonbeliever and a rumored Freemason, and Endecja publicists unleashed a torrent of invective against him as an illegitimate victor foisted upon the country by its undesirables. In December 1922, a week after his election, Narutowicz was shot dead by a nationalist extremist. Representatives of the Church sent distinctly mixed messages in response to the murder. Cardinal Kakowski of Warsaw presided with dignity at the state funeral in his cathedral, but this act of respect attracted less attention than the considerable number of curés who openly applauded the gunman or said masses for him upon his execution. The primate, Cardinal Dalbor, rebuked the renegade priests, but he avoided any direct condemnation of the killing of Narutowicz and remained conspicuously absent from the obsequies. As a whole, the response of the Polish Church to the assassination struck many as scandalous, and many blamed the full-throated politicking of the rightist clergy for helping to create an atmosphere conducive to mayhem.[24]

At the time of the murder of Narutowicz, reasonable observers could, and did, conclude that Poland was coming apart at the seams, and that the Church was doing much of the tearing. The prospect loomed of a permanent split of the country into warring camps: advocates of a "national-Catholic" ideal ranged against their opponents, and the episcopate locked in the smothering embrace of the National Democrats. Convinced that such a fate would benefit neither Poland nor its Church, Pope Pius deepened his resolve to prevent it by the one sure means at his disposal, the capacity to nominate hierarchs. Over the course of his pontificate, by a piecemeal changing of the guard, he persistently strove to break the link between Polish Catholicism and Endecja by replacing deceased or retired rightist bishops with a generation of successors who were younger, apolitical or at least nonpartisan, and more in tune with the outlook and aims of the Holy See than their predecessors.[25]

Already frayed by the violence and acrimony of 1922, relations between altar and throne got no better in the following year when a peasant-Right coalition headed by Wincenty Witos took the reins in Warsaw. The Church and the premier regarded each other with mutual reserve, and no appreciable progress was made toward the concordat during his tenure. In fact, the discord grew more acute that autumn when the Piast partners in the government pushed for an extended land reform including redistribution of mortmain holdings of the Church. The suggestion aroused indignant protests from the Polish episcopate and the Holy See. Cardinals Dalbor and Kakowski were demonstratively summoned to Rome, where they issued statements opposing the legislation with the obvious approval of the pope. The countermeasures of the Church exerted their desired admonitory effect on the Polish Right, contributing to the collapse of the land-reform initiative and the subsequent crackup of the Witos ministry in December.[26]

By this time, the relationship of church and state had sunk so low that it could only go up, and so it did. In the first place, the exit of Witos cleared the path for the formation of a government better suited, by makeup and inclination, to reconcile Catholicism with the republic. Władysław Grabski, a political veteran with a reputation for expertise in economics, returned for a second stint as premier at the head of a nonparty cabinet with a mandate to repair the tattered finances of the country. Grabski was something of a political chameleon, a man with ties to the Right who had managed somehow to avoid becoming anathema to the Left. Intended as a stopgap, the Grabski régime stayed afloat for nearly two years, an eternity by the standards of interwar Poland before 1926. Apart from his economic credentials, the prime minister survived thanks to his considerable gift for slippery adroitness, including a knack for keeping the wheels of government greased with the oil of corruption. Given the advantages of time and a semblance of conditional bipartisan support, the Grabski team managed to complete some of the unfinished business of building Polish statehood, notably a currency reform and, as it happened, the long-promised concordat with the Vatican.

At first, in its absorption with the economy, the Grabski government looked likely to continue its predecessors' habit of treating the concordat as the neglected stepchild of Polish politics. The concordat question had got lost in the shuffle in the three years after passage of the constitution. In Rome, the Polish minister Skrzyński did what he could on his own to lay the groundwork for a treaty, but his superiors back home showed no interest. In 1923 the frontiers of Poland received definitive international recognition, and the Vatican saw this as an opportune moment to begin parleys now that there was assurance that diocesan boundaries could be brought into line with political realities, but Warsaw went on dawdling. By the time the delays dragged into the following year, Pope Pius began to grow irritated at the lack of news on the Polish front. At last Grabski crowded a meeting with Cardinal Kakowski into his schedule and apologized that he had been too busy with the economic emergency to give any attention to church-state affairs. Kakowski replied, in so many words, that there was no time like the present, and that the prime minister could start by putting his older brother in charge of the concordat project.[27]

Stanisław Grabski, a professor of economics, was a sitting National Democratic member of parliament who had served a brief term as minister of religious confessions in the defunct Witos cabinet. Aside from fraternity with the premier, he was a logical candidate to represent Poland in hammering out a deal with the Curia. As Kakowski had said, the elder Grabski was acceptable to the Polish episcopate, which thought of him as a friend of the Church. Further, as a deputy from the largest party in the Sejm, he stood a good chance of gaining the treaty a solid base of support once it came up for a ratification vote. For his part, Grabski was willing to take on the task, so long as he was given full authority to hammer out a deal without the interference of the Polish diplomats assigned to the Vatican. This condition suited Warsaw, which suspected that Skrzyński had got too cozy at St. Peter's and that Grabski might drive a shrewder bargain. In June 1924 the cabinet formally named Grabski as its plenipotentiary for the concordat and sent him off on his errand to Rome, where he soon won the respect of the pope and Cardinal Gasparri as a tough but trustworthy negotiator for Polish interests.[28] As his counterpart, the Holy See selected Mgr. Francesco Borgongini-Duca, but everyone understood that he was little more than a mouthpiece for Pius XI, who took the Polish concordat under his personal care.[29]

By his own account, Grabski entered the concordat talks with a strategy based on the assumption that Poland and the Vatican were natural partners and that he would give in order to get. First, he backed away from the long-standing hankering of the Polish Foreign Ministry after an Austrian-model concordat giving the state broad influence over ecclesiastical affairs, which had proved a stumbling block to an accord. He also conceded at once the full legal autonomy of the Church in Poland, no great loss since it already had been written into the constitution. Having established a tone of cooperation, he sought in return a number of provisions that would recognize Polish state interests in certain sensitive questions where religion and politics intersected. These had to do with reinforcing the claim of Warsaw to its contested frontiers and strengthening the position of Latin Catholic

Poles in areas of the country where they were outnumbered by peoples of other nations or confessions. Neither Germany to the west nor Lithuania to the northeast accepted its border with Poland, so, at a minimum, Grabski wanted diocesan lines redrawn in conformity with the new map, and hoped as well to obtain Polish ecclesiastical authority over the Free City of Danzig. Indeed, one factor that encouraged his brother the prime minister to open the negotiations at last was the calculation that if Poland reached a concordat before its unfriendly neighbors, it might get favorable treatment in Rome ahead of Berlin and Kaunas. The Polish delegate also demanded that his government have a say in the appointment of bishops as a guarantee of their loyalty to the republic. This pertained especially to the kresy of eastern Poland, for Grabski thoroughly shared the National Democratic conviction that the Church should serve as an instrument of Polish assimilation in these regions where Poles were a minority. In further pursuit of this goal, he looked for ways to curb the activities of the Greek Catholic clergy of East Galicia, regarded by Warsaw as a subversive element of Ukrainian separatism, and to obtain the ouster of Jerzy Matulewicz, the Lithuanian bishop of Vilna, whose story will be reserved for a later chapter.[30]

Grabski and Borgongini-Duca haggled over the concordat for four months in a series of twenty-three meetings in Rome beginning in October 1924. Both pledged to barter in a spirit of concord, and so they did for the most part, although on occasion the proceedings got bumpy. At one point, after pointedly stressing the need of the papacy for Polish help in the battle against Bolshevism and the other evils of the day, Grabski raised the threat of a political backlash against Catholicism in Poland if Vatican stubbornness prevented agreement on a treaty; the monsignor stiffly replied that the Church would not buy a concordat at the cost of its freedom. They sparred repeatedly over the items on Grabski's wish list: the Uniate question, Danzig, the nomination of hierarchs, the status of Vilna and Bishop Matulewicz. In the end, the eruption of a crisis in relations between the Holy See and the anticlerical Herriot government of France induced Borgongini-Duca, or his higher-ups, to give way on a few points in order to keep Poland within the fold of reliable friends of the Vatican. Once Pius XI had given "every comma" of the final text his personal blessing, the Polish concordat was signed in Rome on February 10, 1925. The pope had followed the negotiations with care and agreed to terms he considered generous to Poland, and was pleased by the result. In a farewell audience, he told the departing Grabski that he had "granted more power to the Polish state than has been given to state authorities in any other modern concordat," for "it is a necessity for the entire Christian world that [Poland] should be as strong as possible."[31]

By no means all observers shared the pope's judgment that Warsaw had done well for itself in the treaty, but in fact both parties had emerged from the talks able to claim to have achieved their essential goals, at least on paper. For the Church, the document guaranteed its "full freedom" within the Second Republic (Art. 1) and nullified any existing laws that conflicted with the provisions of the concordat (Art. 25), thus putting to rest the nagging worries about the carryover legislation from the prewar regime. In addition, religious instruction was to be mandatory for Catholic pupils in state schools, taught by catechists approved by the Church (Art. 13). By the same token, Poland realized most, if not quite all, of its extensive agenda to assure the political loyalty of the Church and its clergy. An ecclesiastical reorganization of the Polish territories saw to it that no part of the country would be under the jurisdiction of a foreign ordinary and had the desired effect of confining the Greek Catholic rite to East Galicia (Art. 9). The assignment of Danzig to the duties of the papal nunciature to Poland fell short of Grabski's request for outright inclusion of the city within a Polish archdiocese, but still displeased Berlin more than Warsaw (Art. 3). The president of Poland would hold the right of veto over papal nomination of bishops (Art. 11), who also would be required to give an oath of allegiance to the republic (Art. 12). To give the state some leverage with lesser clergy suspected of seditious activity, the government could present its complaints against the offending priest to his bishop for possible sanctions (Art. 20).

Aside from these political clauses, the concordat necessarily dealt at length with material and institutional matters. The document embraced an agreement for state subsidies to cover the salaries and retirement pensions of clergy and religious as well as some of the costs of Church administration and construction. In addition, the treaty included a formula to settle, once and for all, the thorny land reform question by making carefully defined and limited Church holdings eligible for redistribution (Art. 24). "In order to improve the economic and social condition of the agrarian population and to enhance the Christian peace of the country," the state could acquire ecclesiastical properties up to a maximum of one hundred thousand hectares. This theoretical possibility was never carried out, as it happened, so in the end the Polish Church escaped unscathed by land reform altogether during the interwar era.

Now that it had been signed, the concordat required ratification by the Polish parliament before taking effect. By and large, reaction to the compact followed predictable partisan lines. The Right and Center tended to endorse the measure, as did that segment of the press reflecting the view of the governmental and diplomatic elites, though not without reservations. On the other hand, the anticlerical Left and many of the followers of Piłsudski, with greater conviction, urged its defeat on the dual grounds that it gave away too much to the Church and that it might harm relations with Poland's ally France by seeming to take sides with the Vatican in its quarrel with Paris.[32]

Given the narrow margin in Polish politics between friends and foes of the Church, the most potentially damaging opposition to the concordat came from within the divided ranks of the Catholic clergy itself. The Holy See and its representative, Nuncio Lauri, praised the treaty as a "great success," and the two cardinals, Dalbor and Kakowski, went along in solidarity with the papacy. Following this lead, most of the episcopate fell into line and accepted the deal as an equitable compromise that would be good for the Church and good for the country.[33] The opinion was by no means unanimous. The inevitable Galician duo, Bishops Sapieha and Teodorowicz, neither believed a concordat was needed nor trusted Pius XI to look out for the best interests of the Polish Church, and the clergy from former Austrian and German Poland, where ecclesiastical landholdings were most extensive, worried that the economic clauses of the pact might impoverish their dioceses. These doubters were made edgy by the strict secrecy of the negotiations, and when Stanisław Grabski apprised the episcopate of the emerging outlines of the concordat in December 1924, they rose in open rebellion. Protesting that the Church was ceding too much to the state, especially in the selection of bishops, Sapieha and Teodorowicz asked permission to go to Rome to state their case directly to the pope, an offer the Vatican turned down flat. The most visible priest-parliamentarian of Poland, Father Adamski, told Nuncio Lauri that he was "horrified" by the content of the treaty, especially the plans for land reform, and warned that as a senator he did not see how he could bring himself to vote for it. The loud clerical complaints failed to rattle Grabski, who bluntly advised the Curia simply to ignore them and crack the whip of papal authority to make the malcontents toe the line.[34]

With difficulty, the Vatican managed to cajole its balky Polish troops into ranks to back the concordat, and did not bother with subtlety. Meeting with Lauri to discuss strategy for the upcoming ratification fight in parliament, the marshal of the Sejm, the Piast deputy Rataj, told the nuncio the margin for error was slight: although the Jews would abstain for reasons of "propriety," if the dissenting clergy persisted in carping against the concordat, there was no reason for anticlericals to be "more Catholic than the priests," and it might well go down to defeat. "*La chose sera arrangée,*" Lauri assured him, and even as he spoke, Rome and its allies among the Polish episcopate were knocking heads to create at least the appearance of a united front of clerical support for the treaty. Lauri, Dalbor, and Kakowski lobbied for it, pressing doubters not to defy the express will of Pius XI. The nuncio took the precaution of informing the loose cannon Archbishop Teodorowicz that urgent pastoral duties would keep him busy at home in Lwów for the time being, far from Warsaw and the legislative chambers he liked to frequent. As for Father Adamski, he received orders from both the pope and Cardinal Dalbor to turn a complete about-face: not only would he take back his criticisms of the concordat, but he would work actively for its passage. Adamski complied, explaining wanly that his earlier remarks must have been misunderstood. These strong-arm tactics squelched the rearguard mutiny of the Polish clergy by the time the Sejm took up the covenant in the last week of March 1925, and only then did its backers in Rome and Poland grow confident of a favorable outcome.[35]

The make-or-break debate on the concordat in the lower house made a curious spectacle. Leading off the proceedings, the first speaker for the affirmative sounded distinctly apologetic, admitting that the document he was presenting had many flaws and openly regretting that he could not introduce it to his colleagues "with greater enthusiasm." He defended the concordat mainly on the less-than-inspiring grounds that any concordat was better than none. After this soporific performance, the key-note speaker for the nays rolled out all the heavy artillery in the anticlerical rhetorical arsenal, to the cheers of the Left and national minorities. And so it went, lukewarm statements of commendation alternating with passionate condemnations. Few deputies tried to defend the treaty on its merits, instead stressing the constitutional obligation to reach a concordat, or the advantage to be gained by beating Germany or Lithuania to the punch in Rome. While the opponents had the edge in emotion, the supporters had the numbers. After three days of argument, the Sejm approved the concordat by a comfortable margin on March 27, 1925. The final vote was interrupted by jeers and catcalls from the leftist benches, mixed with reproaches against Jewish deputies for tacitly permitting the measure to pass by dint of their abstentions. With far less furor, the Senate followed suit a month later, and the laborious process of working out the formal relationship of the Polish Church with the Second Republic, and of the Republic with the Holy See, had finally reached completion nearly seven years after it had begun.[36]

Carrying out the terms of the concordat, Pius XI issued the bull *Vixdum Poloniae unitas* the following October, promulgating a new ecclesiastical organization of Poland. The decree divided the country into five Latin-rite metropolitanates in accordance with the boundaries of the Republic, the sees of Warsaw, Gniezno-Poznań, and Lwów joined by new archdioceses of Kraków and Vilna. In addition, Lwów retained its status as the archiepiscopal seat of the country's two Eastern-rite congregations, the Armenians and Greek Catholics. This basic structure would remain in place until after the Second World War.

Reaction to the Polish concordat at home and abroad varied according to point of view. Its terms drew objections from Germany and Lithuania for its recognition of the Polish frontiers they disputed, rewarding the keenness of the Grabski government to make a deal with the Holy See before either neighbor had the chance to persuade the pope to draw diocesan lines that might call into question the legitimacy of the postwar political boundaries. German opinion deplored the formation of a separate Diocese of Katowice within Poland as a "second partition of Silesia," but Weimar officialdom muted its disappointment on the pragmatic grounds that the Vatican scarcely could have done otherwise.[37] No such restraint prevailed in Lithuania, driven to fury by a sense of betrayal at the creation of a Polish metropolitanate with its seat in Vilna, seized by Warsaw in 1920. Angry crowds pelted the residence of the papal delegate in Kaunas with eggs. In a huff, the Lithuanian government broke off its own concordat negotiations, recalled its envoy to the Holy See, and bombarded the Curia with irate messages Cardinal Gasparri deemed unworthy of reply. The breach between Catholic Lithuania and the Vatican opened by the Polish concordat would take two years to heal.[38]

At least one of the contracting parties to the treaty, the pope, considered it entirely satisfactory. This was not the first of the many concordats of Pius XI, but it was the first he concluded with a predominantly Catholic land, apart from the special case of Bavaria. Pius saw the concordat with Poland as exactly what he had wanted, a fair bargain and a suitable model to serve as a precedent in future dealings with other governments. Subsequent interwar concordats followed the basic outlines of the Polish exam-

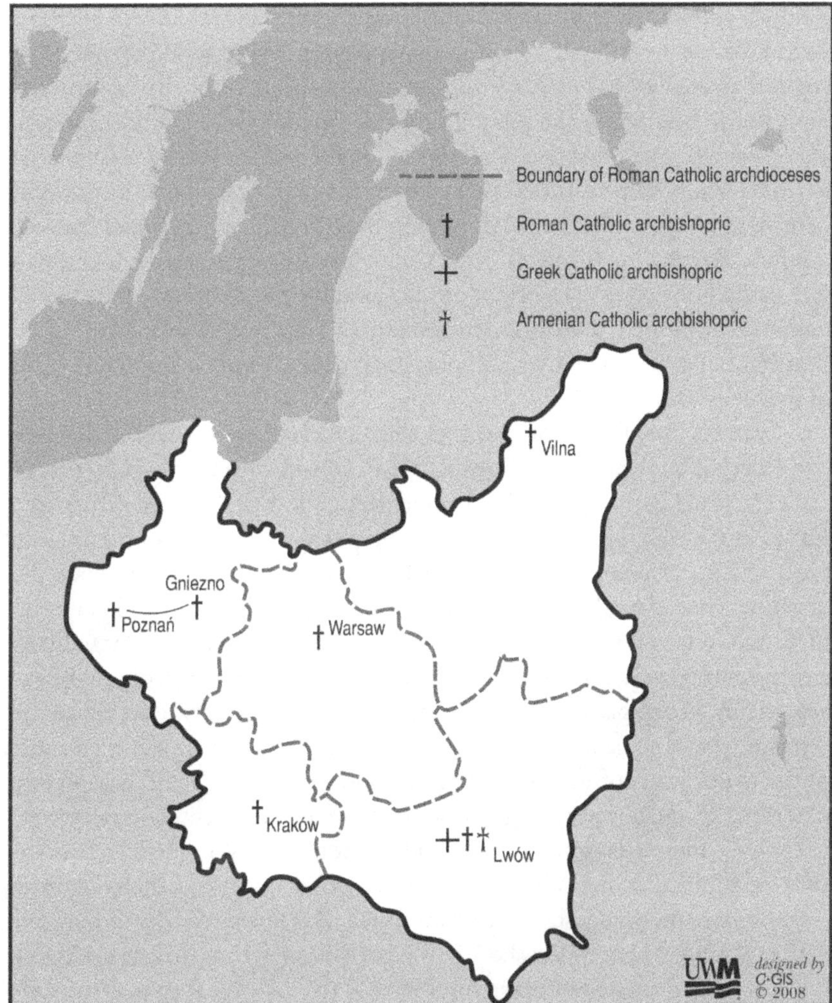

MAP 2. Diocesan organization of Poland, 1925–39. Map by Donna G. Genzmer, University of Wisconsin–Milwaukee. Copyright © 2009 Board of Regents of University of Wisconsin System

ple, and observers claimed to see its influence in the development of concordatory policy through the remainder of the Ratti papacy.[39]

Inside Poland itself, the government and the Polish episcopate also praised the concordat. Prime Minister Grabski hailed it as a "good work of law and an excellent work of policy," although numerous critics disagreed on both counts.[40] Despite some muttering within their ranks, the bishops, or at least most of them, joined in the applause. Those who defended the concordat argued that it was a win-win proposition, mutually reinforcing both Polish patriotism and piety by serving the interest of church and state alike. They pointed out that Warsaw no longer had to worry that a hostile foreign bishop, some future Cardinal Bertram, might meddle to its political detriment by his ecclesiastical dominion over Polish territory, and that the republic now had a means to insist on loyalty from the restive Ukrainian Greek Catholic clergy. The right of secular authority to approve the nomination of bishops would become a standard feature of the concordats of Pius XI, but at the time it struck some analysts as an unusually broad grant of privilege to the state.[41]

Even so, the weight of opinion, then and later, held that the Church had emerged as clearly the winner of the Polish concordat of 1925—that as the stiff price of its gains, the Second Republic had "concede[d] to the Catholic Church an exceptionally strong position in the country."[42] To a great extent, of course, Warsaw had little choice in the matter, since the prominence of the Church in Polish life existed naturally as a primary element and result of national history, and hardly required a concordat to bring it into being. It would have been truer to put it the other way around: the exceptionally strong place of Catholicism in Poland had largely determined the terms of the concordat. The outcome was a document that achieved most of the major goals of the Polish Church and the Holy See and was widely described as one of the most generous concordats of the era in its deference to the altar, indeed as approaching the ideal Catholic view of modern church-state relations. For many Poles, this was a good thing; to others, it was a disappointment, even a scandal. In any event, this interpretation of the concordat as a great victory for the Church became so entrenched that within a few years the primate of Poland felt the need to challenge it as an erroneous conventional wisdom concocted by anticlericals.[43]

Critics of the Polish concordat attacked it as incoherent in form and objectionable in content. Legal commentators charged that sloppy editing and translation had left discrepancies between the official French text and its Polish version. Worse, it was shot through with vague and imprecise language that left several of the most contentious questions of church and state essentially unresolved, still open to guesswork and interpretation. As time went on, such ambiguity would become a recognizably frequent feature of the concordats of Pius XI, accepting blurry compromises to mask unsettled differences, or skirting thorny issues altogether in order to close the deal. While this approach made the political task of negotiation and ratification easier, it meant, in essence, that there was still no real agreement on many points, and was of no help once the real battle could be put off no longer, when the time came to implement the paper concordat into the hard reality of law and procedure. The irony was that the concordat, long awaited as the indispensable instrument that would clarify and define the rights and duties of the Church in Poland, turned out so unclear and indefinite that it left plenty of room for continued wrangling over the very matters it was supposed to settle, and in some respects left things more muddled than ever.[44]

As to the substance of the treaty, the leftist and national minority parties and constituencies that had opposed a concordat from the outset never made their peace with the finished compact. In their eyes, it was a lopsided usurpation of power and privilege by the Church, wrung from a conveniently submissive government that was soft on clericalism. To be sure, many of the detractors would have found any concordat unbearable, no matter what its terms. Still, the striking fact remained that support for the concordat within the country had been broad but not deep, and that the opponents, although a minority, had fought their losing fight with a stronger resolve that remained undimmed even after ratification. These included the Piłsudski loyalists, temporarily diminished as a political force by the withdrawal of their leader from public life, but once the tables turned in Warsaw, this faction would dominate the Second Republic for the remainder of the interwar period and thus assume responsibility for carrying out the concordat it heartily disliked.[45]

While the secular Left in Poland disparaged the concordat as a giveaway to the Church, a substantial segment of the Catholic priesthood, and a handful of bishops, faulted it for rendering unto Caesar that which was God's. Many of the lesser clergy of modest means complained that their salary had been pegged at a precariously stingy level, and worried—without reason, as it happened, since it became a dead letter—that the land reform clause ran the risk of running the Church into the poorhouse. On a higher plane of principle, Bishop Sapieha and a few of his episcopal peers feared that the Church had made needless sacrifices to civil authority and compromised its independence from state power. Several years later, Sapieha confidentially rued the concordat as a "painful subject," at best a *malum necessarium* not to be celebrated, at worst a baited trap to ensnare the Church that the pope and his allies within the Polish hierarchy had stumbled into without due caution.[46]

This was a pessimistic minority reading. In the eyes of the pope and the greater part of the Catholic leadership of Poland, the advantages of the concordat more than justified its cost. Beyond its own merits, they saw it as the culmination of a successful campaign, grueling and lengthy, to win for the Polish Church the assurance of legal protection and benevolent treatment by the state that it had not enjoyed since the eighteenth century and could not take for granted in the Second Republic. The respected bishop of Siedlce, Henryk Przeździecki, rejoiced that 1925 would be remembered as the "year the shackles of slavery fell from our holy Church in Poland."[47] From this perspective, 1918 had marked merely the beginning, not the fulfillment of the liberation of Polish Catholicism, and only now, seven years later, could it call itself truly free.

4 | Papal Blessing

Church and State in the Piłsudski Era, 1926–1935

For nearly the first decade of the Second Polish Republic, the triangular relationship of institutions that determined the ties of church and state had operated according to familiar and predictable patterns. First, the government of Poland functioned as an unsteady, raucous parliamentary democracy that passed the baton of authority from one ineffectual cabinet to another. Among the many factions that jockeyed for power, the largest was the rightist bloc clumped around the National Democrats, who claimed to speak for the interests of Catholicism. Second, Poland also possessed a notoriously combative and politicized Catholic clergy and episcopate that, on the whole, saw nothing wrong with reciprocating the overtures of the nationalists and making common cause with the Endecja of Roman Dmowski. Third, the Holy See, represented almost continuously by Achille Ratti, first as nuncio, then as pope, strove to persuade Warsaw to be more friendly to the Polish Church, and to wean that same Church from its dependence on the rightist camp, which he disliked intensely on grounds of policy and personality alike. The usual result was a muddle: the politics of religion in Poland hovered in limbo, never quite in crisis, but never quite satisfactory to all the principals. This state of affairs turned around abruptly in 1926, the watershed year of interwar Polish history, starting with a pair of leadership changes, one natural, one sudden and violent. Once these shifts took hold, the relations of church and state became, simultaneously, both better and worse than before. This paradox stemmed from the fact that although the nature of the new Polish government that seized control in Warsaw could not help but sharpen conflicts with the Church, these were held in check by the simple but effective buffer of mutual affection and trust between two highly placed men. For almost the next ten years, to a remarkable degree, the decisive factor in keeping the uneasy peace between Catholicism and the Second Republic was the unlikely but unbreakable friendship of Pius XI, the Vicar of Christ, and the strongman of Poland, the onetime revolutionary and apostate whose rule many Polish clerics regarded as their worst nightmare come true.

The first of these transitions began in February 1926 when Cardinal Dalbor, archbishop of Gniezno-Poznań and primate of Poland, died at age fifty-six after a long illness. To the end, the self-effacing Dalbor maintained his tendency to defer to stronger figures within the episcopate, such as Sapieha and Teodorowicz, and permit them to align the Church with the political Right. In failing health, he had yielded most of his duties to his capable suffragan bishop, Stanisław Łukomski, an outspoken supporter of National Democracy who quickly established himself as the rising star of the dominant rightist wing inside the hierarchy. When the death of his superior opened a vacancy for the primacy of the Polish Church, many of his colleagues looked to Łukomski as the natural heir to the position he already had occupied in all but name for the past year.[1] However, the choice belonged not to them, but to the pope, who did not consider the decision so obvious and took his time making his mind.

At about the same time, the surviving Polish cardinal, Archbishop Kakowski of Warsaw, is said to have warned the president of the republic against the danger of an imminent coup d'état by Józef Piłsudski and his followers. This bit of advice scarcely required clairvoyance—if so, Kakowski would not have been the man to supply it—for in the early months of 1926 many Poles sensed the looming breakdown of the "Sejmocracy," the multiparty parliamentary system the country had adopted upon regaining independence and that had produced, in Kakowski's view, little besides "demagogy and anarchy."[2] The crisis erupted on May 12 when Marshal Piłsudski, provoked to emerge from retirement by the formation of a government he found intolerable, marched on Warsaw at the head of troops loyal to him as their commander. After three days of confused fighting in the capital, the insurgents achieved victory, and Piłsudski would spend the remaining nine years of his life as the *padrone* of Polish politics, not quite a dictator but plainly the man who pulled the strings from behind the curtain.

The May coup precisely divides the political history of interwar Poland into phases before and after. Gradually Piłsudski put into place a hybrid structure that retained most of the form of the republic, and much of its content, but imbued it with an authoritarian impatience to push Poland in the direction he wanted it to go. The stated purpose of his government was to accomplish the "cleansing" of the country, or *sanacja,* which became the nickname of the regime. Translated, the slogan meant a reduction of factionalism and the long-range goal of changing the constitution to create a stronger presidency to be filled, naturally, by Józef Piłsudski. The movement forswore ideology, apart from platitudinous calls for civic virtue and national unity, and based its appeal on the charisma and patriotic stature of its founder. In practice, sanacja straddled the middle of the spectrum and relegated other parties to noisy but permanent opposition, including Dmowski's National Democrats. The government dominated the scene by exploiting the genuine popularity of Piłsudski, playing fast and loose with the spirit of democratic practice, if not its letter, and resorting occasionally to repression, albeit trifling by the standards of the true European despotisms of its day. The leader ran the show from the background, choosing to rule through his favorites and military cronies, the so-called Colonels who made up his entourage and took turns filling cabinet posts at his command. By imposing himself on his nation as its stern, grandfatherly tutor, Piłsudski has inspired comparisons with such as Atatürk and de Gaulle, but in the end his approach to statecraft stands sui generis, like the man himself.

The outbreak of civil war in Poland posed a hard question for the Church, both at the Vatican and in the country itself: how would it react to the internecine spilling of blood, to the violation of constitutional order, to the brute usurpation of power by a faction widely regarded as an enemy of Catholicism? By coincidence, Cardinal Kakowski happened to be in Rome when the rebellion broke out. Summoned to confer with the pope and Cardinal Secretary of State Gasparri, he assured them that all would be well in his homeland and, in return, received orders to hurry back to Warsaw with instructions to pour holy oil on the troubled waters. Upon arriving in his pacified but tense see, he pronounced a blessing on Piłsudski and his new regime in the name of the pontiff. Responding to the entreaty of a Piłsudski emissary, he issued a pastoral letter urging the faithful to remain calm and, to boot, forbade priests to use their pulpits to stir up opposition. For his part, the marshal repaid the favor by conveying a message he would repeat several times over the years: the pope had his promise that "so long as Piłsudski rules Poland, no harm will come to the Church."[3] The exchange was a sign of things to come. In short order, Pius XI and Piłsudski had reaffirmed the confidence in each other that dated from the pope's days as nuncio in Warsaw, and they would rely on the lubricant of their well-known personal rapport to prevent friction between church and state from overheating.

In so doing, both chiefs went against the inclinations of their respective camps. The reappearance of Piłsudski as a force in public life after a hiatus of three years revived the long-standing hostility between his followers and the Catholic clergy, raising it to new levels now that the stakes were suddenly higher. They were, of course, in the narrow sense partisan foes after a fashion. Both sides recalled their bitter clashes in the formative phase of the republic, and the Piłsudskiites never shed their opinion of the priesthood as cheerleaders for the Right. Nor was there any shortage of current issues to divide them, such as the recent concordat. All the same, at bottom their animus was more cultural than political, rooted in profound differences of fundamental belief and patriotic ideals. For the Church and its sympathizers, Catholicism was not merely the deepest of truths, but a precious and essential part of Polish identity, hallowed by God and history. Most of them would have endorsed the formula polak-katolik without hesitation, and taken for granted that what was good for the Church was good for Poland.

While sanacja was a motley army united only by allegiance to the marshal, and its ranks included legions of devout Catholics, at the same time the Piłsudski ethos was grounded firmly in a secular conception of citizenship. Religion, or its lack, was a matter for the individual conscience, of no value as a test of Polishness. The typical Piłsudskiite had, at best, mixed feelings about the legacy and influence of the Church in national life even if he was a communicant, and subscribed to the liberal anticlerical outlook to greater or lesser degree. The closer one got to the core of the movement, the more heterodoxy became the norm, a statement of independence and broad-mindedness, practically a badge of clan membership. Protestants and atheists made up a disproportionate share of the Piłsudski entourage. Above all, Catholic opinion fretted about the striking number of Freemasons who populated his inner circle at a time when the Church condemned the secret brotherhood as one of its most dangerous and relentless enemies. Among others, his closest friend, Walery Sławek, his first handpicked premier, Kazimierz Bartel, and his brother, Jan, belonged to the society, and they were not alone.[4] In all, six of the eight men, apart from Piłsudski himself, who served as sanacja prime ministers were Freemasons, not to mention a long list of cabinet ministers and diplomats. The leader looked with indulgence on the ties of his aides de camp with the "royal craft." He tried on occasion to use the Masonic connections of his underlings with foreign lands to Polish advantage, and appears to have regarded the lodge, on balance, as a beneficial force in the country.[5] The Church could not have disagreed more. Even Cardinal Kakowski, otherwise not ill-disposed toward Piłsudski, found the prospect of a government run by his Masonic cronies hard to stomach.[6] This was such a sore point that over the years that whenever a churchman, whether in Poland or Rome, found something to dislike in the actions of sanacja, he would almost always ascribe it to the malicious influence of Freemasonry. On top of everything else, there was the fact that the regime had originated in unconstitutional force. At least one of the few bishops who had supported Piłsudski before the coup turned against him afterward as an insurrectionary with fraternal blood on his hands.[7] In sum, when the Polish Church looked at sanacja, it saw bad policy being made by bad men who had gained power in a bad way, while Piłsudskiite true believers saw the Church as an unfriendly and unenlightened interest group hiding an unwelcome political agenda behind a religion that most of them rejected, and that many of them treated with the special scorn of the fallen away.

Despite these considerable obstacles, both Piłsudski and the pope were resolved to pursue the modus vivendi they had always favored. While much of the sanacja constituency would have relished a war against clericalism, the marshal himself had consistently tried to steer clear of trouble with the Church, and now he had more incentive than ever before. In order to placate and unify the country, he wanted to reach out to conservatives and present himself as a genuine national leader, not just a tinpot junta warlord and darling of the Left. Neutralizing the opposition of the Catholic clergy and allaying the suspicions of the faithful were vital elements of that strategy. For his own reasons, Pius XI hoped to see Piłsudski succeed. The fact that the marshal had overthrown something like a democracy and was in the process of replacing it with something like dictatorship was no object to the pontiff, who held no prejudice in favor of republicanism. The pope still regarded the soldier he had befriended as nuncio as the most impressive of Polish statesmen, and the one whose policies best suited the Vatican. Beyond that, he admired him as an authentic hero of Christian civilization. To a pope increasingly vexed by the peril of Bolshevism and who had witnessed the Battle of Warsaw of 1920, Piłsudski's victory over the Red Army loomed as an event of epic proportions, and he plainly felt that their shared experience in the cauldron of a key historical moment forged between them a unique bond of kinship and fate. *L'Osservatore romano* developed the habit of lauding the virtues of Piłsudski and recounting his exploits in the struggle against Communism, especially when it would do him the most good at home, and Pius seldom passed up any opportunity to regale visiting Polish diplomats and churchmen with his own heartfelt praise of the marshal.[8]

As a first step in the direction of rapprochement between the Polish Church and sanacja, the pope had to select a new archbishop of Gniezno-Poznań and primate of Poland. One part of his equation was easy: Bishop Łukomski, the rightist protégé of Cardinal Dalbor, would not do as a successor. Instead, Łukomski was made ordinary of provincial Łomża, an exile disguised as promotion. This decision effectively removed him from the ranks of hierarchical movers and shakers. Finding a suitable candidate proved trickier. Determined to put his unequivocal stamp on the episcopate, Pius nearly settled on Fr. Stanisław Sopuch, an obscure and unworldly Jesuit who was reputed to be on good terms with Piłsudski and, by some accounts, had made himself useful to the embattled Nuncio Ratti during the humiliating last months of his mission to Poland. This trial balloon never got off the ground. The nominee did not want the post, the Endecja-leaning clergy of the Gniezno-Poznań see objected to his reputed politics, and the Jesuit General Ledóchowski argued that tradition forbade the choice of one of his order as primate and, more particularly, that Sopuch was just not up to the job. His first, unconventional option foreclosed, Pius fell back on another but safer regular, the forty-five-year-old Salesian August Hlond, only recently consecrated as bishop of Katowice. Like Sopuch, Hlond was a religious who enjoyed the personal confidence of the pontiff and had nothing to do with the Dalbor-Sapieha-Teodorowicz clique that had dominated the episcopate since 1918: the similarities clearly show the qualities the pope was seeking in his nominee, above all his insistence on an outsider primate who might breathe fresh air into the overheated atmosphere of the Polish hierarchy. Unlike the Jesuit, Hlond lacked the baggage of association with Piłsudski, or of any known political affiliation at all. Possibly for that very reason, his nomination encountered no resistance. Hlond was installed as ordinary of Gniezno-Poznań in June, received the cardinalate a year later, and occupied the primacy of Poland until 1948.[9]

Getting his bearings and distracted by illness and absence in Rome, Hlond adopted a wait-and-see posture toward the Piłsudski system during his first months as primate amid signs of an approaching clash between sanacja and the Church. Openly suspicious of the crowd of Freemasons and skeptics now inhabiting the governmental headquarters in the Belvedere palace, the clergy spoke in defiantly combative tones to their new rulers and spurned Piłsudski's overtures for a truce. Despite an appearance by freshly elected president Ignacy Mościcki as a goodwill gesture, a Catholic Congress held in Warsaw at the end of August took on the character of an oppositionist rally. Delegates accused the regime of undermining the family by promoting looser marriage and divorce laws, and press accounts described a massive religious procession through the streets of the capital as the first public demonstration against sanacja.[10] No bishop attended the reception held for Piłsudski at the Radziwiłł estate in October, the symbolic high point of his effort to reconcile with the moderate Right. A month later, the episcopate issued an oblique but unmistakable statement of no confidence in the civil authorities, warning that recent events in the country had encouraged Communism and endangered Catholicism and the nation, sounding a call to "defend the rights of the Christian Church, the family, and public morality." Some voices in the press counseled Piłsudski to think twice and heed the bishops' manifesto, but his cheerleaders on the Left charged that it amounted to a clerical declaration of "civil war," and urged him to respond in kind.[11]

For both sides, the status of the concordat of 1925 quickly became the barometer of their relationship, as it would remain throughout the Piłsudski era. Negotiating, signing, and ratifying the concordat had been one thing; carrying it out was another matter requiring the ongoing cooperation of ecclesiastical and state authorities. Practically to a man, the sanacja insiders thought of the concordat as a lopsided giveaway to the Church, and they resented being the unwilling inheritors of what they saw as Stanisław Grabski's pietistic generosity to the cloth. Within their ranks, sentiment ran strong for enacting the accord in the most restrictive fashion possible, crippling it by delay or administrative manipulation, or junking it altogether.[12] Fully aware that many provisions of the concordat were uncomfortably vague and that the government held the advantage of initiative now that fulfillment of the contract depended on its unilateral action, the episcopate girded to fight for its rights and to prod the reluctant state to implement the treaty in its original spirit.[13] Accusations that the Piłsudskiites were dragging their feet or not living up to their obligation to uphold the concordat occupied a prominent place in the polemical offensive of the Church against the new masters in Warsaw.

The mounting discord between sanacja and the Polish Church left an opening for Roman Dmowski, threatened with political oblivion by the Piłsudskiite takeover, to propose a formal marriage of his National Democrats with Catholicism. The two camps had been frequent fellow travelers in the past, but always in spite of the rightist party's heritage of anticlericalism, philosophical materialism, and rejection of religious values. Now that the events of May had given his rival the upper hand and required him to devise a strategy for the survival of his movement, Dmowski responded with a concerted effort to win Catholic support based on the idea of a natural partnership of Endecja and the Church along the lines of the polak-katolik thesis. In part this was a tactical move dictated by the desire to form a common front of the Right against Piłsudski, but it also reflected a gradual evolution within National Democracy itself. By this time, the positivist founders of the party had largely given way to a younger generation of Endek loyalists more sympathetic to Catholicism. In addition, as he grew older, Dmowski became ever more fixated on the dangers posed by Freemasonry and the Jews and saw the Church as an institution willing and able to help defeat these influences in the country.[14] Accordingly, in November 1926 he addressed a Catholic gathering in Poznań and, in the presence of Archbishop Hlond, called for the placing of Poland on Catholic foundations, "for our National Church is the Roman Catholic Church."[15] He elaborated on this theme in 1927 with the publication of his pamphlet *Kościół, Naród, i Państwo,* which contended that for Poles, Church, nation, and state—the trinity of his title—were, or ought to be, intertwined and inseparable concepts. In it he declared that "Catholicism is not an adjunct of Polishness . . . [but] in large degree provides its basis. . . . The Polish state is a Catholic state . . . in the full sense of the term, for our state is a national state, and our nation is a Catholic nation." Taking a clear swipe at sanacja, he warned that forces seeking to reduce the role of the Church in Polish life "strike at the selfsame foundation of the nation."[16] At the same time, Dmowski began to identify himself as Catholic in outlook. The literal sincerity of this claim is open to doubt, for there is no evidence that he had repented his atheism. Upon the appearance of *Kościół, Naród, i Państwo,* a friend is said to have asked the author if, in fact, after all these years, he now believed in God. Dmowski snorted that of course he did not, "but I had no choice but to write that pamphlet."[17] Whatever his private convictions, the essay succeeded in its aim of gaining the attention of Catholic opinion. Some churchmen and lay commentators smelled within it the same odor of opportunism they had always detected in Dmowski's attempts to use religion for political advantage, but others, perhaps a majority, took it as evidence that the Endeks had turned a new leaf, cast off their un-Christian dogma of national egoism, and enhanced their credentials to forge a solid alliance with the Church.[18]

In part to ward off this very possibility, Piłsudski and the pope joined forces to divert church and state from their collision course, and from the end of 1926 into the next year a number of signs made plain that Belvedere and the Vatican were determined to enforce peace and restrain the belligerent instincts of their respective troops. In the wake of the Polish episcopate's very public announcement of grievance against sanacja, Archbishop Hlond followed with a private letter to the marshal expressing willingness to mend fences with the government in return for a show of good faith. He did not have to wait long for an answer. At about the same time, the regime consented to start discussing the implementation of the concordat with the bishops and began a series of minor but noticeable concessions to their interpretation of the document.[19] Gradually the hierarchy observed a new readiness on the part of high officialdom, especially President Mościcki, to meet the Church halfway on matters of religious policy.[20] The warming trend became apparent in July 1927 when the highest representatives of altar and throne gathered in Vilna for a ceremonial coronation of the icon of the Blessed Virgin of Ostrabrama. Piłsudski took advantage of the occasion to extol Pius XI as "a great friend" of Poland and confidentially reaffirmed his promise to the pope never to permit "any legislation harmful to the Church."[21]

By this time, having already chosen a Polish primate he hoped could get along with sanacja, Pius had set in motion another personnel change calculated to encourage the thaw with Warsaw. It soon became plain that the incumbent nuncio to Poland, Lorenzo Lauri, had little use for Piłsudski or his regime, and rumor had it that the marshal made a point of requesting his recall. In an ironic replay of his own experience six years earlier, the pope brought Lauri home in 1927 with the customary reward of a cardinal's biretta. The difference in this instance was that neither pontiff nor nuncio took offense at Warsaw's meddling. It gave Pius his opportunity to replace the appointee of Benedict XV with one more to his liking, and Lauri welcomed both the promotion and the rescue from the Polish weather he detested.[22] The pope took a full year to fill the opening, likely an indication of the low priority he accorded a nuncio in the realm of Polish policy, which he regarded as his own preserve. The eventual selection of the well-traveled curial envoy Francesco Marmaggi raised eyebrows within sanacja ranks since his previous posting to anticlerical Czechoslovakia had ended in the fiasco of a rupture between Prague and the Holy See, and they feared that he had been sent as a watchdog for Catholic orthodoxy. In fact, although Marmaggi never struck his hosts as much of a diplomat, he soon won them over with his evident fondness for Poland and his eagerness to carry out the papal line of benevolence toward the Piłsudski regime.[23] The nuncio arrived in Warsaw with instructions from the Vatican to regard the Polish government as generally well disposed to the Holy See, in spite of difficulties caused by the presence of highly placed secular and anti-Catholic elements: he should cultivate the personal esteem of the marshal for the pope and put this advantage to good use in making progress toward the top priority of policy, the implementation of the concordat.[24]

While building bridges to sanacja, the Polish Church also began to put some distance between itself and the nationalist right wing, which had become used to the benefit of Catholic support. In February 1927 the Church gave its public blessing to the work of the Catholic League, a nonpartisan lay organization that had operated in obscurity since its founding in 1920. At first glance, the Piłsudskiites suspected the bishops of wanting to set up a clericalist monolith of opposition to the government, but breathed easier once they grasped that the primary intent of the move was to provide Catholics with an independent outlet for their political energies and, not incidentally, to pry them away from their attachment to National Democracy. Commentators noted as well that the rise of the League followed on the heels of the papal condemnation of Action Française as an inadmissibly nationalist and materialist ideology hiding behind a veneer of pseudo-Catholicism, a decree they read as a censure, by analogy, of the Endecja. Noting the coincidence of these developments, at least some attentive Polish Catholic publicists took the hint that they should resist the blandishments of the Right and steer clear of those who, "under the name of religion, espouse principles in complete contradiction of it and *who, in adopting the motto of love of country, sow hatred among their fellow citizens.*"[25] The message was clear: the National Democrats were not fit political company for Catholics who took their faith seriously.

All the same, old habits died hard, and as Poland geared up for parliamentary elections to be held in March 1928—the first since the May coup—the Polish Church showed strong signs of reverting to its accustomed partiality to the Right. In December 1927 the episcopate issued a pastoral letter, largely the handiwork of Archbishop Teodorowicz, possibly in collaboration with Dmowski himself, that urged their flock to vote for the "Catholic and national camp." In the past, such language had been code for backing Endecja, and government partisans called foul. In addition, a multitude of lesser clergy gave their vocal support to the National Democrats, as usual. Clearly prompted by the Vatican, the two Polish cardinals did some quick backpedaling to dispel the impression that the bishops remained in the Right's pocket. From Rome, while awaiting the consistory that would formally confer his red hat, Primate Hlond ordered priests from his diocese running for election on the ND ticket to withdraw from the race and also complimented the sanacja regime in a press interview. Cardinal Kakowski denied, implausibly, that the bishops' statement could be construed as an endorsement of the opposition. A prominent Piłsudskiite candidate weighed in to announce, without contradiction, that he enjoyed the tacit support of high Church dignitaries and added that he had reason to know that the pope stood behind Kakowski's exegesis of the disputed pastoral letter. Delighted by this about-face, the government press reminded readers of the well-known special relationship between Pius XI and Marshal Piłsudski and crowed that the pope, in effect, had voted for the sanacja slate. These exertions from the top succeeded in blunting the effect of the December pastoral, but may have done little to stop the lower clergy from electioneering for the Endeks. In the end, the Piłsudskiite front—the so-called Nonpartisan Bloc for Cooperation with the Government (BBWR)—won a plurality of votes and seats, but not the majority it wanted to ram through its agenda. Merely by surviving, the Right could claim a victory of sorts, and its spokesmen attributed their success in part to their Catholic and clerical sympathizers.[26]

In the wake of the confused performance of the Church in the 1928 campaign, Hlond and Kakowski moved to lay down the law to their episcopal brethren, again at the behest of Pius XI. The primate went to Rome for consultations on Polish affairs and, by some accounts, left with a mission and an understanding: the Vatican would do what it took to break the Polish clergy of its habit of partisan politicking and urge the Catholic national minorities of Poland to be loyal to the republic, in return for Warsaw's pledge to honor the interests of the Church and implement the concordat in good faith.[27] Even if the whispers were not literally true, what happened next was entirely consistent with them. At a gathering of the episcopate in Gniezno in September 1928, the cardinals told the bishops that they would have to mend their political ways. Hlond faulted his clergy for carrying over their congenital allergy to civil authority acquired in the days of foreign rule into the era of independence, preventing the Church from maintaining a cordial dialogue with a genuinely Polish state. Dropping the other shoe, Kakowski urged upon his colleagues the wisdom of a reconciliation with sanacja. Despite its reputation, the Piłsudski team posed no threat to the Church, and could be dealt with in constructive fashion. Any expense of

Catholic energy and passion against the legal government of Poland was a diversion from the struggle against the true evils of the day, such as Communism and atheism. Put on the spot, the bishops acquiesced, and with that the lonely efforts of their hierarchical superiors to reach an accommodation with Marshal Piłsudski became a settled policy.[28]

Armed with the manifest imprimatur of the pope, Cardinal Hlond now started to come into his own and take full control over the Polish episcopate with a mandate to end its feud with the Piłsudskiites. So far as can be told, the primate held no strong opinions regarding sanacja, pro or con, but he was willing to get along with it in a spirit of benign impartiality. In essence, he took the position that the post-May *équipe* should be judged by the same standards applied to any legitimate government: so long as it did not trespass against the rights of Catholicism, it should receive the loyalty and respect that was its due. Of course, Hlond had no real choice but to follow this course, since the pope demanded it, but he had his own reasons. In the first place, it appealed to his lively patriotism. He also worried that the bishops had compromised their dignity and teaching authority through excessive partisanship, and that by speaking in more measured voice they might restore their reputation and enhance their influence on public policy. Finally, there was the pragmatic consideration that, even though the National Democrats could now more plausibly call themselves a Catholic party in light of their doctrinal mellowing, they looked like a spent force in a Poland dominated by Piłsudski, and the Church could gain nothing by chaining itself to their sinking ship. To that end, the firebrand Archbishop Teodorowicz was eased out of his accustomed status as primary commentator for the episcopate on political matters that he had held in Dalbor's day, and those duties were assumed by Hlond and Kakowski.[29]

Before long, Primate Hlond acquired a personal prestige and an effective leadership over the cantankerous Polish hierarchy that had eluded his recessive and sickly predecessor. He delegated the tasks of administration of his diocese to suffragans and gave priority to his primatial office and the duties proper to it, such as dealing with the Holy See, and worked assiduously to centralize his authority over his episcopal peers. Reserving to himself the right to speak for the bishops, he took care to comment on public matters in measured and moderate terms, and Warsaw officialdom paid him the compliment of conceding that he was sober and reasonable even when they disagreed with him.[30] His efforts were aided by the widespread opinion that he was a figure of uncommon talent and stature. Grave in demeanor and long-winded, he struck some as ponderous. In 1928, Hilaire Belloc attended a dinner in London given in honor of Hlond and several other accompanying Polish bishops—all of them, he noted, "enormous men, placid and contented" —and gleefully related to a correspondent that the primate's plodding and interminable address caused Francis Cardinal Bourne to "writhe with Boredom."[31] This was a minority view. He impressed many more as "an outstanding personality of great worth," as one foreign diplomat put it. Such was his reputation that his name was occasionally mentioned in curial circles as a potential future Vatican secretary of state, or conceivably even the first non-Italian pope of the modern era, getting the nationality right, if not the man.[32] Hlond was also a good conciliator, able to bridge the disagreements that had led to the notorious factionalism within the episcopate. For one thing, he managed to accomplish the delicate task of cementing a solid working relationship with the only other member of the Latin hierarchy who matched him in ability, Archbishop Sapieha of Kraków, who did not let his National Democratic sympathies or the muzzling of his bosom friend Archbishop Teodorowicz stop him from becoming a loyal associate of the primate despite their sharp differences over political strategy.[33]

The ascension of Hlond's star also made life easier for the other Polish cardinal, Kakowski of Warsaw, who settled into a comfortable niche as junior partner of his younger but more celebrated colleague. During the first decade of independence Kakowski had been the lone wolf of the episcopate, given scant respect by most of the bishops and isolated from them by his soft spot for Piłsudski and his tendency to side with the Holy See in its frequent clashes with the Polish hierarchy. Now that the tables had turned and his minority stand had become Church policy, he took on greater visibility and carved out a role for himself as the deferential lieutenant of Hlond and, in effect, the liaison between the episcopate and the government, which saw him as its friendliest advocate among the senior bishops. The new arrangement also meant that the Vatican could discard its awkward practice of years past of ignoring the primate and treating Kakowski as the head of the Polish Church in all but name out of its lack of confidence in Dalbor: everyone knew that Hlond ran the episcopate and that he enjoyed the full trust of the pope, and Kakowski was content to labor in his shadow. He still drew criticism as a nonentity who toadied to sanacja and showed an unseemly eagerness to show up at Piłsudski family name days. Behind his back, Teodorowicz snickered at him as "our Byzantium" for his servility to the ruling clique.[34] Even Hlond appears to have esteemed the office of archbishop of Warsaw more than its occupant, but they saw eye to eye in most respects and coexisted easily enough, without the chill or turf rivalry that had come between Kakowski and Dalbor.[35]

During this first flush of warming between the Polish Church and the Piłsudski regime, the two sides appeared to reach a breakthrough on the paramount issue that had divided them, the realization of the concordat. By late 1927, a year of periodic meetings between the so-called Papal Commission of Polish bishops and functionaries from the Ministry of Religious Affairs had produced nothing but mutual exasperation. The prelates sent off a complaint to Piłsudski that his minions were obstructing the parleys, while the bureaucrats predictably explained to him that the churchmen were demanding so much that there was no use talking to them.[36] In an attempt to break the logjam, Piłsudski sat in on the next pair of negotiating sessions in January 1928. This was an unusual intervention into the thicket of church-state questions by the marshal during his decade of quasi-dictatorship. As a rule, he devoted himself to foreign and military affairs, leaving other areas of statecraft to be managed by underlings unless and until his decree was needed to resolve a matter of fundamental policy and remove it as an irritant so that he could get back to his specialties. His performance on this occasion was vintage Piłsudski: impatient with the details of a dispute outside the range of his interest and expertise, keen to decide it once and for all with a pronunciamento, charming and blustering at the same time. He, Piłsudski, would personally guarantee that the concordat would be carried out, but if the Papal Commission and his government could not settle their differences about how to do it, then Warsaw would have to decide things on its own, or insist on renegotiating the treaty with the Holy See from scratch.[37] Had such a statement come from anyone else in Poland, Rome would have been aghast, but the Vatican trusted Piłsudski so completely that it put the most favorable interpretation on it. The strongman agreed to meet directly with a representative of the episcopate as needed to talk over issues related to the concordat, and Cardinal Gasparri immediately conveyed his satisfaction that the marshal had taken things into his own hands. A year later, in conversation with Ambassador Skrzyński, Pope Pius spoke of the wrangling over the Polish concordat as a thing of the past now that Piłsudski had made himself its arbiter.[38]

In the meantime, the episcopate continued to toil away at the project of disengaging the Church from the country's political wars. By 1930, with the warm encouragement of the Vatican, the Catholic League had been recast as a Polish branch of Catholic Action, the movement that sought to consolidate Catholic social and political activity under the supervision of the hierarchy. Catholic Action was dear to the heart of Pius XI, who saw it as the embodiment of his ideal of the Church doing its work in the world, beholden to no worldly potentate or creed, and he was fond of calling it the apple of his eye. Catholic Action eventually attained the considerable membership in Poland of nearly a million by 1939, although its impact on public life remained limited, in large degree hampered by an organizational torpor caused by its dependency on clerical guidance. Despite its weaknesses, Catholic Action left a discernible, if literally immeasurable, influence on the future of the Polish Church by mobilizing thousands of committed lay believers in a common purpose of spreading knowledge of modern Catholic social doctrines in a country that had scarcely heard of *Rerum novarum* and subsequent teachings in its tradition. The seeds planted in these years did not have time to blossom in the short span allotted to the Second Republic, but would bear fruit after the Second World War.[39]

Because the fragile truce between the Polish Church and the sanacja regime in Warsaw rested so heavily on the personal understanding of Piłsudski and the pope, it broke down quickly under the pressure of a variety of stresses that came to bear on it, and during the four years from 1928 to 1932 church-state tensions rose to their highest sustained level in the history of interwar Poland. For one thing, neither the Piłsudskiite true believers nor the Catholic clergy had their hearts in an accord. Many of the most zealous followers of the marshal, the loyalists who populated the middle ranks of officialdom and controlled much of the day-to-day working of government, recoiled against the very idea of making common cause with the Church and reasoned that their leader's seeming accommodation was in fact no more than a necessary tactical move in a stealthy "war against clericalism" that might take decades before the religious superstitions of Poles had eroded away.[40] These hostile bureaucrats tended to set the tone of religious policy, for while Piłsudski sincerely meant to do right by the Church according to his lights whenever he thought about it, he did not think about it too often. By the later months of 1928, Church organs began to take alarm at a rising mood of anticlericalism in sanacja circles. These apprehensions deepened the next year with the handing of the religious-affairs portfolio to Stanisław Czerwiński, an apostate and Freemason despised by Catholic opinion. Before the year was out, the pope began to salt conversations with

Poles with warnings against Masonic influence in their country, and to worry aloud that while he knew that Piłsudski would do nothing to harm the Church, he could not say the same about an unsettling number of the men who surrounded him.[41]

So far as the Piłsudskiites were concerned, fault for the touchy relations of church and state fell not on their anticlerical wing, but on the Catholic clergy itself. The bishops might say one thing and speak the language of compromise and cooperation with the government, they charged, but in practice they and their priests did another by continuing to patronize the National Democrats; Warsaw had the best of intentions to treat the Church fairly, but had the right to expect a modicum of goodwill in return rather than abuse as an impious gang of reprobates.[42] From Rome, Ambassador Skrzyński chimed in to warn that the steady defamation of sanacja by the rightist opposition and its clerical allies was making his job of representing Polish interests to the Curia much harder.[43] In April 1930 Nuncio Marmaggi called on Prime Minister Sławek and asked pointedly if his government was "satisfied with its standing in the eyes of Catholics in Poland, that is, the majority of the nation." Since the answer was obvious, Sławek did not bother with the formality of saying no, but turned the question around by charging that the Catholic faithful had been brainwashed against the Piłsudski regime by their pastors, who viewed it "through the hateful eyes of National Democracy."[44]

Amid signs of mounting strain between Warsaw and the Church, the process of implementing the concordat bogged down again, further aggravating hard feelings on both sides. By January 1929, a year after Piłsudski had given his vow to fulfill the concordat, the Polish bishops reported to the Vatican the disquieting news that no progress had been made after all. Not only that, but a palpable increase of anticlerical sentiment in the parliament seemed to place the Church in jeopardy.[45] In its defense, the government responded that working out the concordat was easier said than done, unavoidably delayed by the arduous task of constructing a coherent legal code for the reunited Poland. This was true to an extent, but in confidential moments sanacja officials made plain that they also saw the concordat primarily as a political issue, that they had their own constituencies to keep happy, and that they preferred to walk, not run, to the finish line.[46] In November, with the impasse still unresolved, the pope received Ambassador Skrzyński for a stiff and lengthy audience. The envoy stated that Piłsudski still meant to keep his end of the bargain regarding the concordat, but the marshal would be unable to do so unless the Church understood that co-operation was a two-way street. Pius volunteered the opinion that Freemasonry lay at the root of the difficulty. No, retorted Skrzyński, playing his trump, the problem was that the bishops and clergy of Poland had not changed their ways since the days the Holy Father had been nuncio to the country, and until they saw fit to "alter their behavior," which he remembered only too well, church and state would remain at loggerheads. The interview did not comfort the pope, and he ended it by expressing his growing unease that Catholicism in Poland was under serious threat from inimical forces.[47] Before the year was out, an internal analysis by the Polish Foreign Ministry concluded that both Warsaw and the Vatican were feeling "dissatisfaction and anxiety" about their relationship.[48]

More than just the concordat accounted for the chill in the air between Poland and the Holy See. In particular, Polish officials took offense at what they saw as a pronounced curial tilt toward Germany at their expense. While it was common knowledge that the Vatican looked with sympathy on the Weimar Republic and did not think much of the Versailles settlement, it took no formal position on the various Polish-German controversies, and diplomatic third parties saw no evidence of papal favoritism one way or the other.[49] Of course, Warsaw might have been more inclined to agree if not for the readiness of Cardinal Secretary of State Gasparri to mention his conviction that the Polish Corridor was a standing threat to peace that would have to go, a habit that got on the nerves of the Polish Foreign Ministry over the years.[50] The Poles tried protests, without result, and reminded themselves that the Vatican was at most a nuisance, not a real danger to their interests, but still they did their share of worrying about the need to get friendlier coverage in *L'Osservatore romano,* or to have more Polish cardinals appointed so as to get a better hearing at the papal court.[51]

Even so, the noticeable downturn in relations between Poland and the Holy See did nothing to change Pope Pius's mind about his preferences in the ongoing tug-of-war in Polish politics. In 1930, bent on finally breaking the ability of the opposition to thwart his agenda, Piłsudski braced for a showdown parliamentary election in November that matched his BBWR against the diminished National Democrats and a potentially formidable Center-Left coalition that entertained thoughts of victory. However, in contrast to the inconclusive contest of 1928 that he had waged according to the niceties of democratic rules, this time Piłsudski meant to win, even if it needed playing rough. As before, the Vatican dropped loud hints during the campaign of the pope's high regard for the hero of the Battle of Warsaw, looking the other way as the government jailed rival candidates and resorted to bullying and manipulation to guarantee victory.[52] The thuggish conduct of the election of 1930 is often regarded as the worst blot on Piłsudski's career, but in the short run the BBWR secured the elusive majority it needed to gain control of the legislature at last and consolidate its grip on the country. On the morrow of the balloting, the pope congratulated Piłsudski via diplomatic channels on having defeated factionalism, "which already once has led Poland to disaster," as if fair elections might revisit partition upon the land.[53] The failure of the Polish episcopate to condemn sanacja for its repression incensed the opposition, which accused it of knuckling under to the regime out of opportunism; at least one bishop privately answered that the Church might sympathize, but could not afford to risk higher pastoral priorities by provoking a rupture with the authorities.[54] For his part, Pope Pius discreetly conveyed some qualms about Piłsudski's hamhanded electoral strategy, but placed greater emphasis on his satisfaction that his friend had prevailed and, in the process, prevented the emergence of a leftist government in Warsaw.[55]

With the election out of the way, the focus of church-state relations returned to the issue that would not go away, the seemingly endless argument over the implementation of the 1925 concordat. By this time, even Cardinal Kakowski, normally inclined to give sanacja the benefit of the doubt, had reached the end of his patience: "God only knows," he wrote to himself in 1930, "when or if the state authorities will at last bring the matter to completion."[56] Before long, however, the logjam seemed to break up as the protracted negotiation went into another of its fitful productive phases. After having dragged its heels for several years, Warsaw became more open to discussion with the episcopate's "Papal Commission." By 1933, agreement had been reached on the abrogation of laws contrary to the concordat in former Russian and Austrian Poland, and the pope acknowledged his contentment with the progress of the work.[57] In spite of these promising auguries, from that point the talks bogged down in renewed disagreement, and then ground to a dead halt. The meetings of the government and the Papal Commission would not resume. In the end, the terms of the concordat were never fully and formally incorporated into the law of the Second Republic.

Aside from the concordat, the Church found other grounds for unhappiness with sanacja in the early 1930s as the regime made a push to exploit its hard-won majority in the parliament and enact its program. The centerpiece of the Piłsudskiite design was a new constitution that would strengthen the executive power and create a presidency suitable to be filled by the marshal. When discussions on the project began in the Sejm in 1931, the episcopate raised its eyebrows at the surfacing of proposals to water down the language of the 1921 "March constitution" regarding the Church and reduce the protection of religious influence in the country.[58] Above all, Belvedere and the bishops crossed swords on issues that pitted Catholic ideals of education, morality, and family against the more secularist outlook of the rulers. The inclination of sanacja toward lay and coeducational schools made the episcopate nervous, and it issued periodic warnings against the rise of antireligious tendencies in Polish classrooms and took pains to prevent hindrances to catechetical instruction.[59] In 1931 the government suggested reforms in marital law that would allow divorce and, in some eyes, establish a legal preference for civil marriage over religious nuptials. The initiative spurred protests and failed even to reach the floor of the legislature, shouted down by a chorus of conservative and rightist objections largely inspired by the Church.[60] A year later an official recommendation to revise the penal code aroused Catholic indignation by sanctioning abortion in certain limited circumstances.[61] This, too, never saw the light of day, but the increasingly acrimonious battle to keep offensive statutes off the law books convinced many of the Polish bishops that the Piłsudskiites had launched a determined assault against basic Christian precepts, and that drastic measures should be taken to halt it in its tracks. Possibly to head off rasher action by their colleagues, Cardinals Hlond and Kakowski, with the approval of the Vatican, agreed in 1931 that the primate would issue a pastoral letter on the defense of Catholic principles in Polish politics.[62] Word of the impending epistle leaked out, and as it neared completion after months of preparation, sanacja steeled itself for bad news, expecting a fierce denunciation that might lead to open conflict between church and state.

At that point, to see that things did not come to that, the three key players—Pius XI, Piłsudski, and Cardinal Hlond—arranged a quiet, roundabout understanding to restore harmony by forcing the episcopate of Poland to back down. In January 1932 Ambassador Skrzyński arrived in Warsaw to meet with Piłsudski, his prime minister of the moment, and his *homme de confiance*, Józef Beck, to deliver a message from the pope himself. The pontiff reaffirmed his confidence in Piłsudski and declared, in so many words, that the blame for the worrisome rise in tension belonged to the Polish bishops and the hyperpolitical lower clergy, whose strident opposition to sanacja verged on disloyalty to the state. If the marshal should feel the need to "take a stronger course" in dealing with his antagonists in holy orders, this would trouble neither the pope nor the majority of Poles. In other words, faced with a choice between his cantankerous Polish bishops and the strongman he had trusted for longer than a decade, Pius had cast his lot with Piłsudski in the most emphatic terms. Given the sensitive and startling nature of the conversation, special precautions would be taken to restrict knowledge of it to the highest circles of confidentiality, and to vouch for the authenticity of the written summary of Skrzynski's communication.[63]

One of the few copies went to Cardinal Hlond, and if Marshal Piłsudski did not have to resort to any of the "stronger" measures permitted him by the pope, perhaps the reason was that the primate of Poland read the document, took the papal hint, and quickly set about to look for a way out of the mounting dispute with sanacja. In March, at the request of the pope, Hlond sent to the Vatican a secret report on the discordant politics of religion in his homeland. The root of the problem, he wrote, was that the Piłsudski regime was pushing a laicizing agenda, which the Church opposed, as was its duty, leading inevitably to friction. Still, he admitted, in doing this, Polish Catholics could and should do a better job of showing respect for civil authorities, avoiding excessive partisanship, and leaving no doubt of their allegiance to the republic—the very virtues Pius had found wanting in the Polish bishops and clergy. The best way to accomplish this, Hlond concluded, was to get the Church in Poland to speak with one voice, meaning, no doubt, his own.[64]

Cardinal Hlond released his long-awaited pastoral, "On the Christian Foundations of Public Life," in April 1932, and differing audiences heard the document with different ears. The press called it a stinging rebuke of governmental policies, but the targets of the lecture paid more attention to the subtler nuances they detected between the lines. In fact, its thrust was that of a stern but temperate warning rather than an outright condemnation, and the regime was agreeably surprised to get off so easily.[65] In an uncharacteristically deft move that would have been unthinkable before the time of Hlond, the Polish Church had managed to complete its successful, sustained campaign to defeat the secularist offensive of the Piłsudskiites and uphold Catholic principles while simultaneously opening the door to reconciliation. The Hlond pastoral marked another turning point in the up-and-down relationship of church and state during the Piłsudski era. Both sides felt the relief that follows a collision narrowly averted: the steadily climbing tension of the previous four years broke, and from that point until the death of the marshal three years later, Catholicism and sanacja kept their peace. In effect, the government tacitly agreed to avoid giving affront to Catholic sensibilities, the Church agreed to show a more friendly face to the government, and, where necessary, they agreed to disagree on respectful terms.[66]

This renewed cordiality was encouraged by developments that allayed some of the Piłsudski regime's chronic grievances against the Church of Rome. For one, relations between Warsaw and the Holy See returned to even keel after a patch of rough sailing, aided considerably by a change at the helm of the Vatican foreign ministry. In 1930, the aged Cardinal Gasparri retired as secretary of state after sixteen years of service over two papacies. As his replacement Pius XI picked Eugenio Cardinal Pacelli, the undoubted standout of his diplomatic corps and longtime nuncio to Munich and Berlin, for the express purpose of grooming him to be the next pope. At first the Poles were made uneasy by Pacelli's strong ties to Germany and his well-known fondness for German culture, but they were delighted to see the last of Gasparri, and did not take long to decide that his successor was closer to their own view on the litmus-test issue of their controversial western frontier. As opposed to Gasparri, who rarely passed up a chance to scoff at the postwar settlements in Silesia, Pomerania, and Danzig, Pacelli also urged Poland and Germany to overcome their enmity for the sake of European harmony and civilization, but added the key stipulation that agitation for boundary revision in current circumstances could only lead to "the most dangerous chaos," and hinted that he would try to persuade the German clergy to steer clear of the topic.[67] After the years of slights and scoldings from Gasparri, such words were music to Polish ears, and by 1932 Ambassador Skrzyński reported to Warsaw that the Vatican thought of itself as "our ally in fundamental political questions."[68] This was an exaggeration just as surely as the previous tendency to equate the bluntness of Gasparri with enmity, for the Holy See truly thought of itself as being on no one's side, or perhaps everyone's. But the welcome tact and cordiality of Pacelli did wonders to refresh the stale atmosphere between Poland and St. Peter's.

To their surprise, the Piłsudskiites also began to notice that not even the Polish episcopate angered them so much anymore, thanks to the gradual effect of the pope's patient strategy of stocking the cathedrals of Poland with ordinaries more to his liking than the old guard that had chased him out of the country. The Vatican did not need convincing that the Polish bishops were, as a body, "trop agités," as Gasparri had delicately put it, but on principle resisted Warsaw's periodic demands to sack this or that hierarch.[69] Instead, Rome waited for death or retirement to provide a graceful opportunity to make the change. In practice, Nuncio Marmaggi chose the Polish bishops; the word in the Curia had it that Marmaggi was, if anything, more Catholic than the pope in his sympathy for Piłsudski and took care to vet candidates for their acceptability to the regime. This procedure put a premium, said some, on finding safe, bland nominees rather than men of ability or imagination and did not necessarily raise the quality of the hierarchy.[70] Whether by accident or intent, it also altered the social profile of the episcopate. The collection of bishops inherited by the Second Republic in 1918 had been dominated by its plurality of aristocrats, but a steady infusion of new members of peasant origin shifted the weight of the body toward commoners by the 1930s. In addition, the episcopate became more unified and less contentious over time, as older bishops set in their ways and divided by their differing experiences in the separated zones of imperial partition gave way to younger ones who came to maturity in the conditions of independence, did not share their elders' ingrained habit of regarding the state as an enemy, and were content to follow the firm and respected lead of Cardinal Hlond.[71] Be that as it may, none of these demographic subtleties mattered as much to the sanacja officialdom as the bottom line: that from their point of view "the younger bishops are an improvement over the older generation," meaning more tractable and less inclined to make trouble or challenge the government, and that was enough for them.[72]

In return, the leaders of that Polish hierarchy reciprocated by developing a conditional but genuinely greater appreciation for Józef Piłsudski as he entered the twilight of his momentous life. Piłsudski had seized power in 1926, still near his peak of vigor and ability and determined to create a constitutional and political structure suited to him, but by the time this had been achieved his mind and body began to falter. By the early 1930s he had become ill and aged, and as his faculties dimmed he withdrew more and more from the tasks of governing, shielded from the public eye by his retainers. The customary inquiries of Pope Pius regarding the health of his friend in Warsaw were now no longer a pleasantry, but an expression of real and growing concern.[73] By no means had all Polish Catholics mellowed in their opinions of the marshal in his dotage. To the end, the faithful remained polarized between those who reviled him as an enemy of their

Church and others who admired him as a national hero.[74] For their part, the chief figures of the episcopate chose to accentuate the positive elements of the Piłsudski legacy. In 1933 the two cardinals took turns paying tribute to him while making their rounds in Rome. Kakowski declared that "order and calm exist in the country thanks only to the marshal" and that he deserved the gratitude of all Poles, while Hlond credited him with reducing the threat of Communism and civil unrest.[75] They also saw no acceptable alternative to the centrist sanacja. The idea of a government of the Left was, of course, out of the question, while the Right appeared to them disoriented and dangerously unreliable as much of the National Democratic camp drifted toward extremism or flirted with fascism.[76] Above all, they took assurance from the knowledge that when push came to shove, as Hlond stated, "Marshal Piłsudski will not permit conflicts with the Holy Father," just as the regime, with greater earthiness, counted on the friendship of its commander with the Vicar of Christ as its "trump" for keeping the clergy out of mischief.[77]

The obvious impending close of the Piłsudski era disposed both the government and Church of Poland toward accommodation, and in the opening weeks of 1935 they reached a meeting of minds on two of the main issues that had come between them during the previous decade. In January the parliament passed the new constitution, which had been the highest domestic priority of the sanacja since its inception. The Piłsudski constitution departed from its predecessor of 1921 in shifting power from the legislature to the executive branch, but duplicated its clauses identifying Catholicism as foremost and privileged among Polish confessions and did nothing to contradict the concordat of 1925. This outcome more than satisfied Hlond and Kakowski, who advised the bishops that they might give it their blessing.[78] Regarding the concordat itself, the subject of so much ill-tempered dickering over the years, the two sides decided to go on dickering, but now under streamlined ground rules intended to keep the talks cordial, if nothing else. In place of the prickly meetings of unwieldy governmental and episcopal committees, the revised arrangement called for Hlond to confer privately with the minister of religious affairs to work out questions as they arose, and the concordat faded away as a source of discord.[79] For one thing, the bishops had become used to the now-entrenched regime and were more willing to take its promises of good faith at face value, lessening their sense of urgency for paper guarantees. For another, with the passage of time sanacja itself had come around to the belief that, after all, it could live with the concordat of 1925: the constitution still required one, and since the trend of recent concordats had been to place more burdens on the civil power, not fewer, the handiwork of Stanisław Grabski that the Piłsudskiites had reviled no longer looked like a bad deal for Warsaw.[80]

By this time Józef Piłsudski was visibly failing, and in April 1935 he was diagnosed with the cancer that would kill him a month later. Even while the marshal of Poland still lived, if barely, the assessments began of his peculiar relationship with the faith of his compatriots, his intriguing friendship with Pope Ratti, and their significance for Polish Catholicism. Convinced of the reliability, the good intentions, and, indeed, the sheer greatness of Piłsudski, warts and all, Pius XI had made him the centerpiece of a policy meant to remake the Catholic Church in Poland and shed it of its political habits the pontiff disliked, much as Leo XIII had challenged the French Church of an earlier day, against all its instincts, to submit to his *ralliement* to the Third Republic in the name of higher papal priorities. Catholic commentators recalled Piłsudski's promise to the pope not to allow harm to the Polish Church, and most of them admitted, if grudgingly, that he had kept his word.[81] As the deathwatch in Warsaw commenced, the weightiest dignitaries of Polish Catholicism—Hlond, Kakowski, Sapieha, and, at a distance, Pope Pius himself—all agreed that, once all was said and done, the relations of church and state were on the right path.[82]

After nine years of informal domination by the soldier who had exerted greater impact on the history of Poland than any man of his generation, the country faced an uncertain future. In March, amid the growing realization that the marshal was not long for this world, Cardinal Hlond had issued a pastoral letter containing a veiled but unmistakable warning that no Polish government should dare to lay hands on the Church, as if anticipating possible battles ahead as Piłsudski's heirs in Belvedere picked up his mantle.[83] The dying strongman himself once had said, in his own florid, pungent style, that so long as he lived he would, "no matter what," keep Warsaw on good terms with the Church, "but how it will be in Wanda's time"—speaking of his daughter, and meaning after he was gone—"well, that I just don't know."[84] But then, neither did he know, nor did anyone else, that before five years were out Poland and its Church would face troubles worse than any they might have imagined.

Pope Benedict XV. Library of Congress

Dignitaries attending a field mass on Saxon Square, Warsaw, August 14, 1919. *Seated left to right:* Józef Piłsudski, chief of state of Poland; Mgr. Achille Ratti, papal nuncio to Poland and future Pope Pius XI; and Herbert Hoover, director of the American Relief Administration and future president of the United States. Polish prime minister Ignacy Jan Paderewski stands behind Ratti. Sixty years later, the former Saxon Square was the site of the Victory Square mass celebrated by Pope John Paul II to begin his historic 1979 pilgrimage to his homeland. It is now known as Piłsudski Square. Hoover Institution Archives, Stanford

Nuncio Ratti aboard a Polish hospital ship treating soldiers wounded in war against the Soviet Union, September 1920. Fondo Giordani, *L'Osservatore romano*

Pope Pius XI. Library of Congress

The two Polish cardinals with some of their colleagues at a Vatican occasion, ca. 1935. Conspicuously seated in front center, wearing a cape and looking at the camera, is August Cardinal Hlond, archbishop of Gniezno-Poznań and primate of Poland. From Hlond, the second figure to the right, hands on thighs, palms down, is Aleksander Cardinal Kakowski, archbishop of Warsaw. Fondo Giordani, *L'Osservatore romano*

The devoted admirers of Catholic Poland Hilaire Belloc and G. K. Chesterton (with unidentified third man), 1932. National Portrait Gallery, London

Left to right: Prince Adam Stefan Sapieha, archbishop of Kraków; Andrei Sheptyts'kyi, Greek Catholic archbishop of Lwów; and Józef Teodorowicz, Armenian-rite archbishop of Lwów, ca. 1937.

Prince Adam Stefan Sapieha, archbishop of Kraków, an official portrait photograph taken in 1937, the year of the Wawel incident.

Pope Pius XII broadcasting his appeal for peace over Vatican Radio, August 24, 1939, from Castel Gandolfo. Standing to the right is Mgr. Giovanni Battista Montini, the future Pope Paul VI. Fondo Giordani, *L'Osservatore romano*

Cardinal Hlond, exiled by the German attack against Poland, at Castel Gandolfo, September 30, 1939, to join other Poles in attending an audience of condolence granted by Pius XII. Fondo Giordani, *L'Osservatore romano*

5 ||| The Friends and Enemies of Catholic Poland

In 1927 G. K. Chesterton numbered Poland among a few "certain things in this world that are at once intensely loved and intensely hated." These were things, he said, "of a strong character and either very good or very bad."[1] As one who loved Poland and indeed thought her very good, Chesterton wrote these words as an attempt to explain her to an uncomprehending England, but they say as much about the author as they do the country he admired as the brave bastion of Christianity. Chesterton was the premier English Catholic publicist of the day, and the text and tenor of his tribute to Poland, both authentically Chestertonian, displayed tendencies that might be called distinctively Catholic of his time and place. His expression of definite, unambiguous opinion, his disregard for fashion or conventional wisdom, and the pairing of stark opposites—love, hate; good, bad—reflected a mind, and its creed, anchored in a sure sense of moral absolutes, of right and wrong, of truth and falsehood, of virtue and sin, judged not by the unreliable standards of mortals, but handed down by an omnipotent yet benevolent God who spoke through his Church. In the meantime, however, believers found themselves forced to wage the war for souls against the relentless foes of Christ in this imperfect earthly realm that had been the duty of the Church for two millennia. Some, like Chesterton, relished the challenge and welcomed it with sunny confidence, while others sounded a grim call of alarm from the trenches against the oncoming hosts of wickedness, which seemed inexorably to be gaining the upper hand in a disordered moment of history, and dug themselves in for a desperate struggle before the promised, ultimate victory. In any event, spiritual and intellectual combat was the natural voice of public Catholicism in early-twentieth-century Europe. From the perspective of eternity, only things of strong character were worth bothering about, they were either good or bad, and they were properly loved or hated according to their relationship with divine law.

So Catholicism reacted intensely to the modern world, using Chesterton's revealing adverb, just as he said Poland aroused intense reactions from people of different sorts, and as with Poland, so too with the Polish Church. Chesterton did not say this in so many words, but he might as well have done, for to him Poland was its faith, no more, no less, a particular brand of Catholicism that he applauded but that others found appalling. Polish Catholic culture was traditional, devotional, and doggedly orthodox, better known for solid peasant piety than for sophistication or scholarship, steeped in patriotism through the ages and battle-hardened by long resistance against foreign oppressors, proud of its heritage as *defensor fidei* and guardian of Christian civilization on its eastern outskirts. More than its counterparts in other lands, the Catholicism of Poland took for granted such propositions as its exclusive claim on truth, the tragic misguidedness of rival varieties of Christianity, the principle that error had no rights, and the unique collective stigma borne by Jews as deicides who persisted in their obstinate rejection of the true Messiah and compounded their guilt by their continuing perverse machinations against his Church. It saw Catholicity as the bedrock of Polish nationhood, took no notice of the peoples in its midst that professed other faiths, except to lecture them on their errancy, and looked down its nose at non-Catholic ethnic Poles as stray sheep at best, as betrayers of the national ideal at worst. To Chesterton, and those who agreed with him, this was Catholicism as it was meant to be, a Church that was steadfast and indomitable in belief, that took its theology whole and without watering down, called a spade a spade, and was willing to fight for the right. To others, it was a bigoted, benighted, provincial, and authoritarian anachronism that held back the progress and development of Polish society like a dead weight. Owing to the vehement responses it excited, pro and con, as well as its own sharp-edged and uncompromising mentality, Polish Catholicism lived within a polarized world of extremes, of white and black, a world populated alike by loyal friends and determined enemies.

At the beginning of 1920, the year newly independent Poland barely escaped with its life by beating back the Red Army, Cardinal Kakowski of Warsaw gave an interview to an Italian newspaper on conditions in his recently resurrected country. After acknowledging the journalist's praise of the strength and vitality of Polish Catholicism, the archbishop hastened to add a qualification that plainly came from his heart: "You must not, however, suppose that we have not also our difficulties. Infidelity and Freemasonry have spread their contagion amongst us, as elsewhere. Judaism constitutes with us a danger more serious than elsewhere." Kakowski dwelt most on the threat of Bolshevism, which he described as an updated form of nihilism, destructive to its core and the negation of civilization, and which lurked just beyond the Polish frontier. "In a word," he concluded, "even in Poland, the Church is in a situation of combat, not in that of peaceful and undisturbed possession."[2]

Several things stand out in this extract. In the first place, by contemporary standards it appears jarringly ignorant and primitive, even paranoid. The reference to infidelity strikes the later reader as slightly quaint, but the swipe at the Jews now appears ugly, while the warning against the wiles of the Freemasons sounds unhinged. If the archbishop of Warsaw spoke these words nowadays, the result would be scandal, and he would be regarded as a crackpot by his own Church. But at the time, nothing about the interview would have seemed remarkable, or strange, or even all that controversial, to a Catholic, even if those outside the fold would have found it literally incomprehensible.

But the Catholic mentality of today is not that of 1920. While it has been a long time since any ranking prelate of the Roman Church would have dreamed of talking that way, Kakowski meant no more than to state what was to him a commonplace and unarguable fact: that the Church faced many adversaries, and of these the worst were the forces of Communism, Freemasonry, and the Jews, whether acting on their own or in combination as a sort of unholy trinity. By no means all Catholics subscribed to these views, but they were common enough and constituted a staple of Catholic polemics throughout the world. Such arguments were as familiar to French or Italian Catholics as they were to Poles. The theory took various guises. How many took seriously the notion of a literal Judeo-Masonic-Communist conspiracy is hard to say, but at the least, many would have accepted the idea in an allegorical sense, as a metaphorical expression of the real, if tacit, alliance of antagonists they faced in a spiritual war for the highest stakes, the preservation or fall of Christian civilization. This was not mere rhetoric, but genuine conviction. The outlook of interwar European political Catholicism was profoundly defensive, and its vocabulary and imagery heavily martial, depicting the Church as a hardpressed rampart of righteousness under fire from the combined assault of an assortment of modern evils, foes whose identities tended to merge and blur in the smoke of battle; in the eyes of the defenders, the fact that Jews, Masons, and Communists wore different uniforms, so to speak, was not nearly so vital as understanding that together they formed the bulk of the same hostile army that had been on the march since the French Revolution.

As Kakowski makes clear, Polish Catholicism harbored no illusions that the fabled devoutness of the country made it immune to these plagues. On the contrary, "even in Poland," as he lamented, the ills of the present day were afoot, manifested in so everyday yet pervasive a matter as the growing corrosiveness of popular culture. There, as elsewhere, homilies decried the rise of hedonism, the decline of sexual morality, and the craze for licentious dancing. In 1923 Cardinal Dalbor solemnly condemned the tango, the two-step, and the foxtrot.[3]

Worse yet, Catholic Poland was convinced of its own unique vulnerability to the three mortal archenemies of the Church. Jews made up a tenth of the population, a percentage unmatched in any other part of Europe, and consequently aroused more than the usual quota of complaints of their disproportionate influence in commerce and the professions. Freemasonry had entered the halls of government on the coattails of Marshal Piłsudski. Bolshevism had its lair just next door in Russia. Furthermore, in Poland popular prejudice and anecdotal evidence combined to make the hypothesis of an infernal collusion all the more plausible. After all, on the whole Masons and politically active Jews did support the laicization of Polish education and society, and the noticeable Jewish presence in the Polish Communist movement was axiomatic. These disquieting circumstances lent a special note of urgency to the worldview of the Church of Poland. If Polish Catholicism harped on the dangers of Bolshevism, Freemasonry, and the Jews loudly, monotonously, and to the point of near-hysteria, this was a case of shouting what Catholics in safer zones of Europe had the luxury to discuss more calmly. The difference was that the threats that in other lands were distant or theoretical were in Poland seen as immediate and tangible. The Vatican agreed that Poland faced greater danger from Communism and its Jewish and Masonic accomplices than any other country, and believed that the bond of shared interest in battling the common enemy was the strongest factor working in favor of cooperation between Catholicism and the Second Republic.[4] This vivid consciousness of menace, obvious and overt or stealthily gnawing from within, permeated the political thinking of the interwar Polish Church. After the Polish debacle in the opening campaign of the Second World War in 1939, Cardinal Hlond, a sober and prosaic man, blamed the catastrophe on the baleful effects of secularism and Freemasonry in bringing down the Second Republic, though German tanks and bombers might have come more readily to mind.[5] In other words, even in Poland—perhaps above all in Poland—the Church found itself locked in a relentless combat of ideas, and defeat would exact a heavy cost in this life and the next.

As an organized political force, Communism in interwar Poland was pathetically weak. Although the Marxist revolutionary movement in the Polish lands had a lineage that rivaled any in Europe and had produced such luminaries as Rosa Luxemburg and Feliks Dzierżyński, it never gained much of a following among Poles, who rejected its program of social radicalism, atheism, and proletarian internationalism, as well as its odor of association with Russia. Fatally, the Communists scorned the idea of Polish independence, the one point on which Poles of all other persuasions could agree. The party turned its back on the appearance of the Second Republic, banking instead on the imminence of global revolution, loudly cheered on the Red Army as it invaded Poland in 1920, and never shook its disrepute as a gang of traitors and foreign agents after the Russian Bolsheviks were pushed back. As the saying had it, Poles regarded the Communists not as the party of the Left, but as the party of the east. True to form, the Communist Party of Poland (KPP) declined to register as a legal political entity, led a shadowy existence behind a variety of fronts, and occupied a negligible presence in Polish public life. Its membership numbered only in the tens of thousands, few of them genuine workers, and its conspicuously Jewish composition with Ukrainian and Belorussian admixtures reinforced its alien image. The inglorious career of the KPP came to a grisly end in the Stalin purges of the 1930s, when Moscow shut down the party and murdered most of its leaders who had not the good luck to be sitting in the relative safety of Polish jails.

The external Communist threat was more credible. The Bolsheviks had seized control of adjacent Russia, constantly proclaimed their intention to export their revolution, and already had made one attempt to overrun Poland by armed might in 1920. While that thrust had been parried at the last minute by Piłsudski's last-ditch victory, the harrowing escape left a deep impression on every patriotic Pole, as well as the pope, who had witnessed the Battle of Warsaw. Every now and then, Pius XI or Cardinal Kakowski would pass along to Polish authorities his intuition of an impending Red Army attack to finish the job; this would generally be brushed off as crying wolf, but in the end their mistake was in the timing, not the principle.[6] In 1928, responding to a nervous inquiry from the pope, Piłsudski assured the pontiff that the Soviet Union was in no shape to initiate war with the Second Republic; Moscow might be tempted to pounce only if, at some point, Germany and Poland came to military blows in the west—the basic scenario that would unfold in September 1939.[7] Aside from the standing peril of a frontal assault, the Soviets also notoriously had at their disposal such unorthodox resources as their clandestine operatives and the Comintern, all the more insidious for their secretive nature and their seemingly ubiquitous industry at making mischief and propaganda.

All the same, at bottom, both in Poland and the Vatican, the Church did not fear the Communists so much as the allure of Communism itself. After all, said Cardinal Kakowski, the only Bolsheviks the Polish peasant knew were Russians or Jews, and he did not care for either of them.[8] The problem posed by the doctrine of Communism was something else again, and far more challenging. In the understanding of the Church, Bolshevism was only outwardly the novel political ideology the world considered it to be. At its heart lay the ancient temptation to deny God and his law, now manifested in the most comprehensive human effort yet to overthrow Christian morality and society. As such, it was evil, and thus possessed a dangerous attractiveness, evil being but the perverted image of the good. When Cardinal Hlond said that with Communism "Satan has entered the politics of nations," he meant it.[9] In their more thoughtful moments, Church spokesmen conceded that Bolshevism fed off the grievances bred by real injustices and inequities in the social and economic order, but this point tended to get lost in their haste to condemn the Reds and all their works.

So the Polish clergy kept up a steady din of denunciation of Communism throughout the interwar decades, maintained at a pitch and with a persistence that their secular critics took as evidence of crazed monomania. "Bolshevism," gibed the anticlerical writer Tadeusz (Boy) Żeleński; all the Polish Church had to say was that "everything is bolsheviks."[10] Red-baiting clerical rhetoric was at its rawest at the parish level, but even the more formal official declarations of the episcopate were not bashful about warning of the Communist peril in lurid language.[11] Except perhaps for its volume and intensity, this was hardly a Polish peculiarity, for Bolshevism weighed heavily on the minds of Catholics everywhere in Europe. The anxiety started at the top, for Pius XI grew increasingly preoccupied with the Communist threat throughout his pontificate and singled it out as the worst of the totalitarianisms that emerged on his watch. Pius was no friend of fascism or Nazism, but his encyclicals on those systems, *Non abbiamo bisogno* (1931) and *Mit brennender Sorge* (1937), while strongly worded, emphasized rebukes of their most glaring abuses; by contrast, his *Divini Redemptoris* (1937) damned Communism as such and in toto, on the grounds that Christians could have nothing in common with its creed of atheism, materialism, and class warfare.

Given its fixation on Bolshevism, the Church was slow to recognize Hitler as the more immediate bearer of war and chaos. In 1936 Cardinal Hlond told an Austrian interviewer that "the peace of Europe and of the world depends exclusively on the removal of the Communist factor."[12] This task was seen as imperative, both in Poland and abroad. As Pope Ratti drew near the end of his life, he and his lieutenants became increasingly insistent in lecturing Polish diplomats about the duty of the Second Republic to be vigilant against Communism foreign and domestic.[13] For the time being, in the eyes of many Catholics, Józef Piłsudski had given heroic service to the cause. In great part the basis for Piłsudski's generally tolerable relations with the Church during his decade of informal dictatorship was the conviction at the Vatican and at the top of the Polish hierarchy that, despite his flaws, he had done more than any man of his generation to thwart the ambitions of Bolshevism.[14] In the long run, Hlond believed, the conflict of Catholicism with Communism was not primarily political, but moral and intellectual, and the one sure way to win it was to answer the cries of the poor by attaining the Christian social justice and solidarity outlined in *Rerum novarum* and elaborated in *Quadragesimo anno* (1931), the successor encyclical of Pius XI.[15] Now Communism is gone, even though that ideal remains unachieved. Hlond did not foresee that, but then again, nor did he anticipate the effect of a Polish pope.

Freemasonry began in 1717 with the formation of the first grand lodge in London, a secret fraternal order modeled after medieval stonecutters' guilds and bound by a code of humane ethics and occult ritual. From England it spread widely through Europe during the eighteenth century, appealing especially to literate men of ambition who saw in it a vehicle for social and professional advancement as well as edification and charitable work. Its organizational culture of deism, rationalism, and brotherhood made it a nice fit with progressive opinion of the day, and Freemasonry became one of the principal engines of the Enlightenment. It endured after the French Revolution and became entrenched as the largest, most far-flung, and most influential secret society in the world, a status it holds to this day.

From the start, the Roman Catholic Church found much to dislike in the Royal Craft. With its elaborate trappings of hidden vows and ceremonies revealed only to the initiate, Freemasonry struck the Church as a species of pseudoreligion incompatible with Catholicism. In addition, the fraternity quickly gained a reputation for fostering ideas and activities inimical to Christianity, and came under suspicion of plotting against the Church under cover of its bond of silence and mystery. Pope Clement XII first condemned Freemasonry in 1738, a judgment reaffirmed formally no fewer than sixteen times by seven of his successors. If anything, Catholic animus toward the Masonic lodges deepened in the nineteenth century, when they were seen as crucial components of the liberal and anticlerical tides sweeping Europe, and Rome detected the hostile hand of the Craft at work within the governmental and social elites of Europe, stirring up hatred against the Church. Pius IX denounced Masonry as "the Synagogue of Satan," and in 1884 Leo XIII made it the anathematized subject of his encyclical *Humanum genus.* Catholics were barred from membership in the Masonic brotherhood on pain of excommunication; the ban was not lifted until 1983.

As in other strongly Catholic regions, Freemasonry found its growth in the Polish lands stunted by ecclesiastical disapproval, but managed to establish a salient if small presence. Following its typical pattern, it recruited from among the educated upper strata and so gained a disproportionate representation within the political class that made up the Polish national movement that culminated in the recovery of independence. Masonic activity in Poland reached a peak, relatively speaking, in the early years of the Second Republic, enlisting a new generation of adherents drawn largely from professional ranks, especially educators and the officer corps. In 1920 the Polish followers of the Craft obtained permission from Masonic authorities abroad to found the Grand National Lodge of Poland.[16]

The increasing influence of Masons in national life, numerically tiny but concentrated in strategic quarters of society, disquieted the Polish Church and aroused the deep-seated Catholic dread of conspiracy orchestrated by the secret brotherhood. The foothold of Freemasonry within the military gave it access to one of the most respected of Polish institutions, and not incidentally the entourage of Chief of State Piłsudski, while its appeal to teachers and academics raised the specter of indoctrination of the young. Compounding the anxiety, Masons were known, or suspected, to be highly placed in the early governments of interwar Poland. Gabriel Narutowicz, the assassinated first president of the republic, was a lodge brother, as was the key Peasant parliamentarian Maciej Rataj. A conspicuous number of Freemasons were clustered in the Foreign Ministry and the diplomatic corps, including the historian Maciej Loret, who put in a two-year posting at the Vatican, of all places. For a brief span in 1922, both the prime minister and foreign minister were Masons. Other political luminaries were the targets of false gossip about their membership in the Craft, notably Ignacy Jan Paderewski and Józef Piłsudski himself. In 1925 Bishop Hlond of Katowice, soon to be named primate, lamented that "we know well that Masons hold high office in our Republic, that they have influence over the direction of Polish domestic and foreign policies . . . what is worse, Freemasonry is invading the Polish schools."[17] By the time Hlond was installed as archbishop of Gniezno-Poznań a year later, the Piłsudski coup had made the peril he described all the more acute from the point of view of the Church by sweeping into the halls of state the comrades of the marshal, the most notorious crowd of Freemasons in the land. From then on the Masonic sympathies of the men who surrounded Piłsudski became a preoccupying source of worry for the Polish Church, not to mention Pope Pius XI, and Poles heard no end of clerical admonitions, sometimes subtle, more often not, against the schemes of the Royal Craft.

In the end, Catholicism may be said to have achieved a victory of sorts in its crusade against Freemasonry in interwar Poland, even if the battle amounted to swatting a fly with a sledgehammer. By any rational measure, the Church grossly exaggerated the extent and effectiveness of Masonic activity in Poland, which was more apparent than real but magnified by fearful imagination and the glamour of secrecy.[18] To be sure, the relentless attacks of Catholic spokesmen did much to stifle the work of the brotherhood in the country. Constantly vilified by the Church and the political Right, Freemasonry became not, as in other lands, a means of career advancement, but a mark of opprobrium and suspicion. In all, the core group of active Freemasons in the Second Republic probably approached one thousand, the smallest figure in central Europe. Politics and infighting also contributed to the decline of the Craft. Dismayed by the gradual rightward drift of the Piłsudski regime, the Grand Lodge purged some of its members with sanacja connections, while others left of their own accord. The Masonic ties and leanings of the government grew weaker with the passage of time. In 1938, desperate to cater to the Church and steal the thunder of the rejuvenated right wing after the death of Piłsudski, the sanacja regency banned Freemasonry in Poland. The prime minister who pushed the decree through the Sejm was himself one of the former brothers who had been drummed out. The movement went underground, perhaps not too abnormal a condition for a secret fraternity, and resumed legal existence only with the revival of the Grand Lodge in 1991, after the fall of the Communism that the Church had considered the natural confederate of the Masonic conspiracy.

The interwar Polish Church has earned few commendations from historians for its words and deeds concerning the Jews, and by modern lights it deserves none. For the most part, debate has split along the lines of describing the Church as "long a bastion of anti-Semitism" and branding it one of the chief culprits responsible for the rising tide of animus against the Jews that swept Poland in the 1930s (the majority view) or defending it, after a fashion, as not the most immoderate element in an environment of inflamed ethno-religious passions.[19] The matter is more complicated than that. It is fair to point out that there was no one Polish "Catholic" slant on Jewish issues and that the Church harbored not only bigots, but also advocates of toleration who urged protection of this vulnerable minority.[20] In addition, Christian attitudes and rhetoric regarding Jewry should not be considered in isolation, as most often happens, but rather in the context of the widespread belief that the Jews were just one part of a general modernist assault on Catholic morality and society; an enemy, to be sure, but by no means the only or even the worst enemy.[21]

Still, there was a standard catalogue of European Catholic complaints against the Jews, with which most Polish Catholics would have agreed: that they had too much economic power; that they were disproportionately mixed up in Communism, Freemasonry, and other unsavory practices; and that on the whole they presented a threat to the health and good order of Christian society.[22] Sparingly used in earlier times, anti-Semitic rhetoric had become a prominent theme in Polish Catholic discourse by the early years of the twentieth century.[23] These views were expressed with an unapologetic directness that today takes the breath away. Catholic polemicists of the time had no sense of obligation to treat Judaism with respect, nor any reluctance to speak of the Jews exactly as they thought of them, as a problem. This pertained especially to Poland, where the concentration of Jewish numbers made the issue seem all the more pressing. Even so, Christian teachings and scruples placed limits on the nature and methods of permissible anti-Semitism. At least in theory—and the theory had some bearing on practice—Catholics could not subscribe to blanket condemnations of Jews on racial or biological grounds, had to make distinctions between "good" and "bad" Jews, and were forbidden to use or encourage violence. In short, the Church tried to have it both ways on the Jewish question, by lending its imprimatur to the defamation and marginalization of Jews within Poland, and then disowning the animosities and outrages that predictably resulted.

At best, the standard approach of interwar Polish Catholic spokesmen and hierarchs was to bestir themselves to disapprove only the vilest forms of anti-Jewish thuggery in painfully qualified language while explicitly sanctioning more respectable means of discrimination, such as economic boycotts, and routinely stigmatizing Jews as spiritual and political adversaries. Cardinal Kakowski provided a typically equivocal example of this approach in 1934, when requested by a delegation of rabbis to condemn violence against Jews. The archbishop of Warsaw replied that of course he stoutly opposed any recourse to physical force, "whether from Catholics or Jews" (although Jewish attacks on Christians never had been at issue), but hastened to add that the involvement of Jews in the propagation of atheism, pornography, and other activities offensive to Christians could not fail to arouse justifiable Catholic anger and thus trigger "most regrettable excesses."[24] In this manner Kakowski managed to blame the victims, change the subject from anti-Semitic bullyragging to the misbehavior of Jews, and issue what amounted to a warning that the Jewish populace could expect to be held collectively responsible for the actions of any of its more disreputable members. One guesses that the rabbis were sorry to have asked.

Again, that is about the best that can be said. At worst, Catholic publicists dished out crude anti-Semitic invective, pure and simple. For instance, in 1936 a Polish Jesuit review declared that "the Jews should be eliminated from Christian society."[25] The words make the blood chill in a world that has known Auschwitz, and it is small comfort to realize that the writer meant them in a metaphorical sense, urging the strict separation of Christians and Jews to prevent the spiritual and ethical pollution of the Catholic community. The themes of segregation, exclusion, quarantine, and eradication gained prominence as the years went by. In the middle and late 1930s, Catholic leaders called for an end to coeducation of Jewish and Catholic students in public schools on the grounds that Polish children would acquire "lower morality" from their Judaic classmates, as if they carried a contagious disease.[26] In 1938 a priest admitted in print that a Jew could not help being what he was, but added "neither is the wolf to blame that he is born a wolf, yet we destroy wolves."[27] One might well ask if the publication of such statements in the charged atmosphere of central Europe during the Great Depression amounted to verbal violence that made a mockery of the prohibition against fists and clubs, equivalent to handing a matchbox to an arsonist and then deploring the fires that followed, noting that, of course, everyone should be careful with matches.

Still, the record is not entirely abysmal, and sometimes Polish Catholic commentary on Jewish matters showed signs of struggling toward a more generous response. One measure of the difficulty and complexity of the issue is the fact that this very effort may be clearly detected in the single statement most often cited to prove the contrary, Cardinal Hlond's 1936 pastoral letter, "On Christian Moral Principles." In it, the primate begins his remarks on the Jews with a flat declaration that "a Jewish problem exists and will exist so long as Jews remain Jews." This sentence has been seized on repeatedly to demonstrate the intractable contempt of the interwar Polish Church toward Jewry.[28] However, in context he is plainly not inciting to hatred, but making a theological point that, for Catholics, was literally an article of faith that they were not bashful about espousing: that the ultimate answer to the "Jewish question" lay in the acceptance by Jews of Jesus as their Messiah and fulfiller of their religious expectations. The accusers of Hlond will often add his frowning observation that "it is a fact that the Jews combat the Catholic Church" and bear their share of blame for the evils of the day. On the other hand, they rarely mention his words that follow, and that carry the brunt of his message: "But let us be fair. Not all Jews are such. Very many Jews are devout, honest, fair, kind, and benevolent. . . . [anti-Semitic doctrines] imported from abroad . . . conflict with the Catholic ethic. It is permissible to love one's own nation the more; it is not permissible to hate anyone, including the Jews."[29]

In practical terms, one might object, the primate arrived at the same conclusion as Cardinal Kakowski—sanctioning peaceable means of so-called national defense, while drawing the line only at physical attacks—but there is a discernible difference of spirit between the thinly veiled try by the archbishop of Warsaw to rationalize violence under cover of deploring it and Hlond's emphasis on the duty of Christians to avoid the sin of hatred.[30] This is not much to boast of by later standards, but in its time and place it stands out as one of the pronouncements of the Church on the Jews that has at least some redeeming features.

Hlond's warning against anti-Semitic notions "imported from abroad" —a transparent allusion to Nazi Germany—illustrates the fact that the Polish hierarchy felt some pressure to bring its position on the Jewish question into harmony with the increasing outspokenness of Pius XI late in his life. Achille Ratti appears to have held the conventionally unfavorable views toward Jews for a European Catholic of his generation until, by his own account, his stint as nuncio to Poland awoke in him a new sympathy for the people that had given the world its redeemer: for him the Jew, formerly an abstract concept, now had acquired a human face. The emergence of the Nazi regime with its trademark dogma of racial determinism offended the aging Pope as un-Christian and provoked him to drop several hints of his mounting concern for the welfare of the Jews. The Jewish issue was not central to his criticism of Nazism in *Mit brennender Sorge* (1937), but it was implied, and in 1938 Pius drew much attention with his informal but public declaration that Christians were "spiritual Semites" and thus forbidden to despise Jews. The nuncio in Warsaw reported to his superiors in Rome that Poland had good reason to seek ways to alleviate its Jewish problem by such means as encouraging emigration, but that the leadership of the Polish Church had the duty to speak out and insist that these policies be carried out in humane fashion, in accordance with Christian principles.[31] Catching the drift of things, Cardinal Hlond began to condemn racism along the lines of papal language, as code for Nazi ideologies of blood, and the Polish Catholic press toned down its anti-Semitic rhetoric.[32] Trying to earn points with the pope, the Polish government eagerly alerted the Vatican whenever an opportunity could be exploited to accuse an unfriendly Catholic cleric of encouraging "biological anti-Semitism."[33]

In 1938, as he entered his last year, Pius gave orders for the preparation of a new encyclical, *Humani generis unitas*, that was to go beyond *Mit brennender Sorge* by explicitly damning racism and anti-Semitism. This document, which did not make it past the stage of a rough draft and was never released, entered lore as the "lost encyclical" of Pius XI, supposedly bottled up by a nervous Vatican bureaucracy until the old pope passed on and cooler heads could prevail. By most accounts, the Polish Jesuit General Ledóchowski took the lead in scuttling the pronouncement, fearing that it would enrage Berlin without restraining it, and might touch off a wave of persecution of the Church in Germany. Some commentators lament the obstruction of this last testament of Pius XI as a wasted chance to ostracize Hitler in plain words; others counter that, in the long run, it was better that *Humani generis unitas* never saw the light of day, since it included a stark reaffirmation of Jewish guilt of deicide that would have stood as a sizable obstacle to the renovation of Catholic teaching on the Jews that emerged from the Second Vatican Council.[34]

To say that Maksymilian Maria Kolbe was typical of the interwar Polish Catholic posture toward the Jews would exaggerate—saints are never typical—but his singular story does highlight some of the paradoxes and subtleties of the subject. This Polish Franciscan voluntarily died a miserable death in Auschwitz in 1941 so that his captors would spare the life of another condemned prisoner, a gentile husband and father. For this act of heroic witness, he was canonized in 1982 and extolled by his countryman, Pope John Paul II, as a fitting "patron of our difficult century." However, the elevation of Fr. Kolbe to sainthood aroused protests from many quarters on the grounds that he was an anti-Semite, a charge that appears not to be true, but still raises enough troubling questions that it can be dismissed only upon close examination.[35]

In Kolbe, as in many holy men, the virtue of kindliness popularly considered "saintly" coexisted with a burning faith, an ironclad conviction, and a fierce determination to spread the gospel. As a student in Rome in 1917, he was shocked and galvanized by the antireligious brazenness of a massive Masonic demonstration outside the Vatican walls, and resolved to dedicate his life to converting the sworn enemies of Christ. To further this goal, and in keeping with his profound Marian devotion, he founded the Militia Immaculatae, a Franciscan community that sought to win souls through appeals to the Blessed Mother. In his polemics he routinely used language about the targets of his evangelical exertions, including the Jews, that now would seem offensively disrespectful of Judaism. However, by his lights, lecturing Jews on the inadequacy and incompleteness of their creed was showing them not enmity, but the most radical sort of love, urging them toward the truth that would win them salvation. In any event, Kolbe said little directly about Jewish questions, and most of that was mild, if prone to stereotype: "the Jews are clever, and there is nothing wrong with that; we want to teach the Poles to be clever, too."[36]

The heart of the charge against Kolbe resides not in his own words, but in the Jew-baiting enthusiasm of the journals published by his house from its center at Niepokolanów, his "City of the Immaculate" not far from Warsaw. Above all, his *Mały dziennik*, a mass market national Catholic daily launched in 1935, provides grist for his critics. In its inaugural issue, *Mały dziennik* announced the intention to "lead the struggle against the

Jewish flood in a Christian way, without hatred and without outrages," but the paper soon developed the habit of referring to Jews in terms that defy benign interpretation.[37] In extenuation, it can be said that Kolbe delegated editorial control of these publications to subordinates, that he was out of the country on missionary work for extended stretches, and that on at least one occasion he called a meeting to scold his journalists for their anti-Semitic zeal. Anecdotal evidence also maintains that once the Germans overran Poland, he performed acts of kindness and comfort to Jews in the shadow of occupation, and inside Auschwitz itself. Upon examination, the disparagement of St. Maksymilian as an anti-Semite does not stand up to scrutiny, but the unsavory diatribes served up by those acting in his name continue to provide an opening for those inclined to look for chinks in his armor of holiness.[38]

In the end, the tortuous attempts of the Polish Church to permit Catholics to get their hands dirty hounding the Jews, just so long as they did not get them bloody—"temper[ing] its national feeling with Christian charity," in the sanitized formulation of a foreign sympathizer—yielded few positive results and did it no credit.[39] Some historians argue that the nagging voice of the Catholic ethos restrained the resurgent Polish Right of the 1930s from embracing full-blown fascism.[40] Even if true, this was largely a distinction of political taxonomy. The great majority of the young generation of radical nationalists that emerged in those years considered themselves Catholics but still turned a blind eye to Church teachings against totalitarianism and violent anti-Semitism; without much difficulty, they could either figure out a way around the sometimes halfhearted admonitions of their pastor or find a likeminded priest willing to give his blessing to their escapades.[41] The unpleasant fact is that, as Ronald Modras has written, too many of the Polish Catholic clergy "were not innocent bystanders or passive observers" of the poisonous anti-Jewish mood that gripped the country as the interwar epoch drew near its end, but "were very much integral to it."[42] In 1937 the Polish Catholic Press Agency called for "a statesmanlike solution for the Jewish problem in Poland," words that take on a grim retrospective irony.[43] Of course, the publicist who composed the phrase had no inkling that the "solution" that history would provide would be Hitler's. It is necessary to retain perspective: at its worst, the "Christian" anti-Semitism of Poland, if so we may call it, never approached the genocidal racism of the Nazis, and the record of the Church, sorry as it was, had no direct bearing on the coming of the Holocaust, which was conceived and carried out by a

German regime that cared not a whit for Catholic teachings or sensibilities. Still, if the Church of Poland could undo and reform any single aspect of its long history, the chances are it would want to take back most of what it said and did about the Jews in the years before they perished, leaving the Polish memory haunted by their destruction.

Pope Pius X had famously defined modernism as the synthesis of heresies; in the disapproving judgment of Catholic Poland, the country's interwar intelligentsia might have been described as the synthesis of heretics. In modern Polish tradition, the significance of the narrow social stratum identified as intellectuals far exceeded its numbers. In its Polish usage, the category was understood to include a broad range of socially respected occupations, such as free professionals, civil servants, teachers, the military elite, and the clergy. However, when the Church spoke of the intellectual class, it tended to employ the term in its more restricted understanding as pertaining to thinkers and artists: scholars, writers, publicists, performers, and the like. During the partition era, when Poles had lacked a state and institutions of their own, these creative circles had gained recognition as the collective articulators and defenders of the Polish national ethos, and this prestige had carried over into the days of independence. For this very reason, the Church of Poland regularly scolded the intelligentsia for misusing its customary office as tribune of the people for the purpose of spreading pernicious moral and political messages throughout society. Apart from an avowedly Catholic minority, Polish intellectuals, like their counterparts elsewhere in Europe, were far more inclined to irreligion, anticlericalism, and radical sympathies than the Polish nation as a whole. Because the intelligentsia was also disproportionately Jewish, Masonic, and leftist, the Catholic critique of the cultural elites of Poland overlapped with its rhetorical crusade against the other reputed archenemies of the faith, here concentrated into one unwholesome fraternity, as if to confirm the theory of a malign conspiracy of the ungodly. For their part, the secular intellectuals more than returned the favor by deriding the Church as an anachronistic stronghold of bigotry, reaction, and mumbo jumbo, worthy only of scorn and contempt.

During the interwar years, this traditional rivalry between the Church and the lay intellectuals hardened and intensified even more. The two camps clashed repeatedly over a variety of issues—education, marriage and family law, the prevailing tone of public culture, the role of the Church in politics—that grew out of their irreconcilable views of the fundamental question whether Poles should adhere to Catholic standards of morality and communal ideals. The Church won most of the battles, though not without difficulty, and deepened its mistrust of the intelligentsia as a harmful element within the nation. Cardinal Hlond took the Polish thinkers to task for peddling "the errors of the nineteenth century . . . and disastrous social and political views," and voices inside the Vatican muttered that they were a "Bolshevist-statist" wolf among the Polish flock.[44]

Of course, such charges daunted their targets not at all, and when the intellectuals bothered to respond, they tended to answer in the coin of mockery and disdain for the cloth. One of them, Tadeusz "Boy" Żeleński, the lifelong enfant terrible of Polish letters, made something of a career of poking irreverent fun at the Church and its clergy. Boy-Żeleński staked his claim to recognition as the leader of Polish anticlericals with the publication of his 1933 polemic *Nasi okupanci* (Our Occupiers), reflecting his argument that Poland had regained independence only to turn around and lose it in subjection to the Roman Church, the local branch of a foreign power that fed off the country as a parasite by extracting privileges unknown even in the Middle Ages. In essence, the book was a rehash of tried and true anticlerical chestnuts, along the lines of "Catholicism in Poland is 20% religion and 80% industry, a superbly organized financial concern." He flashed his trademark acid wit in deliberate provocations, such as his suggestion for the founding of a "Bolesław the Brave Society," to honor the memory of the medieval Polish king who had ordered the martyrdom of St. Stanisław, the revered symbol of ecclesiastical resistance against unjust civil power. Boy-Żeleński delighted in his reputation as the chief literary tormentor of Catholicism in Poland, boasting to his readers that the devout had good reason to call him "Antichrist."[45]

The constant bickering of the interwar period deepened the bitter estrangement between the Church of Poland and the leading minds of the country and helped ensure that the rift would carry over into the future. Looking back on the experiences of his youth from a vantage point of six decades, the poet Czesław Miłosz recalled that in the 1930s it was as if Catholicism and the literary and intellectual milieus inhabited different planets.[46] After the Second World War, significant numbers of the surviving Polish intelligentsia, or the younger generation that inherited their worldview, lent their support to the Communist regime that arose in the wake of the Red Army. By 1977 the democratic activist Adam Michnik, a man of impeccable credentials as an *inteligent,* a former red-diaper baby, penned an influential tract that urged his colleagues to overcome their ingrained animus and make their peace with a changed and lately enlightened Church as an essential ally in the task of toppling the PRL dictatorship. True, he allowed, in the days of the Second Republic, opposition to the Church was an essential part of a progressive and humane agenda, but times had changed. At the same time, Michnik ruefully admitted, perhaps the Church had not been entirely mistaken in the old days, after all: "it is not without some painful self-reflection that I read today the prewar comment of then Reverend Wyszyński"—the venerable Catholic primate of Soviet-dominated Poland, honored by many Poles as the modern St. Stanisław—"to the effect that 'our intelligentsia is preparing the groundwork for communism—and the scaffold for itself.'"[47]

G. K. Chesterton had said that Poland was hated, as confirmed by this impressively lengthy list of antagonists, but also that it was loved, and in fact both the Polish nation and its Church found ardent admirers throughout the world, notably among coreligionists who regarded those two things as synonymous. For the most part, these were rock-ribbed west European Catholics of conservative to rightist politics who gave honor to the Second Republic as the worthy inheritor of the age-old Polish mission to defend faith and civilization on the eastern periphery of the continent. Inclined by confessional culture to take the long view and to discern the hand of Providence in the world, they saw current political conditions as a reflection—indeed, an inescapable consequence—of the tragic heritage of schism that had disrupted Christendom; for Poland, standing between the trouble-making powers of Germany and Soviet Russia was simply the present-day manifestation of its destiny to serve as "the advance guard of the Catholic tradition between the Reformation and Orthodoxy."[48] This romantic theory of an idealized Poland as the veritable instrument of God throughout European history lent a supernatural aura to such events as the recovery of Polish independence, with its imagery of resurrection, and Piłsudski's rebuff of the Bolsheviks in 1920, which renewed the reputation of his country as the bulwark of Christianity. In return for its devotion to the Church and its arduous service on the front lines of the struggle against the evils of the day, Poland deserved the gratitude and support of Catholics from all points of the globe.[49]

The two most tireless and visible exponents of this doctrine of religious solidarity with Poland were Hilaire Belloc and G. K. Chesterton, the foremost Catholic public intellectuals of England in their time and the elders among a stellar generation of British Catholic men of letters that included

Graham Greene, Evelyn Waugh, Christopher Dawson, and J. R. R. Tolkien. As a tribe, English Catholics, a minority within their own land hardened in their faith by centuries of persecution, were peculiarly apt to look abroad to find inspiration in the Poles as religious exemplars and comrades in arms. As "papists" in the realm that had martyred More and Campion, they were out of step with their own national history and ethos, and knew it. In Waugh's *Brideshead Revisited,* when the secular Charles Ryder opines, with bland broad-mindedness, that Catholics are just like anyone else, his ambivalently Catholic friend Sebastian protests, "My dear Charles, that's exactly what they're not—particularly in this country, where they're so few. . . . They've got an entirely different outlook on life; everything they think important is different from other people." Keenly, even defiantly aware of their scarcity and their apartness from the normal run of Britons, an apartness defined entirely by religion, and long used to swimming against the tide, English Catholic publicists came naturally by the combative and ultramontane rhetorical style of political Catholicism of the era. Patriots as Englishmen, as Catholics they placed more weight on their citizenship in a larger European spiritual commonwealth: they used the term "Christendom" without irony. In the sphere of religion, their writings are reminiscent of the testaments of exiles yearning for their true homeland. As isolated adherents to the faith stranded, as it were, behind Protestant lines, they looked across the Channel for confessional allies. They trusted in the papacy, and felt special kinship with foreign lands of rich and historic Roman heritage. Famously and heroically devout, Poland appealed to them as the valiant champion of Catholic interests whose enemies—Communists, schismatics, Jews—were also their own. The fact that fashionable British opinion of the interwar years looked down on the Second Republic as a tinpot dictatorship with imperial pretensions that bullied its minorities led them to defend it all the more. In fact, they did not love Poland, which they scarcely knew, so much as their own idea of Poland: the *antemurale,* the shining knight of Christendom and Western civilization, the Church on horseback vigilant against the foe.[50]

Already upon the beginning of the interwar period, Hilaire Belloc and Gilbert Keith Chesterton were friends and collaborators of long standing, so closely identified with each other that they acquired the dual moniker "Chesterbelloc," as if they were a single being that thought with one mind and spoke with one voice. In many respects they were, indeed, birds of a feather, as prolific literary jacks of all trades who dabbled comfortably in genres ranging from detective fiction and children's verse to feuilletons and apologetics, and as stout defenders of the Catholic political and social agenda. All the same, they contrasted in tone and temperament. While much of his work had a light touch, the snobbish, French-born Belloc could become severe and pompous when addressing the solemnity of religion, and as a polemicist tended to lay it on thick. After establishing fame as a youthful literary prodigy, Chesterton entered the Church of Rome in middle age as the culmination of a prolonged and public religious awakening. "GKC" relished a good scrap in the name of orthodoxy—he once explained his attraction to Catholicism by calling it "the one fighting form of Christianity" —but he was a happy warrior, rumpled and roly-poly, whose sunny good humor charmed even adversaries who could not abide his opinions. Chesterton the convert looked up to the older, cradle-Catholic Belloc as a mentor in craft and faith, to the consternation of many who regarded the younger man as both the greater talent and the more generous soul.

For Belloc and Chesterton, the incalculable significance and worth of Poland resided in the singular religious and military mission God had entrusted to it on the outskirts of Europe. Chesterton defined the country as "the Catholic culture thrust like a sort of long sword-blade between the Byzantine tradition of Muscovy and the materialism of Prussia. That is what Poland is; and that is infinitely the most real, practical, determining and important thing that she is."[51] The Poles were a people in arms fighting for faith and freedom against German militarism and Russian despotism, malign legacies of Protestantism and Orthodoxy: their struggle was that of the authentic, healthy Catholic civilization of Europe against the historic threats to its integrity. For the time being, the combat was spiritual and political, but at a moment's notice the gunfire might become literal. To Belloc and Chesterton, the restoration of Poland for the purpose of resuming its watch in the east had been the whole point of the world war. During the conflict, Belloc had lobbied the pope to place the Polish question at the top of his agenda, and upon its end Chesterton warned that failing to fulfill the justified ambitions of the Poles would be to snatch defeat from victory, "to lose the War . . . we have already won."[52] The war, they contended, had swept away an antebellum European order of Protestant hegemony, and reconstruction of a mighty Polish state was the key to furthering the Catholic cause in international affairs and, in light of the dangers still afoot, avoiding ending up with "half Europe and perhaps half Asia on our backs."[53]

Once the interwar Second Republic claimed its place on the map, the two writers continued as its leading champions in Britain, their admiration for the country deepened all the more by its early exploits. In virtually identical language, Belloc and Chesterton hailed the reappearance of Poland as "the chief miracle of modern times."[54] The stunning Polish defeat of the Red Army on the Vistula in 1920, just as all appeared lost, furnished proof for any with eyes to see that Poland remained, now as in centuries past, the "bastion" and "outpost" of the Occident, and that the Marxist doctrine of atheism and determinism could not prevail against the Cross.[55] Chesterbelloc regretted, but did not wonder, that their advocacy fell on deaf ears, especially in Britain, and that the West failed to appreciate Poland and grasp the meaning of its service to mankind. The modern opinion-making elite, they contended, were utterly worldly and ill-disposed toward Catholicism. As a consequence, they misunderstood Poland and what it stood for—or understood it all too well—and so despised and vilified the country; since the larger public read only bad things about the Second Republic, and believed what it read, the Poles received not the recognition and gratitude they deserved, but apathy or outright hostility.[56] According to Chesterton, thus was Poland intensely loved and intensely hated at the same time. He regarded this divide as so basic and telling that he adopted a sort of Polish litmus test: if someone approved of Poland, this was a sign of sound mind, solid judgment, and good moral character.[57]

Each of them undertook an interwar pilgrimage to Poland, separated by only a few months. In 1928 Belloc carried out a journey partially paid for by the Polish government. The traveler made a point of stopping at the famous Marian shrine of Częstochowa; he pronounced it surpassed only by Rome itself, and left behind a copy of a poem he dedicated to the monastery's revered icon of the Black Madonna. Apart from religious motives, he told his hosts, his purpose was to produce a book that would warn English readers that "if a mistake in foreign policy is made about Poland, it will involve the whole of Europe."[58] This followed on the heels of a more elaborate and public sojourn by Chesterton, who enjoyed greater celebrity among Poles as their sympathizer and toured their country for five weeks in 1927 amid fanfare as the honored guest of the national chapter of the PEN literary society. His experiences favorably confirmed all his preconceptions of Polish chivalry and piety from the moment of his arrival in Warsaw, when a cavalry officer greeted him with the gallant salutation that the Englishman could not be called the chief friend of Poland only for the reason that "God is the chief friend of Poland." Chesterton had an audience with Piłsudski, who impressed him as a great man. He also met with Dmowski, who, chided by one of the writer's entourage for anti-Semitism, shot back that he took his faith from Christ, "who was murdered by the Jews." The trip delighted Chesterton and deepened his commitment to the land he had lionized from afar. In the PEN club album he inscribed the words "If Poland had not been born again, all the Christian nations would have died," a statement as heartfelt as it was extravagant. GKC returned home fired with inspiration, more determined than ever to speak as the tribune of the Poles in the Anglo-Saxon world.[59]

The two Englishmen loved Kraków, for its beauty and antiquity, but even more for its value as a symbol of Catholic culture, radiant yet endangered. Belloc had visited Warsaw once, years earlier, when it was a Russian provincial town; he declared it depressingly reminiscent of Omaha, and left the next day, earlier than planned.[60] By contrast, Kraków enchanted him with its spires, its churches, and its aura of "that holy something which inhabits Poland like a secret flame."[61] Like his friend, Chesterton sensed that the city breathed an air of haunted glory that stood for larger things. Valiant but vulnerable, Kraków stood for Poland, stood for all Christendom, in its history as a bulwark against barbarians from the east: "There is little change in the position today; except that the barbarian is called Bolshevism." The hourly sounding of the *hejnał* from the tower of St. Mary's Church, commemorating the legend of the trumpeter slain while calling the town to arms against a thirteenth-century Tatar attack, stirred him to a near-poetic suspension between triumph and melancholy. In the clarion he heard "the defiance of civilization besieged. Only the trumpet peal breaks on the last note. . . . And so odd and moving is the break that a man listening today can fancy that he hears not only the trumpet, but the bolt of the barbarian singing by."[62]

As the interlude between the world wars drew toward its close, this note of foreboding and gathering menace took on a growing prominence in Belloc and Chesterton's literary homilies on the interdependence of Poland and the Catholic cause. Shortly before his death in 1936, GKC rightly predicted that Nazi Germany and Soviet Russia would become collaborators, contrary to general belief—they were natural partners, he warned, equally inimical to Christian civilization—and that Hitler would loose a new war with an assault against the Polish republic.[63] Some years earlier he had penned an essay entitled "Where Poland Stands": the answer, he said, was that Poland stood on the edge of Europe as its protector, heroic but exposed, burdened by centuries of duty as sentinel and soldier—"and the time may come when the protector must be protected."[64] By 1939 he was no longer alive to witness the fulfillment of his somber prophecies, but Hilaire Belloc remained to rally the friends of Poland—intensely loved, intensely hated—to rescue their beleaguered guardian from its enemies and God's. We do not know if he recalled his departed friend's reflections on the trumpeter of Kraków, but its like would have occurred to him naturally, for it was imbedded in his mentality: once again, as so many times in the past, the barbarians were at the gates. Once again Poland, the Christian knight of nations, faced their singing arrows, sounding the alarm for the defense of the West.

6 ||| Vilna and Lwów

The Catholic Minorities of Eastern Poland

One of the many complications of life in interwar Poland, where the terms "Catholic" and "Pole" were widely regarded as synonyms, was that not all of its Catholics were Poles. The Catholic population of the western two-thirds of the country was almost entirely Polish, but in the northeast some eighty thousand Lithuanians, overwhelmingly Latin Catholic, dwelt among a hodgepodge of peoples, while in the southeast corner roughly three million Ukrainians of the Greek Catholic Eastern rite formed a local majority within the Galician districts inherited from the defunct Habsburg Empire. Fragments of the main blocs of Lithuanian and Ukrainian settlement beyond the frontiers, these minorities were a legacy of the bygone Polish Respublica, which had introduced Catholicism into the polyglot expanses of the kresy that stretched eastward toward Russia. Now, in the nationally charged Poland of the Second Republic, their presence became a source of chronic friction at the junction of religion with politics. Their attempts to maintain their identity within a state they did not regard as their own won the sympathy of the Vatican as the impartial shepherd of the faithful, but came into conflict with the resolve of Warsaw to consolidate its grip on the eastern borderlands. Discord over these issues persisted throughout the interwar era, made more dramatic by its focus on two of the most intriguing and controversial figures in modern Polish ecclesiastical history. In their time, both of them were among the most reviled men in Poland: now, Bishop Jerzy Matulewicz is officially numbered by the Church among the citizens of heaven, while the cause for canonization of Archbishop Andrei Sheptyts'kyi received the endorsement of no less an authority than the Polish pope.[1]

Britons and Americans, it is said, are divided by a common language; the Catholic peoples of the Polish east were divided by a common heritage.

For centuries old Poland had ruled the broad reaches of Lithuania and Ukraine, stamping the kresy with the imprint of Polish culture and its religious attribute, Catholic Christianity. Pagan Lithuania had received baptism in the fourteenth century upon entering into federation with Poland, and in 1596 the Orthodox bishops of Polish Ukraine agreed to join the fold of Rome through the creation of the Greek Catholic rite, Eastern in custom but in communion with the papacy. The traditional "Jagiellonian" ideal that conceived of Poland as the shared homeland of its motley inhabitants survived the partitions of the Commonwealth and continued for a time to animate the movement to restore Polish independence, but the emergence of separate nationalisms based on ethnicity caused a gradual estrangement. By the dawn of the twentieth century, significant and growing numbers of Ukrainians and Lithuanians demanded a political destination that parted ways with the Poles. These aspirations were bound to collide, for few Polish patriots could imagine a Poland shorn of the kresy, cherished as a vital part of the national patrimony. The jumbled settlement pattern of the east worked against a neat resolution: Poles and Jews predominated in urban areas, the more numerous non-Polish peasants in the surrounding countryside. This made likely flashpoints of the two great cities of the region, Vilna and Lwów, historic strongholds of Polish population and culture, but also coveted by Lithuanians and Ukrainians, respectively, as their own natural metropolises.

These overlapping claims to the borderlands exploded into urgency at the end of the First World War, when the antebellum empires of eastern Europe fell apart and left their former subjects to fight over the pieces, fights intensified by the simultaneous convulsions of the Russian revolutions. Reborn Poland secured Lwów and East Galicia in 1919, after several months of bitter combat to put down an armed drive to establish a separate Ukrainian state. To the north, Warsaw vied with the Bolsheviks and free Lithuania for control over Vilna and its environs. The city bounced back and forth before being captured by Polish forces in 1920 and annexed two years later. Combined with a military victory of sorts over the Red Army, these successes allowed Poland to take in much of the kresy, but left the country with hostile neighbors outside the eastern periphery of the republic and a multitude of unhappy minorities inside it.[2]

This result also brought within the orbit of interwar Poland the traditional heartlands of Lithuanian and Ukrainian Catholicism, the Latin Diocese of Vilna and the Greek Catholic Eparchy of Halicz-Lwów, as well as the two prelates who came to personify those sees, Jerzy Matulewicz and Andrei Sheptyts'kyi. Though one sprang from humble origins, the other from noble, in other respects their biographies were similar as regulars and embodiments of the ambiguities of nationality in the borderlands. Matulewicz had been born into the Lithuanian peasant family Matulaitis in 1871 near Mariampol. Orphaned as a boy, he was given a Polish upbringing by an uncle. He acquired Polish language and culture, and as a seminarian polonized his name; still, he remained Lithuanian by conviction. Ordained in 1898, Matulewicz entered Polish ecclesiastical life and gained a reputation for holiness and pastoral excellence. In 1911 he became general of the Congregation of Marian Fathers and oversaw the reform of that monastic order. The disruptions of the Great War confined him to the Polish lands, and by 1918 he had returned to Mariampol to direct the restoration of the Marian cloister near his birthplace.

For his part, Sheptyts'kyi had entered the world in 1865 as Count Szeptycki, a Roman Catholic Pole, scion of a prominent aristocratic clan of the Ukraine that had taken on Polish identity over the generations. As a young man, he discerned a call to revert to his family's Ruthenian roots: "I love Poland," he said—a claim many of his Polish detractors would have denied—"but the language of the people among whom I was raised became my speech, its songs my songs."[3] Now a conscious Ukrainian, he also embraced the Greek Catholic rite of his adopted nation, and in 1888 entered the Basilian order, which was the elite training ground of its clergy. Upon ordination, Sheptyts'kyi shot up the ladder of the Uniate hierarchy. By 1900 he had attained the rank of metropolitan of Halicz-Lwów, making him both the spiritual head of Eastern-rite faithful within the Habsburg Empire and, by all odds. the most visible of Ukrainian leaders. While the unworldly Matulewicz shied away from politics or identification with a national cause —in 1911 he had sworn an oath at the tomb of St. Peter that neither he nor his Marians would serve such ends[4]—Sheptyts'kyi saw himself as the tribune of his people, and regarded this service as one of his chief pastoral duties. Throughout his lengthy residence in the Greek Catholic cathedral of St. George in Lwów, time and again he exerted his commanding personality to defend his Ukrainian Uniate flock and to upbraid those he saw as their persecutors, of which interwar Poland would be the next, if by no means the worst. Both shepherd and sheep had endured severe trials during the world war. The Russians subjected Greek Catholics to a hostile Orthodox regime during the occupation of Galicia in 1914–15, and upon their withdrawal in the face of the German advance took Sheptyts'kyi into a captivity that did not end until 1917.

Once the dust from the war settled and Vilna and Lwów along with their Catholics came into the hands of an independent Poland, the religious politics of the region quickly settled into a pattern of national rivalry that changed but little over the next two decades. Up to the Piłsudski takeover of 1926, Polish governments, especially those dominated by the rightist National Democrats, sought to use the Church as an instrument of assimilation of non-Poles in the kresy; afterward, the sanacja regime adopted a more modest policy of trying to prevent minority clerics from lending support to secessionist agitation or engaging in actions deemed disloyal to the state. Warsaw achieved neither goal. In the Vilna diocese, Catholic clergy supplied much of the leadership and energy behind the Lithuanian national movement within Poland, and attracted the wary eye of the authorities. In Galicia, the Greek Catholics presented the same challenge at a considerably higher level of intensity. There the Uniate Church, its numbers robustly expanding, functioned as a sanctuary for Ukrainian national sentiment, and its priesthood as the guiding light of Ukrainian political and intellectual activity, with the formidable Metropolitan Sheptyts'kyi at its summit. It goes too far to say, as many Poles did at the time, that the Greek Catholics were an outright seditious force, but it is also true that their confessional culture breathed a spirit of antagonism to the Second Republic that did much to convince it that the Uniates were an oppositionist element, and to treat them as such, accomplishing little more than the perpetuation of a cycle of mutual distrust. At a personal level, as an apostate in two senses, Archbishop Sheptyts'kyi became a bête noire to Polish nationalists, his very biography an affront.

For its part, the Holy See found itself caught in the middle among the feuding peoples of its Polish faithful, its natural sympathy for Poland and the Poles as the anchors of Catholicism in east-central Europe tempered by worries that, left to itself, Warsaw would be unable to resist taking steps that alienated its Catholic minorities and injured the broader interests of the Church. Achille Ratti tried to present himself as a disinterested conciliator from the opening days of his nunciature in 1918. As papal legate both to Poland and Lithuania, he refused to take sides in their disputes over Vilna. The matter of the Greek Catholics was thornier still. Ratti and his superiors in Rome foresaw that the Polish republic would be tempted to govern the Uniates severely, as a political threat. Further, they understood that the Poles did not regard the Greek Catholics as genuine coreligionists: that "for a Pole, *latin* means Polish and Catholic, while *greek* means Russian and Orthodox . . . and a Uniate is not a fellow Catholic, but something in between a Catholic and a schismatic." Such was the view, by and large, of the Polish Latin clergy as well, which looked down on the Eastern rite as a second-class category within the Church, perhaps useful as a temporary halfway house for conversion from Orthodoxy to "true," Roman, Catholicism, but not for any merit of its own. Although it would not say so aloud, the Vatican recognized that the Polish complaints against the Greek Catholics carried some weight: after a history of persecution, the Uniate Church did require rehabilitation to remedy its acquired defects, and caution would be needed to prevent its inclinations toward Ukrainian nationalism from getting out of hand. Still, the papacy considered the Eastern rite the proper model for Catholicism in the Ukraine, now and in the future, and counted on being able to find ways to permit western and Greek Catholics to coexist within Poland.[5]

But this tangled dynamic came into play only after the emergence of a fully independent Poland; in the early months of 1918 the Vatican still assumed that the world war would end with the victory of the Central Powers in the eastern front, and decided the time was none too soon to begin the job of rebuilding the Church in the war-torn regions that long had borne the heavy hand of tsarist rule but now had been reconstituted as puppet Polish or Lithuanian states within a German sphere of influence. One of the priorities of Rome was to fill the bishopric of Vilna, vacant since 1907, the largest and one of the most populous dioceses in the territories of the old Respublica. The choice required balancing an unusual number of sensitive pastoral and political factors. For one thing, the Christian inhabitants of the district were wildly mixed, mainly Polish and Belorussian with a sizable Lithuanian minority. While the Belorussians had yet to emerge into national consciousness, the new bishop would need to avoid giving offense to either of the rival camps of Poles or Lithuanians who claimed Vilna as their own. To boot, the nominee had to pass muster with the German occupation authorities. Given the exacting criteria of the job description, the Vatican's attention soon turned toward the Marian general, Fr. Matulewicz, who appeared uniquely qualified to fill the bill. This godly monastic suited the preference of the Germans for a Lithuanian who would give them no trouble, while the Taryba, the governing council of the Lithuania, which had arisen under the patronage of Berlin, contented itself that he was a son of the nation. For their part, the Polish bishops reasoned that, under the circumstances, a polonophone Lithuanian was all they could hope for in

Vilna, and recommended him as not merely the best, but indeed the only possible candidate for that see.[6]

Matulewicz himself disagreed, and as soon as the rumor mill began linking his name to the episcopal opening in Vilna, he tried to take himself out of the running. While long tradition regards seemly expression of modesty as good form in aspiring hierarchs, in his case the reluctance was unfeigned. In part, Matulewicz simply preferred the monastic life, but even more he sensed his own unsuitedness to lead a diocese torn by contesting nationalisms. Neither training nor nature prepared him for the predictable conflicts, and he shrank from the prospect. In Vilna, he presciently told a friend, "I would please no one—not the Poles, not the Lithuanians, not the Belorussians—and I would be lost amid political struggles."[7] But his protests of inadequacy only reinforced the opinion of his superiors that Matulewicz was the man for this delicate mission. After vetting his candidacy, an impressed Achille Ratti concluded that "his humility is the very proof that we have chosen well."[8] On Ratti's recommendation, Pope Benedict selected Matulewicz for Vilna in October 1918 and refused to take no for an answer.[9]

Despite the care the Vatican had taken with its decision, Bishop Matulewicz received a chilly reception in his new see. All along, patriotic Lithuanians had considered him a second choice, merely a tolerable substitute for a more forthrightly political hierarch, while the Polish clergy of the city delivered a protest to Rome against the elevation of a Lithuanian as spiritual head of Vilna.[10] Literally from the hour of his installation, the bishop pledged to stay above national antagonisms and to serve all his various flock alike. Matulewicz regularly, even relentlessly, recalled St. Paul's assurances of the irrelevance of ethnicity in the eyes of God and echoed the apostle in vowing to be "for the Poles a Pole, for the Jews a Jew, for the Greeks a Greek . . . all things to all men."[11] Summoning the favorite comparison of those who dream of governing a mixed population in harmony, he hoped to make Vilna an ecclesiastical version of Switzerland, where he had studied as a youth.[12] He ordered his priests to refrain from divisive political activity and, in word and deed, called for evenhanded respect for Poles, Lithuanians, and Belorussians.

Bishop Matulewicz's appeals to create a diocese that rose above national division fell on deaf ears. As he feared, in seeking to avoid favoring any of the peoples under his jurisdiction, he won the trust of none. His scrupulous avoidance of partisan identification led him even to reject overtures from his most likely base of political support, moderate advocates of a renewed Polish-Lithuanian federation.[13] Decided nationalists of both camps had little use for him. Lithuanians considered him derelict in championing their cause. Above all, the Poles of Vilna regarded him, as he noted, as an unwanted and resented "stepfather."[14] In this frontier area the National Democrats set the tone of Polish politics and zeroed in on Matulewicz as an enemy. The Endecja claimed a large following among the Polish clergy of the city, who more or less openly defied their bishop.[15] In Vilna, Matulewicz rued, he had at hand "many nationalist priests, both Polish and Lithuanian, but few Catholic priests."[16]

Any slim chance Matulewicz had of winning even the grudging acceptance of the Poles vanished once the World War ended unexpectedly in a fully sovereign Poland anxious first to secure, and then firmly retain, Vilna and its hinterland. Over the next two years possession of the region shifted with the prevailing winds of combat in the borderlands. Reporting to Nuncio Ratti in October 1920, Matulewicz summarized his woes in dismal arithmetic: since his arrival rule over the city had changed hands seven times, and five different regimes had patrolled the territories of his diocese. "That I have not yet been expelled or clapped into prison," he legibly sighed, "I ascribe to divine mercy alone. I am wearied and exhausted by all of this, and were it not the will of God and the Holy See, I would remain in Vilna not one moment longer."[17] For its part, the government of the fledgling Polish republic did what it could to see that Matulewicz got his wish to depart, for Warsaw made no secret of its desire to procure his ouster. The last of the *coups de main* he enumerated had brought Vilna into Polish hands to stay, until the return of war in 1939. Lithuania refused to concede the loss of its capital, while the winners were keen to cement their hold. Practically from the instant it achieved full independence in November 1918, Poland began to drop pointed hints to Rome that what had sufficed before full statehood would do no longer: the retention of a professed Lithuanian as pastor of Vilna was intolerable.

Nor did Polish opinions of Matulewicz soften with the passage of time. "From its first day," muttered the leading National Democratic daily in summer 1919, "the reign of Bishop Matulewicz has been one constant ordeal."[18] Despite his own unhappiness in the post he had tried to shun, he fought doggedly to ward off his foes. Amply endowed with the self-righteousness that is the frequent defect of the saint's qualities, he considered himself undeservedly defamed by a Polish chauvinist fringe.[19] Nuncio Ratti did his best to defend the bishop he had handpicked for the city of the Virgin of

Ostrabrama against the Endek attacks, but the problem went deeper than simply shrugging off noisy protests from the usual suspects from the nationalist Right; even the members of his Polish flock with no political ax to grind wanted to see their Lithuanian ordinary go.[20] Ratti tried to salvage the situation by suggesting the appointment of a Polish auxiliary in Vilna, a solution seconded by Matulewicz himself, but this expedient failed to satisfy Warsaw.[21] Citing the manifest animus of the city's Poles toward Matulewicz as proof that his very presence offended patriotic sentiment, Poland formally petitioned the Holy See for his removal in 1921 and renewed the request on a regular basis over the next few years.[22]

In the meantime, to the south, another Catholic prelate was exasperating Polish officialdom as the suspected ringleader of a minority people that posed a security risk to the new Second Republic, the Greek rite Archbishop Sheptyts'kyi. As the world war neared its end, Sheptyts'kyi appears to have favored the creation of a Polish-Lithuanian-Ukrainian federation in the Jagiellonian tradition, but when battle erupted in East Galicia over the question of its inclusion within Poland, the metropolitan and the bulk of the Uniate clergy lent their moral support to the cause of an independent West Ukraine. The bloodshed appalled the Vatican, which begged for restraint from both sides but placed more blame on the Poles. For the duration of the conflict, the Polish authorities placed Sheptys'kyi under careful watch, at times approaching conditions of house arrest in his residence in Lwów.[23]

Toward the end of 1920, after Poland had subdued East Galicia but not yet won international recognition of its eastern frontiers, Sheptyts'kyi asked Warsaw for permission to journey to Rome for his *ad limina* report to the pope required of bishops every five years. The request was granted, with unease. Polish diplomats at the Vatican kept close, nervous tabs on Sheptyts'kyi's talks with Benedict XV and Curia officials, and the Polish episcopate sent two of its own, his fellow Galicians Sapieha and Teodorowicz, to the Eternal City to counter the metropolitan's influence. The unease turned to alarm when, instead of returning to Lwów upon completion of his Roman errand, perhaps fearing arrest upon entering Poland, Sheptyts'kyi obtained the pope's blessing to pay apostolic visits to Greek Catholic colonies in other parts of the world. For most of the next two years he traveled to the United States, Canada, South America, and various ports of call in western Europe before ending up in Rome once more at the end of 1922. Along the way, Sheptyts'kyi preached his favorite theme of the special mission of Uniatism in the reunification of Christendom, but he also made plain his refusal to accept the finality of Polish rule over East Galicia. He met with numerous dignitaries of state, including the presidents of France and the United States, but studiously avoided contact with representatives of Poland, lest it be interpreted as acknowledgment of citizenship; in general, he conducted himself as the spokesman for a people under the heel of foreign masters.[24]

Of course, Poland complained bitterly to the Vatican about Sheptyts'kyi's activities, but gained little satisfaction, for the Ukrainian church and its formidable archbishop enjoyed the protection and high regard of the papacy. Rome granted that Sheptyts'kyi could try the patience of any government that had to deal with him, but esteemed him as a man "of great abilities, of vast plans and hopes," a key figure in the future of Catholicism in eastern Europe.[25] For his part, Nuncio Ratti and his aides had seen enough to conclude that the root of the problem in East Galicia was not Ukrainian rebelliousness but Polish arrogance and hostility toward the Uniates.[26] So when the Poles voiced their grievances about the Greek Catholics, curial officials would respond with a standard, noncommittal reply: the Vatican would do what it could to urge the Eastern-rite Ukrainians to behave as loyal Polish subjects, but Warsaw must do what was needed to earn their loyalty.[27]

What galled the Polish government most about Matulewicz and Sheptyts'kyi was its resentful conviction that the two bishops prevented the Second Republic from using Catholicism to solidify its tenuous hold on the eastern borderlands. At bottom, this had less to do with their influence on the Lithuanians and Greek Catholics, already written off as unreliable citizens, than with their effect—or rather, their lack of effect—on peoples of the region still up for grabs. In the Vilna precincts, Warsaw looked to the Belorussians as an ethnically malleable peasantry that might be transformed into Poles with the help of the Church, but only under the leadership of a suitably inclined Polish bishop, not an unworldly Lithuanian. As for East Galicia, Poland objected to the Vatican policy of encouraging conversions from Orthodoxy into Uniatism rather than the western observance: the Latin Church, it was believed, set the convert on the road to becoming a Pole, while the Eastern rite preserved his native, non-Polish identity, contrary to the interests of the state.[28] The logic of this line of argument failed to persuade Rome, which resolutely opposed allowing the Church to be enlisted as an instrument of Polish assimilationist pressures in the kresy.[29]

Even so, Poland might have got its way in engineering the removal of these two troublesome prelates if not for an untimely transition of the papacy. While the Holy See took a dim view of governmental lobbying to oust bishops for political reasons, Polish diplomats at the Vatican found Benedict XV open to hearing out Warsaw's side on the Vilna and Lwów questions, and willing to meet them halfway. He at least hinted at the possibility of finding different responsibilities for Sheptyts'kyi, far away from Galicia, and Cardinal Gasparri pledged that Rome would lean on the Greek Catholic clergy to behave themselves and steer clear of sedition.[30] The pope also quietly agreed to shift Matulewicz out of Vilna after the decent interval of awaiting formal international approval of the Polish claim to the city.[31] But Benedict died in 1922 with these changes still unmade, and when the former nuncio to Poland succeeded him, Warsaw soon learned that the new pontiff was made of stern stuff and held strong opinions, among them that Matulewicz and Sheptyts'kyi were both right where they belonged. Pius XI remained settled in his conviction that the unassuming Marian he had personally chosen to be bishop of Vilna should stay at his post, and he also had a soft spot for Sheptyts'kyi and the Uniates. Under Benedict, Poland had tried to solve its Sheptyts'kyi problem by persuading the Vatican to kick him upstairs into a Curia sinecure; after Pius took charge, Warsaw shelved this strategy for fear that this steely pope, if anything, would only replace Sheptyts'kyi as archbishop of St. George with someone worse.[32]

For its part, the Holy See wanted badly to broker a solution to the impasse between Sheptyts'kyi and Poland that would allow the absentee bishop to return to his Ukrainian flock from his de facto exile. An opportunity for breakthrough appeared to open in the spring of 1923, after the Council of Ambassadors recognized the eastern frontier of the Second Republic—and with it, Polish rule over Vilna and East Galicia—and so ruled out any lingering possibility of Ukrainian independence. By midyear, the three parties seemed to have worked out a deal: Sheptyts'kyi was to write a pastoral letter expressing allegiance to Poland and urging Greek Catholics to follow suit; in return, Warsaw would assure Pius that the metropolitan would be permitted passage to Lwów without incident. Sheptyts'kyi produced a letter judged acceptable by both the pope and Poland's minister to the Holy See, Skrzyński. The Polish Foreign Ministry thereupon issued instructions that the prelate was being granted permission to go home and that there was to be no trouble upon his return to the country.[33]

At that point, politics and confusion combined to upset the carefully orchestrated plans for the homecoming of Archbishop Sheptyts'kyi.[34] In Warsaw the government of Władysław Sikorski fell and was replaced by a Center-Right coalition headed by the Peasant chieftain Witos but bearing the strong imprint of the National Democrats, who pushed a hard line against the Uniates. The new foreign minister, Marian Seyda, took a second look at the Sheptyts'kyi file and concluded that his predecessor, the pope, and Poland's man at the Vatican all had erred in letting the archbishop off the hook too easily. Whether Seyda may have been swayed by protests from Endecja followers who detested Sheptyts'kyi is hard to say. At any rate, practically at the last minute the Witos cabinet turned about face and decided to deny the metropolitan reentry until he swore a more satisfactory oath of loyalty. By that time, Sheptyts'kyi's train from Rome was already under way, and the upshot was a clumsy little standoff at the Polish frontier.

As the night of August 22 turned to morning, the train bearing Archbishop Sheptyts'kyi crossed from Czechoslovakia into Poland at Dziedzice. Polish troops then isolated and occupied his wagon. There he remained in detention in his car on the border for three days, nursemaided by a delegation of Polish officialdom. On August 24 these functionaries informed Sheptyts'kyi that, for his own good and that of public order, he would not be free to proceed to his see in Lwów for the time being. Instead they whisked him to Poznań, where he was confined to a monastery for several weeks, against his wishes.[35] Poland tried hard to portray the internment of Sheptyts'kyi as something other than what it was, claiming that he had arrived at the border in poor health—true enough, as far as it went—and badly in need of lengthy recuperation, in a restful spot, under watchful supervision, far from Lwów; but the involuntary nature of his enforced convalescence was plain to see.

This highhanded treatment of a distinguished and prominent hierarch aroused a storm of reaction from various quarters. In Poland, rightist opinion cheered the government for having given Sheptyts'kyi what he had coming to him, while the Center-Left opposition decried the move as a hamhanded provocation that risked inflaming the combustible Ukrainian question.[36] Meanwhile, back in Rome, Pius XI lost his storied temper at the news, naturally concluding that Warsaw had played dirty and double-crossed him. He blistered the ears of the luckless Polish envoy and dispatched Cardinal Kakowski to intercede with Seyda to obtain Sheptyts'kyi's freedom.[37] Having made its point, Poland consented to break the deadlock, but not without making the archbishop carry out an ostentatious reenactment of his submission to Polish authority. In the first days of October, Sheptyts'kyi traveled to Warsaw for an audience with the president of the Second Republic, where he gave a publicly reported statement of loyalty; then, and only then, was he allowed to continue on to Lwów, bringing an end at last to his nearly three-year sojourn.

In the short term Poland paid a price for its decision to break its word to Pius XI and play fast and loose with the terms for readmission of Metropolitan Sheptyts'kyi for the sake of pleasing the Endek rank and file, if that was behind it. Some observers sized up the episode as a bungle typical of Seyda's brief and artless tenure as foreign minister.[38] Of course, by seizing and harassing the Uniate archprelate, the Poles could have done no more to bolster his moral authority among disaffected Ukrainians had they tried.[39] But the episode did no lasting damage. As in earlier disagreements, papal annoyance with Poland was acute but fleeting, and in the years to come the government of the Second Republic would find the renewed presence of Archbishop Sheptyts'kyi inside the country to be more a manageable nuisance than the menace it had feared.

While Warsaw was making Sheptyts'kyi take a roundabout and difficult itinerary into Lwów, it was also doing its best to hand Bishop Matulewicz a one-way ticket out of Vilna. Now that Polish ownership of the city was confirmed, over the course of 1923 the government peppered the Vatican with more insistent demands for the removal of the Lithuanian ordinary of the diocese it considered a key ethnic battleground. The genuine official motivation, as before, was the belief that a Polish bishop was needed in Vilna to advance the polonization of the region, but care was taken to hide this aim behind arguments that might sound more respectable within the Curia —that he had not taken Polish citizenship, or that his original choice had been imposed by Germany.[40] Rome dismissed these complaints as false, irrelevant, or trivial. This left Polish representatives with few cards to play, given that Matulewicz was a model of personal and pastoral virtue and had prudently followed a path of correct, if distant, behavior toward secular authority. The problem, as the Polish minister to the Holy See privately noted, was that Warsaw could present no proof that the bishop of Vilna had done anything to harm legitimate state interests.[41] On top of that, the Church now had as its pope the former nuncio to Poland, who counted himself the friend and patron of the beleaguered hierarch. Pius XI considered Matulewicz the finest of the bishops of Poland and assured him that, at bottom, "the Poles have only one charge to make against you: that you are a Lithuanian."[42] Polish churchmen sent to Rome to support their government's case against Matulewicz got only the back of the pope's hand or the lash of his temper as he turned his back on them in disgust or asked tartly how their consciences could permit them to carry out their errand.[43] After a year of issuing crude demands for the sacking of Matulewicz and getting nowhere, in 1924 the Polish foreign ministry decided, for a change, to try an approach to the subject that had some intelligence behind it: let it be for the time being, and wait to insert it into the mix of the horsetrading soon to take place over the anticipated concordat with the Holy See.[44]

This was sound thinking, for the concordat talks that began later that same year furnished the ideal occasion for Poland to attempt to solve its Lwów and Vilna problems gracefully within the context of a general reorganization of the Church within the country. Warsaw made good use of the opportunity. Indeed, for the Poles, reaching a satisfactory resolution of these issues was the main attraction of a concordat, and the Vatican had dangled this very possibility as bait to coax them to the table.[45] Thus encouraged, the Polish negotiator, Stanisław Grabski, took care to keep these two sore points front and center during the parleys. His papal counterpart resisted but gave way in the end, and Grabski got what he was looking for. In the first place, the concordat of 1925 gave the Second Republic the means to hold Catholic clergy accountable to standards of loyalty to the state, a measure largely aimed at Lithuanians and Ukrainians. As regards the Uniates, the treaty disappointed Sheptyts'kyi by restricting the Greek Catholic Church to its traditional Galician territory, depriving it of a role in Rome's plan to foster conversions from Orthodoxy in former Russian lands, and by incorporating the Eastern rite into the Polish episcopate without any separate or autonomous status.[46]

The Matulewicz question was trickier and required much haggling before an accord could be reached. Grabski presented his government's case with nearly disarming candor: even though Matulewicz "might be the finest pastor, and . . . he does nothing illegal," for political reasons he simply could not stay in Vilna. His opposite number, speaking for the pope, alternately stood on principle or tried to change the subject, but left the door ajar for a deal.[47] Finally, the two sides put together an intricate gentlemen's agreement. Grabski came up with the acceptable formula: the Vilna diocese would be redrawn and made a metropolitanate, notwithstanding the advice of the Polish episcopate to the contrary, technically creating a hierarchical vacancy for an archbishop that the incumbent would not fill. Matulewicz would be shifted to other duties in the time-honored manner of imposing what appeared to be a promotion. The Vatican negotiator balked at first, but Grabski enlisted the aid of Ledóchowski, the Polish Jesuit General, and in the end the pope consented to the arrangement.[48] For Pius it must have been a bitter pill to swallow. The Holy See naturally disliked governmental pressures to fire bishops, especially this pope, and especially this bishop, and perhaps only the occasion of a much-desired Polish concordat could have persuaded Rome to pay this price and provided the necessary cover for the maneuver.[49]

The details of the Vilna understanding were carried out without delay, even before the promulgation of the papal bull of 1925, which formalized the reorganization of the Church in Poland hammered out in the concordat. Though not privy to the talks in Rome that already had decided the matter, Matulewicz could put two and two together and gather that his days in Vilna were numbered. Beyond that, he now recognized that most of his Polish flock, not just its hardcore Endek wing, wanted him gone. In June, bowing to the inevitable and wishing to spare the Holy See embarrassment, he submitted his resignation to the pope, who named him a titular archbishop as recompense.[50] Having won their objective, Polish officials gave Matulewicz assurances of no hard feelings: Warsaw had nothing against him as a man or as a bishop, but for reasons of state could not abide his presence in Vilna or the kresy. They pointed out, accurately enough, that the government had proposed installing him as bishop of Częstochowa, the famed Marian shrine city, as a tribute to his devotion to the Virgin.[51] Making Matulewicz the Lithuanian ordinary of an entirely Polish diocese made little sense on its face, but to Warsaw that did not matter, for he could do no harm in Częstochowa: what did matter was that he could not be tolerated as pastor of a region, such as Vilna, where the government counted on the Church to help place a definitively Polish stamp on the area.

Apart from his resentment at having been hounded out of Vilna, Matulewicz cannot have been entirely unhappy to escape a see that for six years had given him little more than an endless routine of antagonism and abuse, with the occasional death threat to break the monotony.[52] As his successor in the city of Ostrabrama, Rome, as expected, chose Archbishop Jan Cieplak, recently released from captivity and a brush with martyrdom at the hands of the Russian Bolsheviks, but the weakened appointee died before setting foot in Vilna. By this time, Matulewicz himself had but little time left to live, and he devoted it to a final assignment that was fitting, ironic, and scarcely less challenging than the one he had just vacated. Named apostolic visitor to Lithuania, he was handed the thankless task of soothing that country's rage that the Vatican had signed the concordat, which both recognized Polish rule over the Vilna diocese and indirectly made him its former bishop.

Matulewicz remained a lightning rod for criticism to the end of his days: instead of welcoming him as a returning son of the nation, Lithuanian opinion faulted him for having given in and stepped down as bishop of Vilna rather than holding on to the bitter end.[53] Still, he managed to placate Kaunas and prepare the ground for a Lithuanian concordat, but his health had always been fragile, and he died in 1927 after an attack of appendicitis. In one of his last letters he wrote, "Truly today I can say that the Catholic Church is my only homeland, and I am its patriot alone."[54]

Although it succeeded in dislodging Matulewicz from Vilna, the Second Republic had to bear the presence of Metropolitan Sheptyts'kyi in Lwów for the rest of its free existence, but in the years to come the Uniate archbishop rendered a grudging, conditional allegiance to the Polish state that had extracted from him a pledge of fealty. After his return to Lwów in 1923, Sheptyts'kyi kept his word and counseled Ukrainians to make their peace with Poland. The Greek Catholic bishops followed his lead and ended their collective refusal to consider themselves members of the Polish episcopate. For the next decade and a half, the bishop of St. George tried to tread a ticklish middle path through a complex set of contradictory pressures. On the one hand, he sought to fulfill his obligation to acknowledge and obey Polish authority, a duty Rome regularly reminded him of, without compromising his commitment to protect his Ukrainian flock or permitting Warsaw to coopt his authoritative voice for its own ends. Beyond that, among the Greek Catholic clergy he represented the predominant consciously "Ukrainian" orientation, but had to coexist with a greater than negligible number of churchmen who favored a more forthrightly friendly stance toward the Polish state. Finally, within the sharply divided milieu of Ukrainian politics, he occupied a moderate position opposed to the extremes of revolutionary Left and violent nationalist Right. Forced to address all these differing audiences, Sheptyts'kyi spoke a clear and consistent public message during the interwar era: Ukrainians owed loyalty to Poland, but Poland owed justice to the Ukrainians, and the government would hear from Sheptyts'kyi if it did not keep its end of the covenant.[55]

The difficulty of this intricate balancing act showed clearly in such instances as the Ukrainian "pacification" of autumn 1930, when Marshal Piłsudski sent cavalry units into East Galicia to subdue a wave of sabotage and terrorism set off by the militant Organization of Ukrainian Nationalists, and cow the local inhabitants while they were at it. In response, Sheptyts'kyi shot protests to Warsaw against its resort to force and joined with other

Greek Catholic hierarchs in issuing a pastoral letter that chastised the Ukrainian rebels but also reproached the Polish government so severely that the text ran afoul of the state censor.[56] This performance infuriated the Polish Right as treacherous and triggered a series of tense exchanges between Warsaw and the Vatican trading charges of Polish mistreatment of Greek Catholics and papal favoritism toward the Ukrainians.[57]

Double-edged conduct of this sort set Poles' teeth on edge and led them to regard Metropolitan Sheptyts'kyi either as a barely tolerable annoyance at best, or as an unreconstructed, all-but-declared enemy of the Second Republic. The sanacja regime of Piłsudski credited itself with greater broad-mindedness toward national minorities than its pre-May predecessors, but never quite made up its mind whether Sheptyts'kyi was a legitimate spokesman for Ukrainian concerns or a security risk, while his colleagues within the Polish episcopate treated him with an uncomfortable mix of respect and reserve. No such ambiguities moderated the opinion of the National Democratic Right, which detested the Uniate archbishop as the "evil spirit of St. George," a malign presence within the country and the moral inspiration behind Ukrainian sedition.[58] For his part, Sheptyts'kyi denied these accusations and claimed always to be true to a Poland true to its own heritage. "They make me out to be a traitor," he is reported to have said, "but . . . I would never do anything against the Rzeczpospolita"—perhaps leaving open the question whether he thought the interwar incarnation of Poland measured up to the best traditions of the multiethnic Commonwealth of yore.[59]

Despite his qualms, Sheptyts'kyi gradually became more willing to advise the Ukrainians of Galicia to accept Poland as their homeland with fewer qualifications, if only as the least unpalatable of a grim set of alternatives. An upsurge of OUN terror in the mid-1930s prompted him to condemn political violence flatly as an offense against Christian morality. In addition, the horrors taking place across the frontier in Soviet Ukraine made Poland, whatever its faults, appear a safe haven for Greek Catholics by comparison, a point the Holy See missed few opportunities to impress upon him.[60] On September 1, 1939, as the German invaders swarmed into Poland, the Metropolitan of Halicz-Lwów would call on Ukrainians to defend the state he had sorely tried for the past two decades.[61]

By that time, although Matulewicz had been dead for more than a decade and Sheptyts'kyi had more or less made peace with the Second Republic, nothing Poland had tried had managed to pacify its restive Catholic national minorities. Rome eventually replaced Matulewicz as bishop of Vilna with his mirror image, Romuald Jałbrzykowski, a Pole who spoke Lithuanian and caused no worry in Warsaw, yet the governmental watchdogs continued to compile dossiers on suspect Lithuanian clergy.[62] Tensions between Sheptyts'kyi and the authorities over Ukrainian questions rose to boiling point once again in 1938, and little more than a month before Germany would unleash Fall Weiss, the Polish ambassador to the Holy See was still bending the ear of anyone in the Vatican who would listen about the danger posed to Poland not by the Nazis, but by the Uniates of Galicia.[63]

Just as the conditions of interwar Poland were unsuited to harmony among its nationalities, so were Polish contemporaries seldom able to evaluate the bishops Matulewicz and Sheptyts'kyi with dispassion. For years Matulewicz was described both as a Lithuanian zealot and as a saint, often in the same breath.[64] Cardinal Kakowski, scarcely the most ungenerous of men, reflected the outlook of his era in his memoirs when he conceded the holiness of Matulewicz, but added matter-of-factly that "as a Lithuanian he favored the Lithuanians over the Poles, and for that reason . . . he had to resign."[65] The image of Andrei Sheptyts'kyi as a son of Poland gone bad, a baleful apostate in both a religious and national sense and therefore doubly perfidious, likewise persisted for decades in Polish memory, perpetuated by unfriendly polemicists or historians eager to portray him in the most forbidding light.[66] But the passage of time and the dramatic political transformation of east-central Europe at the end of the Cold War seem to have eased the ethnic rivalries that gripped the borderlands in the first half of the twentieth century and softened Polish views of the pair of Catholic prelates who had incarnated those old quarrels. Fr. Maciej Zięba suggests that the figure of Metropolitan Sheptyts'kyi, formerly a stark symbol of division between Poles and Ukrainians, may in time more properly be seen as a sign of the intimate historical ties between the two peoples.[67] As for Jerzy Matulewicz, when the Catholic Church proclaimed him blessed in 1987, marking the six hundredth anniversary of the baptism of Lithuania, Polish Catholic commentators used the occasion to offer historical amends for the indignities their nation had done him during the 1920s. As the Polish pope pronounced the formula of beatification in St. Peter's Square, in his former see of Vilna, not quite yet freed from the yoke of Soviet rule, Poles and Lithuanians alike gathered in six modest masses of celebration.[68] One imagines that the Blessed Jerzy would have approved.

7 ||| Poland, the Orthodox, and the Conversion of Russia

In 1917, as the world war continued to ravage Europe, several things happened that, taken together, foreshadowed the most ambitious and complex theme of the relationship between Poland and Catholicism during the two decades that followed. On May 13, three Portuguese shepherd children received the first of what many came to believe were a series of miraculous visitations from the Virgin Mary at Fatima; their testimony has fired the Catholic imagination ever since. Just two days earlier, Pope Benedict XV had issued a formal statement promoting Catholic missionary work in the Christian East and establishing the Congregation for Eastern Churches, devoted to that very task. In the meantime, the country that had been the colossus of Orthodoxy careened through revolutionary upheaval, from the collapse of the Romanov dynasty to the advent of the Bolsheviks. The leadership of the Catholic Church read these as converging signs pointing to the imminent realization of one of the grandest and most enduring of Roman dreams, one that the Fatima visionaries declared that Mary had promised would come true if her warnings and requests were heeded: the conversion of Russia to the Catholic faith.

What did this immense project of trying to herd the Orthodox masses into the flock of Peter have to do with the Second Polish Republic after it emerged unexpectedly in 1918? An essential, natural, and even providential part, in the eyes of the keepers of the dream. To those inclined to view the world through the eyes of the Church, the revived homeland of the devoutly Catholic Polish nation appeared to be a state largely founded on the rejection of all things Russian, including the religion of the ousted foreign overlords. Hilaire Belloc applauded the postwar demolition of a massive Russian Orthodox cathedral on Saxony Square in Warsaw "with everything about it utterly un-Polish. It was like a seal of conquest. . . . Its complete disappearance was one of the first tasks of the new Poland"—a perfect expression of Polish political and spiritual emancipation and independence. Echoing his friend, G. K. Chesterton observed that "If the erection of a building is a symbol or memorial, the destruction of a building can be a symbol and a memorial also"—a token, in this case, of the welcome restoration of the supremacy of Catholicism in one of its historic strongholds, and possibly of further advances yet to come.[1] Just as Catholicism had conquered Orthodoxy in Warsaw, so might it elsewhere as well, and undo the schism of 1054.

For the religious fault line of Europe ran through the heart of the Second Republic. Once the boundaries of the country were fixed, nearly four million Orthodox dwelt in the regions east of the zone of Polish and Catholic settlement, chiefly Ukrainians and Belorussians in the Volhynia, Polesie, and Nowogródek districts. Beyond the eastern frontier lay Russia itself, the great prize. Inevitably, any Catholic campaign to woo the Orthodox would count on the cooperation of Poland in fostering the conversion of its own Eastern Christians and serving as a base for the evangelization of the Russian expanses.

The plan failed, for many reasons, one being that the government of Poland refused its assigned role in the enterprise. The Church might yearn to win souls, but in calculating its own interests Warsaw preferred that its Orthodox subjects stay Orthodox rather than become Catholic on the terms offered by the Vatican, and did its best to frustrate the efforts of the pope and his men to extend the reach of Catholicism into Soviet Russia. Although the direct opposite of what might be expected of a country renowned as semper fidelis, these policies made unanswerable sense to all the various governments of the Second Republic, which might have agreed on almost nothing else, and underscored the general point that during the interwar period, the purposes of Catholicism and of a free Polish state proved harder to match than most might have guessed in 1918.

This story begins with the convulsion of Russia by war and upheaval, and the hopeful belief within the hierarchy of the Catholic Church that the dangers and evils of the revolution, however great, were outweighed by the greater opportunity it afforded to redraw the religious map of Christendom to their gain. Ghastly though the war had been, by destroying the antebellum order it seemed to have opened dazzling possibilities for historic initiatives in the regions that lay beyond the traditional sphere of Catholicism. "Now begins a new era in the east," noted Nuncio Ratti's chargé a few days before the armistice. "Without the Turkish Empire, without the Austrian Empire, without tsarism, the situation takes a completely novel and mysterious turn."[2] Above all, the Russian case combined peril and promise. The breakup of the empire and the resulting liberation of its Polish and Lithuanian subjects had reduced the number of Catholics in Russia from fifteen million to one-tenth the prewar total, mostly Latin-rite Poles. This remnant soon felt the heavy hand of Bolshevik antireligious persecution. Their spiritual head, Archbishop Eduard von der Ropp, bemoaned to Ratti the "terrible circumstances" of his church shortly before being deported to Poland by the Red authorities in 1919 on charges of espionage.[3] Still, Catholic leaders tended to underestimate both the durability and the ferocity of the Communists and to assume that the future of their confession in the Russian lands had to be better than its past. In 1920 Cardinal Kakowski of Warsaw gave rosy assurance to an interviewer that "whatever be the régime which Russia will eventually obtain, it will be impossible ever to return to the religious intolerance which, under the Tsar's régime, prevailed against Catholics. Religious liberty will remain an accomplished fact in the history of that country."[4] From this perspective, far more significant than the momentary tribulations of the Church in Russia was the momentous fact of the toppling of the imperium that had been the pillar of Orthodoxy, clearing the way at last to Catholic evangelization efforts in the largest of Christian countries.

Although a consensus had quickly formed within the Vatican, warmly encouraged by Pope Benedict himself, that the hour had struck to pursue the conversion of the Orthodox of Eastern Europe, opinions differed on how to go about it. The decision makers of the Church debated two differing ideas, each with its own thrust and potential drawbacks. Since 1907 the papacy had authorized the Greek Catholic metropolitan of Lwów, the redoubtable Archbishop Sheptyts'kyi, to serve as its point man in efforts to restore communion with Orthodox Slavs, endorsing the argument that he had made his life's cause: that the future of the Church in the lands of the quondam Russian Empire depended on an expansion of its Eastern rites tailored to suit the culture and ecclesiastical traditions of its inhabitants. Sheptyts'kyi dreamed in grand terms of nothing less than the full reunion of the churches of West and East, based on the model of his own Ukrainian observance, and took the fall of the tsardom as the signal to begin in earnest. But by no means all agreed on the wisdom of relying on Sheptyts'kyi, or his Uniate strategy. As we have seen, the government of the new Poland frowned upon any extension of the influence of the Greek Catholics, or their archbishop, in its own eastern marches, as did most of the Polish Latin-rite bishops: if the Orthodox of the kresy were to become Catholic, they should be brought into the Western rite, which would assimilate them into Polish nationality, not the Ukrainian church Warsaw regarded as a troublemaking school for separatism. This view won the qualified support of the exiled Archbishop von der Ropp, who urged a two-track approach of biritual conversion in Russia and the Polish kresy to Western or Uniate Catholicism, as local conditions dictated, but subject to the Polish Latin hierarchy, not to Sheptyts'kyi, who, he cautioned, was "infatuated with politics."[5] Of course, the obvious rejoinder to this line of thought was to point out that to the extent that the East Slav Orthodox saw the hand of the Latin Poles behind the invitation to join the Catholic fold, the more they were likely to spurn it. Weighing the alternatives, Benedict reaffirmed the papal preference for the Uniate approach, but chose not to press the issue, out of respect for the objections of the Polish bishops.[6]

But by this time the pontificate of Benedict XV nearly had run its course, and in fact the future eastern policy of the Catholic Church was taking shape in Poland, where the pope in waiting, Nuncio Ratti, was getting a firsthand crash course in these matters. Being Achille Ratti, he forged ironclad convictions on the subject, which he took home with him to Italy and eventually to the Vatican Palace. From his Polish vantage point, he acquired a fascination with Russia and the implications of its revolution. He did what he could to intercede on behalf of the beleaguered Russian Catholics, and helped to secure the safe release of Archbishop von der Ropp, who became a personal mentor on eastern problems.[7] The prospect of coaxing the Orthodox into the embrace of Rome, he believed, was both realistic and imperative, and he favored the Piłsudski conception of a vast Polish-led east European federation precisely for its usefulness in facilitating the work of evangelization. As for the contentious question of which rite to emphasize as a vehicle of conversion, Latin or Uniate, Ratti decided that the Polish distaste for the Eastern Catholics was a national bias rooted in cultural arrogance that did not serve the broader interests of the Church. As an adjacent Catholic and Slavic country, Poland would make the ideal base for the courting of the Orthodox of Russia, but the venture could not afford to appear either "*troppo 'polacca'*" or "*troppo 'romana'*": in other words, it must stress the Uniate option.[8] Nevertheless, Ratti doubted whether the task should be entrusted to Sheptyts'kyi and the Greek Catholics, given their hostility toward Poland and tendencies toward Ukrainian nationalism, and concluded that the answer was to start fresh with a new Eastern-rite specially made to order to house the Orthodox of Russia and the formerly Russian kresy of Poland.[9]

One considerable complication in these discussions was that in the meantime, the Polish Republic was working out a scheme for handling its Orthodox that had little in common with the thinking of Achille Ratti, or any of the other Catholic churchmen. They took as a given that the Orthodox ought to be converted, on grounds of religious principle; Warsaw did not, on grounds of pragmatic statecraft. The reasoning of Polish officialdom, upheld consistently throughout the interwar years, ran along these lines: if, in the best of cases, the Orthodox Belorussians and Ukrainians of eastern Poland could be converted to Latin Catholicism, the time-tested passageway into Polish identity, well and good, but nine centuries of schism suggested that this was a long shot. The worst alternative—and regrettably, the one favored by the Vatican—would be to promote their conversion into Eastern-rite Catholicism, regarded by the Poles as hostile to their culture and state.[10] For that matter, nor could Warsaw see anything but trouble coming from Rome's pet notion of displacing Orthodoxy with Uniatism in Russia, whether Red or not.[11] In the meantime, Poland had to manage an Orthodox population of its own of four million historically dominated by a small minority of Russians who openly yearned for the restoration of the Russian Empire. As insurance against the probability that the *prawosławni* could not be induced to become western Catholics, Warsaw came up with an agreeable backup plan: try to turn a negative into a positive by emancipating the non-Russian Orthodox Slavs of the Polish kresy from their Russophile leadership through the creation of an autocephalous Orthodox church within the country that, not incidentally, would be dependent on, and loyal to the Second Republic. Chief of State Piłsudski affirmed this policy publicly in 1922, and in that same year a bare majority of the Orthodox bishops of Poland, with governmental prodding, voted to endorse autocephaly and break ties with the Metropolitanate of Moscow.[12]

The decision of Poland to patronize the establishment of a separate national Orthodox church under its thumb ran into several obstacles. In the first place, it scandalized many within the ranks of Orthodoxy. A Russian monk slew the pro-Polish metropolitan Georgi of Warsaw as an apostate, and large numbers of the faithful spurned the new *cerkiew* as illegitimate. In addition, the government found itself ensnared against its better judgment in what would become an endless no-win dispute over ownership of church properties that did much to spoil its hopes of currying goodwill among the Orthodox. Many of the functioning Orthodox houses of worship in the new Poland originally had belonged to Uniate Catholic parishes, only to be seized for use by the conqueror's religion during the era of rule by Russia, which had suppressed Uniatism in the nineteenth century. Naturally, the Vatican and the Polish Church demanded their return, and in the first flush of independence, as anti-Russian passions ran high, Warsaw tacitly permitted the Catholics to begin the repossession of these properties willy-nilly, provoking horrified, sometimes violent resistance from the Orthodox worshippers. Once they realized they wanted to win over their Orthodox citizens, not repel them, the Polish authorities thought better of it and tried to put a stop to this grassroots war over churches so obviously at odds with their larger purposes in the kresy. In 1922 the government declared that the contested holy buildings belonged to the state, and hoped the whole mess would just go away. Undaunted, the Catholic Church flooded the court system with hundreds of lawsuits to regain these ex-Uniate assets, and also badgered Warsaw for a favorable political ruling that might settle the matter at a single stroke. The Second Republic tried as it might to stall this revindication controversy into oblivion, but it developed an inconvenient habit of resurfacing, and the longer it dragged on, the more it deepened Orthodox misgivings about the intentions of their Polish rulers.[13] Most awkward of all, the choice of Poland to support Orthodoxy over Uniate Catholicism on both sides of its eastern boundary could only dismay the Vatican and prompt accusations that the Poles were betraying their duty to the faith. Be that as it may, Warsaw pressed ahead with its bet that a compliant autocephalous Polish Orthodox church could serve its goals of religious and ethnic tranquility in the borderlands.

One of the explanations of their lack of enthusiasm for Catholic missionary activity in Russia was the wish of the Poles to avoid unnecessary irritation of their relations with this dangerous neighbor, and by Holy Week of 1923 they found out just how irritable the Communist dictatorship could be when it came to dealing with the "opiate of the masses." Now firmly in place after prevailing in revolution and civil war, the Soviet regime ramped up its assault on religion, including the Catholic confession, so easily identifiable with the Polish enemy. In 1922 a wave of closure of churches, plunder of their valuables, and desecration of relics elicited unavailing protests from Warsaw. The campaign reached a climax in 1923 with the arrest, show trial, and condemnation to death of two prominent Catholic clergymen, both Poles, Archbishop Jan Cieplak, the de facto head of the Church in Russia, and his assistant, Monsignor Konstantin Budkiewicz. Following worldwide calls for mercy, Cieplak was spared execution, but Budkiewicz was shot on Easter eve as a Polish spy; opinions split, then and in later retellings, whether the Sikorski ministry of Poland made things worse and helped to seal the fate of Fr. Budkiewicz by ignoring Soviet hints of a prisoner exchange and issuing unwisely heated and public demands for clemency, despite counsels of discretion from the Vatican.[14] By the time Archbishop Cieplak, weakened unto death, was sent into exile in 1924, the Catholic Church in the Soviet Union had been all but shut down.[15]

Such was the state of affairs when the new Pope Pius XI, two years removed from the nunciature in Poland that had kindled his belief in a future Catholic Russia, announced his program for the evangelization of the Orthodox in the encyclical *Ecclesiam Dei*, issued in November 1923 on the three-hundredth anniversary of the martyrdom of the Uniate missionary St. Josaphat. By now Pius had recruited an additional voice into the ongoing discussion within the inner circles of the Church over the conversion of the East, that of the French Jesuit Michel d'Herbigny. Born in 1880, d'Herbigny devoted himself from youth to study of Russia and its culture and to the cause of winning that country over to Catholicism. As archbishop of Milan, Cardinal Ratti had taken this promising Jesuit under his wing as a like-minded consultant on Russian affairs, and he called him to Rome upon assuming the papacy in 1922.[16] During the decade that followed, d'Herbigny would rank as the right-hand man of Pius XI in this undertaking so dear to the pontiff's heart, the supreme architect of the eastern policy of the Vatican. He was also destined to be remembered as one of the most fascinating and enigmatic figures in the recent history of the Church, a man—according to one who knew him well—of manifest idealism and prodigious if erratic energy, who attained great power and influence only to end in "the most humiliating disgrace."[17]

By no coincidence, d'Herbigny's view of the most effective way to appeal to the Orthodox mirrored that of Pius himself: Uniatism, but with a novel twist that removed Archbishop Sheptyts'kyi and his Greek Catholics from any part in the Russian venture that had been his cherished goal. Rather than bank on Sheptyts'kyi's millennial vision of the reconciliation of the western and eastern Churches, d'Herbigny and his pope thought instead in terms of millions of individual conversions, "sheep-stealing" on an unheard-of scale. Apart from this basic difference in philosophy, the Ukrainian

Catholics were ruled out as objectionable both to the Russians, the intended targets, and to the Poles, whose collaboration would be needed. This was a bitter pill for Sheptyts'kyi to swallow, but he understood and loyally accepted the decision. The solution, d'Herbigny convinced Pius—who required little convincing, already having come to roughly the same conclusion—was to place the burden of proselytization on a new Eastern rite carrying no unwanted historical baggage, and to entrust the cultivation of this Slavonic church to his own Jesuit order, the traditional missionaries to peoples of exotic cultures.[18]

From the outset, eastern Poland had been seen as the starting point of this "neounion" strategy, and an occasion to launch a pilot project there soon arose. In 1923 the respected Latin Catholic bishop of Siedlce in Polesie, Henryk Przeździecki, reported that he had received a delegation of Orthodox peasants who declared themselves fed up with the internal quarrels within their church over the issue of autocephaly, and improbably asked the Catholic ordinary to provide them with genuine priests of their faith. Interpreting the request broadly, the Vatican directed Przeździecki to initiate within his jurisdiction a new Eastern rite in communion with Rome. As opposed to the partially westernized Greek Catholic liturgy, this Byzantine-Slavonic Church would duplicate the profile of Orthodoxy virtually intact except for a celibate clergy placed under authority of the local Latin bishop. The experiment got under way in 1924 with the opening of a Jesuit mission in the tiny village of Albertyn, combining the first Byzantine-Slavonic parish with a center for training members of the order for the work of winning souls in the Polish kresy and, eventually, Russia itself. By the next year the neounion had been introduced in other dioceses in eastern Poland as well.[19]

The timing of the decision to set up the Slavonic rite had much to do with an emerging sense of Catholic dissatisfaction with the early results of the postwar drive to evangelize the Orthodox.[20] Many had blithely expected an easy windfall of "returns to Rome" from among the Orthodox of the Polish borderlands, since most of them were descendants of Eastern-rite Catholics forcibly converted by the Russians; but the anticipated torrent turned out to be a trickle, a disappointment in some quarters blamed on past and present missteps of the Poles themselves. Deploring the traditional Polish stance of disdain and antagonism toward both the Orthodox and the Uniates, one observer asserted that "were it not for Poland, Russia would now be Catholic."[21] Having done their worst through the centuries to make Catholicism anathema to their eastern neighbors, now the Poles were erring in the opposite direction by promoting an autocephalous Orthodox church of their own creation. Bishop Przeździecki reproachfully asked a government dignitary why "Poland is rescuing Orthodoxy, which is collapsing in Russia."[22]

Unmoved, Warsaw received the news of the inauguration of the neounion in its territories with distaste. As always in its consideration of questions dealing with eastern Catholicism, the Second Republic worried that it would retard or even prevent the assimilation of the non-Poles of the kresy, all the more so in this case because the Slavonic rite seemed to hold the potential to gain a considerable following.[23] No sooner had the Jesuits set up shop in Albertyn than the ministries of foreign and religious affairs worked out a policy on the neounion that would change only in degree over the next decade and a half. The unanimous verdict of officialdom was that the East Slav rite flatly contradicted Polish interests. Conversion of the Orthodox, if done at all, should be done directly to the Western rite. The growth of the Slavonic Uniate Church would reduce Polish cultural influence in the borderlands and provide a rallying point for Ukrainian and Belorussian nationalist malcontents, becoming a counterpart, and possibly worse yet, a political ally, of the Greek Catholics in the southeast. Still, Poland could not afford to oppose the missionary pet project of the Church openly, lest it anger the Vatican by coddling schismatics. So Warsaw should mute its criticisms, for the most part, but quietly drag its feet and think of ways to tie up the venture in delay and red tape.[24]

But while the left hand of Poland looked for ways to hinder the spread of the Slavonic rite in its formerly Russian provinces, its right hand missed its best chance to do just that in the haggling over the 1925 concordat with the Holy See. The Poles demanded, and obtained, the consent of the Vatican to confine Sheptyts'kyi's Greek Catholics to the Ukrainian regions inherited from Austria, thus preventing their extension into the territories gained from Russia—not much of a concession, given that Rome already had made the same decision on its own. However, the East Slav rite figured nowhere in the text of the treaty, although it came up repeatedly in the negotiations, whether directly or implied within verbal sparring over the conflicting intentions of the parties concerning the borderlands. Weighing in for Poland, Stanisław Grabski insisted that "in the Polish kresy any government must concern itself with religious questions and support the Latin rite as an element of Polishness," only to be told by his opposite number that any successful approach to the Orthodox would require a rite "that has nothing in common with Polishness." In the end they let the subject drop; possibly Grabski hoped to preserve the Republic's freedom of action concerning the neounion.[25] At any rate, Warsaw came to rue the omission, for its real effect was to grant d'Herbigny and the pope carte blanche to implant the new rite in the ex-Russian districts of Poland as they saw fit with no concordatory restrictions.

Having established a beachhead of the neounion in eastern Poland, the Vatican now began a series of exploratory probes into the main objective, the Russia now under Communist rule. Pius XI sent his designated eastern expert Michel d'Herbigny on a reconnoitering journey into the Soviet Union in 1925, traveling incognito to assess the conditions of the country, where, they believed, an unsavory gang of atheist thugs had done them the unwitting favor of knocking Orthodoxy off its pedestal and leaving it ripe for the taking. Looking beyond the bleak present, d'Herbigny brought back with him a forecast of a bright future for Catholicism in Russia after a short Bolshevik interlude. More convinced than ever that his handpicked Jesuit protégé was the man to spearhead the mission to the Orthodox, Pius established within the Congregation for Eastern Churches a special papal Commission on Russia (Commissio pro Russia) with d'Herbigny as its head. Next, in 1926 the pope had d'Herbigny consecrated a bishop and authorized him to undertake two more clandestine journeys into the Soviet Union for the purpose of reviving the moribund Russian hierarchy necessary to maintain the sacramental life of the Church in the country. While there, d'Herbigny named four bishops of the Western rite, but underestimated the degree of caution needed to avoid the notice of the watchdogs of the Soviet regime, who became aware of his activities and of the existence of his fledgling underground Church.[26] Unaware that its secret plan had been compromised in its inception, and cut off from regular communication with the USSR, the Vatican remained for some time under the illusion that all was well. Two years later, flush with confidence, d'Herbigny predicted—not for the last time—that the impending conversion of Russia would open all of Asia to the advance of Catholicism.[27]

But before long, stern reality began to intrude on these Roman reveries as evidence mounted that the rate of Orthodox conversions to Catholicism in the Polish kresy—in the mind of the Vatican, the essential prelude to the push into Russia—had slowed nearly to a dead stop. By the later 1920s no more than twenty thousand Polish Orthodox had rallied to the neounion, usually in the form of entire parishes following the lead of their pastor. This figure amounted to considerably less than 1 percent of the Orthodox population of the country, less, in fact, than the number of conversions from Uniate Catholicism to Orthodoxy.[28] In other words, far from making historic gains at the expense of the Orthodox in eastern Poland, Rome was actually losing ground.

The reasons for the failure of the Byzantine-Slavonic rite to gain traction in the Polish kresy were many and complicated, starting with the tense mixture of religion and national unrest in the region, with its dense intermingling of rival peoples and confessions. The introduction of the autocephalous Polish Orthodox church sponsored by Warsaw opened a bitter rift between its adherents and the "true" Orthodox, who disdained the upstart cerkiew. While the two Orthodox parties fought each other, both also locked horns with the Uniates, turning eastern Poland into a zone of ongoing religious strife luridly described by the *Times* of London as a peasant battleground of "churchyard riots and churchdoor murders."[29] Beyond that, Orthodox opinion lodged complaints against the Byzantine-Slavonic rite in particular, charging it with carrying out forced conversions and acting as a covert agent of westernization and Polonization of Ukrainians and Belorussians.[30] In addition, the unresolved issue of the Catholic claims for repossession of the ex-Uniate Orthodox churches in the kresy reached a crescendo as the Church filed a host of last-minute lawsuits to meet a government-imposed deadline to begin all such proceedings by 1929, fanning Orthodox suspicions that they were being ill-used by the ruling Poles and their Roman religion.[31]

If the intended converts found little to like in the Catholic neounion, neither did the Polish political and spiritual leadership, to the displeasure of the Holy See. By this time Piłsudski had taken charge in Warsaw, and his government outdid its predecessors in its skepticism concerning the far-reaching Vatican plans in the east. For the most part, the marshal left management of religious policy to his bureaucrats, who thought the Orthodox kresy were best left Orthodox, and grumbled that Rome had played dirty by waiting until after the concordat to foist the unwanted Byzantine-Slavonic rite on Poland. Prime Minister Bartel, in a meeting with representatives of the Polish episcopate, expressed fears that the neounion would harm state interests; he was answered with reassuring words.[32] But in fact, not a few of the Catholic bishops of the country harbored doubts of their own about the East Slav rite, and one glaring cause of the unimpressive progress of the neounion in the borderlands was the refusal of some ordinaries to promote it in their dioceses.[33] At the end of 1928 the pope felt the need to get his Polish troops in line, calling on the bishops of Poland to do all in their power to support the important work of converting the Orthodox of the country, an implicit admission both that the work was not going as well as it might and that he thought the bishops were not trying to help as hard as they might.[34]

It was typical of Pius XI that the puny harvest of souls in the Polish kresy did not make him alter his course in any way, except to persuade him that what was needed was to accelerate the mission to the Orthodox into higher gear and to hand over its direction entirely to Michel d'Herbigny and his Vatican office rather than count on the uncertain assistance of local bishops. As the decade of the twenties neared its close, d'Herbigny held firm to his confidence in the immediate conversion of the Russians and prevailed on the pope to give him the tools and the clout to reach the goal. Pius XI was not one to stop at half measures. In 1929, at d'Herbigny's suggestion, he established a Pontifical Russian College, the Russicum, to train priests for mission work in Russia, and addressed a letter to all seminarians appealing for volunteers for this calling, especially from among the Jesuits. The Russicum was placed under the protection of the recently canonized patroness of missions, St. Thérèse of the Child Jesus, and partially funded with contributions from her own Carmel of Lisieux. Next, in a *motu proprio* of 1930, the pontiff removed the Commissio pro Russia headed by d'Herbigny from the oversight of the Congregation for Eastern Churches: his star still rapidly ascendant, the French Jesuit now had consolidated complete personal control over the papal campaign to convert the Orthodox in Russia and all nearby countries, and would report directly to Pius himself. As he marshaled his forces to launch his peaceful crusade to the East, that same year the pope called on the faithful in all lands to pray for Russia and its conversion to Catholicism, as Our Lady of Fatima had requested in 1917.[35]

This flurry of papal decrees made d'Herbigny the second-most-powerful man in the Vatican, and also gave him dictatorial sway over the Roman drive to coax the Orthodox of eastern Poland into the neounion, much to the alarm of the Polish Second Republic. Internal official assessments described the new charter of the Commissio pro Russia, in terms of near panic, as an infringement on the right of the state to govern its own territories, and ticked off a host of reasons why it was bad for Poland: the effort to implant the East Slav rite would impede the Polonization of the kresy, stimulate Communist and national separatist agitation in the borderlands, and likely make the job of managing relations with the Soviet Union, challenging at best, all the more difficult.[36] Warsaw held d'Herbigny and his coterie of other French Jesuits within the Commissio in deepest mistrust, regarding them as zealots hell-bent on using Poland as a pawn in their Russian game "without the slightest concern for the requirements of the Polish raison d'état in the kresy."[37] In short, the Poles saw nothing to like in the pro Russia, even down to a thin-skinned objection to its name, as implying that their eastern provinces remained more genuinely Russian terrain than part of an independent Poland. D'Herbigny tried to convince the Polish envoys to the Holy See that their government had nothing to fear from the neounion, that they could be sure that the pope who had resided in Poland held the best interests of the Second Republic at heart, but his entreaties fell on deaf ears.[38] Warsaw complained to any and all in the halls of the Vatican that Rome had unwisely placed its eastern policy, a subject calling for delicacy and careful judgment, in the incautious hands of "people like Bishop d'Herbigny, beguiled by a mirage of a great, united Russia," but found few sympathetic listeners there.[39] For one thing, because many in the Curia saw Poland as the obstructionist culprit responsible for the slow start of the Slavonic rite, they gave little credence to advice from that quarter.[40] Further, as Poland's men at the Vatican soon discovered, the new autonomy of the Commissio pro Russia shielded it from normal bureaucratic oversight and rendered their own protests against its activities pointless. In frustration, they grumbled that although "Mgr. d'Herbigny makes trouble for us all the time," they could do nothing to stop him: the Frenchman answered to the pope, and the pope alone, and so long as he enjoyed the complete confidence of Pius XI, there was little chance of reining in the pro Russia.[41]

The mounting tension between Warsaw and the Holy See over the neounion came to a head in November 1930 when the Polish ambassador Skrzyński obtained a papal audience to deliver a message from Marshal Piłsudski himself, making one of his infrequent interventions into the arena of religious affairs. Speaking through his proxy, Piłsudski bluntly told his old friend the pope that his government "must oppose the propagation of this artificial and ephemeral movement, which creates anti-Polish centers in the eastern territories," and had no choice but to refuse to cooperate in the organization of a Slavonic-rite hierarchy on Polish soil. Flashing his trademark temper, Pius interrupted the messenger with a sharp retort: he, the pope, whose fondness for the Polish republic could not be questioned, declared that the neounion would be good for the Church, and good for Poland, because the newly converted Catholics of the Polish kresy would not wish to return to Russian rule. Looking for silver linings, Skrzyński reported to his superiors that the frosty interview at least had made plain to the pontiff the depth of Piłsudski's objections to the East Slav rite, but held out no hope that Pius would change his mind.[42]

Warsaw did not have to wait long for the papal reply to the Piłsudski démarche. Upon the turn of the new year 1931, Rome announced that the pope had consecrated the Ukrainian Redemptorist Fr. Mykola Charnets'kyi a bishop and named him apostolic visitor to the Slavonic-rite Catholics of Poland.[43] In other words, if the Second Republic would not exercise its concordatory right to work with the Vatican in finding mutually acceptable candidates for bishops of the neounion, Pius would do it himself, without consultation. Neither the nomination of Charnets'kyi nor its peremptory character pleased the Poles. They considered the newest member of the Polish hierarchy a Russophile, confirming their gloomiest apprehensions of the tendencies of the Byzantine-Slavonic Church. When Charnets'kyi arrived in Poland, he received an icy reception from both its government and its episcopate, and in Rome Ambassador Skrzyński warned d'Herbigny that the Vatican was running the risk of triggering the wrath of Marshal Piłsudski.[44]

Whenever the Holy See and the Second Republic neared the brink of crisis in their relations, these two uncomfortable but necessary partners pulled back and sought to make amends, and so they did now. D'Herbigny offered to meet with Piłsudski to set his mind at ease about the neounion.[45] The Polish envoys at the Vatican advised Warsaw to swallow its annoyance, that nothing could be gained from challenging the pope on the East Slav rite he regarded as a favored child, and to take him at his word that he would not permit it to be used to harm the interests of Poland.[46] The Poles also received relief of a sort from an unexpected source, the apostolic visitor Charnets'kyi, who, upon inspecting his Slavonic Church at first hand, informed the Vatican that it suffered from serious defects—some, to be sure, of Warsaw's making, but others that showed that the Polish complaints about the new rite had some basis. Soon after hearing this sober assessment, Pius quietly passed word to Skrzyński that Poland could expect to see changes in the handling of the neounion movement that it considered an unwelcome imposition.[47]

As a result, over the course of the next year, Warsaw and the Vatican seemed to make some progress toward reaching an understanding that would reduce their differences over the Byzantine-Slavonic rite. Even as sanacja officialdom continued to voice their frustration with the neounion in public and private fora, behind the scenes steps were being taken to arrive at an accommodation.[48] In March 1932 the primate of Poland, Cardinal Hlond, speaking on behalf of both his government and his episcopate, addressed a letter to the Holy See respectfully requesting a series of reforms in the East Slav rite and the manner of its propagation in their country, including a greater say in decision-making. On this occasion, instead of brushing aside their objections, Rome responded with signs of willingness to meet the Poles halfway. Cardinal Pacelli, the secretary of state, and Bishop Charnets'kyi admitted that mistakes had been made in the hurried formation of the neounion, but pledged that they would be put right. Bishop d'Herbigny offered himself for a soothing interview in a Kraków newspaper, and Warsaw began to notice, for the first time, a welcome readiness on the part of his pro Russia to try to avoid treading on Polish toes in carrying out its work in the kresy.[49] By the autumn of 1932 Pius had taken actions to dilute the Russianness of the Slavonic rite that Poles found threatening and offensive, and announced that Hlond and two other Polish bishops would join the Congregation for Eastern Churches.[50] As the year drew to a close, the prospects appeared good that the main players in the sluggish crusade to convert the Orthodox of Poland might find common ground at last. Having been shown their lead by Cardinal Hlond, the Latin bishops of the country put aside their qualms about the neounion and fell into line behind their pontiff.[51] For his part, from his Roman perch, Ambassador Skrzyński expressed optimism that Poland and the Holy See could work out an approach to the vexed subject that both sides could live with: the pope would be willing to bend only so far—"he does not regard as good Catholics those who oppose the propagation of the Eastern rite"—but in the end he would settle for compromise rather than insist on ramming his policy down Polish throats.[52]

Isolated by distance and lengthy residence in Italy from the mood of the country he represented to the Vatican, Skrzyński underestimated the force of a swelling popular outcry in Poland against the Byzantine-Slavonic Church and its sponsor, Bishop d'Herbigny. Solid majorities of Poles of all persuasions looked down on Uniates as bogus Catholics and dubious citizens and could not fathom the papal insistence on making more of them, especially nationalist circles in the eastern provinces directly targeted by the pro Russia. The stepped up pace of neounion proselytization in the kresy starting in 1930 prompted an ongoing wave of criticism in the influential rightist press of the region that rose steadily in scope and stridency. By 1932 the journalistic assault against the East Slav rite had grown so severe that the head of the flagship Jesuit neounion mission in the country rushed into print a pamphlet claiming to spell out "the truth about Albertyn," defending the Uniate experiment against the charges of its ruinous impact in the borderlands.[53] However, this lonely voice was drowned out by the furor surrounding the nearly simultaneous appearance of H. I. Łubieński's *Droga na wschód Rzymu* (Rome's road to the east), a broadside indictment of the Vatican's bet on Uniatism as both misguided and ineffective that called on Polish Catholics to oppose it for the good of both the nation and the faith.[54] The self-published screed did little more than rehash the standard catalogue of arguments against the neounion widespread in Polish opinion and might have receded into quick obscurity if Cardinal Kakowski had not transformed it into a cause célèbre by announcing in October that he had placed it on the Index of forbidden writings.[55] Naturally, it was generally assumed that the archbishop of Warsaw took this action on papal orders; in fact, he probably did it on his own. Kakowski had a gift for bumbling, and he appears to have issued the decree in an ill-advised excess of zeal to demonstrate the recent commitment of the Polish episcopate to uphold the Slavonic rite project, and without reckoning on the backlash of angry public reaction against the ban within Poland. Speaking in confidence, the Vatican disowned Kakowski's edict as a clumsy overreaction, but said nothing for the record out of reluctance to undercut his authority as bishop, thus reinforcing the impression that Rome had engineered the incident in a heavy-handed attempt to stifle legitimate debate on a contentious issue of pressing importance to the Second Republic.[56] The Polish press erupted in outrage against the condemnation of the Łubieński book, stirring popular animus toward the neounion to new heights.[57] More quietly, but just as firmly, the Warsaw government remained entrenched in its belief that the spread of the East Slav rite was "at odds with the fundamental interests of the state."[58]

The journalistic fraternity of Poland now aroused and ready for combat against the eastern policy of the Vatican, a bizarre turn of events within the Commissio pro Russia handed them an opening made to order for them to have a field day at the expense of none other than its mastermind,

Bishop d'Herbigny. In 1932 Fr. Alexander Deubner, a Russian-born minor functionary in the pro Russia, disappeared shortly after a cache of secret documents turned up missing from its Vatican office. Putting two and two together, Polish ecclesiastical sources inspired the rumor that Deubner was a Soviet agent who had spirited the papers to Moscow.[59] Elements from the vanished priest's biography seemed to confirm the worst Polish suspicions of the dangerous folly of the pro Russia approach banking on Uniatism: his Russian origins, the fact that he was a distant relative and protégé of the despised Greek Catholic archbishop Sheptyts'kyi, and his current duties as an aide to d'Herbigny. The Deubner story gained some fleeting attention elsewhere, but the Polish press seized on it and splashed it across its front pages on a regular basis over the first quarter of 1933, featuring lurid charges of espionage leading to the arrest and execution of Catholic clergy in Russia, and of the exposure of the Slavonic rite Church as a Communist plot. By comparison, the official *Gazeta polska* showed restraint in tut-tutting that the Deubner revelations were nothing more than the logical outcome of the wrongheaded incompetence of d'Herbigny, who "trusts no one except those who should not be trusted. . . . The concentration in the hands of Father d'Herbigny, a man imprudent at best, of matters important to Poland cannot leave us indifferent."[60] Stung by the accusations, d'Herbigny asked Warsaw to issue a public rebuke of the scandalmongering in the papers, a request seconded by the Jesuits and other curial dignitaries. Ambassador Skrzyński replied, in so many words, that if d'Herbigny did not like reading his press clippings, that was his problem.[61]

The circumstantial case against Fr. Deubner was strong enough to persuade some later historians that he was indeed a GPU plant, but the likelier explanation is that the Russian priest was a man of delicate and unstable character, something of a lost soul who impulsively went into seclusion as the result of a personal crisis; upon hearing his name mentioned in connection with the purloined pro Russia papers, he stayed underground out of fright.[62] For what it is worth, the Polish diplomats in Moscow and at the Vatican concluded on the basis of their own inquiries that Deubner was no Soviet spy.[63] The fugitive eventually resurfaced in Rome in July 1933 and reported to d'Herbigny, who sent him off to a monastery for temporary safekeeping. By that time Deubner's misadventure had cost his chief dearly. The bad publicity had sullied the reputation of the Commissio pro Russia and tarnished d'Herbigny himself. The incident almost surely denied him the cardinalate Pius XI had been expected to confer upon him that same year and emboldened the growing company of his detractors inside the Vatican and out.[64]

The Deubner affair had weakened d'Herbigny and shaken though not yet shattered the trust of Pius XI in his favorite, but the final ruination of the French Jesuit who personified the Roman pursuit of the Orthodox was near at hand. During his term of eminence as the pope's indispensable lieutenant, d'Herbigny had run up a long list of enemies. His abundant talents were rendered less attractive by an overbearing conceit, an unnerving relish for intrigue, and a shortage of prudent judgment. In addition to the notorious friction between him and Poland, the government of Italy had its own reasons to dislike the suzerain of the pro Russia. Within the walls of the Vatican Palace, he rubbed many colleagues the wrong way by trading on his familiarity with Pius XI and, so they suspected, passing off his own opinions and ideas as those of the pontiff himself for his own advantage.[65]

Most unfortunately for d'Herbigny, his brashness and incaution lost him the support and protection of the leadership of his own Society of Jesus. When d'Herbigny was riding high and Polish envoys to the Vatican searched high and low for ways to hold him in check, they recognized that the one chink in his armor of impregnability was his belonging to an order that bound him with vows of obedience, and on occasion they managed to gain some limited leverage on the pro Russia by making use of sympathetic Polish Jesuit contacts.[66] Of course, in those days a Pole still commanded the Jesuits, and over time d'Herbigny got on the wrong side of his superior, Father General Ledóchowski. It has been said, and may well be true, that Ledóchowski came to resent his younger subordinate's ambition, his taste for the spotlight, and his direct access to the ear of the pope, but he also had weightier motives than jealousy for wanting to bring d'Herbigny to heel.[67] As head of the Jesuits, Ledóchowski originally had approved the decision to launch the neounion rite in his native Poland and to embark upon the conversion of the Orthodox of eastern Europe and the Soviet Union as a missionary endeavor of his order.[68] But the passage of time demonstrated ever more plainly that the audacious design of d'Herbigny to plant the seeds of a future Catholic Russia in conspiratorial fashion under the noses of the Bolsheviks had ended as a fiasco. The Soviet authorities had caught on to his catacomb church at once, and as the newly consolidated Stalin regime redoubled the Communist war on religion, its clergy were systematically subjected to harassment, arrest, or worse. The very fact that the rout of Catholicism in the country was so thorough had accounted for the deduction of the Polish envoys on the scene that Alexander Deubner had not been a GPU agent: Moscow already knew all there was to know about the workings of the pro Russia, and there was no more Russian Church left to roll up.[69] Not only had d'Herbigny gambled and failed in Russia, at enormous cost, but as a Polish patriot Ledóchowski swung over to the view that the neounion, and the method of its implementation in the kresy, was doing more harm than good in the land of his birth. By the time of the founding of the Russicum toward the end of the 1920s, he told the pope frankly that he did not have high hopes for the success of the Russian venture in the near future and that he would prefer that the task not be assigned to his order.[70] According to most accounts, by the end of 1931 the Jesuit general began a whispering campaign in the Vatican corridors to urge and arrange the deposition of Bishop d'Herbigny.[71]

The downfall of d'Herbigny followed hard on the heels of the Deubner scandal and brought him not only demotion but disgrace. To this day the circumstances of his abrupt dismissal remain obscure and disputed, giving rise to speculation that some grave moral offense or bungled freelance Russian faux pas might have been the last straw that broke the patience of Pius XI.[72] There was also, as we have seen, no shortage of plausible candidates for identification as the individual or capital responsible for slipping the knife into d'Herbigny's back. Still, many suspected the hand of higher-ups in the Polish political or ecclesiastical sphere, or some combination of the two. One theory is that in September 1933 Ledóchowski approached the pope—possibly at the instance of Marshal Piłsudski, or speaking on behalf of a once-again fed-up Polish episcopate—and persuaded him that it was time for d'Herbigny to go. At that point, Pius informed the mystified director of pro Russia that it was the will of the father general that he should be sent to Brussels for medical treatment. Once d'Herbigny arrived in Belgium, Ledóchowski ordered him to resign from all of his Vatican duties.[73] While the historical record cannot confirm this scenario in all its details, in broad outline it probably comes reasonably close to the truth. Certainly when the news of his exile became known in 1934, most observers, including d'Herbigny himself, took for granted that maneuvers of Polish origin lay at the bottom of it.[74] At any rate, Michel d'Herbigny would be afforded ample time to ponder the causes of the flameout of his meteoric Roman career as he lived out the remainder of his days in the obscurity of Jesuit residences until his death in 1957.

The sacking of d'Herbigny did not mean that Pius XI had lost any of his ardor for the conversion of Russia; to the contrary, the fundamental explanation of the dismissal of the Frenchman, minus its sensational aspects, may simply be that at the time he was fired the eastern policy he had conceived and overseen lay in shambles. After ten years the neounion Byzantine-Slavonic rite had won no more than thirty thousand adherents in eastern Poland, at the cost of affronting the government of the country and pushing its Catholic episcopate near to rebellion. In Russia d'Herbigny's rash throw of the dice to push for an immediate restoration of the Church in anticipation of a quick dissolution of the Communist regime resulted in disaster. By the mid- to later thirties, as the Stalin terror neared its peak, the secret hierarchy set in place by d'Herbigny had been annihilated, and only two Catholic priests remained at liberty in the USSR, down from two hundred in 1924.[75] The Polish Jesuit General Ledóchowski now took greater control over the missionary efforts of his order among the Orthodox, steering them along more cautious lines. In 1937 he told the Polish-American novice Walter Ciszek that the time was not right to send priests into Russia: instead, he assigned the eager young volunteer for Russian duty to put in a few years at Albertyn, safely on the Polish side of the frontier, and await a more opportune moment to fish for Russian souls.[76]

The disappearance of d'Herbigny also led straight to the emasculation of the Vatican office that had been created for him to carry out his now-shipwrecked design for converting the Orthodox, and to a general reorganization of the neounion project. After having functioned autonomously since 1930 as the bailiwick of d'Herbigny, the Commissio pro Russia was subordinated to the Secretariat of State in December 1934 and its competency limited to Latin Catholics in Russia. Meanwhile, the Congregation for Eastern Churches took over responsibility for the Byzantine-Slavonic rite. In effect, Poland had seen the last of pro Russia activities within its boundaries. The Vatican took these steps at least in part to satisfy what it thought were the Polish objections to the procedures of the d'Herbigny years, but soon discovered, to its surprise and annoyance, that there seemed to be no pleasing the Poles on this subject. Polish representatives tartly expressed their lack of confidence in the Eastern Churches bureau as well, based on their unhappy experiences of its supervision of the Ukrainian Greek Catholics, and contended that the central issue was whether basic decisions on religious policy in their country would be made in Rome, or in Warsaw where they belonged.[77]

None deterred, the papacy stuck to its guns and resolved to push ahead with the neounion experiment in the Polish east. The last nuncio of the interwar era reported to duty in Warsaw bearing instructions to revive the faltering project. The new rite would have made more progress, the Vatican reasoned, but for the opposition of the Polish government and its misguided unwillingness to help convert the Orthodox, the lukewarm reaction of the Latin clergy of Poland, and the daunting expenses of the missionary work. Still, despite these obstacles, the new rite remained a high priority of the pope, who wanted his emissary to press the Second Republic to see the light and bring its policies into line with the evangelistic imperatives of the Church.[78]

In response, the Polish government of the later 1930s, managed by the uninspired inheritors of the deceased Józef Piłsudski, whose unlikely friendship with Pius XI had smoothed over the rough patches in relations with the Holy See, threw up its hands and elected to go its own way in dealing with the Orthodox of the kresy, whether the pope liked it or not. Poland had its fill of trying to humor what it saw as the Vatican's fruitless and injurious pipedream of converting the Orthodox to Uniatism, scorning it as "the illusion of Rome."[79] From now on, Warsaw would revert to the two-track policy it had always preferred and resolve to make it stick: it would continue to patronize its lapdog national autocephalous Orthodox church and was prepared to assist conversion of Belorussians and Ukrainians to Western-rite Catholicism, but would drop all pretense of cooperation with the East Slav neounion.[80]

Having asserted a free hand in handling Orthodox questions, Poland went on to demonstrate that, with the assistance of the Polish Church, it was perfectly capable of being as clumsy and incompetent in this field as Michel d'Herbigny had been. The approach it regarded as more realistic than the Vatican's was no less delusional, and was incoherent and self-contradictory to boot: if the previous decade and a half had not done enough to estrange the Orthodox inhabitants of eastern Poland from their government for good, the series of botches committed by Warsaw in the last two years more than sufficed to finish the job. First, it agreed to a settlement in the long-simmering dispute over the disposition of contested church properties that did little to satisfy the Orthodox that they had received their fair share. After being tied up in a protracted limbo of litigation, the issue returned to the political realm when the Polish supreme court ruled in 1934 that it was properly not a matter of law, but of direct negotiation between the Republic and the Catholic Church. Forced to come to grips with an interconfessional quarrel its instincts had correctly warned it to shun as long as possible, Poland reluctantly entered into on-again, off-again talks with Cardinal Hlond and the papal nuncio. The parties reached a deal in June 1938 on terms that even some Catholic voices from abroad criticized as unreasonably tilted against the Orthodox Ukrainians of southeastern Poland. The Catholics gained title to all properties in their de facto possession, including those appropriated in vigilante style after the First World War, and withdrew most of their other claims in return for compensation, while Warsaw pledged to begin granting them unused Orthodox buildings currently held by the state.[81]

To make matters worse, the ink barely had dried on the accord before many of the Orthodox structures slated for handover to the Catholics were set ablaze by the Polish army.[82] In 1938 Poland sent military units in to "pacify" Ukrainian unrest in East Galicia, resulting in the destruction of the majority of Orthodox churches and chapels in the region. At the same time, the Catholic Church authorities in Poland, with state encouragement, began efforts to recruit conversions of both Orthodox and Uniates into the Latin Catholic rite, in flat contradiction of longstanding Vatican directives.[83]

This combination of affronts, following in quick succession, provoked a storm of Ukrainian outrage. The Greek Catholic archbishop Sheptyts'kyi, raising his voice on behalf of Orthodox Ukrainians, condemned the wave of church burnings and warned against the use of pressure tactics to drum up converts to Western-rite Catholicism as both unjust and harmful to the goal of religious reunion. Ukrainian deputies in the Sejm levied charges of persecution, including allegations of compulsory conversions in the countryside. Spokesmen for the sanacja regime and the Polish Church shot back with heated denials of wrongdoing, stressing the need to put down sedition in Galicia, and the rightist press added fuel to the church fires by congratulating officialdom for having set the torch to "130 dens of Ukrainianism."[84]

As its hopes to secure the loyalty of its Orthodox Ukrainian and Belorussian populace literally went up in smoke in Galicia, Warsaw engaged in one last sterile round of bickering with the Vatican over the Byzantine-Slavonic neounion. The two sides exchanged grievances along familiar and by now predictable lines, the papal nuncio to the country imploring the Poles not to put roadblocks in the path of the East Slav rite and hearing in rejoinder complaints that the "union was a misfortune for Poland."[85] The Vatican scapegoated the departed d'Herbigny for any and all past defects in the neounion in particular or eastern evangelization activities in general, and assured Poland that from now on nothing important would be decided or done without checking with Jesuit General Ledóchowski.[86] But so far as the governors of the Second Republic were concerned, it did not matter who ran the policy if the policy was simply wrongheaded and unacceptable. Almost plaintively, Warsaw pointed out that in the past fifteen years, one quarter million Polish Orthodox had adopted Latin Catholicism, ten times the number that had rallied to the Uniate Slavonic rite; why on earth would the Vatican not draw the proper conclusion of arithmetic and history?[87] To Foreign Minister Józef Beck, a jaundiced observer, the answer was that the lure of Russia possessed a unique, age-old power to entrance and befuddle the Vatican, shown in its stubborn commitment to a method —conversion via the Uniate rites—"thanks to which it has not reached Russia but only weakened the Polish state and Catholic life in Poland and confused the Church in Poland."[88] One could only wonder if and when Rome would recognize its mistake. "In the eyes of the Church, a century is not a long time," Beck noted in characteristically acid tone, "but three centuries must count for something."

In the end Poland managed to outlast the Vatican in its prolonged test of wills over the future of Christianity in east Europe when Pius XI died in February 1939. The pope who had entered the rarefied circles of his Church on the heels of his nunciature in Warsaw had been the creator and guardian of the Byzantine-Slavonic rite and the champion of its use as the key to unlock the Polish borderlands and ultimately Russia to Catholicism. The Poles wasted no time sounding out his presumptive successor, Cardinal Pacelli, about his views on the matter, and after his election quickly concluded that they would find him much easier to work with on eastern matters than his iron-willed predecessor.[89] In May the Vatican showed a flash of its old fire when it threatened sanctions against any Polish cleric found to be pushing Uniates into the Latin observance, but by summertime the Polish ambassador felt secure in predicting that the pontificate of Pius XII would relegate the troublesome neounion to a much lower level of priority.[90]

Of course, the eruption of the Second World War soon overpowered all other concerns and presented both Poland and the Vatican with far more pressing and desperate preoccupations than their running disagreement over the Eastern rites. Looking back over the previous twenty years, neither could claim to have succeeded in its approach to the Orthodox. The Second Republic had hoped to win the allegiance of the Orthodox of its kresy, and failed dismally; the Holy See had hoped to enlist them en masse into the Catholic neounion, but no more than twenty-five thousand souls rallied to the new rite, and atheist Communism still held Russia in its harsh grip. In 1941, writing from wartime exile in London, the Polish journalist-politician Stanisław Cat-Mackiewicz lamented that "nothing more plainly convinced me of the immaturity of the men who governed Poland than the issue of the Orthodox Church." The Orthodox inhabitants of the east, he said, might easily have been made into reliable citizens with anything like proper handling. "The loyalty of the Orthodox was so great and sincere that only a miracle could have turned the Orthodox clergy away from that path. This miracle appeared in the form of the stupidity of our rulers."[91] For his part, in 1942 and 1952, in separate acts ten years apart, Pope Pius XII consecrated first the world and then the people of Russia to the Immaculate Heart of Mary, carrying out the request of the last surviving visionary of Fatima, who declared this the wish of Jesus Christ. The conversion of Russia to Catholicism, so recently seen as near at hand, had become once more a matter not of policy but of prayer.

8 | Post Mortem

Piłsudski Lies Uneasy in the Grave

WHEN MARSHAL JÓZEF PIŁSUDSKI DIED on May 12, 1935, the ninth anniversary of his rebellion that had brought him to power, the life also went out of the Polish regime that had based its claim to legitimacy on the mortal foundations of his personal authority and leadership. During the few years of peace left to the Second Republic, the mediocrities who ruled Poland as his political inheritors tried but failed to fill the shoes of their departed hero as the country slid toward dictatorship and disastrous war. Bereft of its animating chieftain, the sanacja government, which had depended on the living Piłsudski, now came to depend on Piłsudski dead, making him the object of a cultlike devotion. His passing likewise reopened the question of the relationship of church and state in Poland. While scarcely the most devout of Catholics, Piłsudski had made a point of keeping peace with the confession that was a national institution; his presence had provided a guarantee of something like official good behavior toward the Church and checked the visceral anticlerical instincts of his followers. Now that he was gone, the terms of the uneasy coexistence of Catholicism and the Second Republic went up for grabs again. The result was an unstable and anxious fluctuation between harmony and tension, ultimately traceable to a twofold question: was the Church showing due respect for the memory of Marshal Piłsudski, and would it support the sanacja regency, which saw itself as his faithful executor? In this setting, it was symbolically fitting that the fragile church-state accord that had prevailed in interwar Poland for nearly two decades almost fell to pieces under the stress of a brief but intense public storm over the proper repose of the bones of Józef Piłsudski himself.

Upon learning of the death of Marshal Piłsudski, Prince Adam Stefan Sapieha, the archbishop of Kraków, telephoned the offices of Cardinal Kakowski of Warsaw to ask whether the deceased had departed this world reconciled with God—not an idle question, given the Polish strongman's disputable attachment to Catholicism. Sapieha was informed that Piłsudski would receive a Catholic funeral in the capital. The next day Kakowski returned the call to urge Sapieha to grant a request soon to be delivered to him in the name of the president of the republic: that he permit the interment of Piłsudski within the crypts of his own venerable Royal Cathedral of Sts. Wacław and Stanisław on Wawel Hill in Kraków, the national pantheon of Poland.[1]

Sapieha had expected this very petition from the government, though not gladly. In fact, Kakowski had warned the bereaved sanacja courtiers that they might encounter resistance from the doughty aristocrat, who was widely recognized as one of the foremost opponents of Piłsudski within the Polish hierarchy.[2] While the prince-bishop of Kraków and the first marshal of Poland had been longtime, though mutually respectful, antagonists, Sapieha's objections had nothing to do with personal animosity, but arose from his prickly sense of responsibility as caretaker of Wawel and its illustrious catacomb. In 1927 Warsaw had proposed the reburial in the cathedral of Piłsudski's favorite poet, the renowned nineteenth-century bard Juliusz Słowacki. Sapieha had given grudging consent, with the stipulation that the decision was his to make and that from now on the royal crypts were to be considered closed.[3] Still, Sapieha knew that he would be asked to make an exception to his rule for the man officially regarded as the founding father of the Second Republic. Indeed, in 1933 Piłsudski had toured the Wawel sepulchers and told Sapieha of his wish to be entombed there.[4] Now that the time had come, Sapieha might have found plausible reasons to refuse posthumous entry to the marshal. The not-inconsiderable forces of the Polish political opposition might—and, in fact, did—take offense at the prospect of the admission of their old adversary into the shrine reserved for the greatest sons and daughters of Poland. Further, he had a written pledge from Piłsudski himself that Słowacki would be the last luminary interred in the cathedral recesses. All the same, Sapieha required no arm-twisting before deciding to honor the presidential request. By his lights, Piłsudski had not been much of a Catholic, and his career not without blemish, but he had rendered honorable service to the nation, and a solid majority of his compatriots would regard him as worthy of a resting place in Wawel.[5]

The Church lent the dignity of its imprimatur to the lavish obsequies orchestrated for Piłsudski. The primate, Cardinal Hlond of Gniezno-

Poznań, praised him as the rescuer of Christendom from Bolshevism by dint of his victory at the gates of Warsaw in 1920, and called for solemn observances in every parish in the country.[6] Cardinal Kakowski officiated at the state funeral mass at the capital's St. John Cathedral on May 17. The next day a train bore the flag draped coffin to Kraków. A dutiful if reluctant principal in the ceremonies, Archbishop Sapieha led the cortège through the streets of the old city to Wawel Hill. There he conducted one last liturgy in the cathedral and presided over the commendation of the body of Józef Piłsudski to its repose in St. Leonard's crypt beneath the nave of the structure.

Some of the foes of sanacja and its late commander, lay and clerical alike, found the extensive involvement of the Church in the official mourning hard to stomach. They muttered that the participating prelates had shown hypocrisy by bestowing fulsome blessings on Piłsudski and pretending that he had lived a Christian life, or died a Christian death.[7] Such charges may well have contained a measure of jaundiced truth, but the same could not be said of Pope Pius XI, who felt genuine sorrow at the news of the passing of the sometime socialist and apostate he had come to esteem both as a European soldier-statesman of historic merit and, on a human level, as a friend. In an audience that summer with the Polish ambassador, the pope tapped a finger to his head, saying, "One would have to be not quite right here not to understand how great a loss was the death of the Marshal," and he continued to volunteer private affectionate tributes of this sort to Piłsudski on a regular basis for the remaining three years of his life.[8] Not all within the Vatican apparatus retained such benign memories of the departed. An internal assessment of the Secretariat of State duly noted Piłsudski's "entirely personal" respect for Pius XI, but sniffed that his regime had been like the man himself, "crude and violent and utterly lacking in religious or civic culture": his rule of Poland had not been good for Catholicism in that country, on balance, and better things should be expected of his successors.[9]

While most observers agreed that Piłsudski had left the scene with church-state relations in Poland in reasonably good repair, his departure left open the question of the future direction of the government in this, as well as other matters of policy.[10] The reigning sanacja had been a loose coalition held together by the person of the marshal, and in his absence it fragmented into factions vying for leadership of the movement. At heart it was anticlerical, a tendency Piłsudski had managed to temper. Fearing the worst, Archbishop Teodorowicz predicted darkly that the orphaned regime now would resort to "terror," cracking the whip to hold the Church in line.[11] As it happened, the early advantage in the jockeying within the ruling elite went to a group headed by President Ignacy Mościcki and General Edward Rydz-Śmigły, who challenged the predominance of the inner circle of Piłsudski cronies. Among other things, Mościcki and Rydz-Śmigły hoped to court the Church and enlist it as an ally of their government, going against the grain of the Piłsudskiite rank and file. Despite the shifting balance of power inside sanacja, diplomacy remained the bailiwick of one of the old guard, Colonel Józef Beck, a longtime favorite of Piłsudski, who in 1932 had installed his younger protégé into the post of foreign minister, for which he had been groomed. Beck took personal charge over relations with the Holy See. Intent on increasing the leverage of the Second Republic over the Church without going so far as to provoke a "Kulturkampf in Poland," as he put it a bit ominously, Beck preferred to shorten the typical chain of bureaucratic communication by dealing one-on-one with the papal nuncio to work out issues as they arose.[12] This was not necessarily an improvement so far as the Vatican was concerned, for neither Pius XI nor Cardinal Secretary of State Pacelli found much to like in Beck or his policies. The foreign minister was a Protestant, and as the future would show, it did not require much to bring to the surface his barely submerged antagonism toward the Catholic Church or its dignitaries. However, the pope took some reassurance from the knowledge that Beck had been the trainee of Piłsudski, and hoped that the influence of the mentor had rubbed off on his apprentice.[13] Within Poland itself, the Catholic episcopate as well, though still wary, soon came to understand to its relief that the successors of Piłsudski were not bent on picking fights with the Church.[14]

Even so, old habits of mutual suspicion persisted, so fights did not take long to break out. As an indication of things to come, the first of them grew out of the ruling clique's touchy sense of protectiveness toward the memory of Marshal Piłsudski. Partly out of conviction, partly because it could think of no better idea to justify its continued existence, sanacja cultivated a veneration of the dead man that was hyperbolic to the verge of morbidity, and reacted with special indignation to any slights against his good name coming from the direction of the pulpit. During the time of the death and funeral, the government had kept a sharp lookout for evidence of disrespect within the Catholic hierarchy, and took umbrage at the openly insulting demeanor of Bishop Augustyn Łosiński of Kielce. Łosiński had ordered clergy and religious of his diocese not to pay respects to the

Piłsudski funeral train as it stopped at Kielce, and forbade the ringing of church bells on that occasion. Infuriated, Warsaw determined to make an example of him. The marshal had been in his grave scarcely two weeks before the Polish ambassador to the Holy See, acting on the instructions of Colonel Beck, presented Cardinal Pacelli with a demand for the summary removal of Bishop Łosiński.[15]

This sort of thing had happened often enough in the past so that by now it followed a script that was predictable, practically routinized. The Poles would state their angry case; the Vatican would offer to appease the Polish unhappiness in some way that would not baldly violate the principle that ordinaries should not be fired on political grounds; and there it would end. Even in the exceptional and awkward instance of Bishop Matulewicz in Vilna, a graceful, face-saving accommodation was worked out. But this time was different. Poland went on the hunt for Łosiński for months with dogged single-mindedness, refused to accept any compromise that stopped short of humiliating both the bishop and the Holy See, and for good measure insisted that only a settlement of this single issue on its own nonnegotiable terms could prevent a breakdown of church-state relations. While no one at the Vatican seemed eager to deny that the ordinary of Kielce had behaved badly, neither did any of them take kindly to ultimata and threats.

After its initial complaints about Łosiński drew no more than the standard perfunctory response, Warsaw decided to show that it meant business. The Foreign Ministry tried applying raw pressure to the papal nuncio, Francesco Marmaggi, sizing him up as a timid soul who might permit himself to be pushed around rather than risk unpleasantness that could derail his expected appointment as cardinal. Accordingly, Beck and his deputy obtained interviews with the unsuspecting Marmaggi and used them as occasions to bully him about Łosiński. They rejected out of hand his placatory suggestions that they try to meet halfway or that they simply allow nature to take its course with the aging and ill bishop of Kielce. Marmaggi diplomatically expressed his eagerness for further conversations with his Polish counterparts, but considering the surly tone of the grilling he had just endured, he cannot have meant it.[16]

When leaning on Marmaggi did not produce the desired ouster of Łosiński, the Polish representatives at the Vatican took turns hectoring both Pacelli and the pope into the autumn, even after Pius made clear that he had heard all he cared to hear from them.[17] Rome attempted to solve the problem in December 1935 by appointing an auxiliary for Kielce, a classic means of enabling an aggrieved government to avoid dealing with an *episcopus non gratus,* but the gesture failed to satisfy the Poles, who would settle for nothing less than Łosiński's head. As the impasse dragged on into the next year, the cabinet of Prime Minister Marian Zyndram-Kościałkowski came close to deciding to withhold payment of state subsidies to the Kielce diocese, in open violation of the concordat, but held off for fear that the Vatican would retaliate by mobilizing the Polish clergy to take its side against the regime.[18]

In March 1936 Warsaw took out its frustrations on the freshly minted Cardinal Marmaggi, now winding up his stint as nuncio and packing his bags to return to Rome to close out his career. He paid a farewell call on a Polish Foreign Ministry official to review the status of religious affairs in the country. If he was expecting an agreeable good-bye, he soon found out otherwise. Not mincing words, the functionary said that church-state relations were not good, that they would not be good so long as Łosiński remained in Kielce, and that unless Marmaggi could conjure up a solution satisfactory to Poland before his departure, the result would be the "complete failure" of his nunciature.[19] But the Vatican had the last word. Three weeks later Cardinal Pacelli declared the topic closed once and for all, telling the Polish ambassador that under no circumstances would the pope cashier Łosiński.[20] What he might have added, but did not, was that by electing to badger Pius and back him into a corner, the Poles had all but guaranteed that he would do the opposite of what they wanted.

The drawn-out quarrel over Bishop Łosiński both reflected and fed a growing suspicion among sanacja adherents that the Polish Church was shifting toward resumption of its old tacit alliance with their rightist National Democrat opponents that had gone on hiatus during the Piłsudski decade. After its prolonged exile in the political wilderness, once its old nemesis the marshal had passed into history, the Endecja emerged with renewed vitality and gained visibly in public appeal at the expense of the ruling party. For one thing, the Endeks caught the wave that lifted the fortunes of the Right in much of Europe, and adroitly borrowed bits and pieces from the vocabulary and substance of fascism. For another, the National Democrats at least had the advantage of standing for identifiable ideas and positions at a time when sanacja had become no more than the party that had been the party of Piłsudski, now without Piłsudski and without a clear message or direction. What is more, this "new" Endecja of the thirties now presented itself squarely as a movement of Catholic character, completing the gradual makeover that had discarded its original heritage of anticlericalism and elevation of nation over Christian scruple. In particular, the younger generation of Endek activists identified themselves as both nationalists and Catholics with equal fervor, claimed to draw programmatic inspiration from the social encyclicals of the Church, and supplied Catholic Action with much of its manpower and energy. As if to symbolize the latter-day baptism of National Democracy, its founding elder, Roman Dmowski, nearing the end of a hitherto unchurched life, received his first communion in 1937.[21] These overtures from the Right made a favorable impression in many Catholic circles and convinced much of the sanacja rank and file that the Church they had always regarded, deep down, as an enemy now was showing its true colors. Cardinal Hlond himself, it was said, was quietly encouraging clerical backing for the Endecja from the top of the hierarchy.[22] By the end of 1936, the mounting partisan tension over the influence of the Church in Polish public life spilled over into back-and-forth ill-tempered name-calling in the press, one side accusing the clergy of cozying up to fascists, the other complaining of a Masonic cabal at the helm in Warsaw.[23]

While an angry anticlerical mood gathered within the excitable base of the Piłsudskiite party, its more cautious leadership still wanted to make Catholicism work for it, not against it. Responding to the signs that the Polish episcopate might be swinging over to the National Democrats, the alliance of President Mościcki and Marshal Rydz-Śmigły at the apex of the regime looked for a way to pull the pendulum back in its direction. Recognizing its weakness, the government made a showy to-do of appearing to rejuvenate itself by repackaging the stale coalition and trying to expand the range of its support, including the extension of an offer of partnership to the Church. This formed part of a broader strategic maneuver by sanacja in its decrepitude to tack rightward in hopes of stealing the thunder of the resurgent Endeks. In 1936 Rydz-Śmigły had authorized Colonel Adam Koc to redesign the Piłsudski political vehicle along the lines of the "patriotic fronts" introduced elsewhere in Europe, which aped but did not duplicate fascism. In February 1937, after months of preparation, Koc announced the formation of the Camp of National Unity (OZN), intended to "consolidate all the constructive forces of the nation," among them the Church that millions of Poles considered a pillar of their identity. The OZN platform stopped short of declaring Catholicism the official religion of the land, as some had anticipated during the prolonged buildup to its unveiling, but its flattery of the Church as an indispensable patriotic institution on a par with the army went far beyond any precedent in the Piłsudskiite annals.[24] Long on bloated rhetoric but short on specifics, the OZN project yielded meager results in spite of the strenuous labors of official propagandists to gin up enthusiasm. Rightist opinion saw through the stunt, recognizing it as a pale imitation of the genuine Endek article. For its part, the Polish episcopate politely but plainly turned down the invitation to align itself with OZN, not wishing to forfeit its independence by accepting the partisan embrace of sanacja.[25] Courted by government and opposition alike, the Catholic hierarchy preferred to avoid becoming the captive of either, a posture that made sense in pragmatic terms as well as principle.

Even though the bishops chose to steer clear of OZN, on the whole the Polish Church and the regime seemed to be getting on better with one another than at any time since the death of Piłsudski. One nagging source of discord was removed by the definitive resolution of the Kielce dispute, which, as Cardinal Marmaggi put it, "the Lord settled" through the death of Bishop Łosiński in March 1937.[26] Warsaw also took note of a recent tendency of both the Vatican and the episcopate to give the government plaudits for its strong stand against Bolshevism, as well as the unquestioned affection of Pius XI for Poland, and concluded that, apart from minor irritations, its strategy of strengthening ties with the Church was starting to pay off.[27] Marmaggi was ending his tour of duty as nuncio to the Second Republic, and Pius offered the post to Archbishop Roncalli, but the future John XXIII declined; as his second choice the pope turned to Archbishop Filippo Cortesi, a seasoned Sicilian diplomat whose appointment to Spain had fallen through with the outbreak of civil war. Cortesi pleaded with the pontiff to let this Polish cup pass from him—both the temperature and the tongue of the country would be too much for him, he said—but in the end he assented.[28] The Secretariat of State encouraged the reluctant appointee with optimistic instructions that the post-Piłsudski leadership of sanacja was trying harder than the late marshal to show a friendly approach to Catholicism and that his mission was to cultivate the good intentions of Rydz-Śmigły and his allies.[29] Upon arrival in Warsaw in May 1937, Cortesi met with President Mościcki, who assured him that church-state relations were on solid footing, troubled only by occasional "misunderstandings"; following up, the deputy foreign minister advised the nuncio that he would do well to ignore the loudmouthed oppositionist contingent among the lower clergy, but that the government had few complaints anymore about the bishops.[30] One of them, Prince Adam Sapieha, had just received the most prestigious decoration of the state to mark his completion of twenty-five years of service as ordinary of Kraków. As if to confirm the growing sense of cooperation, that same month Poles in Rome held a requiem mass for Józef Piłsudski on the second anniversary of his death, attended by Cardinal Hlond and the Polish ambassadors to Italy and the Holy See.[31]

This interlude of rapprochement was fleeting, for a month later the on-again, off-again truce between the Catholic Church and the sanacja regime came close to breaking down for good in a bitter and noisy wrangle that broke out at their most sensitive and symbolically potent meeting point: the tomb of the same Marshal Piłsudski in Wawel Cathedral. The uproar took the country by surprise, but it had been building quietly out of public view for two years. From the moment Piłsudski had been laid to rest within the bowels of Wawel, his grave site had become a magnet for thousands of pilgrims. These throngs were not always notable for religious decorum nor always well behaved, and at its worst the press of crowding and clutter could make the interior of the church seem more like a marketplace than a historic house of worship. Archbishop Sapieha did not take long to decide that the commotion inside Wawel could not go on. Before Piłsudski was two months dead, Sapieha began telling the sanacja authorities that St. Leonard's crypt could not hold the numbers trooping in to pay tribute to their founder and that the only solution was to move the sarcophagus to another location inside the building to divert traffic and reduce the racket to bearable levels. By the end of 1935, Warsaw had accepted his proposal that a private sepulcher for Piłsudski might be constructed beneath the adjoining Tower of the Silver Bells, where a separate outside entrance would afford his devotees access to the tomb without the need to go through the cathedral proper.[32]

The government set up a committee to oversee the preparation of the Silver Bells burial chamber, but being a government committee, it addressed its task too slowly to suit a testy archbishop anxious to return his church to normal. Hindered by artistic disagreements between the political appointees and their hired architect, Adolf Szyszko-Bohusz, the project dragged on into springtime of 1937. Prodded to speed its labors to completion, the panel said it would need yet more time to put the finishing touches on the elaborate design it had chosen. Unimpressed by its taste for the ornate, Sapieha fumed that the board seemed to have forgotten that it was building a tomb, not a boudoir. By now the delays and snags had exhausted the prince-bishop's limited reserves of patience. Worse, they persuaded him that the true, hidden preference of Polish officialdom was that the Piłsudski shrine should remain where it was, in its original St. Leonard's niche, meaning the permanent disruption of the sacred dignity of the cathedral. At that point fate intervened in the form of Szyszko-Bohusz, speaking on his own without the knowledge or authorization of his bosses on the commission, who told Sapieha that the Silver Bells crypt was ready for occupation.[33] Hearing this, the archbishop made up his mind to force the issue and proceeded to impose his fiat with a breathtaking absence of tact. After inspecting the new grave site himself, Sapieha matter-of-factly informed the memorial committee on June 17 that he would order and carry out the long-postponed transfer of Piłsudski's casket into its Silver Bells site within the next few days, standing on his customary prerogative and responsibility as custodian of Wawel. The startled board objected, but Sapieha paid it no heed. Stymied, the commission sought hurried rescue from President Mościcki, who respectfully asked the bishop to stay his hand, but to no avail. Sapieha tartly turned him down, insisting that the move must take place immediately and adding for good measure that the dampness of the St. Leonard's vault was taking a toll on the integrity of Piłsudski's corpse.[34] As word of the archbishop's intention spread within the small circle privy to the matter, he turned a deaf ear to urgent counsels that he had embarked upon a perilous course and would do well to turn back. Having unwittingly set the chain of events in motion, the mortuary architect Szyszko-Bohusz warned Sapieha that relocating Piłsudski's casket without state sanction would open the door to "countless difficulties."[35] On June 23 the papal nuncio, Archbishop Cortesi, just completing his first month on assignment in Poland, made a last-minute appeal to the ordinary of Kraków to bow to the presidential request, both to show due regard for civil authority and to shield the Church from unnecessary trouble.[36] Sapieha would not be moved. That very night he had the sarcophagus transported without ceremony into the Silver Bells tower, giving only post facto notice to the Piłsudski family.

So far as Archbishop Sapieha was concerned, he had done no more than exercise his right and duty as caretaker and guardian of Wawel Cathedral and its royal tombs, and he had no inkling that what he regarded as a clear-cut issue of internal housekeeping would bring a wave of official and public wrath down upon him and threaten a rupture between his government and his Church. Only a select few knew, or cared, about the complicated twists and turns of the Piłsudski burial arrangements or the niceties of jurisdiction: as the world saw it, what counted was that a churchman notorious as an opponent of Piłsudski, with no warning and for no apparent reason, had chosen to deliver a gratuitous affront to his mortal remains and to the leaders of the republic that had beseeched him not to tamper with its holy of holies. What is more, since the public was unaware of the plans for eventual transfer of Piłsudski's remains into the Silver Bells tower, many drew the conclusion that Sapieha was pursuing a personal vendetta against the dead man by banishing his bones from the cathedral.

In short, Sapieha had managed to insult, or appear to insult, the Piłsudskiite camp on both sides of the divide between this world and the next, and the regime and its legions exploded in an outcry of anger that was genuine, if not free of histrionic excess. The very next day, the premier, General Felicjan Sławoj-Składkowski, tendered his resignation on the theatrical grounds that the midnight outrage in Kraków had occurred on his watch; President Mościcki declined the gesture, to no one's surprise. On a more serious level, Warsaw instantly decided that Sapieha could not be allowed to get away with thumbing his nose at the clearly voiced wishes of the state, on this of all subjects. Ironically, representatives of the ruling group recently had inspected the Silver Bells chamber, found it worthy, and likely would have agreed to the transfer had the archbishop approached them in more obliging spirit, but sanacja was not willing to swallow his fait accompli or excuse his flat rejection of a personal entreaty from the president of the republic to postpone the reinterment of the body.[37] While they were at it, neither were they inclined to concede the principle that Sapieha took as established fact, that he, and he alone, was curator of the Wawel graves and could administer them as he saw fit.[38] With these points on their agenda, Foreign Minister Beck and the Polish diplomats at the Vatican began talks with the Holy See on June 24, the day after Sapieha had carried out his unilateral decision.

At the same time, Polish governmental spokesmen announced the news from Wawel in tones of horror and indignation and drummed up a campaign of public vilification of the offending archbishop. Official newspapers expressed "profound disgust" at what they called an "unpardonable insult to the Polish nation," and speculated that Sapieha's serious illness with pneumonia must have addled his judgment. Meanwhile, the authorities confiscated or shut down papers sympathetic to the bishop. Across the country, military veterans' associations and other Piłsudskiite organizations staged rallies of protest against Sapieha, given benevolent cooperation from the police and generous publicity by the sanacja mouthpieces.[39]

These attacks fazed their target not at all. Writing to inform Cardinal Hlond that his health would prevent him from attending a bishops' conference, Sapieha relegated mention of the "completely laughable fuss" over the Wawel tombs to an airy afternote at the bottom of his letter: there was no reason for concern, and if newly arrived nuncio Cortesi thought otherwise, that was just his poor knowledge of Poland speaking.[40] But in fact it was Sapieha who had misread the situation, and before long the fracas threatened to spin out of control and do real political and diplomatic harm. In the first place, it injected an awkward complication into Poland's relations with an ally. At month's end the country would host a state visit from King Carol II of Romania. Not only was the royal traveler Orthodox, but he was so famously dissolute as to have incurred the ban of his own church. His notoriety as the "playboy king," especially his colorful liaison with Madame Magda Lupescu, provided abundant fodder for lurid tabloid headlines. As part of his itinerary, Carol wished to pay homage to Piłsudski at his tomb while touring Kraków on June 30. The circumstances naturally inspired gossip that Sapieha had rushed the transfer of Piłsudski's remains into the Silver Bells annex to avoid the indignity of having to receive the disreputable and non-Catholic monarch within his cathedral. The Vatican, as well as Polish governmental and ecclesiastical authorities, all scurried to deny these sensational whispers for the sake of appearance, but their problem was that the whispers were all too obviously true. With the brutal lack of subtlety that typified his approach to the entire Wawel affair, the prince-archbishop had made abundantly plain in his official correspondence that one reason he had set his abrupt deadline was to keep the presence of the "schismatic" sovereign from sullying the sacred confines that housed the relics of St. Stanisław. The timing alone spoke volumes, but Sapieha made sure no one could miss his point by issuing a transparent public statement that justified his action on the grounds that pilgrims "of other creeds" coming to honor Piłsudski no longer could be permitted to "disturb . . . the peace of the consecrated place." In the face of these unpromising omens, strenuous efforts at damage control got under way to salvage what could be salvaged from King Carol's suddenly scandal-imperiled Polish tour.[41]

On top of that, the more impassioned footsoldiers of the Piłsudskiite political armies, anticlerical to the core, showed signs of getting out of hand. The Wawel incident brought out into the open the emerging divide between the moderate sanacja leadership, which had sought to sweet-talk the episcopate and still wanted to settle the Sapieha matter neatly behind closed doors, and the Piłsudski true believers, whose ire against the Church had been mounting steadily for some time and who now saw their chance to settle old scores with the cloth. Having given these elements their signal to go on the attack through its own rhetorical assault against Sapieha, Warsaw now found itself hard-pressed to rein them in. Incensed protesters smashed the windows of the episcopal residence in Kraków on June 26, and might have done the same to the nuncio's palace in Warsaw had police not preemptively dispersed the converging crowd. In both cities rowdies sacked the offices of Catholic newspapers. In full cry, parliamentary backbenchers and journalistic cheerleaders for the government called variously for the offending prelate's removal, arrest, or exile. Others went further and threatened reprisals against the institution he represented, urging the nationalization of Wawel, declaration of "open war" with the Church, and the unilateral amendment or annulment of the concordat of 1925. With such hot-headed proposals in the air, the Sejm announced plans to convene an extraordinary session to deal with the emergency: the hazard now loomed that inflamed and unpredictable legislators would take the delicate construct of church-state relations into their rough hands.[42]

The cooler heads within the Polish government wanted no part of the drastic measures of street toughs and grandstanding parliamentarians, but the Foreign Ministry itself strayed into perilous territory by reverting to habit and directing its embassy at the Vatican to demand the ouster of Archbishop Sapieha from the Kraków see that had been his for a quarter century.[43] The entire affair came as an unwanted and unexpected headache for Stanisław Janikowski, the deputy chief of mission, who was minding the store during the untimely absence of Ambassador Skrzyński. On a personal level, Janikowski got along well with Sapieha, and so found himself in an uncomfortable position; more importantly, he saw nothing but trouble ahead if he tried to act on his instructions. Warsaw had tried to have bishops sacked before, but never so starkly in public. The Polish diplomats on the scene feared that their higher-ups had not carefully calculated the risks of adding fuel to this particular fire: the request might well inflame Pius XI, for all his long-standing animus toward the ordinary of Kraków and his abiding affection for the memory of Piłsudski, and likewise ignite the equally combustible Sapieha, with regrettable results. Janikowski reasoned that the situation called for a bit of judicious procrastination. Doing what Skrzyński had done on occasion in his place, he sat on his orders from the Ministry and waited for Warsaw to recover its temper.[44]

Through it all, the Polish clergy also opted for discretion. Though keeping silent in political debates was not their habit, this time they kept their heads low as the winds of controversy blew about them. While a gathering of delegates of Catholic organizations called on the faithful to rally behind Sapieha, the episcopate gave their beleaguered colleague no more than perfunctory support. The primate, Cardinal Hlond, stayed in the background during the fray, saying nothing for the record and trying to mediate behind the scenes.[45] In part, this collective reticence amounted to a natural defensive response to the sudden and fierce wave of attacks against the Church, but it also reflected a tacit admission that their brother bishop from Kraków had acted highhandedly and discourteously, even if technically within his rights, and so could not entirely escape reproach. Besides, the hierarchy had no choice but to defer to Rome, for all observers understood that a solution to the impasse depended on the intervention of the Holy See.

For its part, the Vatican agreed that Poland had solid grounds for complaint and assured the Poles that they would receive satisfaction and that this would include forcing Archbishop Sapieha to eat humble pie. Privately, the pope's men in the Secretariat of State pronounced themselves aghast. The sostituto, Giuseppe Cardinal Pizzardo, admitted to Janikowski that he could not explain Sapieha's conduct, "being unable to determine a priori that he has gone mad," and the two diplomats drafted a joint communiqué voicing strong disapproval of the "deplorable incidents" surrounding the furtive nocturnal migration of Piłsudski's corpse.[46] However, before the declaration could see the light of day, Pius XI decided to handle the matter in more understated fashion. With a hint of embarrassment, Cardinal Pacelli primly informed Janikowski that the pope had expressed "*quelques doutes*" regarding the comportment of the bishop of Kraków and had told the nuncio to Warsaw, Archbishop Cortesi, to see to it that things were put right.[47]

Not since the days Pope Ratti himself had spent in Poland had a nuncio to the Second Republic taken on a challenge equal to this one, and Archbishop Cortesi tackled the job with businesslike despatch. He understood that his superiors wanted him not just to straighten out the diplomatic disarray, but also to teach a "lesson" to Sapieha, an extra assignment he seems not to have minded, since it gave him the chance to exact some revenge for the bishop's condescending brushoff of his own advice to think twice before shifting the Piłsudski casket.[48] On June 28 Cortesi sent Sapieha summary notice that he would go to Kraków himself to take charge of the situation before it got any worse. He closed with the barbed assurance that although it was true that he had only newly arrived in Poland, as Archbishop Sapieha had been so quick to point out, he knew what he was doing.[49] His most pressing task was to devise a speedy and graceful way of enabling King Carol to pay his respects to Piłsudski with some shred of dignity. As it happened, Sapieha's pneumonia, while genuine enough, furnished a plausible occasion for the pope to appoint Cortesi to stand in as canon of Wawel during the resident archbishop's indisposition. This expedient of having Cortesi assume temporary command over the Metropolitanate of Kraków in turn put him in position to accept the convenient invitation of the government to act as host to the Romanian monarch as he saluted Piłsudski, neatly solving that problem. By shunting Sapieha into the background, it also cleared the way for the nuncio and Foreign Minister Beck to work out a satisfactory resolution of the Wawel imbroglio on their own.[50]

With the potential trainwreck of King Carol's visit averted, the negotiators could focus on settling the broader issues of the affair, and Warsaw and the Vatican together fashioned a deal both sides could live with. For Pius XI and Cardinal Pacelli, the key was to chasten and correct the bishop of Kraków without appearing to undercut his office. In their eyes, Sapieha's episcopal authority to shepherd his diocese required defense as an inviolable principle, but the prince-archbishop had committed a gross error of judgment and good manners; the Polish republic deserved an apology and promises that nothing of the sort would happen again. If the manner of making amends caused Sapieha personally to be taken down a peg, that would not distress the pope, who remembered this particular bishop as one of the plagues of his Polish nunciature.[51]

These terms suited Poland, which likewise wished to close the books on the episode as quickly as possible. The regime wanted merely to make its point and extract some limited penance from Sapieha, not to risk making an enemy of the Church.[52] Moreover, sanacja, sensing danger on both its right and left flanks, had its own political motives for wanting to put the Wawel ruckus to rest and damp down the passions it had ignited. The government grew suspicious that two separate factions, for different reasons, were fanning the flames of the controversy to exploit it for their own purposes by provoking an irreparable breach between Catholics and Piłsudskiites: the usual suspects, its nationalist opponents, who wanted the Church on their side, and the raucous anticlericals within the sanacja party itself, who wanted to put a stop to the efforts of their current leaders to get the Church on theirs. Prolongation of the affair, so Beck told foreign diplomats, "would only work to benefit Fascist forces in Poland."[53] Between them, Cortesi and Beck put together a mutually acceptable package. The transfer of Piłsudski's coffin into the Silver Bells tower would stand and the archbishop of Kraków would incur no legal penalty or ecclesiastical discipline, but Sapieha would write a letter of explanation to President Mościcki, expressing regret for any offense and pledging in future not to alter or rearrange the Wawel tombs without first gaining the assent of the head of state. Cortesi then imposed the conditions of the agreement upon Sapieha.[54]

The stiff-necked archbishop bridled at being made to swallow his pride as the price for escaping his predicament, and the Polish and Vatican authorities who had made the deal over his head had to put him through the wringer to get him to comply. Coaxed by both Cortesi and Hlond, Sapieha produced his prescribed note to Mościcki, dated July 6, but its tone reflected no hint of admission of fault. Instead, he stressed that his actions had been defamed and misrepresented by ambiguously identified "anti-Catholic and anti-national elements." In brusque reply, the president said, in so many words, that this was no apology at all, and Warsaw publicly rejected it on July 10.[55] That same day, the pope himself instructed Cortesi to suggest strongly to the bishop of Kraków that he dig deeper within himself to summon the contrition expected of him. A second, more conciliatory letter followed at once, and this one the Polish government deemed satisfactory. On July 15 an official response accepted the archbishop's extorted request for pardon, pronounced the vindication of the underlying principle that the Wawel pantheon was "the common property of the State and the Church," and on that basis declared the affair over.[56]

To the relief of many, the settlement of the dispute at the diplomatic level mooted the possibility of action by the Sejm, but still the special "Wawel session" convened on July 20 to permit the sanacja deputies to play to the galleries by belaboring Sapieha for the record. With the threat of mischievous legislative retaliation against the archbishop and the Church headed off, the majority in the chamber put its rubber stamp of approval on the government's handling of the incident and devoted the bulk of the day to an orchestrated display of grandiloquent high dudgeon. The lawmakers stood in tribute to Piłsudski as the vice-marshal of the assembly eulogized the deceased and deplored the disrespect shown his mortal remains. "For all time," he intoned, "the history of the Kraków Metropolitanate will bear the gloomy page written on June 23, indelibly linked with the name of Metropolitan Adam Sapieha. Nothing will erase it from history."[57]

This bombastic prediction to the contrary, the dust from the affair settled pretty quickly, leaving few traces, apart from inflicting some lingering bruises on its episcopal protagonist. Archbishop Sapieha smarted over a sense of having been misunderstood and ill used. He had gone through the motions of confessing his own mistakes, as ordered, but believed in his heart that he had done no more than discharge his rightful duties, only to be waylaid by sanacja elements looking for any excuse to assail the Church.[58] A scant week after tendering his apology to Mościcki—"my sacrifice," he called it—Sapieha asked Cortesi for permission to issue a pastoral letter telling his side of the story of the affair. Of course, this was the very last thing the nuncio wanted him to do, so he answered no without thinking twice.[59] While in Rome the following spring, the bishop endured a frosty audience with Pius XI, who gave the visitor an angry piece of his mind about the past summer's events in Kraków.[60] Only in his later years, after the passage of time had taken away the sting of the experience, was Sapieha able to look back on the Wawel altercation of 1937 with rueful amusement.[61]

The row over the resting place of the bones of Piłsudski bore more than a few touches of the droll, and mystified many, especially foreigners who lacked a sense of its context. Reporting to Washington, the American ambassador to Poland, A. J. D. Biddle, described this "most curious and unparalleled incident" in the fascinated but superior tone of an explorer observing a bizarre aboriginal rite.[62] In its aftermath, the lasting impression left of the episode was the undeniable air of strangeness that clung to it. Later commentators and historians, captivated by these antic aspects, tended to laugh it off as a weird example of eastern European exotica—in the words of one, an "almost ridiculous brouhaha."[63] But its oddness masked the serious issue that lay at its heart. That was no laughing matter, and it might have upset the precarious balance of church and state in interwar Poland had not Warsaw and the papacy made haste to ensure that things would not reach the tipping point. They knew from experience that keeping the peace between altar and throne in Poland was not as easy as it appeared to casual onlookers, who took for granted the secure and comfortable fit of the Catholic confession within the political framework of *Polonia semper fidelis.* At its birth, the Second Republic had inherited a legacy of deep division in Polish public life between those who honored the Church as the age-old guardian and definer of national values and those who upheld a secular vision of patriotic virtue, regarding Catholicism as a secondary or even suspect influence. More often than not during the interwar decades, to repeat the saying, Poland had a government that was less Catholic than the nation as a whole, a fact institutionalized by the monopolization of rule by Piłsudski and his followers. Forced to coexist, Church and regime had worked out a modus vivendi that papered over their deep-seated uneasiness in each other's company. The arrangement had been difficult but manageable, but more than any other event during the interwar era, the Wawel incident threatened to lay bare the unresolved tensions in Polish culture over the role of the Church in national politics, and came closest to overturning the tacit working agreement not to risk bringing these divisive questions into the light of day. To keep matters in perspective at this time of civil war in Spain and the rise of hostile totalitarianisms, the Vatican faced much bigger problems in Europe than Poland, just as Warsaw faced much bigger problems than the Catholic Church: all the more incentive for both of them, perhaps, to nip the Wawel unpleasantness in the bud before it could reach critical dimensions and add to their list of troubles. A few months later Cortesi reported to Cardinal Pacelli that Poland was coping reasonably well with the array of political, social, and economic ills that were threatening to spin out of control elsewhere in Europe, thanks to the effective collaboration of officialdom and Catholic forces in the country.[64] It was as if the Wawel incident never had happened.

Once it had passed without inflicting too much harm, the contretemps in Kraków had the effect of clearing the air and permitting the sanacja government and the episcopate to resume their efforts to inch their way toward a wary mutual understanding. The bishops still jealously defended the independence of the Church and reserved the right to take the authorities to task when they saw fit, but as a body, according to the bottom-line reckoning of the regime, they had become a much tamer lot than in days past, and now one could work with them. Over the long haul the logical and intended result of the methodical changing of the guard Pope Pius had carried out over the years had been to make the Polish episcopate less political and cantankerous and more acceptable to the Piłsudski équipe running things in Warsaw—in other words, everything it had not been when he had been in Poland as nuncio. For instance, in Kielce, the same Augustyn Łosiński who had blatantly refused to mourn the passing of Piłsudski was succeeded as ordinary by the younger and much more accommodating Czesław Kaczmarek.[65] This sort of substitution, duplicated many times over, produced the desired effect, demonstrated most clearly in cases of the dog that did not bark: for one, the collective restraint shown by the bishops in response to the considerable provocation of the Wawel ruckus would have been unimaginable a decade earlier.

Another reason that inclined the Polish hierarchy to make its peace with sanacja was that it saw no alternative. In spite of the open invitation from the National Democrats, who now paraded their Catholicity, and the obvious preference of the lesser clergy for the Endeks, the hierarchs of the Church in Poland felt deep qualms about giving in to the blandishments of the nationalist Right. To some extent these were imposed on them by Pius XI, who issued *Mit brennender Sorge,* his encyclical against the excesses of Nazism, in March 1937. Even at their anti-Semitic worst, the National Democrats were not Nazis, but the comparison was too close for comfort, and in the wake of the papal slap at Hitlerism, the Polish episcopate followed suit with a series of condemnations of totalitarianism, chauvinism, and racism, all of which could be read as implicit rebukes of Endecja.[66] But even without the prodding of the Holy See, a majority of the bishops concluded that these "new" National Democrats, though more overtly religious than their predecessors, were still up to their party's old tricks of trying to manipulate the Church for their own ends, and balked at anointing them as the standard-bearers of political Catholicism in the country. So the episcopate maintained neutrality in Polish partisan warfare, but in practice a neutrality that winked in the direction of the Piłsudskiite regency. Cardinal Hlond privately accused the Right of pushing a line of policy "leading to absurdities," and the primate obliquely endorsed the OZN ticket in elections in 1938 by urging Catholics to vote as their civic duty in the face of opposition calls to boycott the polls.[67] These tendencies naturally pleased the sanacja government, and even persuaded it to reverse its habitual approach to managing the Church: while in his day Piłsudski had counted on the Holy See to use its influence to keep the Polish bishops in line, by 1939 Warsaw placed more confidence in the episcopate than in the Vatican.[68]

To be sure, to some extent this turnabout was a testament less to Poland's high esteem for the bishops than to its growing annoyance at the papacy. Genuine policy differences, particularly the chronic arguments over Uniate and Russian questions, had put a chill into the atmosphere, then the decision of the Polish foreign minister to get even for a personal slight put the relationship into the deep freeze. In January 1938 Beck offered the seasoned diplomat Jan Gawroński the ambassadorship to the Holy See recently vacated by the death of the incumbent-for-life, Władysław Skrzyński. Gawroński declined, in part because now the frustrations of a Vatican posting seemed to outweigh the attractions, but also because it was common knowledge within the Polish diplomatic corps that their boss would soon ask the embassy there to make an impossible request of Pius XI, and he wanted no part of it.[69] Colonel Beck planned to make a state visit to Italy in March, and wished to pay a call on Pope Pius while in Rome. He and the Vatican always had regarded each other with misgivings, but the Holy See gave him high marks for his deft handling of the Wawel incident, and *L'Osservatore romano* greeted his arrival in the Eternal City with praise for his effective and constructive statesmanship.[70] However, the divorced and remarried Beck wanted to obtain a papal audience in the company of his uncanonical wife. As a matter of course, the pope would not consent to receive the couple in these circumstances: this was elementary, well-understood Vatican protocol, so much so that insiders, including even some of Beck's own subordinates, wondered what could have possessed him to court such sure embarrassment. The pope excused himself with illness transparently, and Cardinal Pacelli went to the unusual length of trying to let the Polish visitor off easy by extending an invitation to meet with him instead. Beck took hot offense at the snub, never forgave it, and repaid it many times over with implacable vindictiveness. He refused to see Pacelli, answering with the calculated insult of proposing to send the Polish chargé as his stand-in. Upon returning to Warsaw, he made Archbishop Cortesi wait several weeks before finally agreeing to give the nuncio the chance to try to smooth ruffled feathers. For the rest of his tenure as arbiter of Polish foreign policy, Beck gave the Vatican the back of his hand and held his country's relations with the papal state hostage to his pique.[71] In case anyone needed it spelled out, the Polish acting chief of mission at the Holy See took leave of the embassy for an extended spell, for no apparent reason, and Beck ostentatiously left the position of ambassador unfilled until after the death of the pope who had given him and his spouse the cold shoulder.[72]

He had not that long to wait. As he entered his eighty-second year, Pius XI grew steadily and visibly weaker. In his decline, the old pope whose lengthy term as successor to St. Peter and autocrat of the Catholic Church could be said to have originated in Poland found occasion to speak of the country of his former nunciature in tender and elegiac words. He expressed contentment with the status of the Church in the Second Republic, in pointed contrast to conditions in Nazi Germany.[73] Just before the new year of 1939, in a final conversation with chargé Janikowski, Pius voiced the hope that God might allow Poland to "maintain inner peace, so difficult to preserve in such times as these."[74] He died six weeks later. On hearing the news, Mussolini crowed that "at last, that obstinate old man is dead."

The pontiff some had called *il papa polacco* was accompanied into death, within a few months on either side, by many of the notables of the history of interwar Polish Catholicism. Sister Faustyna Kowalska, the visionary of Divine Mercy, died in October 1938, and Mother Urszula Ledóchowska, whose brother was the Polish Jesuit general, the following May: both would be canonized by their countryman pope, John Paul II. Archbishop Teodorowicz of Lwów, the epitome of the firebrand Polish hierarch of his era, breathed his last in early December 1938. On December 30 Cardinal Kakowski of Warsaw succumbed to illness. Three days later Roman Dmowski, the patriarch of National Democracy, died in the bosom of the Catholic Church he had only recently made his own. Cardinal Hlond denied the wish of Dmowski's devotees that he be interred in Poznań Cathedral, the burial place of the first rulers of Poland.[75] The generation that had dominated the story of the Church in Poland between the wars was passing away, and the giants who would take their place after the Nazi onslaught gave way to prolonged Soviet captivity were just coming into maturity: when Pope Ratti died in February 1939, Stefan Wyszyński was a thirty-seven-year-old priest in Włocławek much concerned with rural and labor issues, and Karol Wojtyła was a promising youth of eighteen in his first year of studies in Polish language and literature at the Jagiellonian University in Kraków. A few days earlier the city's archbishop, Adam Sapieha, weighed down by advancing age, poor health, and the death of his close friend Archbishop Teodorowicz, had submitted to Pius XI his resignation as ordinary of the diocese and caretaker of the tomb of Józef Piłsudski within the Silver Bells tower of Wawel Cathedral. His letter never reached the eyes of the dying pope. In April Sapieha renewed his request to step down in an audience with the newly elected pontiff, Pius XII. According to John Paul II, Pius replied, "War is coming; you will be needed." A month later Archbishop Cortesi, last occupant of the office of papal nuncio to the Second Republic that first had been held by Achille Ratti, reported that Sapieha had agreed to remain at his post "in this moment of great danger for Poland."[76] By the time his own earthly span ended in 1951, Sapieha would have shepherded the Metropolitanate of Kraków through not one, but two world wars.

9 ılı Oratio pro Pace

Pius XII and the Coming of the Second World War

In 1932 G. K. Chesterton, the foremost Catholic publicist of his day, predicted that the most terrible war in human history would break out before long on the frontier of the Second Polish Republic he lauded as the bulwark and hope of Christendom.[1] Seven years later his prophecy came true, visiting ruin upon the country and plunging Europe into a nightmare half decade of violence and destruction. As the invading German and Soviet armies overran and partitioned the land Stalin's foreign minister reviled as the "ugly bastard of Versailles," the newly enthroned bishop of Rome, the pope of the Church most Poles regarded as their own, made anguished reference to the calamity in his first encyclical. "The dread tempest of war is already rising despite all Our efforts to avert it," he wrote. "When we think of the countless disasters that are happening . . . the pen might well fall from Our hand. . . . The blood of countless human beings raises a dirge over Our dear Poland which, by its fidelity to the Church, by its exertions on behalf of Christian civilization . . . has a just claim on the generous and brotherly sympathy of the whole world."

The pontiff voiced his prayerful belief that Poland would attain "the hour of resurrection" through the intercession of Mary, Help of Christians, and added that none could doubt his own fatherly sorrow and care for his Polish flock in their affliction.[2] But in fact great numbers of Poles in all stations of life shared a sense of dismay that their pope had denounced in plain words neither the evil done to them nor the evildoer by name. The disappointment damaged the prestige of the papacy in Polish opinion for years to come and played into the hands of Communist propagandists eager to blacken the reputation of the Church they saw as a political and ideological rival.[3] Pius XII is the most controversial of modern popes; the debate focuses almost entirely on what he said or did, or did not say or do, in the face of the Nazi German genocide of European Jews. Often overlooked is the fact that the papal "silence"—if so it can fairly be called—in response to the Shoah was preceded and foreshadowed by the analogous and painfully cautious reaction of the Holy See to the German assault on Catholic Poland that touched off the Second World War. For reason of these similarities, examination of the approach taken by the Vatican to the shattering of European peace in 1939—well meaning, but helpless and ineffectual in the end—also can shed light on the more publicized disputes regarding his pontificate that have inspired the flurry of polemics some have called the "Pius wars."[4]

As the cardinals of the Catholic Church gathered in Rome in February 1939 to designate one of themselves as successor to the deceased Pope Pius XI, some speculated that the choice might fall upon the primate of Poland, Archbishop Hlond of Gniezno-Poznań.[5] This was flattery or idle chatter, as Hlond himself understood: to him it was obvious that the next pontiff would be Italian, and would have to be well versed in politics and diplomacy so as to deal with the challenge posed by the aggressive German dictator, Adolf Hitler, who was both "genius" and "madman." In his view this could only improve the prospects of the odds-on favorite, the sitting secretary of state, Eugenio Cardinal Pacelli.[6] So stellar seemed the qualifications of this ascetic Roman aristocrat that Pius XI had openly groomed him for the papacy, contrary to established Vatican protocol, steadily building up his résumé to make his eventual elevation to the Chair of Peter a foregone conclusion. When the decisive moment arrived, the vote of the Sacred College was a mere formality. Pacelli received election as pope with near-record speed, on the first day of the conclave, and took the same name as his predecessor whose right-hand man he had been.

Foreign capitals greeted the advent of Pius XII with approval or distaste, depending on their reading of his stance on matters touching their own interests, and in 1939 one issue, and one only, dominated the agenda of Europe: the mounting appetite of Hitler. As if to drive the point home, three days after the formal inauguration of the Pacelli pontificate on March 12, Germany swallowed the rump Czechoslovakia that had been the remnant of the Munich accord of the previous year. Increasingly anxious over the threat posed by Berlin, England and France had quietly encouraged the selection of Pacelli, while Poland—the latest target of Hitler—took satisfaction from the new pope's profession of high regard for that country, "so very Catholic, worthy, and devoted to the Church," and especially beloved of Pius XI.[7] On the other hand, Germany had hoped the cardinals would choose anyone but Pacelli, and when that did not happen the regime-controlled press denounced the outcome of the conclave; one Nazi paper, summoning the worst insult in its lexicon, sneered that Catholics had handed over leadership of their church to "a full Jew."[8]

That the arrival of Eugenio Pacelli to the papal throne would offend the Nazi dictatorship and hearten those made uneasy by its ambitions seemed the natural conclusion to be drawn from his lengthy career in Vatican diplomacy. In 1917, aged forty-one and already touted as a future pope, he had been consecrated an archbishop and appointed nuncio to Germany. After a twelve-year residence in Munich and Berlin, Pacelli took a deep knowledge and admiration of things German with him when he returned to Rome to receive his double promotion as cardinal and secretary of state to Pius XI. From the start, his duties as the papal foreign minister called on him to make use of his expertise in issues relating to Germany, including the chronic tension over the desire of the Weimar Republic to recover lands lost to Poland and the Free City of Danzig after the First World War. The Vatican consistently had regarded the Versailles order as flawed and foreseeably temporary and had not been shy to advise Warsaw to give in to the German demands, both as a matter of justice and to avoid the risk that Berlin might end up doing a deal with Soviet Russia at Polish expense. The Poles had feared that Pacelli would mean more of the same, given his prolonged exposure to German views, but he had pleased them by emphasizing instead his vision of a reconciliation between the two countries that did not depend on territorial revision.

The German question took on greater urgency in 1933 when the tottering republic surrendered power to the National Socialists. The Holy See had no clear idea how to handle a Germany now ruled by Hitler, meaning that over the next six years the policy of the government of the Church toward the Third Reich was just as confused and inconsistent as that of its worldly counterparts. Like most other European capitals, the Vatican blew hot and cold on the Nazi despotism, alternately hoping for the best and fearing the worst. On one level, the new masters of Germany repelled Pius XI and his lieutenants as neopagan bullyboys whose boorish habits included a vulgar anticlericalism; as for Pacelli himself, precisely his high regard for German culture led him to express his private "disgust" at those who had seized control in the country that had become his second home. Still, the papacy had a long history of holding its nose and doing business with regimes it deemed unsavory, and its first inclination was to look for redeeming features in the Nazis, chiefly their professed hatred of Communism. In March, Pius declared to the startled Polish ambassador that "Hitler is the one head of state in the world who lately 'speaks of Bolshevism as the Pope speaks.' . . . That Bolshevism is not one of the problems or one of the foes, '*mais que c'est l'ennemi*,'" adding the "purely fatherly" suggestion that Warsaw should not consider the loss of the Polish Corridor too high a price to pay for German friendship. This was but one of several occasions during 1933 when the Vatican urged Poland to join with its western neighbor, even in its worrisome National Socialist incarnation, to defend Christian civilization against the Soviet threat to the east. In July, Berlin and the Holy See raised eyebrows by announcing that they had concluded a concordat. Despite misgivings, Pacelli negotiated and signed the agreement on the grounds that in order to protect the Church in Germany, any concordat was better than none. Be that as it may, historical opinion has harshly judged the treaty as having lent unfortunate international legitimacy to the Third Reich, and at the time it prompted grumbling from some quarters in Polish opinion that the papacy had granted Hitler, of all people, easier terms for a concordat than it had given Catholic Poland in 1925.[9]

The Vatican had assumed that the responsibilities of power would tame the Nazis, but disillusionment set in quickly, and before long the mood in the apostolic palace had turned sharply against the Hitler regime. By the end of 1933, Cardinal Pacelli was telling his subalterns within the Secretariat of State that the overlords of Germany were "ferocious brutes." If anything, at this time his one superior was expressing himself on the subject with more vehemence. The pope deplored the "horrible, catastrophic mentality" revealed in Hitler's *Mein Kampf*, and pointed to the Nazi government as reason to suspect that the German nation, unlike the Poles, was "neither humane nor Christian." Although Pius gave his blessing to the Polish-German declaration of nonaggression in 1934 as a step in the right direction toward easing the hostility between the two countries, some of his diplomats voiced their doubts to Warsaw about the wisdom of the move—not the only time that the Vatican would offer Poland conflicting counsel about its stance toward Nazi Germany. Archbishop Marmaggi, the nuncio to Poland, warned that "God cannot bless any discussions with these Germans," and Pacelli hinted at his regret that Marshal Piłsudski had handed Hitler a lifeline to escape his increasing diplomatic isolation, as if the *Reichskonkordat* had not done much the same thing.[10]

As Germany began to build up its military muscle and throw its weight around in Europe, the Holy See stepped up its behind-closed-doors campaign of warning against the Nazi peril. By 1935 the Polish ambassador to the Vatican reported that his hosts had come to regard the Third Reich as "a catastrophe for religion and civilization." Pius XI began to sense the approach of war and to revise his initial belief that Hitler would not be the cause of it. Now he started to suggest to the Poles that they might do well to prepare themselves to resist German advances against the Corridor he had earlier advised them to yield. After Hitler reoccupied the Rhineland by force in March 1936, the pope accurately predicted that Germany would go on to grab at a series of targets in central Europe, including Danzig and Pomerania: "only the chronology" was open to question.[11]

At the same time, inside the Vatican this growing mistrust of Berlin coexisted uneasily with a prevalent conviction that Communism presented the greater long-term threat and that the Nazis, though dangerous, might still be persuaded to make useful contributions to the front of opposition to revolution and its Soviet sponsors. Pacelli, who knew them better than his colleagues, warned that the National Socialists were "false prophets with the pride of Lucifer" and that Hitler's vaunted anti-Bolshevism was all just empty talk, but he still did not abandon hope that the European powers might compose their differences to shield Western civilization from the Communist menace. Pius XI wasted few opportunities to lecture the Poles on the need for vigilance against Russia and its doctrines and urged them to do all that they could to maintain tolerable relations with Germany so as to serve that higher priority.[12] Echoing the papal exhortations, the Polish primate, Cardinal Hlond, agreed that his country should regard the Third Reich as a difficult but necessary partner in the common resistance against the true enemy to the east.[13]

In the twilight of his life, Pius XI grew bolder in his warnings about Nazi Germany as it launched its drive to bring central Europe under its heel. Provoked by flagrant and ongoing violations of the concordat of 1933, the pope in 1937 issued the encyclical *Mit brennender Sorge*, which rebuked the Hitler regime for its mistreatment of the Church and its ideological offenses against Christian morality. This scolding from the Vatican angered the Nazis and cemented their mistrust of Pacelli, the presumed mastermind behind the encyclical, but in fact the pope needed no prodding to upbraid the ruffians who ran Germany, and true to form, he came closer to stating frankly the opinions that his secretary of state kept to himself. In

May 1938, two months after the German takeover of Catholic Austria and on the eve of a state visit to Rome by Hitler, Pius whisked Pacelli away with him to the papal retreat at Castel Gandolfo to spare himself—so he said in public audience—the sight of "another cross not that of Christ" given honor in the Eternal City.[14] As his strength ebbed, the pope clung to the hope that war might be avoided, but some of those who served him in the Vatican wondered whether the statesmen scrambling to preserve the peace in Europe were up to the job. Assessing the dismal implications of the mutilation of Czechoslovakia decreed by the Munich conference, the Curia insider Fr. Domenico Tardini told the Polish chargé that no doubt British Prime Minister Chamberlain meant well, "but his actions must be judged on the basis of their results."[15]

By the time Pacelli broadcast a radio appeal to the world for peace on his first full day as pope in March 1939, he had established a reputation as a discreet but decided foe of Nazism, and the Holy See appeared on the verge of an all-but-open alignment against the German dictatorship. The initial moves of the new pontificate seemed to confirm these impressions. The nomination of Luigi Cardinal Maglione, a former nuncio to Paris, as secretary of state was taken as a sign of papal preference for the Franco-British bloc, and chatter in the hallways of the Vatican continued to disparage Hitler as "that motorized Attila," and fascist governments such as his as "the work of the devil."[16] But meanwhile, Pius XII decided that the time had come to attempt to improve at least the tone of the contentious dialogue with Germany and to shore up the credentials of the papacy as an impartial and conciliatory influence in world affairs. With the wisdom of hindsight, historical opinion has praised the aging Pius XI for having made his disapproval of Hitler and his regime plain to see, but at the time many within the Curia thought of this candor as an exasperated old man's liberty best interred with him. The new pope spoke more cautiously and signaled his readiness to restore a more cordial relationship with the Third Reich, not out of sympathy with its nature or aims, but as a dictate of prudence and the needs of the moment. A diplomat by training and instinct, Pacelli concluded that continuing the outspokenness of his predecessor would be futile and even counterproductive. The Nazis were what they were: lectures from Rome would not get them to mend their ways, and might well backfire by inciting reprisals against the Church in Germany or leading to the dead end of a complete rupture of relations between Berlin and the Vatican. Above all, he believed, with Europe teetering on the brink of war, that the duty of the Holy See was to put itself in position to serve as a credibly disinterested conciliator and peacemaker, if needed, as Benedict XV had tried to do a quarter century earlier.[17]

Pius XII hardly could have been blamed for fearing that the drastic deterioration of the European international order would require him to take on that duty sooner rather than later. Germany had instigated the emergency by demanding that Poland agree to the incorporation of Danzig within the Reich, ominous concessions in the Polish Corridor, and effective relegation to the status of a vassal of Berlin. Warsaw vowed to resist rather than bow to extortion, and received halfhearted pledges of support from Britain and France by the end of March 1939. Hitler responded to this show of defiance by resolving to crush Poland by military force, and began to beat the drums of war as he had done to such unnerving effect in the run-up to the dismemberment of Czechoslovakia. In its alarm, the Vatican reacted to the sudden intensification of the crisis in a babel of conflicting voices. The Secretariat of State sostituto, Fr. Montini, a former staffer of the Warsaw nunciature and future Pope Paul VI, assured a functionary of the Polish embassy that if Poland were to find itself forced to fight to defend its "rights and territory, it would be a just war," leaving the mistaken impression he was stating official policy, not his personal conviction. His superior, Cardinal Maglione, told the Poles that trying to talk with Hitler was useless, and *L'Osservatore romano* warned that if given Danzig, Germany would simply step up its campaign of strong-arming its eastern neighbors.[18] However, these signs to the contrary, the papal ambassador Archbishop Cortesi gave a more accurate indication of the thinking of the Vatican in a gloomy mid-April conversation with Polish deputy foreign minister Szembek. The nuncio voiced the opinion that a war over Danzig could not be localized, but must widen into a repeat of the calamity of 1914. Noting that the population of the Free City was predominantly German, he wondered aloud whether "the world would understand why [Poland] would unleash the dogs of war for the sake of this non-Polish object . . . and whether the world would stand by [her] side," and asked if Warsaw instead might consider attempting to meet Hitler halfway on Danzig. Szembek said no, and Cortesi changed the subject, but it has been claimed that the Holy See continued to encourage suggestions along these lines through back channels.[19] In any event, Cortesi had unveiled the idea that became the guiding principle of the counsels and actions of Pius XII in the summer of 1939: that general war would be the worst of all outcomes, to be avoided at all costs, and that if necessary, Poland should make any concessions needed to keep the guns silent, both for her own sake and that of European civilization.

In early May, the pope made his first attempt to offer his good offices as a mediator, advancing the idea of an international conference of five pivotal states—England, France, Poland, Germany, and Italy—to be devoted to hammering out a pacific solution to the Danzig question and other contested issues.[20] The overture appealed to Mussolini, Hitler's reluctant ally, who had no stomach for rushing into combat in 1939, but the other four principals declined the invitation, keeping their true motives prudently out of public view.[21] Hitler had his own reasons: he was already bent on the destruction of Poland by military force and wanted no part of parleys that could have no purpose but to stop him short of that hidden goal. The fact that Mussolini and the pope were singing from the same hymnal troubled Colonel Beck, the Polish foreign minister, who suspected the pontiff of acting more as an Italian patriot than as a high-minded nonpartisan. He sent back word to Pius that the best way to guarantee peace was for the Poles and their coalition partners to remain steadfast.[22] Beyond that, for Poland and its British and French allies, the specter of a summit meeting convened to haggle over the boundaries of a central European country threatened by Hitler bore too close a resemblance to a similar recent gathering that already had become a byword for the failure of appeasement: as if in unison, all insisted they wanted nothing to do with "another Munich."[23] As the pope realized that his five-power-talks initiative was going nowhere, he accepted the graceful way out presented to him by Hitler, who told the nuncio to Germany that war was not imminent and that Berlin had no grievances that could not be satisfied amicably. Accentuating the positive, the Vatican announced the withdrawal of its proposal of a grand peace conference, on the tortuously reasoned grounds that the constructive responses of all the governments asked to participate meant that no such assembly was needed.[24]

Rebuffed in its first try at facilitating a comprehensive settlement to arrest the slide into war, the Holy See hovered on the edges of the anxious maneuvering among the capitals of Europe that dragged on through the next three months, and looked for any chance to pour holy oil on the troubled waters of the continent. During this jittery interlude, papal diplomacy largely amounted to providing a forum for the circulation of rumor, speculation, and threats. By dint of its reputation as a listening post, the Vatican heard things, and would be fed bits of information in the expectation that those snippets would be passed on through the grapevine, as they generally were. Cardinal Secretary of State Maglione and his emissaries understood that they were being manipulated, but the pope's determination to spare no effort in the quest for peace left them no choice but to play along. So Hitler's foreign minister preened and blustered before the nuncio to Berlin, boasting that the Wehrmacht would make quick and deadly work of Poland if given the chance, and hinting at his master's readiness to come to terms with Stalin if the Western democracies did not watch their step. Goebbels crowed that Danzig would return to the Reich within weeks. For their part, the British and French asked Maglione to convince Mussolini that they meant business in standing by the Poles. In carrying out these errands as go-between, the Vatican took for granted that it could exert no influence on Berlin, and little on London or Paris, but that it might be able to make some headway with Rome and Warsaw, since the Italians did not want war and the Catholic Poles might listen to their pope.[25] Following this line of reasoning, Maglione saw grounds for optimism despite the dangers, and the opportunity for the Holy See to perform a helpful service: assuming that England and France held their ground, if Mussolini could be persuaded to talk sense to Hitler, and if Poland could be kept from making a fatal mistake out of rashness or panic, all might yet be well.[26] As the key element of this strategy, at the start of June the Holy See began an intense effort to get Italy on board, so that the two governments on either side of the Tiber could act in concert to keep the peace. The Quirinale responded by subjecting the papal representatives to the diplomatic equivalent of the good-cop/bad-cop treatment, posing as the voice of reason imploring Europe to let his hotheaded German friend get his way before he resorted to violence. The Duce tried to shake up the Vatican with scare tactics, warning that war was inevitable unless the pope could manage to "calm the Poles," as if they were the troublemakers who had to be brought into line. A few days later, his foreign minister, Count Ciano, used more honeyed words to arrive at the same conclusion: he had it on good authority that any German attack on Poland was at least six months away, meaning there was still time to work out a solution for Danzig; the Holy See should direct its energies toward advising Warsaw to grasp the gravity of its situation and to do what was needed to spare itself the wrath of Hitler.[27] Making the wish father to the thought, Maglione took Ciano's statement as gospel and had Archbishop Cortesi pass it on personally to the Polish foreign minister without delay. Colonel Beck did not think much of the Ciano theory, or, presumably, its implicit corollary that the Second Republic should try to buy its way out of trouble by giving way on Danzig. He saw no reason to believe that Mussolini's son-in-law knew what he was talking about; and Poland would be prudent, but would not back down.[28] This answer left the Secretariat of State with no option but to hope that Ciano was right after all and to issue repeated appeals for restraint to the Axis powers, as well as the Polish government and Catholic clergy.[29]

All that the Vatican accomplished through these exertions was to heighten the suspicions of Poland and its allies that the Holy See had got too chummy with Italy to be trusted as a truly honest broker. None doubted that Pius XII sincerely desired peace, but all three members of the coalition worried that he also had an ulterior agenda that they had best beware. Maglione had to deny French and British conjecture that he had cooked up a plan for an agreement that would allow the Reich to absorb the Free City after a decent interval. A friendly source inside the Curia tried, but failed, to assure a nervous Polish contact that the papacy would not turn its back on his country for the benefit of the Nazi regime that persecuted the Church inside its borders, but the Poles surmised that the pontiff, known to be a Germanophile, might well wish to see Danzig go to Hitler on grounds of sentiment or high politics. Beck guessed that whatever he might say, the pope regarded Poland as a pawn in a bigger game, and that his real aim was to extricate Mussolini from a tight spot or to curry favor with Berlin in hopes of bringing relief to hard-pressed German Catholics.[30]

Of course, if the foreign minister of Poland had cared much what the pope thought, he would have seen that his government put an ambassador in place to plead its case with the Holy See at this tense hour, instead of indulging a private grudge against the papacy by refusing to appoint one. Incensed that he and his wife had suffered what they took as a personal slight at the hands of Pius XI, Beck had flaunted his anger by declining to fill the Vatican post, which had stood empty since 1937. After months of embarrassed advice from subordinates that the feud had gone on long enough and was starting to damage the interests of the state, Beck grudgingly agreed to send someone to Rome, but specified that the designee should be a second-rater not cut out for more important work: "let him quarrel there with bishops and cardinals."[31] In the end he gave the dubious honor to Kazimierz Papée, a diplomatic warhorse whose previous stints in Danzig and Czechoslovakia allowed him to speak with some credibility on the overriding topic of the summer of 1939. Papée arrived in the Eternal City in late July and spent his first days on the job in a series of audiences with the pope, Maglione, and Father General Ledóchowski, among others. Apart from increasing concern that Germany and the Soviet Union might upset the balance of forces by striking a predatory bargain, the message the new ambassador gathered from all of these eminences was sympathetic and encouraging: firmness was the way to deal with the Nazis, and Poland merited praise for its composure under immense pressure. The belief of the Holy See, reported Papée, was that "we [Poles] will solve Hitler."[32]

Perhaps Papée had heard only what he chose to hear, but within a fortnight the Vatican was singing a different tune. Having drawn revised, grimmer conclusions about the direction things were headed, the pope's men began taking soundings for possible last-ditch steps to avert the war now in sight. Warned by Cortesi from Warsaw on August 14 that the crisis had taken a sudden turn for the worse, Maglione arranged a meeting at Castel Gandolfo with Ambassador Papée, who repeated his declarations of Polish resolve and confidence in the support of the Western democracies. The secretary of state agreed with Papée's argument that the German saber-rattling over Danzig now stood revealed as no more than a pretext masking a plan to swallow up all eastern Europe, but came away convinced that the Poles were living in a fool's paradise and grossly underestimating the disastrous contingency he had come to consider a near certainty: that Stalin would decide to join with Hitler in partitioning the Second Republic. Maglione directed Cortesi to ask Poland if the Apostolic See could assist in any way as a mediator, an offer politely turned down.[33] Warsaw being unwilling to take his hint that the time had come to try to reach terms with Berlin, Maglione approached the British, who replied that any proposal for negotiation based on a priori acceptance of the German claim to Danzig was out of the question.[34] Running out of options, Vatican diplomats began to pass the word that if the situation became truly dire, with no discernible prospect of rescue through secret talks, as a last resort the pope would start to issue public calls for peace. Pius XII made his first declaration of this sort on August 19, speaking to pilgrims at Castel Gandolfo.[35] The next day the French ambassador told Fr. Tardini that rather than voice general appeals to all nations without distinction, the pontiff should remove all doubt about where he stood by stating flatly that Germany was in the wrong and must cease its misdeeds—the anticipation of a reproach that would be leveled against this pope many times during the hostilities soon to commence.[36]

August 21 brought the news the Vatican had both feared and expected: the German and Soviet dictators had agreed to conclude the nonaggression treaty they formally announced two days later. Doggedly, and incredibly, the Polish ambassador insisted to Tardini that the Ribbentrop-Molotov pact changed nothing.[37] The Holy See knew better, realized that if war came, Poland was lost, and largely for that reason was all the more resolved that war must be headed off.[38] Out of ideas, the British urged the pope to exert his unique moral authority by making a dramatic open appeal for peace, and to do it without delay; the Vatican agreed, more out of a sense of duty than any real expectation that the papal intervention would do any good, and assured Papée in advance that the pontiff would say nothing to disquiet Warsaw.[39] On the evening of August 24, Pius XII broadcast a radio address to the world, beseeching the European powers to sheathe their swords and spare their peoples the disaster that hung over the continent. The impassioned heart of his speech, apparently inspired by Montini—"The danger is imminent, but there is yet time. Nothing is lost with peace: all may be with war" —ranks among the most remembered words of his lengthy pontificate.[40]

That same evening Montini declared to a staffer of the Polish embassy that his country had justice on its side, but the Poles and their allies were left dissatisfied and nonplused at the studied evenhandedness of the statement of the pope himself.[41] Pius had named no names, nor given any hint of censure of Hitler or of defense of the rights of an innocent Catholic state menaced by an aggressive neopagan dictator. Old Vatican hands began to mutter that Pius XI would have shown more spine in saying exactly what he thought of the Nazi-Soviet accord and its obvious malevolent implications.[42] Both Papée and the French ambassador asked for a pledge that if war came, as now seemed inevitable, the pope would denounce the German assailant and make plain his solidarity with the Polish cause. When the request was relayed to him, Pius told his diplomats that he could do no such thing without exposing forty million Catholics under Nazi rule to unacceptable risk, and that in any case he had "already expressed himself, and clearly."[43] Instead, the Vatican responded with a series of desperate last-minute initiatives that Foreign Minister Beck made a point of deploring in his memoirs as an affront to the sentiments of his Catholic compatriots for pressing upon them the need to back down and allow Hitler to walk off with Danzig.[44]

The tame historians of People's Poland had a pat, ideologically handy explanation for this: Pius XII, who had lived in Germany, spoke German, esteemed German civilization, and kept Germans within his inner circle, wanted to see Germany get the Free City—in short, he was in fact the "Hitler's pope" of John Cornwell's venomous description.[45] The decisions and actions of the 257th successor to St. Peter in the crucible of war are by no means beyond criticism, but fairness—not always the highest priority of his detractors—compels one to recognize that his reasons for counseling the Poles to surrender without a fight had nothing to do with a fictitious soft spot for the Nazi tyranny. It is trite, but true, that above all Pope Pacelli sought the keeping of the peace nearly to the exclusion of any other end. Beyond that, he was convinced that by accepting combat, Poland would seal its own annihilation within days at the hands of a devastating German juggernaut.[46] In effect, he would ask Warsaw to render a Christian sacrifice to spare itself and the world the greater evil of war. Some of his subordinates recognized that further attempts to lean on Poland to make concessions rested on faulty assumptions, or ran the risk that the motives of the Holy See would be misunderstood. Pius thought that Danzig really was the point of the crisis and that its cession to Germany might solve it, while his Secretariat of State recognized that the Free City was just a cover for Hitler's more grandiose project of conquest.[47] Tardini warned that the Vatican could be seen as "playing Hitler's game," suspected of trying to engineer "a new Munich" in cahoots with Mussolini.[48]

But the pope had the last word, and on August 30 he told Cardinal Maglione to instruct Nuncio Cortesi in Warsaw to convey to the Polish government a last-gasp proposal recommended to the Holy See by Mussolini: if Poland consented to permit the return of Danzig to the Reich and to negotiate certain other German grievances, Hitler might be willing to talk.[49] Strictly speaking, Cortesi was to act merely as a courier of information rather than an advocate for the idea, but there was no mistaking that his real mission—as Montini later described it—was to tell the Poles, on behalf of the pope, that it was "better to undergo pain today than to lose your life tomorrow."[50] The nuncio advised against taking this step, because Poland had categorically declared its resolve to fight rather than give an inch and would take umbrage at what it would consider unwelcome papal meddling; Maglione ordered him to carry out his assignment.[51] The next day, as Pius voiced a final call to Poland, Germany, and the other European powers, "in the name of God," to reach a "just and peaceful" resolution of their differences, Cortesi managed to get a hearing with Szembek, the harried deputy foreign minister. Szembek agreed to pass on the nuncio's communiqué to Colonel Beck immediately, and promised a reply on the morrow.[52]

By the time Beck telephoned his curt and negative answer to Cortesi, in a tone so caustic that it jarred the Vatican, the Second World War was already underway.[53] Shortly after dawn on September 1, as he prepared for morning mass, Cardinal Hlond heard the explosion of German aerial bombs falling on Poznań.[54] At about the same time, Cardinal Maglione informed Pius XII that Germany had unleashed an all-out attack on Poland. Silent and ashen, the pope retired to his private chapel to pray.[55]

Now that the war it dreaded had erupted, the Holy See evaded repeated and urgent invitations to proclaim its moral support of a Catholic country beset by a brutal and unprovoked military assault. With the invasion of Poland still in its first hours, French ambassador Charles-Roux asked for a Vatican condemnation of the German aggression, but Maglione replied that there was no need, as "the facts speak for themselves."[56] On September 2, the Polish envoy Papée met with the pope, who avowed his sympathy for the Poles but carefully avoided going beyond that, explaining that he "must not forfeit the possibility of influencing Germany in the future."[57] Over the next two weeks, as the German forces routed the Polish defenses and terrorized the civilian population, France and friends of Poland inside the Vatican sought to extract an unqualified gesture of papal backing for the beleaguered Second Republic, but to no avail.[58]

The Holy See thought it had reasons for refusing to take sides in these opening days of the conflict, and thought it best not to say them out loud. For one thing, the Vatican had drawn the early impression from its testy eleventh-hour dealings with Beck that Poland, though clearly more sinned against than sinning, had stubbornly thrown away its last chances to avert bloodshed without giving a fair hearing to alternatives, and so might not be entirely absolved of responsibility for helping to set Europe aflame. While real enough, this "blame-the-victim" strain of thinking was kept out of sight, confined to corridor gossip or veiled hints in *L'Osservatore romano.* More importantly, the pope clung to the illusion that the war could be kept short and local and that he must preserve his eligibility to be called in as an impartial arbitrator. Rumors swirled during September that after Germany inflicted a limited defeat on its eastern neighbor, Hitler might be coaxed into a compromise peace settlement, perhaps even including a partial restoration of Poland and Czechoslovakia. So long as he retained the faintest hope of this possibility, Pius resolved to say or do nothing to jeopardize his suitability as a disinterested broker.[59] The pope waited two weeks before making comment on the war for the record, and allowed himself to go only so far, and no further, to suggest his private concerns for the Poles. On September 13, he drafted a brief statement for publication in *L'Osservatore romano* that he had done all in his power to prevent the outbreak of hostilities. The next day, greeting a newly arrived ambassador at Castel Gandolfo, he mentioned the "unparalleled catastrophe" of the combat now raging in Europe, and lamented the miseries it had brought upon "a Catholic Nation."[60]

By that time, the unnamed Catholic nation was plainly in extremis, illustrated by the hazardous itinerary under fire of the primate of Poland and the papal nuncio to Warsaw. On September 3, at the recommendation of the Polish authorities, Cardinal Hlond fled eastward to the capital before his see of Poznań was engulfed by the German advance. Two days later the government and diplomatic corps evacuated Warsaw to fall back farther to the southeast; Cortesi complied, with the blessing of Maglione, and prevailed upon Hlond to accompany him. The two prelates joined in the chaotic retreat toward the Romanian frontier, dodging German bombardment along the way. By September 13, Hlond had determined to make his way to Rome, there to plead the Polish cause to the pope and await the opportunity to return to the homeland. He crossed into Romania the next day, declining invitations to be designated president or prime minister while abroad; the cardinal would not set foot on Polish soil again for the duration of the war.[61] Cortesi stayed on for the time being, as the Polish army made its last stand, and managed to anger Colonel Beck yet again by toying with the idea of retracing his steps to Warsaw, implying a readiness to accept the fait accompli of the German conquest. As it was, the nuncio followed the government of the Second Republic into exile on September 18, and eventually repaired to Rome himself.[62] The decisions of Hlond and Cortesi to vacate their posts in this critical hour, depriving the wartime Church in the occupied country of its two most visible figures of leadership, were received badly in Poland and, it is said, in the Vatican as well, as a violation of the principle that the shepherd should not abandon his endangered flock.[63]

Cortesi and the Polish authorities had exited the country one day after the Red Army entered it uninvited, as the Soviet Union pocketed the eastern half of Poland allotted it by the secret protocol of the Hitler-Stalin pact. In marked contrast to its hesitant and muted reaction to the German attack, the Vatican denounced the Russian incursion in no uncertain terms.[64] The differences had to do with matters of conviction and tactics alike. In the eyes of the papacy and the Catholic world, the fall of Polish territory to Germany was a dreadful though potentially remediable misfortune, but the fall of Polish territory to Communist Russia was sheer disaster. The horrors that Nazi rule would bring to its subjugated populations lay in the future:

the Soviet yoke, it was assumed, would be far harsher, and the westward advance of the Bolshevik tyranny threatened the further spread of atheistic revolution. Beyond that, the Holy See felt constrained to talk softly about Germany in hopes of wheedling Berlin to the bargaining table, but had no corresponding incentive to mind its tongue about the misdeeds of the Red dictatorship, which lay beyond any conceivable influence of the Roman pontiff. At the same time, the Vatican understood, to its chagrin, that the Soviet entry into the war lessened the chance that the fray could be localized, limited, and brought to a quick end that salvaged some semblance of a Poland.[65]

Cardinal Hlond arrived in Rome on September 18 and met with Pius XII three days later, a delay read by some as a clear sign of papal unhappiness that the primate of Poland had not chosen to remain with his countrymen.[66] If so, the snub escaped the notice of the archbishop, who recorded in his journal that the pope received him in a spirit of abundant warmth and compassion for the Polish plight.[67] On the other hand, Hlond was taken aback to encounter many churchmen inside the Vatican "thinking with the brain of Goebbels," as he put it, convinced that the Poles had brought their ruin upon themselves by foolishly opting for a war they could not win.[68]

Despite these internal doubts about the wisdom of Polish policy, the Holy See began to look for ways to demonstrate its sympathy for the Second Republic as the German and Soviet onslaught neared its unstoppable completion. On September 28, Hlond was granted access to the airwaves of Radio Vatican to deliver a pastoral message to his homeland. The cardinal used this opportunity to broadcast a patriotic call for resistance, declaring, "You have not perished, Poland," echoing the lyrics of the national anthem. "By the will of God, you will revive in glory, my beloved, martyred Poland!" To those schooled in its nuanced customs, the Vatican had removed any mystery about its true allegiance by allowing Hlond the use of its facilities to utter words of this sort.[69]

Two days later, the pope tried to underscore the point by means of his definitive personal authority, but he would have done better to leave well enough alone. At Castel Gandolfo, he received a delegation of Poles, including Cardinal Hlond, Father General Ledóchowski, and Ambassador Papée. Pius offered his audience the balm of consolation and trust in divine Providence, straining for the upper reaches of his distinctive brand of saccharine eloquence. He extolled the virtues of afflicted Poland, implicitly blessed its military effort, and reminded the saddened expatriates of the promise of faith and resurrection. "We do not say to you: 'Dry your tears!' Christ . . .

gathers them, and one day will give recompense for the tears you shed for your dear dead, and for your Poland, which can never die."[70]

Years later, after passions had cooled, the pope's comments were commended by some of those who heard them as fitting and heartfelt, but at the time they fell flat on ears that burned to hear not just condolences for the victim, but stern denunciation of the transgressor. Condemning the sin but not attributing it to a sinner, the statement failed to satisfy the British and French and bitterly disappointed Papée. The reaction surprised Pius. The pontiff confessed to one of the Polish diplomats that he had sensed a certain chill in the air during the course of his remarks, and his face fell when told that the Poles had expected him to give them "words of justice" as well as commiseration.[71] Within a few days, the opinion that the pope had failed to speak up for Poland gained traction. Behind the scenes, the French ambassador tried to shame the Vatican into action, and Papée detected signs that some papal advisers were urging their sovereign to throw off his self-imposed restraints. Stung, the pope privately defended himself against the accusations of his indifference to the fate of Poland. "You know which side my sympathies lie. But I cannot say so. . . . I could not say more than I did. There are in Germany fifty million Catholics and plenty of Poles, who would suffer . . . for the curses which they asked me to pronounce."[72] In an effort to limit the damage, on October 15 *L'Osservatore romano* published a leading article, vetted by Pius himself, that stressed his genuine sorrow for the trials of the Polish republic, but added that the bishop of Rome had no choice but to act as a spiritual father to all nations without favor.[73]

The pope had continued to parse his words with a caution many found bewildering or distasteful, because he still remained convinced into the first week of October that the war could be ended within days and that he could best help by staying quiet, calm, and soothing. Italy floated proposals that Britain and France agree to a settlement that recognized the German spoils of battle. This meant acknowledging the dissolution of Poland: although Pius deplored the idea, he favored peace on any terms, even these. Only after London and Paris rejected these conditions did he bow to the inevitable and conclude that nothing more could be done to prevent a prolonged conflict of continental scale.[74]

The opening salvos of what would become World War II brought a calamitous end to the free existence of the Second Polish Republic and meted out a crippling blow to the Catholic Church both in that unfortunate land and in the wider world. The September campaign had subjected Poland, and its roughly twenty-four million Catholics, to a condominium of totalitarian regimes hostile to Christianity. In stark illustration of the collapse of the high aspirations of the Holy See regarding eastern Europe in the twentieth century, and of its worst nightmares for the future, on October 17, Red Army units entered the village of Albertyn in what had been the Polish kresy, shut down the Jesuit mission established there as a base for the conversion of Russia, and converted it into a barracks.[75] The Vatican saw little but gloom on the horizon. In its view, the most likely scenario was a rapid victory of the German-Soviet alliance over England and France, then, after a falling out, a climactic war to the death between the Hitler and Stalin dictatorships, with who knew what consequences.[76]

A reign of terror began to descend upon the Poles, and few within the vicinity of St. Peter's believed that it would be lifted soon or that much could be done about it in the meantime. The Radio Vatican started to broadcast news of German atrocities in the occupied country, then suspended them when Polish bishops reported that the transmissions only led to repressions more severe.[77] For his part, Cardinal Hlond gradually realized that he could not return to Poland so long as the Nazis held sway, and reconciled himself to an extended residence in the Eternal City. His absence from the homeland during its wartime hardship would diminish his own reputation and elevate that of his de facto stand-in as bulwark of the Polish Church under siege, Archbishop Sapieha of Kraków, who would be recalled as the "steadfast prince . . . the strength and mainstay . . . of the whole nation" by the Polish pope who began seminary studies under his protection.[78] Reflecting the prevailing funereal mood in Rome, one cardinal told Hlond, "You will rise again, but in 150 years," possibly thinking it was a comfort; the exiled primate of Poland retorted that the day of liberation would arrive during the reign of Pius XII.[79]

Meanwhile, the pope chose this glum interlude to issue the first encyclical of his pontificate, *Summi pontificatus,* on October 20. Now released, in a sense, from the inhibiting anxiety that he would do more harm than good by speaking his mind, the pontiff used the occasion to reflect on the war, its causes, and its tragic effects as openly as his diplomatic second nature would permit. The document bore the subtitle "On the limitations of the Authority of the State," and its elaborations on that theme took direct aim at the claims of totalitarian government in general, though it admonished none in particular. Pius mentioned one country only. At the suggestion of Cardinal Hlond, he inserted a poignant and sorrowful passage on the tribulations of Poland, coupling lament for the present woes of that nation with assurances of eventual emancipation.[80] The message was clear enough for readers with any grasp of the habitual subtleties of papal idiom. Nazi Germany had no doubt that it was the intended target of the reproaches of *Summi pontificatus,* while Ambassador Papée reported that the pope, at last, had let the world know that at heart, he stood by Poland.[81] A few days later Polish chargé Janikowski met with Pius and summarized his own interpretation of the lessons of the encyclical: that its criticisms applied equally well to Nazism and Bolshevism, that the partnership of the dictatorships that had ganged up to crush the Second Republic amounted to the "alliance of two demons," and that civilized men should hope that the war would bring an end to "demonism." As usual, Pius had left it to others to employ words of crystal clarity without volunteering them himself, but agreed, with some prodding, that Janikowski had not misconstrued the thrust of his message.[82]

But by that time, nothing that he might say in even thinly veiled language, or in diplomatic confidence, would change the fact that many would remember Pius XII as having failed to act in a manner befitting the vicar of Christ when the coming of the Second World War called on him to give prophetic witness to the elementary principles of morality and justice. Rather than do this, the pope had maintained a public reticence based on a variety of reasons he thought compelling: his sincere belief that any kind of peace was preferable even to the most virtuous of wars, an adherence to a somewhat rigorous conception of the impartiality of the papacy, a well-intentioned if illusory determination to preserve the ghost of a chance that the Vatican might be able to step in as a peacemaker acceptable to all, the fear that pronouncing an anathema on the German conquerors would simply worsen the lot of the Poles now in their power. In many ways, the dilemma Pius faced in 1939 anticipated and strongly resembled the circumstances of his later and more notorious wartime "silence" when confronted by the inhuman crimes of the Nazis. Here, too, he took the path of discretion imposed on him, so he thought, by cautious wisdom and the best interests, fully considered, of the unfortunates in the grip of Hitler. For this, he now is widely disparaged as a weakling or even a villain, in spite of the considerable evidence of his clandestine opposition to Nazi Germany and assistance to endangered Jews. One may question whether Pius XII made the correct choices of policy during the war, but he chose them with honorable intentions, and it appears that he was mainly "guilty" of having been pope at the wrong historical moment, and one ill matched to his talents and personality. A comparison with John Paul II—justifiably renowned for his success in exerting the influence of the papacy in world affairs—is instructive. For one thing, Stalin's famed cynical dismissal of the effectiveness of the pope's divisions is half right, measured by his own brutal standards: the moral authority that is the principal asset of the Petrine office was a much more effective weapon in cold war, contending with the likes of civilized adversaries such as Gorbachev and Jaruzelski, than in the most total of hot wars, trying to moderate the behavior of Hitler. Neither do the accidents of personal style work to the advantage of Pius XII. On paper, Pope Wojtyła's declarations on political topics appear little more direct than those of Pope Pacelli. But the Polish pontiff was a man of enormous warmth, a gifted orator whose trademark was an ability to hold vast throngs spellbound in a variety of tongues, and practiced in the art of nuance from long experience at getting around the restrictions of Communist censorship. By way of contrast, Pius XII was the last of the popes of the old style, who cultivated an aura of oracular inapproachability, accentuated in his case by an otherworldly demeanor that came across as studied and cold. Moreover, he had something of a tin ear for rhetoric, with a penchant for grandiloquence that could impress but rarely inspire. The magnetic John Paul had the knack for giving people the sense, often rightly, that when he addressed them, in the flesh, on touchy matters of politics, he meant more than he could prudently say. When the remote Pius XII released a statement about Poland in 1939, he left people with the hollow sense that he had said less than he meant.

A week and a day after the promulgation of *Summi pontificatus*, the Jesuit weekly *America* published an article entitled "Poland, the Bastion of Our Civilization." Its author was Hilaire Belloc, who had celebrated the rebirth of an independent Poland at the end of one world war, and now mourned its passing at the outset of another. As he and G. K. Chesterton had done so often over the preceding two decades, Belloc discerned a universal significance in the destiny of that country. The Polish question of the grave present day, he asserted, was nothing less than "the test of Europe": "If we cannot [restore Poland] it will mean that. . . . our descendants will no longer be able to call themselves civilized men. . . . We stand or fall by Poland; and 'we' means all our art, literature, philosophy, all the mighty heritage now at stake." Once again, as before, Belloc wrote, Catholic Poland found itself under the heel of enemies of the faith. Upon its deliverance depended the future of Christendom.[83]

Strictly speaking, Cardinal Hlond had been correct to predict that Poland would return to the map of Europe before the pontificate of Pius XII had ended, but not in the full sense he intended, for he could not have foreseen the scale and duration of the ordeal that lay before his homeland. The war inflicted horrific suffering on the Polish lands and their inhabitants. It sorely tested the Catholic Church in the country, which won back its reputation for patriotic valor in national adversity it had dissipated in the interwar partisan squabbles, at the cost of the lives of almost one-third of its clergy.[84] Peace brought not freedom, but the prolonged Soviet captivity. The authentic liberation of Poland, as Hlond meant it, did not arrive until fifty years had passed since 1939, when a Pole occupied the Chair of St. Peter previously held by Pius XII, and both he and the Church of his Poland would receive much credit for inspiring the bloodless overthrow of dictatorship in Central Europe.[85]

The idea that Polish Catholicism would emerge in time as a leading sponsor of a historic advance of democracy and enlightened civic virtues would have seemed incredible during the twenties and thirties, when progressive opinion disparaged it—with some exaggeration, but only some—as the antithesis of both. Of course, there is much more to the Church than simply politics. In the broad sweep of things, the matters discussed in these pages meant less to the story of Christianity in Poland and abroad than the founding of the Catholic University of Lublin, the life of an obscure nun named Faustyna Kowalska, or even the decision of the recently widowed Karol Wojtyła the elder to take his son with him on pilgrimage to the shrine of Kalwaria Zebrzydowska. Still, ecclesiastical involvement in public affairs is no small thing in the Catholic tradition, and there is no disputing that in the decades between the world wars Polish Catholicism possessed a distinctive identity—the "strong character" that Chesterton had praised—that exerted considerable influence on political questions both inside Poland and beyond its frontiers. The issues of the proper place of Catholicism within a Polish republic, and of Poland within the universe of Catholicism, stirred up controversy and trouble from the outbreak of the First World War to the opening guns of the Second.

As Martin Conway has pointed out, understanding the politics of Catholicism in the first half of the twentieth century requires a combination of the general and the specific: the prevailing outlook of the Catholic world at the time, and the local circumstances of each particular country.[86] In that era, European Catholics maintained a solid front of group identity, shared beliefs, and common purpose that transcended national boundary lines. They knew who they were, what they stood for, and what and whom they favored and opposed in the arena of civic affairs. They mistrusted the modern age as hostile to their religion and what it held dear, and nursed a sense of past persecution at the hands of non-Catholic regimes, as well as a fear of its resumption. Catholic political consciousness and activity arose as a movement of defensive reaction against this catalogue of grievances, and sought to restore or uphold the interests and values of the Church and its members.[87]

In Poland, an environment of peculiar intensity had distilled this potent mixture of Catholic insecurity, conviction, and resentment into highly concentrated form. There geography, recent history, and clashing visions of moral and national ideals had come together to push the theme of conflict between the Church and its real or imagined enemies to its limits. Catholic Poland had known the discriminatory rule of Protestant and Orthodox conquerors, and the embattled, fortress-mentality worldview of its brand of political Catholicism had been forged in the fire of resistance against oppression during the era of partition.

One of the verities of ecclesiastical history is that the Christian church always appears at its noblest in times of persecution, and at its worst in times of privilege. The advent of the Second Polish Republic did not bring out the better qualities of the Catholic Church within the new polity. Before and after the decades between the wars, the Polish Church won renown as a stalwart pastor of its hard-pressed flock, while the conditions of independence and something like official preferment gave it the luxury of a considerably less heroic absorption with the task of repairing and looking after its institutional prerogatives and well-being. Emerging into the unfamiliar setting of statehood and pluralism after long subjection to hostile alien authority, the Catholic Church in Poland resolved to assert and reclaim what it saw as its due place in the life of the nation. It set about doing this with an insistent, truculent single-mindedness that reflected no sense of confidence, but rather its perception of acute vulnerability, of being uniquely exposed to the dangers posed by Communists, Jews, and Freemasons, and threatened by the control over the apparatus of government by an undevout political class. Where the Church saw only its own weakness, opponents saw only imposing and aggressive strength and dug in their heels, so they thought, to ward off clericalist hegemony. Usually sooner than later, debates over the role of the Church in the affairs of the Second Republic became pitched battles of ideology that defied easy or amicable solution. Many Polish Catholics had imagined that their creed was the natural uniting principle of the reborn Rzeczpospolita. It was not. It divided. In a Poland that was one-third not Polish and one-third not Latin Catholic, it could not do otherwise; it divided party from party, nation from nation, and patriot from patriot.

This habit of discord, albeit generally tempered by the polite conventions of high office, also typified the relationship of the trio of elites whose job was to manage the harmonious coexistence of church with state inside Poland and in the international sphere. The government of the Second Republic, the Catholic hierarchy of Poland, and the Holy See had broadly similar but by no means identical sets of agendas and interests. This produced a pattern of frequent and recurring strain, and disagreement barely contained, within a larger framework of uneasy cooperation that none of them could afford to do without, in spite of the vexations of the triangular partnership. Their interaction was complex and variable, as each of the three aligned itself with or against the others depending on the particular issue at stake, often turning out counterintuitive results. Thus, for example, did Pius XI force the Polish bishops to give grudging loyalty to the regime of Józef Piłsudski, which he commended and they deplored; thus did Warsaw and the Polish episcopate collaborate to jettison the same pope's ambitious project to convert the Orthodox of Russia; and thus did the Second Republic reproach the papacy for failing to appreciate and support the raison d'état of Poland, and the papacy fault the Second Republic for failing to live up to its obligations to the overriding cause of the mission of Catholicism in the twentieth century.

This was the political profile of Polish Catholicism of a given age, the one that ended suddenly in 1939. Change had begun already by degrees between the wars with the gradual transfer of leadership of the Church of Poland from an older generation that had been schooled, for better and worse, in the rigors of foreign bondage in the nineteenth century, to successors who were, as a group, broader and fresher in outlook and less overtly political or prone to partisan enthusiasm—a process mandated by Pius XI himself, who thought it a necessary medicine to cure the Polish Church of ills acquired during its subjugation, and encouraged on the spot by Cardinal Hlond, acting as his deputy.[88] Thereupon followed the half century of "trial by fire," in the metaphor of Bohdan Cywiński, which engulfed the Catholics of central Europe. The irony is that it was the experience of war and Communism that made the Catholic Church in Poland in fact, at least for a crucial forty-five-year span, what it had only claimed to be during the interwar years: the genuine and generally acknowledged representative and moral voice of the Polish nation.

The title of this book is meant to be taken with a grain of salt. It is a phrase taken from a newspaper article of 1932 that reflected a piece of conventional wisdom of the day, that Poland was the Catholic country nonpareil, ready and willing to do the bidding of the Church. This was the myth that was neither entirely true nor entirely false. Perhaps the larger truth is that the interplay of Christianity with the state is challenging under any and all circumstances. Drawing the line separating the rightful realms of God and Caesar is never easy, even in Poland, called by many, now as then, the most faithful daughter of Rome.

Notes

Chapter 1

1. Stanisław Grabski, *Pamiętniki* (Warsaw: Czytelnik, 1989), 2:109; Wincenty Witos, *Moje wspomnienia* (Paris: Instytut Literacki, 1964), 2:239–41.

2. *L'Osservatore romano,* July 26, 1960.

3. Charles Loiseau, "The Vatican and the New States of Central Europe," *Living Age,* November 8, 1919, 323–24.

4. Maisie Ward, *Gilbert Keith Chesterton* (New York: Sheed and Ward, 1943), 428.

5. Tadeusz Marynowski to Sylwin Strakacz, April 26, 1919, *Archiwum polityczne Ignacego Paderewskiego* (APIP), ed. Halina Janowska (Wrocław: Zakład Narodowy im. Ossolińskich, 1974), 2:116.

6. *New York Times,* August 28, 1932.

7. Georges Castellan, *Dieu garde la Pologne! Histoire du catholicisme polonais, 1795–1980* (Paris: Robert Laffont, 1981), 121.

8. For some of the complications of the meaning of Catholicism in Polish history, see Brian Porter, "The Catholic Nation: Religion, Identity, and the Narratives of Polish History," *Slavic and East European Journal* 45, no. 2 (2001): 289–99.

9. Wincenty Urban, *Ostatni etap dziejów Kościoła w Polsce przed nowym tysiącleciem, 1815–1965* (Rome: Hosianum, 1966), 475–76.

10. Cited in Szymon Rudnicki, "Nacjonalizm i religia," *Przegląd historyczny* 78, no. 1 (1987): 94. Brian Porter, *When Nationalism Began to Hate: Imagining Modern Politics in Nineteenth-Century Poland* (New York: Oxford University Press, 2000), sheds light on the ambiguous relationship of Catholicism with the early National Democracy.

11. Cited in Janina Barycka, *Stosunek kleru do Państwa i oświaty* (Warsaw: Nasza Księgarnia, 1934), 19–20. Pope John Paul II beatified Archbishop Bilczewski in 2001, and his canonization followed in 2005.

12. Stewart A. Stehlin, *Weimar and the Vatican, 1919–1933: German-Vatican Diplomatic Relations in the Interwar Years* (Princeton, N.J.: Princeton University Press, 1983), 3–21.

13. Max Liebmann, ed., "Les conclaves de Benoît XV et de Pie XI, notes du cardinal Piffl," *La revue nouvelle* 38, nos. 7–8 (1963): 45.

14. Maxime Mourin, *Le Vatican et l'URSS* (Paris: Payot, 1965), 29.

15. Secretariat of State to Bishop Adam Sapieha, April 9, 1915, Archive of Mons. Achille Ratti, Archivio Segreto Vaticano, Vatican City (ASV); Tomasz Schramm, "Watykan wobec odbudowy państwa polskiego," in *Szkice z dziejów papiestwa,* ed. Irena Koberdowa and Janusz Tazbir (Warsaw: Książka i Wiedza, 1989), 239; Francesco Vistalli, *Benedetto XV* (Rome: Tipografia Poliglotta Vaticana, 1928), 174; Stanisław Dzierzbicki, *Pamiętniki z lat wojny, 1915–1918* (Warsaw: Państwowy Instytut Wydawniczy, 1983), 96.

16. Castellan, *Dieu garde,* 102.

17. Wacław Jędrzejewicz, ed., *Kronika życia Józefa Piłsudskiego* (London: Polska Fundacja Kulturalna, 1989), 3:13–14; Aleksandra Piłsudska, *Wspomnienia* (Warsaw: Novum, 1989), 186.

18. Bronisław Bozowski, "Ks. Kardynał Aleksander Kakowski," *Więź* 5 (May 1973): 107; Walerian Meysztowicz, *Gawędy o czasach i ludziach* (London: Polska Fundacja Kulturalna, 1983), 168–69.

19. Bożena Krzywobłocka, *Chadecja, 1918–1938* (Warsaw: Książka i Wiedza, 1974), 46.

20. Robert Speaight, *The Life of Hilaire Belloc* (New York: Farrar, Straus and Cudahy, 1957), 359.

21. J. C. H. Aveling, *The Jesuits* (London: Blond and Briggs, 1981), 344; Thomas E. Hachey, ed., *Anglo-Vatican Relations, 1914–1939: Confidential Annual Reports of the British Ministers to the Holy See* (Boston: G. K. Hall, 1972), 16; Roberto Morozzo della Rocca, *Le nazioni non muoiono: Russia rivoluzionaria, Polonia indipendente, e Santa Sede* (Bologna: Il Mulino, 1992), 136.

22. Hachey, *Anglo-Vatican Relations,* 4; Fernand Hayward, *Un pape méconnu, Benoît XV* (Tournai: Casterman, 1955), 87–88.

23. Roman Dmowski, *Polityka polska i odbudowanie państwa* (Warsaw: Perzyński, Niklewicz, 1925), 136–37; Schramm, "Watykan," 244–45.

24. Jan Skarbek, "W dobie rozbiorów i braku państwowości (1772–1918)," in *Zarys dziejów Kościoła katolickiego w Polsce,* by Jerzy Kłoczowski, Lidia Müllerowa, and Jan Skarbek (Kraków: Znak, 1986), 284; Edward J. Pałyga, *Polsko-watykańskie stosunki dyplomatyczne: Od zarania II Rzeczypospolitej do pontyfikatu papieża-Polaka* (Warsaw: Instytut Wydawniczy Związków Zawodowych, 1988), 22; Schramm, "Watykan," 246.

25. Roman M. Zawadzki, "Biskup Adam Stefan Sapieha podczas pierwszej wojny światowej," in *Kardynał Adam Stefan Sapieha,* ed. Stanisław Stępień (Przemyśl: Południowo-Wschodni Instytut Naukowy w Przemyślu, 1995), 150.

26. Benedict XV to Polish episcopate, July 16, 1921, Archiwum Prymasów Polski (APP), Archiwum Archidiecezjalne w Gnieźnie, Gniezno.

27. Hayward, *Pape méconnu,* 104; Józef Wołczański, "Adam Stefan Sapieha w korespondencji z biskupami Galicji (Małopolski) w latach 1900–1939," in Stępień, *Kardynał,* 123–24. Fr. Ledóchowski served on the small curial committee that drafted the "Peace Note." Hachey, *Anglo-Vatican Relations,* 16.

28. Sapieha to Archbishop Teodoro Valfré di Bonzo, March 25, 1917, in *Achilles Ratti (1918–1921),* vol. 1, *25 IV–31 VII 1918,* ed. Stanisław Wilk, Acta Nuntiaturae Polonae 57 (Rome: Institutum Historicum Polonicum, 1995), 332–33.

29. Castellan, *Dieu garde,* 108; Bogdan Hutten-Czapski, *Sześćdziesiąt lat życia politycznego i towarzyskiego* (Warsaw: Hoesick, 1936), 2:418; Cardinal Aleksander Kakowski, unpublished memoir, "Z niewoli do niepodległości," Archiwum Archidiecezjalne Warszawskie, Warsaw, 2:76–77; Janusz Pajewski, *Odbudowa państwa polskiego, 1914–1918* (Warsaw: Państwowe Wydawnictwo Naukowe, 1978), 204–6.

30. Terzo Natalini, ed., *I diari del cardinale Ermenegildo Pellegrinetti, 1916–1922* (Vatican City: Archivio Segreto Vaticano, 1994), 183; Ratti to Gasparri, October 14, 1918, in Wilk, *Achilles Ratti,* vol. 2, *1 VIII–11 XI 1918,* 219.

31. Ratti to Gasparri, August 17, 1918, in Wilk, *Achilles Ratti,* 2:48.

32. "50. rocznica śmierci Arcybiskupa Józefa Teodorowicza," *Tygodnik powszechny,* January 8, 1989.

33. Valfré di Bonzo to Gasparri, January 13, 1918, in Wilk, *Achilles Ratti,* 1:361–62; Ratti to Gasparri, September 1, 1918, in Wilk, *Achilles Ratti,* 2:129; Gasparri to Ratti, September 28, 1918, in Wilk, *Achilles Ratti,* 2:199; Wołczański, "Adam Stefan Sapieha," 124.

34. Benedict XV to Kakowski, October 15, 1918, APP.

35. Polish episcopate to the Polish nation, in *Kościół w czasie wojny polsko-bolszewickiej, 1919–1920,* ed. Marian Marek Drozdowski and Andrzej Serafin (Warsaw: Polska Akademia Nauk, 1995), 49–51.

36. Kakowski, "Z niewoli," 5:8–9; Bozowski, "Kakowski," 107; Natalini, *Diari Pellegrinetti,* 177, 185, 188; Ratti to Gasparri, October 24, 1918, in Wilk, *Achilles Ratti,* 2:241–44.

37. Dalbor to Ratti, January 19, 1919, Ratti Papers; Hutten-Czapski, *Sześćdziesiąt lat,* 2:605–6; *Times* (London), February 15, 1919.

38. *Times* (London), December 2, 1918.

39. Jean-Marie Mayeur, "Les églises et les relations internationales: L'Église catholique," in *Histoire du Christianisme des origines à nos jours,* vol. 12, *Guerres mondiales et totalitarismes (1914–1958),* ed. Jean-Marie Mayeur (Paris: Desclée-Fayard, 1990), 313.

40. For instance, that of Antoni Sujkowski, cited in Kłoczowski, Müllerowa, and Skarbek, *Zarys dziejów Kościoła,* 295.

41. Ermenegildo Pellegrinetti, "Relazione finale," July 1921, in *L'Archivio di Mons. Achille Ratti, visitatore apostolico e nunzio a Varsavia (1918–1921): Inventario,* ed. Ottavio Cavalleri (Vatican City: Archivio Segreto Vaticano, 1990), 185.

42. Ibid., 179–80.

43. Józef Wierusz-Kowalski to Władysław Skrzyński, September 1, 1919, APIP, 2:314; Wierusz-Kowalski to Piłsudski, October 20, 1919, Archiwum Adiutantury Generalnej Naczelnego Dowództwa (Archiwum Belwederskie) (AGND)

64/1773, Sterling Library, Yale University; Natalini, *Diari Pellegrinetti,* 187–88, 215, 228, 230; Ratti to Gasparri, November 4, 1918, in Wilk, *Achilles Ratti,* 2:277–79.

44. Jules Laroche, *La Pologne de Pilsudski: Souvenirs d'une ambassade, 1926–1935* (Paris: Flammarion, 1953), 98; Daniel Stone, ed., *The Polish Memoirs of William John Rose* (Toronto: University of Toronto, 1975), 152; Francesco Tommasini, *La risurrezione della Polonia* (Milan: Fratelli Treves, 1925), 10; Pellegrinetti, "Relazione finale," 192; Meysztowicz, *Gawędy,* 261.

45. Maciej Rataj, *Pamiętniki* (Warsaw: Ludowa Spółdzielnia Wydawnicza, 1965), 53; Pellegrinetti, "Relazione finale," 190–91; Natalini, *Diari Pellegrinetti,* 210; Wołczański, "Adam Stefan Sapieha," 136–37.

46. Istruzioni della S. Congregazione Orientale, [1936–37], ASV, Affari Ecclesiastici Straordinari: Polonia.

47. Francis McCullagh, *The Bolshevik Persecution of Christianity* (New York: E. P. Dutton, 1924), 313.

48. Quoted in Ryszard Torzecki, "Z problematyki stosunków polsko-ukraińskich," *Dzieje najnowsze* 17, no. 2 (1985): 155.

49. Krzysztof Krasowski, "Między Warszawą a Watykanem: Episkopat Polski wobec rządu i Stolicy Apostolskiej, 1918–1939," in Koberdowa and Tazbir, *Szkice,* 271.

50. Jerzy Kłoczowski, "Catholiques et protestants dans l'Europe du centre-est," in Mayeur, *Histoire du Christianisme,* 712; Jerzy Kłoczowski and Lidia Müllerowa, "W dwudziestym stuleciu (1918–1980)," in Kłoczowski, Müllerowa, and Skarbek, *Zarys dziejów Kościoła,* 292–93.

51. Laroche, *La Pologne de Pilsudski,* 85.

52. *Times* (London), January 3, 1920.

Chapter 2

1. Robin Anderson, *Between Two Wars: The Story of Pope Pius XI (Achille Ratti), 1922–1939* (Chicago: Franciscan Herald Press, 1977), 25; Lillian Browne-Olf, *Their Name Is Pius: Portraits of Five Great Modern Popes* (Milwaukee, Wisc.: Bruce, 1941), 320; Thomas B. Morgan, *A Reporter at the Papal Court: A Narrative of the Reign of Pope Pius XI* (New York: Longmans, Green and Co., 1937), 143–47; Angelo Paredi, "I tre anni di Achille Ratti in Polonia (1918–1921)," in *"Polonia Restituta": L'Italia e la ricostruzione della Polonia, 1918–1921,* ed. Marta Herling (Milan: Centro di Studi sull'Europa Orientale, 1992), 117; Walter H. Peters, *The Life of Benedict XV* (Milwaukee, Wisc.: Bruce, 1959), 198–99; Cardinal Aleksander Kakowski, unpublished memoir, "Z niewoli do niepodległości," Archiwum Archidiecezjalne Warszawskie, Warsaw, 4:725.

2. Charles Loiseau, "La politique du Saint-Siège en Europe centrale (1919–1936) —II," *Le monde slave* 14, no. 1 (1937): 103–4; Gasparri to Ratti, May 4, 1918, in

Achilles Ratti (1918–1921), vol. 1, *25 IV–31 VII 1918*, ed. Stanisław Wilk, Acta Nuntiaturae Polonae 57 (Rome: Institutum Historicum Polonicum, 1995), 36–49; Gasparri to Ratti, June 30, 1918, Archive of Mons. Achille Ratti, Archivio Segreto Vaticano, Vatican City.

3. Bogdan Hutten-Czapski, *Sześćdziesiąt lat życia politycznego i towarzyskiego* (Warsaw: Hoesick, 1936), 2:551. By 1920, Ratti's responsibility for the lands of "former Russia" had been reduced to exclude Finland and Ukraine, which were assigned their own apostolic visitors.

4. Paredi, "I tre anni," 118.

5. Gasparri to Ratti, September 7, 1919, Ratti Papers.

6. *L'Osservatore romano*, July 26, 1960; Carlo Confalonieri, *Pio XI visto da vicino* (Turin: Editrice S.A.I.E., 1957), 321–22; Ratti to Dalbor, Archiwum Prymasów Polski (APP), Archiwum Archidiecezjalne w Gnieźnie, Gniezno; Władysław Skrzyński to Józef Beck, February 10, 1934, Poland—Ambasada (Catholic Church), Hoover Institution Archives, Stanford, Calif. (HIA); Terzo Natalini, ed., *I diari del cardinale Ermenegildo Pellegrinetti, 1916–1922* (Vatican City: Archivio Segreto Vaticano, 1994), 142; William Teeling, *Pope Pius XI and World Affairs* (New York: Frederick A. Stokes, 1937), 67; Benedict Williamson, *The Story of Pope Pius XI* (New York: P. J. Kennedy and Sons, 1931), 54.

7. *Times* (London), January 28, 1919.

8. Piotr Szczudłowski, "Polityczna działalność abpa Józefa Teodorowicza w okresie II Rzeczypospolitej," *Nasza przeszłość* 81 (1994): 117.

9. Ermenegildo Pellegrinetti, "Relazione finale," July 1921, in *L'Archivio di Mons. Achille Ratti, visitatore apostolico e nunzio a Varsavia (1918–1921): Inventario*, ed. Ottavio Cavalleri (Vatican City: Archivio Segreto Vaticano, 1990), 191, 193.

10. Bronisław Bozowski, "Ks. Kardynał Aleksander Kakowski," *Więż* 5 (May 1973): 100, 108; Stanisław Wilk, *Episkopat Kościoła katolickiego w Polsce w latach 1918–1939* (Warsaw: Wydawnictwo Salezjańskie, 1992), 74–75, 429.

11. Wacław Jędrzejewicz, ed., *Kronika życia Józefa Piłsudskiego* (London: Polska Fundacja Kulturalna, 1977), 1:460.

12. Maciej Rataj, *Pamiętniki* (Warsaw: Ludowa Spółdzielnia Wydawnicza, 1965), 53.

13. Kakowski, "Z niewoli," 5:30.

14. Aleksandra Piłsudska, *Wspomnienia* (Warsaw: Novum, 1989), 233.

15. "Opis podróży nuncjusza Rattiego do Wilna i Kowna," *Tygodnik powszechny*, March 28, 1993. See also Wacław Jędrzejewicz, *Józef Piłsudski, 1867–1935: Życiorys* (London: Polska Fundacja Kulturalna, 1993), 65, and John Murray, "St. Andrew Bobola and Poland," *Month*, July 1938, 27–28.

16. Pellegrinetti, "Relazione finale," 160; Kakowski, "Z niewoli," 5:33.

17. Pellegrinetti to Gasparri, August 23, 1921, Ratti Papers.

18. Daniel Stone, ed., *The Polish Memoirs of William John Rose* (Toronto: University of Toronto Press, 1975), 102.

19. Francesco Tommasini, *La risurrezione della Polonia* (Milan: Fratelli Treves, 1925), 96–97.

20. Stanisław Janikowski to Beck, January 5, 1938, Ambasada RP przy Watykanie A.44.122/17, Instytut Historyczny im. Generała Sikorskiego, London (IHGS).

21. Mgr. Walerian Meysztowicz, "La nunziatura di Achille Ratti in Polonia," in *Pio XI nel trentesimo della morte (1939–1969): Raccolta di studi e di memorie,* ed. Carlo Colombo (Milan: Ufficio Studi Arcivescovile, 1969), 195. Also Skrzyński to August Zaleski, June 27, 1931, IHGS A.44.122/7; Walerian Meysztowicz, *Gawędy o czasach i ludziach* (London: Polska Fundacja Kulturalna, 1983), 169, 261.

22. Natalini, *Diari Pellegrinetti,* 184, 237, 241.

23. Skrzyński to Zaleski, November 8, 1929, IHGS A.44.122/2; Pellegrinetti, "Relazione finale," 192; Rataj, *Pamiętniki,* 53.

24. In the Ratti Papers, see the file "Concordato, 1918 July–1920 March," and "Osservazioni sul 'Projet de l'organisation de l'Église Catholique dans le Royaume de Pologne'" [1919?]. In addition, Rataj, *Pamiętniki,* 54, and Tommasini, *La risurrezione,* 98.

25. Pellegrinetti to Gasparri, July 23, 1921, Ratti Papers; Sapieha notes on concordat, November 8, 1931, Cardinal Sapieha Papers, Archiwum Kurii Metropolitalnej, Kraków; Krzysztof Krasowski, "Między Warszawą a Watykanem: Episkopat Polski wobec rządu i Stolicy Apostolskiej, 1918–1939," in *Szkice z dziejów papiestwa,* ed. Irena Koberdowa and Janusz Tazbir (Warsaw: Książka i Wiedza, 1989), 295–97; Roberto Morozzo della Rocca, *Le nazioni non muoiono: Russia rivoluzionaria, Polonia indipendente, e Santa Sede* (Bologna: Il Mulino, 1992), 297; Wilk, *Episkopat,* 96–97.

26. Angelo Tamborra, "Benedetto XV e i problemi nazionali e religiosi dell'Europa orientale," in *Benedetto XV, i cattolici e la prima guerra mondiale,* ed. Giuseppe Rossini (Rome: Edizioni 5 Lune, 1963), 868.

27. Szczudłowski, "Polityczna," 124, 135.

28. In *Archiwum polityczne Ignacego Paderewskiego* (APIP), ed. Halina Janowska (Wrocław: Zakład Narodowy im. Ossolińskich, 1974): Sapieha to Paderewski, May 11, 1919, 2:150, Jan Ciechanowski to MSZ, June 30, 1919, 2:231, Wierusz-Kowalski to Skrzyński, September 1, 1919, 2:314–16, Maciej Loret to Paderewski, November 4, 1919, 2:363; Meysztowicz, *Gawędy,* 259; Konstanty Skirmunt to Komisja Likwidacyjna Polskiego Komitetu Narodowego, May 23, 1919, in *Watykan a stosunki polsko-niemieckie w latach 1918–1939,* ed. Jarosław Jurkiewicz (Warsaw: Książka i Wiedza, 1960), 21–22.

29. Wierusz-Kowalski to Paderewski, [July 1919], APIP, 2:291–92.

30. Francesco Vistalli, *Benedetto XV* (Rome: Tipografia Poliglotta Vaticana, 1928), 297; Stewart A. Stehlin, *Weimar and the Vatican, 1919–1933: German-Vatican Diplomatic Relations in the Interwar Years* (Princeton, N.J.: Princeton University Press, 1983), 71.

31. Gasparri to Ratti, May 23, 1920, Ratti Papers.

32. Hansjakob Stehle, *Eastern Politics of the Vatican, 1917–1979* (Athens: Ohio University Press, 1981), 19; Stehlin, *Weimar,* 126.

33. Rataj, *Pamiętniki,* 87.

34. Morozzo della Rocca, *Le nazioni,* 285–86.

35. Jędrzejewicz, *Kronika życia,* 1:503.

36. *Kościół w czasie wojny polsko-bolszewickiej, 1919–1920,* ed. Marian Marek Drozdowski and Andrzej Serafin (Warsaw: Polska Akademia Nauk, 1995), 96–102; Jędrzejewicz, *Kronika życia,* 3:33.

37. Wierusz-Kowalski to MSZ, July 12, July 16, August 6, August 8, 1920, 67b/4264 and 68a/4506, Archiwum Adiutantury Generalnej Naczelnego Dowództwa (Archiwum Belwederskie) (AGND), Sterling Library, Yale University; *L'Osservatore romano,* August 8, 1920; *Times* (London), August 13, 1920.

38. For this paragraph, [Skrzyński ?] to Beck, August 26, 1933, HIA; Eustachy Sapieha to Ratti, August 13, 1920, Ratti Papers; Kakowski to clergy of Archdiocese of Warsaw, August 10, 1920, in Drozdowski and Serafin, *Kościół w czasie wojny,* 108–9; Morozzo della Rocca, *Le nazioni,* 289; Georges Roche and Philippe Saint Germain, *Pie XII devant l'histoire* (Paris: Robert Laffont, 1972), 40; Stehle, *Eastern Politics,* 20; Tamborra, "Benedetto XV," in Rossini, *Benedetto XV,* 867–68; Wincenty Witos, *Moje wspomnienia* (Paris: Instytut Literacki, 1964), 2:287, 310–11.

39. Benedict XV to Polish Episcopate, September 8, 1920, in Drozdowski and Serafin, *Kościół w czasie wojny,* 42–43; *Times* (London), August 30, September 7, September 9, 1920.

40. Janina Barycka, *Stosunek kleru do Państwa i oświaty* (Warsaw: Nasza Księgarnia, 1934), 36–38. In Drozdowski and Serafin, *Kościół w czasie wojny,* see the statements of Polish prelates giving thanks to God and the Blessed Virgin for the victory but omitting mention of the commander, 123–30. In his memoirs, Cardinal Kakowski characteristically tried to walk down the middle of the road by stating that "the Miracle on the Vistula was certainly an act of Providence, but also of the army and the entire nation." "Z niewoli," 5:49.

41. Wierusz-Kowalski to Skrzyński, November 15, 1919, APIP, 2:371; *Kurjer lwowski,* December 21, 1920; Stehlin, *Weimar,* 104–13, 117; Tytus Komarnicki and Józef Zarański, eds., *Diariusz i teki Jana Szembeka (1935–1945)* (Szembek) (London: Polish Research Centre, 1964), 1:335–36.

42. In AGND: Wierusz-Kowalski to MSZ, December 16, 1919, 65a/2137, March 8, 1920, 65b/2937, March 16 and 17, 1920, 70/5797; Kazimierz Rędziński, "Watykańscy komisarze a plebiscyt górnośląski," *Człowiek i światopogląd* 7–8 (1985): 89; Zygmunt Zieliński, "Udział Adama Stefana Sapiehy w sprawie Śląskiej podczas plebiscytu w roku 1921," in *Księga Sapieżyńska,* ed. Jerzy Wolny (Kraków: Polskie Towarzystwo Teologiczne, 1986), 2:95.

43. Wierusz-Kowalski to MSZ, February 3, 1920, AGND 65a/2476; Ratti to Gasparri, August 23, 1920, Ratti Papers; *Przegląd wieczorny,* October 7, 1920; Stehlin, *Weimar,* 114; Tommasini, *La risurrezione,* 100.

44. Peters, *Benedict XV,* 200–201. See also Stanisław Sierpowski, "Nieznane listy nuncjusza apostolskiego w Polsce—Achillesa Rattiego z lat 1920–1921," *Życie i myśl* 39 (1991): 52.

45. MSZ to Sapieha, September 15, 1920, Sapieha Papers.

46. In AGND: Wierusz-Kowalski to MSZ, October 3, 1920, 68b/5072, Loret to MSZ, October 18, 1920, 69b/5478; Naczelna Rada Ludowa na Górnym Śląsku to MSZ, March 11, 1922, Ministerstwo Wyznań Religijnych i Oświecenia Publicznego (MWRiOP), no. 415, Archiwum Akt Nowych (AAN), Warsaw; Browne-Olf, *Their Name,* 326–27; Zieliński, "Udział," 94–95.

47. Ratti to Bertram, November 26, 1920, Ratti Papers; Stehlin, *Weimar,* 127–28; Kakowski, "Z niewoli," 5:199.

48. Gasparri to Pellegrinetti, July 3, 1921, Ratti Papers. Also Józef Bańka, "Dekret ks. kard. Adolfa Bertrama z 21 XI 1920 roku a ks. Achilles Ratti, późniejszy Papież Pius XI," *Nasza przeszłość* 36 (1971): 287–306; Rędziński, "Watykańscy komisarze," 62–66; Stehlin, *Weimar,* 121–22; Tommasini, *La risurrezione,* 101; Zieliński, "Udział," in Wolny, *Księga,* 96–98.

49. Eustachy Sapieha to Ratti, December 29, 1920, Ratti Papers; France, Ministère des Affaires Étrangères, *Bulletin périodique de la presse polonaise* (BPPP), no. 97.

50. In AGND: Przeździecki memorandum, November 21, 1920, 70/5752, Wierusz-Kowalski to MSZ, December 4, 1920, 71/6030, Maj. Kierzowski memorandum, December 14, 1920, 71/6124; Rataj, *Pamiętniki,* 191–92.

51. Poland, Sejm, *Sprawozdanie stenograficzne z posiedzenia Sejmu Rzeczypospolitej,* November 30, 1920; *Times* (London), December 8, 1920; Rataj, *Pamiętniki,* 119.

52. Ratti to Gasparri, December 5, 1920, Ratti Papers.

53. Gasparri to Ratti, November 24 and December 28, 1920, Ratti Papers.

54. Morozzo della Rocca, *Le nazioni,* 171, 243; Rędziński, "Watykańscy komisarze," 82. Also see Sierpowski, "Nieznane listy," 53–54.

55. In AGND: Wierusz-Kowalski to MSZ, November 22, 1920, 72a/6389, November 23, 1920, 72a/6388, December 3 and December 11, 1920, 71/6203.

56. Teodorowicz memorandum on Upper Silesia, [1938?], Sapieha Papers; Natalini, *Diari Pellegrinetti,* 248; Rataj, *Pamiętniki,* 53–55.

57. Szczudłowski, "Polityczna," 125–30; Zieliński, "Udział," in Wolny, *Księga,* 100–102.

58. Teodorowicz to Benedict XV, March 19, 1921, Gasparri to Sapieha, April 8, 1921, Sapieha Papers; Gasparri to Ratti, April 12, 1921, Ratti Papers.

59. Edward J. Pałyga, *Polsko-watykańskie stosunki dyplomatyczne: Od zarania II Rzeczypospolitej do pontyfikatu papieża-Polaka* (Warsaw: Instytut Wydawniczy Związków Zawodowych, 1988), 50. See as well Pellegrinetti to Gasparri, June 19, 1921, Ratti Papers; Natalini, *Diari Pellegrinetti,* 246; Szczudłowski, "Polityczna,"

132–33; Tommasini, *La risurrezione,* 97; Wołczański, "Adam Stefan Sapieha," in Stępień, *Kardynał,* 125–26.

60. Meysztowicz, *Gawędy,* 262; Morgan, *Reporter,* 153–54; Paredi, "I tre anni," 122.

61. Skrzyński to MSZ, July 3, 1921, Ambasada RP w Londynie, no. 879, AAN. Also Wierusz-Kowalski to MSZ, June 10, 1921, AGND 74b/7903; Rataj, *Pamiętniki,* 53–55.

62. Benedict XV to Polish episcopate, July 16, 1921, Ratti Papers; Skrzyński to MSZ, September 30, 1921, AAN-MWRiOP, no. 432. Also Stanisław Kętrzyński, report of MSZ Political Department on Polish-Vatican relations, January 29, 1921, reprinted in Jurkiewicz, *Watykan a stosunki,* 27–32; Stehle, *Eastern Politics,* 19.

63. Kakowski, "Z niewoli," 5:201.

64. Ibid., 131–33. See as well Meysztowicz, *Gawędy,* 263.

65. Meysztowicz, "La nunziatura," 197–98; Meysztowicz, *Gawędy,* 262; Tommasini, *La risurrezione,* 101.

66. Anderson, *Between Two Wars,* 57; Max Liebmann, ed., "Les conclaves de Benoît XV et de Pie XI, notes du cardinal Piffl," *La revue nouvelle* 38, nos. 7–8 (1963): 50–51.

67. *Le messager polonais,* February 21, 1925.

68. *Times* (London), February 8, 1922.

69. Kakowski, "Z niewoli," 5:202; BPPP, no. 115.

70. M. Pernot, *Le Saint-Siège, l'Église catholique et la politique mondiale,* 2nd ed. (Paris: Armand Colin, 1929), 153, quoted in Georges Castellan, *Dieu garde la Pologne! Histoire du catholicisme polonais, 1795–1980* (Paris: Robert Laffont, 1981), 123.

71. BPPP, no. 115.

72. Natalini, *Diari Pellegrinetti,* 264.

73. Wierusz-Kowalski to Skrzyński, September 1, 1919, APIP, 2:313–15; Rataj, *Pamiętniki,* 54; Meysztowicz, *Gawędy,* 305–6.

74. For instance, Carlo Falconi, *The Popes in the Twentieth Century: From Pius X to John XXIII* (Boston: Little, Brown, 1967), 172; J. Derek Holmes, *The Papacy in the Modern World, 1914–1978* (London: Burns and Oates, 1981), 91; Anthony Rhodes, *The Vatican in the Age of the Dictators, 1922–1945* (New York: Holt, Rinehart and Winston, 1973), 19.

75. Tommasini, *La risurrezione,* 97.

76. Henri Daniel-Rops, *A Fight for God, 1870–1939* (London: J. M. Dent and Sons, 1966), 272. Also see Meysztowicz, "La nunziatura," 201, and Stehlin, *Weimar,* 81–84.

77. Jędrzejewicz, *Kronika życia,* 2:51.

78. François Charles-Roux, *Huit ans au Vatican, 1932–1940* (Paris: Flammarion, 1947), 31.

79. Witold Malej, "Kardynał Aleksander Kakowski w świetle własnych wspomnień," *Nasza przeszłość* 8 (1958): 266.

80. Report of Polish minister to the Vatican, April 10, 1922, Ambasada RP w Londynie, no. 879, AAN.

Chapter 3

1. Since the point is often misunderstood, it may be worth noting that a concordat is not tantamount to alliance of the Apostolic See with the corresponding state, or approval of its policy. In other words, the fact that the Vatican reached a concordat with Nazi Germany in 1933 does not in itself suggest friendly relations between those two governments, any more than arms control treaties indicated friendly relations between the United States and the Soviet Union during the Cold War. Indeed, the root of any concordat is a mutual recognition of the potential for conflict over the welfare of Catholics and their Church that must be settled by negotiation and treaty and cannot be left to trust or goodwill. In practice, the ability to contemplate or conclude a concordat requires a certain minimum of compatibility, at least in the sense of being able to do business, but the papacy could, and did, reach such agreements with regimes with which it did not see eye to eye. Again, Nazi Germany is a prime example. See Frank J. Coppa, ed., *Controversial Concordats: The Vatican's Relations with Napoleon, Mussolini, and Hitler* (Washington, D.C.: Catholic University of America Press, 1999).

2. Stanisław Wilk, *Episkopat Kościoła katolickiego w Polsce w latach 1918–1939* (Warsaw: Wydawnictwo Salezjańskie, 1992), 97. See as well Krzysztof Krasowski, *Episkopat katolicki w II Rzeczypospolitej* (Warsaw: Redakcja Naukowa, 1992), 42–43.

3. Leszek Kuk, "A Powerful Catholic Church, Unstable State and Authoritarian Political Regime: The Christian Democratic Party in Poland," in *Political Catholicism in Europe, 1918–1945*, ed. Wolfram Kaiser and Helmut Wohnout (London: Routledge, 2004), 150–71.

4. Cardinal Aleksander Kakowski, unpublished memoir, "Z niewoli do niepodległości," 5:152, 160, 173–76, Archiwum Archidiecezjalne Warszawskie, Warsaw; Wincenty Urban, *Ostatni etap dziejów Kościoła w Polsce przed nowym tysiącleciem, 1815–1965* (Rome: Hosianum, 1966), 468.

5. Maciej Rataj, *Pamiętniki* (Warsaw: Ludowa Spółdzielnia Wydawnicza, 1965), 52–53; Piotr Szczudłowski, "Polityczna działalność abpa Józefa Teodorowicza w okresie II Rzeczypospolitej," *Nasza przeszłość* 81 (1994): 148; Francesco Tommasini, *La risurrezione della Polonia* (Milan: Fratelli Treves, 1925), 98; Wincenty Urban, "Kościół wobec reformy rolnej w Polsce odrodzonej," in *Kościół w II Rzeczypospolitej*, ed. Zygmunt Zieliński and Stanisław Wilk (Lublin: Katolicki Uniwersytet Lubelski, 1980), 65–67.

6. Poland, Sejm, *Sprawozdanie stenograficzne z posiedzenia Sejmu Rzeczypospolitej*, November 4, 17, 19, 1920; Władysław Abraham, "Konstytucja a stosunki wyznaniowe i Kościół," in *Nasza konstytucja*, ed. Michał Rostworowski et al. (Kraków: By the author, 1922), 115–16.

7. Bohdan Cywiński, *Ogniem próbowane—I: Korzenie tożsamości* (Rome: Papieski Instytut Studiów Kościelnych, 1982), 68.

8. Abraham, "Konstytucja," 128–32.

9. Ministerstwo Wyznań Religijnych i Oświecenia Publicznego (MWRiOP), no. 400, Archiwum Akt Nowych (AAN), Warsaw; Charles Loiseau, "La politique du Saint-Siège en Europe centrale (1919–1936)—II," *Le monde slave* 14, no. 1 (1937): 105; Władysław Leopold Jaworski, "Kościół Rzymsko-Katolicki a Konstytucja polska," *Ruch prawniczy* 2, no. 1 (1922): 3–4.

10. Krasowski, *Episkopat*, 65.

11. Polish episcopate, "Memorjał dla Rządu Rzeczypospolitej," January 17, 1922, Cardinal Sapieha Papers, Archiwum Kurii Metropolitalnej, Kraków; Bożena Krzywobłocka, *Chadecja, 1918–1938* (Warsaw: Książka i Wiedza, 1974), 60; MSZ to Jerzy Madejski, March 6, 1922, Ambasada RP w Berlinie, AAN, no. 1556.

12. Henri Daniel-Rops, *A Fight for God, 1870–1939* (London: J. M. Dent and Sons, 1966), 260–61; Thomas E. Hachey, ed., *Anglo-Vatican Relations, 1914–1939: Confidential Annual Reports of the British Ministers to the Holy See* (Boston: G. K. Hall, 1972), 85.

13. Jan Gawroński, *Moja misja w Wiedniu, 1932–1938* (Warsaw: Państwowe Wydawnictwo Naukowe, 1965), 151; Walerian Meysztowicz, *Gawędy o czasach i ludziach* (London: Polska Fundacja Kulturalna, 1983), 325.

14. Meysztowicz, *Gawędy*, 318, 321, 331–32. For an example of official Polish grumbling about Vatican policy, see Stanisław Kętrzyński, report of MSZ Political Department on Polish-Vatican relations, January 29, 1921, in *Watykan a stosunki polsko-niemieckie w latach 1918–1939*, ed. Jarosław Jurkiewicz (Warsaw: Książka i Wiedza, 1960), 27–32.

15. Karolina Lanckorońska, "Władysław Skrzyński," *Tygodnik powszechny*, March 10, 1996. See also Alfred Wysocki, *Tajemnice dyplomatycznego sejfu* (Warsaw: Książka i Wiedza, 1988), 216.

16. Meysztowicz, *Gawędy*, 319; Terzo Natalini, ed., *I diari del cardinale Ermenegildo Pellegrinetti, 1916–1922* (Vatican City: Archivio Segreto Vaticano, 1994), 254.

17. Meysztowicz, *Gawędy*, 319. Montini appears to have found Warsaw tedious, and this may have contributed to the brevity of his posting there. Frank J. Coppa, "The Contemporary Papacy from Paul VI to Benedict XVI: A Bibliographical Essay," *Catholic Historical Review* 92, no. 4 (2006): 604.

18. Janikowski to Beck, July 24, 1936, and Skrzyński to Beck, December 4, 1936, Ambasada RP przy Watykanie A.44.122/15, Instytut Historyczny im. Generała Sikorskiego, London (IHGS); Tytus Komarnicki and Józef Zarański, eds., *Diariusz*

i teki Jana Szembeka (1935–1945) (Szembek) (London: Polish Research Centre, 1964), 2:312–13.

19. The quotations are from Rataj, *Pamiętniki,* 235–36, and Józef Beck, *Final Report* (New York: Robert Speller and Sons, 1957), 128. Also Meysztowicz, *Gawędy,* 287–88.

20. A Cologne newspaper praised Pius XI as "the most German pope in history." Daniel-Rops, *Fight for God,* 272.

21. Wacław Jędrzejewicz, ed., *Kronika życia Józefa Piłsudskiego* (London: Polska Fundacja Kulturalna, 1986), 2:66; in AAN-MWRiOP: MSZ to Wojewoda Rymer, Katowice, October 31, 1922, Hlond to MWRiOP, January 27, 1923, Silesian Provincial Government to MSZ, February 9, 1924, no. 415, and MSZ to MWRiOP, May 4, 1925, no. 455.

22. Harold Williamson to Charles Evans Hughes, October 19, 1922, Hugh Gibson Papers, Hoover Institution Archives, Stanford, Calif. (HIA); Wilk, *Episkopat,* 328–29.

23. Teodorowicz memo on candidacy to Senate, [1938], Sapieha Papers, no. 9; Meysztowicz, *Gawędy,* 306; Anthony Rhodes, *The Vatican in the Age of the Dictators, 1922–1945* (New York: Holt, Rinehart and Winston, 1973), 15; Wilk, *Episkopat,* 329.

24. Gibson to Hughes, March 1, 1923, Gibson Papers, HIA; Marian Aleksandrowicz, "Edmund Dalbor," in *Na stolicy prymasowskiej w Gnieźnie i w Poznaniu: Szkice o prymasach Polski w okresie niewoli narodowej i w II Rzeczypospolitej,* ed. Feliks Lenort (Poznań: Księgarnia Św. Wojciecha, 1982), 302.

25. Jerzy Kłoczowski and Lidia Müllerowa, "W dwudziestym stuleciu (1918–1980)," in *Zarys dziejów Kościoła katolickiego w Polsce,* by Jerzy Kłoczowski, Lidia Müllerowa, and Jan Skarbek (Kraków: Znak, 1986), 335; Jerzy Kłoczowski, "Catholiques et protestants dans l'Europe du centre-est," in *Histoire du Christianisme des origines à nos jours,* vol. 12, *Guerres mondiales et totalitarismes (1914–1958),* ed. Jean-Marie Mayeur (Paris: Desclée-Fayard, 1990), 712.

26. Tommasini, *La risurrezione,* 98–99.

27. Kakowski, "Z niewoli," 5:217–18; report of Bishop Szelążek meetings with pope and Cardinal Gasparri, [ca. August 1924], AAN-MWRiOP, no. 458; Tadeusz Górski, "Odrodzona Litwa i Stolica Apostolska," *Tygodnik powszechny,* September 12, 1993; Kazimierz Szwarcenberg Czerny, "Jak to było z konkordatem polskim z 1925 r.?" *Tygodnik powszechny,* September 12, 1971.

28. Stanisław Grabski, *Pamiętniki* (Warsaw: Czytelnik, 1989), 2:232; Szwarcenberg Czerny, "Jak to było?"; report of Bishop Szelążek meetings with pope and Cardinal Gasparri, [ca. August 1924], AAN-MWRiOP, no. 458. One of the many controversies surrounding the Polish concordat through the years has to do with the choice of Stanisław Grabski as negotiator and his performance in that capacity. Contemporary opponents of the concordat unleashed volleys of ad hominem attacks on Grabski, a National Democrat seen by many leftists as a partisan enemy

and a toady of clericalism. Among other faults, they charged him with incompetence, lack of preparedness, excessive deference to the Church, and seeking to use the concordat talks as a means of advancing his political ambitions. These criticisms were repeated by the official Marxist Polish historians of the Communist era, for instance Jerzy Wisłocki, *Konkordat polski z 1925 roku* (Poznań: UAM, 1977), 82–85. Unsurprisingly, his brother the prime minister defended him against such attacks. Władysław Grabski, *Dwa lata pracy u podstaw państwowości naszej (1924–1925)* (Warsaw: Hoesick, 1927), 141. Maciej Rataj, a peasant politician closely acquainted with the concordat project from its inception, also praised his work. Rataj, *Pamiętniki,* 325. In 1992, Krasowski, *Episkopat,* rejected most of the charges against Grabski as groundless or exaggerated, 78.

29. Kakowski, "Z niewoli," 5:203.

30. Stanisław Grabski, *Pamiętniki,* 2:230–34; Władysław Grabski, *Dwa lata,* 141.

31. Stanisław Grabski, *Pamiętniki,* 2:233, 238. See as well Rataj, *Pamiętniki,* 304. The Polish summaries of the negotiating sessions between Grabski and Borgongini-Duca are held in IHGS A.44.122/1 and Poland—Ambasada (Catholic Church), HIA.

32. France, Ministère des Affaires Étrangères, *Bulletin périodique de la presse polonaise* (BPPP), no. 152.

33. Adamski to Sapieha, March 11, 1925, Sapieha Papers. In the same collection, see Sapieha notes on concordat, November 8, 1931.

34. Adamski to Lauri, February 26, 1925, Archiwum Prymasów Polski (APP), Archiwum Archidiecezjalne w Gnieźnie, Gniezno. Also Adamski to Dalbor, January 23, 1925, APP; protocol of meeting of Polish episcopate, December 4–6, 1924, pro memoria of Polish episcopate, December 12, 1924, summary of meeting between Grabski and Borgongini-Duca, January 9, 1925, Poland—Ambasada (Catholic Church), HIA; Rataj, *Pamiętniki,* 304, 325.

35. Rataj, *Pamiętniki,* 308, 327. In addition, Bishop Henryk Przeździecki to Dalbor, March 11, 1925, Lauri to Dalbor, March 12, 1925, Adamski to Lauri, April 1, 1925, APP; Kakowski, "Z niewoli," 5:219–20.

36. *Sprawozdanie,* March 24–27, 1925. Also, Stanisław Grabski, *Pamiętniki,* 2:238; *Times* (London), March 30, 1925.

37. John B. Stetson Jr. to Frank Kellogg, January 5, 1926, 860c.00/305, State Department Decimal File, RG 59, National Archives, Washington, D.C. See as well Stewart A. Stehlin, *Weimar and the Vatican, 1919–1933: German-Vatican Diplomatic Relations in the Interwar Years* (Princeton, N.J.: Princeton University Press, 1983), 135–38, 415–16.

38. Polish Foreign Ministry to Polish Embassy, London, May 21, 1925, Ambasada RP w Londynie, Joseph Piłsudski Institute of America, New York (PIA); *Times* (London), March 12, 1925; Hachey, *Anglo-Vatican Relations,* 85–86.

39. Mgr. Valérien Meysztowicz, *L'Église Catholique en Pologne entre les deux guerres (1919–1939)* (Vatican City: n.p., 1944), 20.

40. Władysław Grabski, *Dwa lata,* 141.

41. Herbert Bednorz, *Le concordat de Pologne de 1925* (Paris: Domat-Montchrestien, 1938), 198–99; Kazimierz Gołąb, "Concordats between Poland and the Holy See," in *Poland in Christian Civilization,* ed. Jerzy Braun (London: Veritas, 1985), 585–86; Hubert Jedin et al., eds., *History of the Church,* vol. 10, *The Church in the Modern Age* (New York: Crossroad, 1981), 183–84; Wiktor Piotrowicz, *Z zagadnień wyznaniowych w Polsce* (Vilna: Lux, 1929), 18–22; Urban, *Ostatni etap,* 537.

42. *Times* (London), February 26, 1925.

43. Adam Gerstmann, ed., *Konkordat Polski ze Stolicą Apostolską* (Lwów: Bibljoteka Religijna, 1925), 26–27; Onio Giacchi, "La politica concordataria di Pio XI," in *Pio XI nel trentesimo della morte (1939–1969), raccolta di studi e di memorie,* ed. Carlo Colombo (Milan: Ufficio Studi Arcivescovile, 1969), 521; Krasowski, *Episkopat,* 77; Krzysztof Krasowski, "Między Warszawą a Watykanem: Episkopat Polski wobec rządu i Stolicy Apostolskiej, 1918–1939," in *Szkice z dziejów papiestwa,* ed. Irena Koberdowa and Janusz Tazbir (Warsaw: Książka i Wiedza, 1989), 309; Piotrowicz, *Z zagadnień,* 22.

44. BPPP, no. 152; Daniel-Rops, *Fight for God,* 261; Gerstmann, *Konkordat,* 5–6; Gołąb, "Concordats," 584; Krasowski, *Episkopat,* 82.

45. A latter-day version of this line of argument became an obligatory part of Polish Marxist historiography of the Communist interlude of 1945–89. Indeed, disparagement of the concordat as an abject surrender to the cloth ranked as Exhibit A of the Communist critique of interwar church-state relations. Writings from the Stalinist phase are worthless, of course. The work of historians of the post-1956 "thaw," such as Jarosław Jurkiewicz and Wiesław Mysłek, may be used with caution, but are still heavily weighted with ideological bias. Even the more sophisticated scholarship of Jerzy Wisłocki, the principal Marxist analyst of the concordat, published in the later 1970s, seriously overstates the chumminess of the Second Republic with the papacy and the Polish Church of its day.

46. Sapieha notes on concordat, November 8, 1931, Sapieha Papers. See also Andrzej Biernacki, "Książę-metropolita krakowski," *Tygodnik powszechny,* July 2, 1989; Władysław Grabski, *Dwa lata,* 141; Krzysztof Skubiszewski, "Adam Stefan Sapieha a zawarcie Konkordatu polskiego," in *Księga Sapieżyńska,* ed. Jerzy Wolny (Kraków: Polskie Towarzystwo Teologiczne, 1986), 2:22–24; Wilk, *Episkopat,* 111–12.

47. Wiesław Mysłek, *Kościół katolicki w Polsce w latach 1918–1939: Zarys historyczny* (Warsaw: Książka i Wiedza, 1966), 34.

Chapter 4

1. Krzysztof Krasowski, "Między Warszawą a Watykanem: Episkopat Polski wobec rządu i Stolicy Apostolskiej, 1918–1939," in *Szkice z dziejów papiestwa,* ed. Irena Koberdowa and Janusz Tazbir (Warsaw: Książka i Wiedza, 1989), 313;

J. Pietrzak, "Czy kardynał August Hlond był zwolennikiem sanacji?" in *Kościół w II Rzeczypospolitej,* ed. Zygmunt Zieliński and Stanisław Wilk (Lublin: Katolicki Uniwersytet Lubelski, 1980), 76.

2. Witold Malej, "Kardynał Aleksander Kakowski w świetle własnych wspomnień," *Nasza przeszłość* 8 (1958): 262. Also Andrzej Ajnenkiel, *Od rządów ludowych do przewrotu majowego: Zarys dziejów politycznych Polski, 1918–1926* (Warsaw: Wiedza Powszechna, 1978), 400–401.

3. Andrzej Micewski, *Z geografii politycznej II Rzeczypospolitej* (Warsaw: Więź, 1964), 189–90. See as well Wacław Jędrzejewicz, ed., *Kronika życia Józefa Piłsudskiego* (London: Polska Fundacja Kulturalna, 1986), 2:232, and Cardinal Aleksander Kakowski, unpublished memoir, "Z niewoli do niepodległości," 5:58–68, Archiwum Archidiecezjalne Warszawskie, Warsaw.

4. Leon Chajn, *Polskie wolnomularstwo, 1920–1938* (Warsaw: Czytelnik, 1984); Ludwik Hass, *Masoneria polska XX wieku: Losy, loże, ludzie* (Warsaw: Polczek, 1993).

5. Władysław Baranowski, *Rozmowy z Piłsudskim, 1916–1931* (Warsaw: Zebra, 1990), 77; Ryszard Świętek, "Les contacts entre la franc-maçonnerie polonaise et française (visite de Józef Piłsudski en France en 1921)," *Acta Poloniae historica* 54 (1986): 167–85.

6. Stetson to Kellogg, July 24, 1926, 860c.404/17, State Department Decimal File, RG 59, National Archives, Washington, D.C. (SDNA).

7. Marek Ruszczyc, "Niepokorny biskup," *Tygodnik powszechny,* November 18, 1990.

8. In Ambasada RP przy Watykanie A.44.122, Instytut Historyczny im. Generała Sikorskiego, London (IHGS): Skrzyński to Zaleski, November 27, 1929, Tytus Komarnicki, memorandum of audience with Pius XI, [June 28, 1930], Skrzyński to Zaleski, June 27, 1931, no. 2, 4, 7; Jędrzejewicz, *Kronika życia,* 2:348.

9. Skrzyński note of conversation with Fr. Sopuch, January 22, 1931, IHGS A.44.122/6; Jerzy Kłoczowski and Lidia Müllerowa, "W dwudziestym stuleciu (1918–1980)," in *Zarys dziejów Kościoła katolickiego w Polsce,* by Jerzy Kłoczowski, Lidia Müllerowa, and Jan Skarbek (Kraków: Znak, 1986), 337; Stanisław Kosiński, "August Hlond," in *Na stolicy prymasowskiej w Gnieźnie i w Poznaniu: Szkice o prymasach Polski w okresie niewoli narodowej i w II Rzeczypospolitej,* ed. Feliks Lenort (Poznań: Księgarnia Św. Wojciecha, 1982), 337; Krzysztof Krasowski, *Episkopat katolicki w II Rzeczypospolitej* (Warsaw: Redakcja Naukowa, 1992), 27; Bożena Krzywobłocka, *Chadecja, 1918–1938* (Warsaw: Książka i Wiedza, 1974), 61; Pietrzak, "Czy kardynał August Hlond," 76–79.

10. Stetson to Kellogg, August 30, 1926, SDNA 860c.404/19; *New York Times,* August 31, 1926.

11. France, Ministère des Affaires Étrangères, *Bulletin périodique de la presse polonaise* (BPPP), no. 171.

12. Memorandum of conversation with Jerzy Paciorkowski of Polish Interior Ministry, October 5, 1928, and memorandum of conversation between Littauer of Press Division of Polish Foreign Ministry and unnamed U.S. diplomat, November 3, 1928, SDNA 860c.404/28; Anna Cienciała, ed., *Polska polityka zagraniczna w latach 1926–1939: Na podstawie tekstów Józefa Becka* (Paris: Instytut Literacki, 1990), 185; Wacław Jędrzejewicz, *Wspomnienia* (Wrocław: Ossolineum, 1993), 223.

13. Polish episcopate to Bartel, October 18, 1926, Ministerstwo Wyznań Religijnych i Oświecenia Publicznego (MWRiOP), no. 402, Archiwum Akt Nowych (AAN), Warsaw; Sapieha to Hlond, March 31, 1930, Acta Hlondiana, vol. 5, pt. 10, 229, Archiwum Archidiecezjalne w Poznaniu.

14. Bogumil Grott, *Nacjonalizm i religia: Proces zespalania nacjonalizmu z katolicyzmem w jedną całość ideową w myśli Narodowej Demokracji, 1926–1939* (Kraków: Uniwersytet Jagielloński, 1984), 16; Teodor Mistewicz, "Stosunek Romana Dmowskiego do religii i Kościoła," *Studia historyczne* 32, no. 1 (1989): 57–72; Jerzy Janusz Terej, *Rzeczywistość i polityka: Ze studiów nad dziejami najnowszymi Narodowej Demokracji* (Warsaw: Książka i Wiedza, 1971), 54.

15. Roman Wapiński, *Roman Dmowski* (Lublin: Wydawnictwo Lubelskie, 1988), 346.

16. Roman Dmowski, *Kościół, Naród i Państwo* (Warsaw: Perzyński, Niklewicz, 1925), 21, 32.

17. Terej, *Rzeczywistość i polityka,* 56. See also Szymon Rudnicki, *Obóz Narodowo-Radykalny: Geneza i działalność* (Warsaw: Czytelnik, 1985), 25.

18. Grott, *Nacjonalizm,* 15; Andrzej Micewski, *Roman Dmowski* (Warsaw: Verum, 1971), 324–27; Mistewicz, "Stosunek," 67–72; Rudnicki, *Obóz,* 25.

19. Antony Polonsky, *Politics in Independent Poland, 1921–1939: The Crisis of Constitutional Government* (Oxford: Oxford University Press, 1972), 210–12.

20. Kakowski, "Z niewoli," 5:95–96.

21. Ibid., 5:74. Also BPPP, no. 177, and Jędrzejewicz, *Kronika życia,* 2:277. The ceremony led the *New York Times* correspondent to conclude, with apparent distaste, that "Poland lives now under the shadow of the Vatican," July 10, 1927.

22. Maciej Rataj, *Pamiętniki* (Warsaw: Ludowa Spółdzielnia Wydawnicza, 1965), 459–60.

23. Walerian Meysztowicz, *Gawędy o czasach i ludziach* (London: Polska Fundacja Kulturalna, 1983), 320.

24. Istruzioni per Monsignor Francesco Marmaggi, February 29, 1928, Affari Ecclesiastici Straordinari: Polonia, Archivio Segreto Vaticano, Vatican City (ASV).

25. BPPP, no. 173. Quotation from *Czas* (Kraków), February 23, 1927 (emphasis in original).

26. BPPP, no. 181–83; Krasowski, "Między Warszawą a Watykanem," 328–29; Pietrzak, "Czy kardynał August Hlond," 83–87; Rudnicki, *Obóz,* 39–42.

27. J. Webb Benton to Kellogg, [1928], SDNA 860c.404/27.

28. Krasowski, "Między Warszawą a Watykanem," 275, 330–31.

29. Ibid., 317–18, 328; Bohdan Cywiński, *Ogniem próbowane—I: Korzenie tożsamości* (Rome: Papieski Instytut Studiów Kościelnych, 1982), 71; Pietrzak, "Czy kardynał August Hlond," passim; Stanisław Wilk, *Episkopat Kościoła katolickiego w Polsce w latach 1918–1939* (Warsaw: Wydawnictwo Salezjańskie, 1992), 352–53.

30. Memorandum of [Stetson?] conversation with officials of Polish Ministry of Interior, November 10, 1928, SDNA 860c.404/29; Cywiński, *Ogniem*, 71; Krasowski, *Episkopat*, 28; Tytus Komarnicki and Józef Zarański, eds., *Diariusz i teki Jana Szembeka (1935–1945)* (Szembek) (London: Polish Research Centre, 1964), 2:221.

31. Robert Speaight, *The Life of Hilaire Belloc* (New York: Farrar, Straus and Cudahy, 1957), 462.

32. Jules Laroche, *La Pologne de Pilsudski: Souvenirs d'une ambassade, 1926–1935* (Paris: Flammarion, 1953), 98. Also Skrzyński to Beck, April 7, 1934, IHGS A.44.122/12, John Willys to Henry L. Stimson, April 28, 1931, SDNA 860c.011/33, François Charles-Roux, *Huit ans au Vatican, 1932–1940* (Paris: Flammarion, 1947), 259–60, and Szembek, 4:497–98.

33. Stanisław Kosiński, "Kard. August Hlond i Adam Stefan Sapieha w latach 1926–1948," in *Księga Sapieżyńska*, ed. Jerzy Wolny (Kraków: Polskie Towarzystwo Teologiczne, 1986), 2:44.

34. Krasowski, "Między Warszawą a Watykanem," 318. Also Willys to Stimson, April 28, 1931, SDNA 860c.011/33, and Wincenty Witos, *Moje wspomnienia* (Paris: Instytut Literacki, 1965), 3:340–41.

35. Krasowski, "Między Warszawą a Watykanem," 316; Wilk, *Episkopat*, 77, 429.

36. Papal Commission to Piłsudski, November 17, 1927, J. i A. Piłsudskich, no. 7, AAN; Krasowski, *Episkopat*, 80.

37. Protocols of meetings of Papal Commission with representatives of Polish government, January 12 and 15, 1928, AAN-MWRiOP, nos. 405, 456.

38. Janikowski telegram, January 15, 1928, J. i A. Piłsudskich, no. 7, AAN; Istruzioni per Monsignor Francesco Marmaggi, February 29, 1928, ASV, Affari Ecclesiastici Straordinari: Polonia; Skrzyński to Zaleski, February 23, 1929, IHGS A.44.122/2.

39. Gasparri to Hlond, April 10, 1929, Acta Hlondiana, vol. 5, pt. 1, 86–88; Jerzy Kłoczowski, *Dzieje chrześcijaństwa polskiego* (Paris: Éditions du Dialogue, 1991), 2:137–39; Daniel Olszewski, "Czym była Akcja Katolicka?" *Tygodnik powszechny*, April 30, 1995.

40. In SDNA 860c.404/28: memorandum of conversation with Jerzy Paciorkowski of Polish Interior Ministry, October 5, 1928, Stetson to Kellogg, November 3,

1928, and memorandum of conversation between Littauer of Press Division, Polish Foreign Ministry, and unnamed U.S. diplomat, November 3, 1928. The quotation is from the last document.

41. Skrzyński to Zaleski, September 23, 1930, IHGS A.44.122/5; Chajn, *Polskie wolnomularstwo,* 229.

42. "Confidential Information," October 27, 1929, and note on the stance of the government, same date, Franciszek Potocki, no. 10, AAN.

43. Alfred Wysocki, *Tajemnice dyplomatycznego sejfu* (Warsaw: Książka i Wiedza, 1988), 215.

44. Note of conversation between Sławek and Marmaggi, April 8, 1930, AAN-MWRiOP, no. 432.

45. Bp. Adolf Szelążek to Gasparri, January 29, 1929, Archiwum Prymasów Polski (APP), Archiwum Archidiecezjalne w Gnieźnie, Gniezno.

46. Anonymous memorandum (October 1929), Franciszek Potocki, no. 9, AAN; memorandum of conversation between Paciorkowski and unnamed U.S. diplomat, March 4, 1929, SDNA 860c.404/30.

47. Skrzyński to Zaleski, November 8, 1929, IHGS A.44.122/2.

48. Memorandum of Political Department, Polish Foreign Ministry, for Zaleski, December 1929, in *Watykan a stosunki polsko-niemieckie w latach 1918–1939,* ed. Jarosław Jurkiewicz (Warsaw: Książka i Wiedza, 1960), 33–41.

49. Willys to Stimson, January 7, 1931, SDNA 860c.404/39; Thomas E. Hachey, ed., *Anglo-Vatican Relations, 1914–1939: Confidential Annual Reports of the British Ministers to the Holy See* (Boston: G. K. Hall, 1972), 86; Stewart A. Stehlin, *Weimar and the Vatican, 1919–1933: German-Vatican Diplomatic Relations in the Interwar Years* (Princeton, N.J.: Princeton University Press, 1983), 158.

50. In IHGS A.44.122/3: Skrzyński to Zaleski, January 27, 1930, and Alfred Chłapowski to Zaleski, [January 1930]; Stehlin, *Weimar,* 320–21, 326, 343–44.

51. In IHGS A.44.122: Zaleski to Skrzyński, February 9, 1929, no. 2, Ministry of Religious Affairs to Foreign Ministry, February 14, 1930, no. 3, Wysocki memorandum of conversation with Marmaggi, [July 28, 1930?], no. 4, and Janikowski to Janusz Jędrzejewicz, September 21, 1931, no. 7.

52. Janikowski to Zaleski, August 30, 1930, IHGS A.44.122/4; John C. Wiley to Stimson, October 15, 1930, SDNA 860c.00/503.

53. Skrzyński to Zaleski, November 20, 1930, IHGS A.44.122/5.

54. Witos, *Wspomnienia,* 3:340–42.

55. In IHGS A.44.122: Skrzyński to Zaleski, December 30, 1930, no. 5, and April 22, 1931, no. 6; Wiley to Stimson, February 28, 1931, SDNA 860c.404/40.

56. Kakowski, "Z niewoli," 5:322–23.

57. Skrzyński to Zaleski, April 22, 1931, IHGS A.44.122/6; Wiley to Stimson, July 29, 1931, SDNA 860c.404/42.

58. Observations of the episcopate of Poland in the matter of revising the constitution, April 24, 1931, APP; Joseph Flack to Stimson, February 8, 1932, SDNA 860c.404/45.

59. *Tablet,* October 11, 1930.

60. Flack to Stimson, February 8, 1932, SDNA 860c.404/45; BPPP, no. 218; Krasowski, *Episkopat,* 191–98.

61. [Skrzyński?] to [Beck?], September 28, 1932, IHGS A.44.122/9; *Tablet,* December 24, 1932.

62. Hlond to Marmaggi, November 20, 1931, and Marmaggi's reply, November 21, 1931, APP.

63. Riservata: Memoria rilasciata all'archivio del Ministero degli Esteri di Varsavia, [1932], ASV, Affari Ecclesiastici Straordinari: Polonia.

64. Hlond to Pacelli, "Informazioni Secrete sulla situazione religioso-politica in Polonia," March 15, 1932, ASV, Affari Ecclesiastici Straordinari: Polonia.

65. BPPP, no. 223; Krasowski, "Między Warszawą a Watykanem," 338–41.

66. Krasowski, "Między Warszawą a Watykanem," 341. In his *Episkopat Polski w II Rzeczypospolitej,* Krasowski interprets the bishops' defeat of the sanacja attempt to laicize education and marriage and family law as one of the notable successes of an attempt on their part to build a "Catholic Poland." In his analysis, following the advent of their foe Piłsudski, the hierarchy set out to consolidate the faithful under its leadership and maintain the status of the Church in the country by ensuring that its law would be guided by Catholic doctrine. At first this was a tacit strategy adopted as a defensive reaction against the rise of the Piłsudskiites, but it became an explicit program after the issue of the landmark social encyclical of Pius XI, *Quadragesimo anno,* in 1931. The long-range goal was to hold the line until the day Poland would once again have a genuinely Catholic government. While not entirely without basis, the argument strikes me as overstated, speculative, and short on proof. There is no evidence of any conscious design to construct a "Catholic Poland" in a social-political sense, as the author describes it, and one is hard pressed to find anything like a master plan in the bishops' policy. The opposition of the Church to the sanacja proposals in conflict with Catholic tradition and teaching is explicable on its face, and mirrors the normal approach adopted by the Church in response to the introduction of laicizing legislation in virtually any predominantly Catholic country. Moreover, it exaggerates the hostility of the hierarchy toward Piłsudski and ignores the role of the pope, whose favorable view of the marshal had a decisive impact on the bishops. The relationship of the Polish episcopate with the sanacja regime was a good deal more complex, and far less systematic, than Krasowski maintains.

67. Skrzyński to Zaleski, November 17, 1931, IHGS A.44.122/7. See also Skrzyński to Zaleski, March 3, 1930, and March 8, 1930, IHGS A.44.122/3 and

March 10, 1931, IHGS A.44.122/3,6; Janikowski to Zaleski, September 10, 1930, in Jurkiewicz, *Watykan a stosunki,* 42–43.

68. Skrzyński to Zaleski, September 27, 1932, IHGS A.44.122/9.

69. Skrzyński to Zaleski, January 30, 1932, IHGS A.44.122/8.

70. Cienciała, *Józefa Becka,* 186–87; Skrzyński to Beck, February 10, 1933, in Jurkiewicz, *Watykan a stosunki,* 44–47; Meysztowicz, *Gawędy,* 322.

71. Kłoczowski, *Dzieje,* 131; Krasowski, *Episkopat,* 15–17.

72. Szembek, 4:200. Also Skrzyński to Beck, February 17, 1934, IHGS A.44.122/12.

73. Skrzyński to Beck, March 11, 1933, reprinted in Jurkiewicz, *Watykan a stosunki,* 52–56; Skrzyński to Beck, January 5, 1935, IHGS A.44.122/14.

74. Georges Castellan, *Dieu garde la Pologne! Histoire du catholicisme polonais, 1795–1980* (Paris: Robert Laffont, 1981), 131.

75. Skrzyński to Beck, March 11, 1933, in Jurkiewicz, *Watykan a stosunki,* 52. See as well Skrzyński to Beck, April 19, 1933, Ministerstwo Spraw Zagranicznych, no. 52, AAN (AAN-MSZ).

76. Skrzyński to Beck, March 11, 1933, in Jurkiewicz, *Watykan a stosunki,* 52–56; Andrzej Micewski, "Wokół Kościoła," *Tygodnik powszechny,* January 5, 1992.

77. In IHGS A.44.122: Skrzyński to Beck, November 17, 1934, no. 13, and [Skrzyński?] to Beck, November 7, 1932, no. 9.

78. Hlond to Polish bishops (confidential), January 23, 1935, APP.

79. Marmaggi to Szembek, January 14, 1935, and Szembek's reply, March 18, 1935, APP.

80. Szembek, 2:86.

81. Kakowski, "Z niewoli," 5:74; Micewski, *Z geografii,* 189–90.

82. Skrzyński to Beck, November 17, 1934, IHGS A.44.122/13; Skrzyński to Beck, April 5, 1935, AAN-MSZ, no. 2836.

83. Wiesław Mysłek, *Kościół katolicki w Polsce w latach 1918–1939: Zarys historyczny* (Warsaw: Książka i Wiedza, 1966), 66.

84. Stanisław (Cat) Mackiewicz, *Historja Polski od 11 listopada 1918 r. do 17 września 1939 r.* (London: M. I. Kolin, 1941), 187.

Chapter 5

1. G. K. Chesterton, "Two Words from Poland," in *Generally Speaking* (Freeport, N.Y.: Books for Libraries, 1968), 49.

2. *Tablet,* January 17, 1920, 69–71.

3. Krzysztof Krasowski, *Episkopat katolicki w II Rzeczypospolitej* (Warsaw: Redakcja Naukowa, 1992), 193.

4. Secretariat of State instructions for Cortesi, May 5, 1937, Affari Ecclesiastici Straordinari: Polonia, Archivio Segreto Vaticano, Vatican City (ASV).

5. August Hlond, *Na straży sumienia narodu* (Ramsey, N.J.: Don Bosco, 1951), 211–16.

6. Tytus Komarnicki, memorandum of audience with Pius XI held on June 26, 1930, [June 28, 1930], Ambasada RP przy Watykanie A.44.122/4, Instytut Historyczny im. Generała Sikorskiego, London (IHGS); Maciej Rataj, *Pamiętniki* (Warsaw: Ludowa Spółdzielnia Wydawnicza, 1965), 459–60.

7. Marmaggi to Gasparri, "Colloquio riservatissimo Pilsudski-Marmaggi," July 12, 1928, ASV, Affari Ecclesiastici Straordinari: Polonia.

8. Georges Castellan, *Dieu garde la Pologne! Histoire du catholicisme polonais, 1795–1980* (Paris: Robert Laffont, 1981), 164.

9. Hlond, *Na straży*, 77.

10. Tadeusz Boy-Żeleński, *Nasi okupanci* (Warsaw: Bibljoteka Boya, 1932), 38.

11. France, Ministère des Affaires Étrangères, *Bulletin périodique de la presse polonaise* (BPPP), no. 171; *Tablet,* October 24, 1936, 562; Bohdan Cywiński, *Ogniem próbowane—I: Korzenie tożsamości* (Rome: Papieski Instytut Studiów Kościelnych, 1982), 72.

12. *Tablet,* December 19, 1936, 871.

13. In IHGS: Janikowski to Beck, November 17, 1933, and Skrzyński to Beck, June 24, 1936, A.44.122/11 and 15; Jarosław Jurkiewicz, ed., *Watykan a stosunki polsko-niemieckie w latach 1918–1939* (Warsaw: Książka i Wiedza, 1960), 71–74, 80–86.

14. Skrzyński to Beck, April 19, 1933, Ministerstwo Spraw Zagranicznych, Gabinet Ministra, no. 52, Archiwum Akt Nowych, Warsaw (AAN-MSZ); Skrzyński to Beck, February 10, 1933, in Jurkiewicz, *Watykan a stosunki,* 44–47.

15. *Tablet,* December 19, 1936, 871, and February 19, 1938, 237.

16. For background on Freemasonry in Poland, see Leon Chajn, *Polskie wolnomularstwo, 1920–1938* (Warsaw: Czytelnik, 1984), and Ludwik Hass, *Masoneria polska XX wieku: Losy, loże, ludzie* (Warsaw: Polczek, 1993).

17. Hass, *Masoneria,* 7.

18. Jerzy Kłoczowski and Lidia Müllerowa, "W dwudziestym stuleciu (1918–1980)," in *Zarys dziejów Kościoła katolickiego w Polsce,* by Jerzy Kłoczowski, Lidia Müllerowa, and Jan Skarbek (Kraków: Znak, 1986), 335.

19. Ezra Mendelsohn, *The Jews of East Central Europe between the World Wars* (Bloomington: Indiana University Press, 1983), 71–72.

20. Arthur L. Goodhart, *Poland and the Minority Races* (New York: Brentano's, 1920), 120–21; Kłoczowski and Müllerowa, "W dwudziestym stuleciu," 306.

21. Ronald Modras, *The Catholic Church and Antisemitism: Poland, 1933–1939* (Langhorne, Penn.: Harwood, 1994), 398–99.

22. *First Things* 99 (January 2000): 39–40.

23. Robert Blobaum, "The Politics of Antisemitism in *Fin-de-Siècle* Warsaw," *Journal of Modern History* 73, no. 2 (2001): 275–306; Brian Porter, "Antisemitism and the Search for a Catholic Identity," in *Antisemitism and Its Opponents in Modern Poland,* ed. Robert Blobaum (Ithaca, N.Y.: Cornell University Press, 2005), 103–23; Brian Porter, "Making a Space for Antisemitism: The Catholic Hierarchy and the Jews in the Early Twentieth Century," in *Jewish Popular Culture and Its Afterlife,* ed. Michael C. Steinlauf and Antony Polonsky, Polin: Studies in Polish Jewry 16 (Oxford: Littman Library of Jewish Civilization, 2003), 415–29.

24. *Tablet,* June 30, 1934, 834.

25. Castellan, *Dieu garde,* 165.

26. Jerzy Tomaszewski, "Niepodległa Rzeczpospolita," in *Najnowsze dzieje Żydów w Polsce w zarysie (do 1950 roku),* ed. Jerzy Tomaszewski (Warsaw: Państwowe Wydawnictwo Naukowe, 1993), 244.

27. Włodzimierz Sznarbachowski, "Totalizm, terroryzm, katolicyzm," *Tygodnik powszechny,* October 31, 1993.

28. For example, the commentary by Flora Lewis in the *New York Times,* September 3, 1989.

29. Hlond, *Na straży,* 164.

30. *Tablet,* February 4, 1939.

31. Cortesi to Pacelli, January 7, 1938, ASV, Affari Ecclesiastici Straordinari: Polonia.

32. Hlond, *Na straży,* 169–70; Szymon Rudnicki, *Obóz Narodowo-Radykalny: Geneza i działalność* (Warsaw: Czytelnik, 1985), 226.

33. In IHGS A.44.122/15, 17: Skrzyński to Beck, June 27, 1936; Polish *aide-mémoire* to Vatican Secretariat of State, March 31, 1938; Janikowski to Beck, August 1, 1938.

34. Frank J. Coppa, "The Hidden Encyclical of Pius XI against Racism and Anti-Semitism Uncovered—Once Again," *Catholic Historical Review* 84, no. 1 (1998): 63–72; Robert A. Hecht, *An Unordinary Man: A Life of Father John LaFarge, S.J.* (Lanham, Md.: Scarecrow, 1996), 103–24; Georges Passelecq and Bernard Suchecky, *L'Encyclique cachée de Pie XI* (Paris: Découverte, 1995), 114.

35. For example, *Our Sunday Visitor,* July 17, 1983, compiled a long list of objections raised against the canonization of Kolbe based on his prewar activities that touched on Jewish issues.

36. Diana Dewar, *Saint of Auschwitz: The Story of Maximilian Kolbe* (San Francisco: Harper and Row, 1982), 7–8, 37.

37. *First Things* 99 (January 2000): 40.

38. Dewar, *Saint of Auschwitz,* 7–8; Modras, *Catholic Church and Antisemitism,* 397–98.

39. *Tablet,* February 4, 1939, 134.

40. Adam Michnik, "Conversation in the Citadel," in *Letters from Prison and Other Essays* (Berkeley and Los Angeles: University of California Press, 1985),

324; Szymon Rudnicki, "Nacjonalizm i religia," *Przegląd historyczny* 78, no. 1 (1987): 100.

41. Sznarbachowski, "Totalizm."

42. Modras, *Catholic Church and Antisemitism,* 396.

43. *Tablet,* February 6, 1937, 194.

44. Kłoczowski and Müllerowa, "W dwudziestym stuleciu," 335; [Skrzyński to Beck?], October 13, 1932, IHGS A.44.122/9.

45. Boy-Żeleński, *Nasi okupanci,* passim.

46. "Debata u Łowczego," *Tygodnik powszechny,* May 21, 1995.

47. Adam Michnik, *The Church and the Left* (Chicago: University of Chicago Press, 1993), 43.

48. Castellan, *Dieu garde,* 167.

49. G. M., "Poland and Christendom," *Month,* December 1931, 544–47.

50. In 2007 the *Chesterton Review* published, as part of its vol. 33, a "special Polish issue" (Spring/Summer) that reproduced a sampling of extracts demonstrating the special regard of English Catholics for Poland, among others, Chesterton, Belloc, Dawson, and Waugh.

51. G. K. Chesterton, "The Modern Hypocrisy," in *The End of the Armistice* (London: Sheed and Ward, 1940), 122. "For Poland Belloc had a kind of historic passion. . . . What Belloc admired in Poland was the flame of a military Christendom not yet extinct." Robert Speaight, *The Life of Hilaire Belloc* (New York: Farrar, Straus and Cudahy, 1957), 461–63.

52. Michael Coren, *Gilbert: The Man Who Was G. K. Chesterton* (New York: Paragon, 1990), 201. The intellectual, apart from political, objection of British Catholic apologists to Russian Bolshevism is obvious; their objection to Germany less so. Belloc and Chesterton blamed Germanic culture for the invention and dissemination of modern schools of philosophy that treated human beings as objects, an approach they saw as derivative from Protestantism and antithetical to the Catholic spirit. Patrick Allitt, *Catholic Converts: British and American Intellectuals Turn to Rome* (Ithaca, N.Y.: Cornell University Press, 1997), 180–83.

53. Maisie Ward, *Gilbert Keith Chesterton* (New York: Sheed and Ward, 1943), 428. See also Hilaire Belloc, "The Two Cultures of the West," in *Essays of a Catholic* (Freeport, N.Y.: Books for Libraries, 1967), 318–19.

54. G. K. Chesterton, "A Crucial Hour for Poland, " in *The Collected Works of G. K. Chesterton,* vol. 34, *The Illustrated London News, 1926–1928,* ed. Lawrence J. Clipper (San Francisco: Ignatius, 1986), 330; Hilaire Belloc, *Return to the Baltic* (London: Constable and Co., 1938), 146–47.

55. Chesterton, "Two Words from Poland," 53; Belloc, *Return,* 152, 175.

56. G. K. Chesterton, "Why Poland Is Hated," in Clipper, *Collected Works,* vol. 5, *The End of the Armistice,* 612; Jay P. Corrin, *G. K. Chesterton and Hilaire Belloc: The Battle against Modernity* (Athens: Ohio University Press, 1981), 175. In a letter from the period, Belloc stated that he wrote on Poland only with a Catholic

audience in mind "because I think it is impossible to explain the Polish question to the average English reader," who lacked a developed sense of religion. *Letters from Hilaire Belloc,* ed. Robert Speaight (London: Hollis and Carter, 1958), 282.

57. Przemysław Mroczkowski, "Don Kiszot zdrowego rozsądku: W 50 rocznicę śmierci G. K. Chestertona," *Tygodnik powszechny,* June 29, 1986.

58. Belloc to Skirmunt, January 5, 1929, Ambasada RP w Londynie, no. 969, AAN. My thanks to Thomas S. Dyman for this reference. Also Speaight, *Life,* 462–63. The book eventually appeared in 1938, under the title *Return to the Baltic.*

59. G. K. Chesterton, *The Autobiography of G. K. Chesterton* (San Francisco: Ignatius, 1986), 306; Chesterton, "Two Words from Poland," 50; Coren, *Gilbert,* 245–48.

60. Speaight, *Life,* 333.

61. Belloc, *Return,* 159.

62. "On New Capitals," in *Generally Speaking,* 60–62.

63. Corrin, *Chesterton and Belloc,* 185.

64. *End of the Armistice,* 137.

Chapter 6

1. I have called these two churchmen by the names they preferred. In Lithuanian, Matulewicz is rendered as Jurgis Matulaitis, or Matulevičius-Matulaitis. In Polish, Sheptyts'kyi is known as Andrzej Szeptycki.

2. Timothy Snyder, *The Reconstruction of Nations: Poland, Ukraine, Lithuania, Belarus, 1569–1999* (New Haven, Conn.: Yale University Press, 2003), is useful for background, especially chapters 3 and 7.

3. Ryszard Torzecki, "Z problematyki stosunków polsko-ukraińskich," *Dzieje najnowsze* 17, no. 2 (1985): 155. See also Benedykt Heydenkorn, "Polityka działalność Metropolity Szeptyckiego," *Zeszyty historyczne* 72 (1985): 101, and Andrzej Zięba, "Ewangelia, Ukraina," *Gazeta świąteczna,* November 5, 2000.

4. Z. S. Siemaszko, "Biskup wileński (1918–1925) Matulewicz na tle ówczesnych stosunków polsko-litewsko-białoruskich," *Zeszyty historyczne* 84 (1988): 11.

5. Congregation "Pro Ecclesia Orientali" for Ratti, May 18, 1918, in *Achilles Ratti (1918–1921),* vol. 1, *25 IV–31 VII 1918,* ed. Stanisław Wilk, Acta Nuntiaturae Polonae 57 (Rome: Institutum Historicum Polonicum, 1995), 77. Also Ratti to Gasparri, November 10, 1918, in Wilk, *Achilles Ratti,* vol. 2, *1 VIII–11 XI 1918,* 296–98; Charles Loiseau, "The Vatican and the New States of Central Europe," *Living Age,* November 8, 1919, 321–27; Roberto Morozzo della Rocca, *Le nazioni non muoiono: Russia rivoluzionaria, Polonia indipendente, e Santa Sede* (Bologna: Il Mulino, 1992), 132.

6. Tadeusz Górski, "Biskup Matulewicz a rząd Polski," *Tygodnik powszechny,* February 13, 1972; Matulewicz journal (October 1918), in Jerzy Matulewicz, *Pisma*

wybrane (Warsaw: Wydawnictwo Księży Marianów, 1988), 33–34; Francesco Tommasini, *La risurrezione della Polonia* (Milan: Fratelli Treves, 1925), 99–100.

7. Matulewicz to Fr. Leon Kułwiec, April 6, 1918, *Pisma*, 95.

8. Stanisław Stomma, "Dla sprawiedliwego miejsca nie było," *Tygodnik powszechny*, March 1, 1987.

9. Gasparri to Ratti, October 14, 1918, and Ratti to Matulewicz, October 18, 1918, Archive of Mons. Achille Ratti, Archivio Segreto Vaticano, Vatican City; Matulewicz journal (October 1918), *Pisma*, 34.

10. Bronisław Makowski, *Litwini w Polsce, 1920–1939* (Warsaw: Państwowe Wydawnictwo Naukowe, 1986), 79; Górski, "Biskup Matulewicz."

11. Matulewicz journal, November 20, 1919, *Pisma*, 52.

12. Tadeusz Górski, "Beatyfikacja arcybiskupa Jerzego Matulewicza," *Tygodnik powszechny*, July 5, 1987.

13. Siemaszko, "Biskup wileński," 14–15.

14. Matulewicz journal, January 5, 1919, *Pisma*, 43.

15. Ibid., April 25, 1919, 50–51.

16. Makowski, *Litwini w Polsce*, 80.

17. Matulewicz to Ratti, October 23, 1920, *Pisma*, 104.

18. *Gazeta warszawska*, August 16, 1919. Among his offenses, according to *Gazeta*, was his use of an automobile of the same colors as the Lithuanian flag.

19. Matulewicz journal, April 25 and December 16, 1919, March 20, 1921, *Pisma*, 50–51, 56–57.

20. Polish Foreign Ministry to Ratti, October 1919, Gasparri to Ratti, November 29, 1919, Ratti Papers; Mons. Ermenegildo Pellegrinetti, "Relazione finale," July 1921, in *L'Archivio di Mons. Achille Ratti, visitatore apostolico e nunzio a Varsavia (1918–1921): Inventario*, ed. Ottavio Cavalleri (Vatican City: Archivio Segreto Vaticano, 1990), 99–100; Tommasini, *La risurrezione*, 100; Wiktor Piotrowicz, *Z zagadnień wyznaniowych w Polsce* (Vilna: Lux, 1929), 45–46, 59.

21. Ratti to Gasparri, November 4, 1918, in Wilk, *Achilles Ratti*, 2:277–79; Ratti to Gasparri, July 4, 1919, and Gasparri to Ratti, September 24, 1919, Ratti Papers.

22. Fragmentary undated reports (1919, 1921–22), Ambasada R.P. przy Watykanie A.44.49/61, Instytut Historyczny im. Generała Sikorskiego, London (IHGS).

23. Morozzo della Rocca, *Le nazioni*, 123, 129; Terzo Natalini, ed., *I diari del cardinale Ermenegildo Pellegrinetti, 1916–1922* (Vatican City: Archivio Segreto Vaticano, 1994), August 20, 1919, 222; George J. Perejda, *Apostle of Church Unity: Metropolitan Andrew Sheptytsky* (Winnipeg: Redeemer's Voice, 1960), 28–31; Zięba, "Ewangelia."

24. Skrzyński to Jan Dąbski, June 9, 1921, Ambasada R.P. w Londynie, no. 879, Archiwum Akt Nowych, Warsaw (AAN); Torzecki, "Z problematyki," 156, 158.

25. Pellegrinetti, "Relazione finale," 190.

26. Maria Klachko, "Podróż metropolity Szeptyckiego do zachodniej Europy i Ameryki w latach 1920–1923," in *Metropolita Andrzej Szeptycki,* ed. Andrzej Zięba (Kraków: Polska Akademia Umiejętności, 1994), 158.

27. Pellegrinetti to Gasparri, June 13, 1921, Ratti Papers.

28. In Ministerstwo Wyznań Religijnych i Oświecenia Publicznego (MWRiOP), AAN, Walery Roman report, May 11, 1923, no. 422, and Provincial Government, Nowogród, to MWRiOP, May 14, 1923, no. 457; Ewa Maj, "Religia i Kościół rzymskokatolicki w myśli politycznej Narodowej Demokracji," in *Religia i Kościół rzymskokatolicki w polskiej myśli politycznej, 1919–1993,* ed. Jan Jachymek (Lublin: Wydawnictwo Uniwersytetu Marii Curie-Skłodowskiej, 1995), 49–50.

29. Pellegrinetti, "Relazione finale," 179.

30. In AAN: Polish Foreign Ministry report, "Watykan a Polska," January 29, 1921, Ministerstwo Spraw Zagranicznych (MSZ) Ref. Wyznań, no. 2834; extracts from report of Polish minister to the Holy See, December 7, 1921, Ambasada R.P. w Paryżu, no. 186; Skrzyński to Skirmunt, December 5, 1921, MWRiOP, no. 458.

31. Skrzyński to Zamoyski, May 4, 1924, AAN-MWRiOP, no. 457.

32. Skrzyński to Aleksander Skrzyński, April 26, 1923, AAN-MWRiOP, no. 458.

33. MSZ to MWRiOP, March 9, 1923, Skrzyński to Aleksander Skrzyński, April 24, 1923, Skrzyński to [Aleksander Skrzyński?], [before July 1923], MSZ to Ministerstwo Spraw Wewnętrznych, July 1923, AAN-MWRiOP, no. 458; Heydenkorn, "Polityczna działalność," 101–3; Klachko, "Podróż," in Zięba, *Metropolita,* 166–68; Mirosława Papierzyńska-Turek, *Sprawa ukraińska w Drugiej Rzeczypospolitej, 1922–1926* (Kraków: Wydawnictwo Literackie, 1979), 94–95, 198–200; in State Department Decimal File, RG 59, National Archives, Washington, D.C. (SDNA): Boal to Hughes, September 5, 1923, 860c.404/6, and September 24, 1923, 860c.404/7.

34. Tommasini, *La risurrezione,* 104–5.

35. Head of the Information Service, Swolkień, to Ministerstwo Spraw Wewnętrznych, August 22, 1923, AAN-MWRiOP, no. 458.

36. France, Ministère des Affaires Étrangères, *Bulletin périodique de la presse polonaise* (BPPP), no. 136.

37. MSZ to MWRiOP, August 21, 1923, AAN-MWRiOP, no. 458; Witold Malej, "Kardynał Aleksander Kakowski w świetle własnych wspomnień," *Nasza przeszłość* 8 (1958): 264; Cardinal Aleksander Kakowski, unpublished memoir, "Z niewoli do niepodległości," Archiwum Archidiecezjalne Warszawskie, Warsaw, 2:76–77, 5:152–54.

38. Tommasini, *La risurrezione,* 75–76.

39. Bohdan Budurowycz, "Sheptyts'kyi and the Ukrainian National Movement after 1914," in *Morality and Reality: The Life and Times of Andrei Sheptyts'kyi,* ed.

Paul R. Magocsi (Edmonton: Canadian Institute of Ukrainian Studies, 1989), 54; Heydenkorn, "Polityczna działalność," 103.

40. In AAN-MWRiOP: Sikorski to Józef Mikułowski-Pomorski, February 9, 1923, no. 454, Council of Ministers to MSZ, October 31, 1923, no. 457, Dmowski to Skrzyński, November 9, 1923, no. 457; Górski, "Biskup Matulewicz"; Górski, "Beatyfikacja."

41. In AAN-MWRiOP, no. 457: Skrzyński to Seyda, June 21, 1923, and Skrzyński to Zamoyski, May 4, 1924.

42. Matulewicz to Fr. Józef Kukta, August 2, 1923, *Pisma*, 118.

43. Walerian Meysztowicz, *Gawędy o czasach i ludziach* (London: Polska Fundacja Kulturalna, 1983), 193–94, 206; Maciej Rataj, *Pamiętniki* (Warsaw: Ludowa Spółdzielnia Wydawnicza, 1965), 235–36.

44. Internal MSZ memorandum for Zamoyski, January 25, 1924, AAN-MWRiOP, no. 457.

45. Stanisław Grabski, *Pamiętniki* (Warsaw: Czytelnik, 1989), 2:231; Rataj, *Pamiętniki*, 202.

46. Edward Prus, *Władyka świętojurski, rzecz o arcybiskupie Andrzeju Szeptyckim (1865–1944)* (Warsaw: Instytut Wydawniczy Związków Zawodowych, 1985), 95–97; Zięba, "Ewangelia"; Andrzej Zięba, "Metropolita Andrzej Szeptycki," *Kwartalnik historyczny* 92, no. 4 (1985): 895.

47. Report of fifth and seventh meetings of Grabski and Borgongini-Duca, October 15 and 18, 1924, IHGS A.44.122/1.

48. Stanisław Grabski, *Pamiętniki*, 2:237; Bolesław Kumor, "Projekty zmian w organizacji metropolitalnej i diecezjalnej w Polsce (1918–1925)," in *Kościół w II Rzeczypospolitej*, ed. Zygmunt Zieliński and Stanisław Wilk (Lublin: Katolicki Uniwersytet Lubelski, 1980), 60.

49. Skrzyński to Zaleski, February 3, 1927, AAN-MSZ, Gabinet Ministra, no. 52.

50. Matulewicz to Pius XI, June 27, 1925, and Matulewicz to Fr. Lucjan Chalecki, August 19, 1925, *Pisma*, 137–42.

51. Matulewicz journal, August 6, 1925, and Matulewicz to Fr. Franciszek Buczys, November 9, 1925, *Pisma*, 58–59, 148.

52. Matulewicz to Buczys, October 27, 1924, cited in "'Nie opuszczaj rąk . . . ,'" *Tygodnik powszechny*, September 12, 1993.

53. Siemaszko, "Biskup wileński," 24.

54. "Na beatyfikację abpa. Jerzego Matulewicza: List pasterski Episkopatu Polski," *Tygodnik powszechny*, July 19, 1987.

55. Budurowycz, "Sheptyts'kyi," 54; Papierzyńska-Turek, *Sprawa ukraińska*, 94–96; Zięba, "Ewangelia"; memorandum of conversation of Stetson (?) with Paciorkowski and Suchenek of Polish Ministry of Interior, November 10, 1928, SDNA

860c.404/29; Heydenkorn, "Polityczna działalność," 103; *Times* (London), May 29, 1925.

56. BPPP, no. 208; Stanisław Stępień, "Stanowisko metropolity Szeptyckiego wobec zjawiska terroru polityczna," in Zięba, *Metropolita*, 114–15; Zięba, "Ewangelia."

57. In AAN-MSZ: Ref. Wyznań, Wysocki to Polish Embassy, the Holy See, [April 3?] 1930, Wysocki note of conversation with Marmaggi, July 28, 1930, no. 2859, Skrzyński to Zaleski, November 19, 1930, November 24, 1930, December 8, 1930, December 9, 1930, no. 2860; internal memorandum concerning Greek Catholic clergy, May 1930, AAN-MWRiOP, no. 435; Willys to Stimson, January 7, 1931, SDNA 860c.404/39; Thomas E. Hachey, ed., *Anglo-Vatican Relations, 1914–1939: Confidential Annual Reports of the British Ministers to the Holy See* (Boston: G. K. Hall, 1972), 193–94; reports on Greek Catholic clergy, [1930], Poland—Ambasada (Catholic Church), Hoover Institution Archives, Stanford, Calif. (HIA); Skrzyński to Zaleski, January 27, 1930, IHGS A.44.122/3; Skrzyński to Ottaviani, January 23, 1930, Segretario di Stato, Rapp. Pontificie: Polonia, Archivio Segreto Vaticano, Vatican City.

58. Zięba, "Ewangelia." Also Andrzej A. Zięba, "Sheptyts'kyi in Polish Public Opinion," in Magocsi, *Morality and Reality*, 385–88.

59. Meysztowicz, *Gawędy*, 265. Also Ryszard Torzecki, "Sheptyts'kyi and Polish Society," in Magocsi, *Morality and Reality*, 81.

60. *Tablet*, December 24, 1938; Tytus Komarnicki and Józef Zarański, eds., *Diariusz i teki Jana Szembeka (1935–1945)* (Szembek) (London: Polish Research Centre, 1964), 4:469–70; Andrzej Friszke, *O kształt niepodległej* (Warsaw: Więź, 1989), 5.

61. Stępień, "Stanowisko," in Zięba, *Metropolita*, 116–17.

62. Reports on political activities of Lithuanian clergy, [1934–35], AAN-MSZ, Ref. Wyznań, no. 2852.

63. Papée to Beck, August 2, 1939, IHGS A.44.122/19; Józef Beck, *Final Report* (New York: Robert Speller and Sons, 1957), 128–29; *Tablet*, March 12, 1938, and October 8, 1938; T.C.H.Y., "Polish Problems," *Commonweal*, June 3, 1938, 150; Budurowycz, Sheptyts'kyi," 57–59.

64. Górski, "Beatyfikacja"; Kazimierz Szwarcenberg Czerny, "Jak to było z konkordatem polskim z 1925 r.?" *Tygodnik powszechny*, September 12, 1971.

65. Kakowski, "Z niewoli," 5:256.

66. For a notable example, see Prus, *Władyka świętojurski.*

67. Zięba, "Ewangelia."

68. Adam Boniecki, "Wielki dzień Kościoła litewskiego," *Tygodnik powszechny*, July 19, 1987.

Chapter 7

1. Hilaire Belloc, *Places* (London: Cassell and Co., 1942), 89–90; G. K. Chesterton, "A Crucial Hour for Poland," in *The Collected Works of G. K. Chesterton,* vol. 34, *The Illustrated London News, 1926–1928,* ed. Lawrence J. Clipper (San Francisco: Ignatius, 1986), 331.

2. Terzo Natalini, ed., *I diari del cardinale Ermenegildo Pellegrinetti, 1916–1922* (Vatican City: Archivio Segreto Vaticano, 1994), 182.

3. Ropp to Ratti, October 4, 1918, in *Achilles Ratti (1918–1921),* vol. 2, *1 VIII–11 XI 1918,* ed. Stanisław Wilk, Acta Nuntiaturae Polonae 57 (Rome: Institutum Historicum Polonicum, 1996), 205.

4. *Tablet,* January 17, 1920, 69–71.

5. Natalini, *Diari Pellegrinetti,* 247. Also article by Abp. Ropp, January 21, 1922, in files of Affari Ecclesiastici Straordinari: Russia, Archivio Segreto Vaticano, Vatican City (ASV); Roberto Morozzo della Rocca, *Le nazioni non muoiono: Russia rivoluzionaria, Polonia indipendente, e Santa Sede* (Bologna: Il Mulino, 1992), 23–24; Stanisław Wilk, *Episkopat Kościoła katolickiego w Polsce w latach 1918–1939* (Warsaw: Wydawnictwo Salezjańskie, 1992), 166–67; Maciej Mróz, "Działalność unijna metropolity Andrzeja Szeptyckiego w Rosji i w Polsce w latach 1917–1922," in *Metropolita Andrzej Szeptycki,* ed. Andrzej Zięba (Kraków: Polska Akademia Umiejętności, 1994), 175–76; Léon Tretjakewitsch, *Bishop Michel d'Herbigny SJ and Russia: A Pre-ecumenical Approach to Christian Unity* (Würzburg: Augustinus Verlag, 1990), 124–28.

6. Maria Klachko, "Podróż metropolity Szeptyckiego do zachodniej Europy i Ameryki w latach 1920–1923," in Zięba, *Metropolita,* 157–60.

7. Mgr. Walerian Meysztowicz, "La nunziatura di Achille Ratti in Polonia," in *Pio XI nel trentesimo della morte (1939–1969), raccolta di studi e di memorie,* ed. Carlo Colombo (Milan: Ufficio Studi Arcivescovile, 1969), 189; James J. Zatko, *Descent into Darkness: The Destruction of the Roman Catholic Church in Russia, 1917–1923* (Notre Dame: University of Notre Dame Press, 1965), 78–79; Lillian Browne-Olf, *Their Name Is Pius: Portraits of Five Great Modern Popes* (Milwaukee, Wisc.: Bruce, 1941), 325.

8. Ratti to Gasparri, February 22, 1921, Archive of Mons. Achille Ratti, Archivio Segreto Vaticano, Vatican City. See also Carlo Felice Casula, *Domenico Tardini (1888–1961): L'Azione della Santa Sede nella crisi fra le due guerre* (Rome: Studium, 1988), 105.

9. Skrzyński to MSZ, December [1931], Poland—Ambasada (Catholic Church), Hoover Institution Archives, Stanford, Calif. (HIA).

10. Morozzo della Rocca, *Le nazioni,* 240; Jules Laroche, *La Pologne de Pilsudski: Souvenirs d'une ambassade, 1926–1935* (Paris: Flammarion, 1953), 86–87.

11. Cyrille Korolevskij, *Métropolite André Szeptyckyi, 1865–1944* (Rome: Ukrainian Theological Society, 1964), 228.

12. Wacław Jędrzejewicz, ed., *Kronika życia Józefa Piłsudskiego* (London: Polska Fundacja Kulturalna, 1989), 3:42; report on organization of the Orthodox Church in Poland, March 28, 1920, Archiwum Adiutantury Generalnej Naczelnego Dowództwa (Archiwum Belwederskie) (AGND) 82/4299, Sterling Library, Yale University; Edward D. Wynot Jr., "Prisoner of History: The Eastern Orthodox Church in Poland in the Twentieth Century," *Journal of Church and State* 39, no. 2 (1997): 320.

13. Gasparri to Ratti, May 19, 1919, Ratti Papers; Wynot, "Prisoner," 321–24; H. E. Wyczawski, "Cerkiew prawosławna w II Rzeczypospolitej," in *Kościół w II Rzeczypospolitej,* ed. Zygmunt Zieliński and Stanisław Wilk (Lublin: Katolicki Uniwersytet Lubelski, 1980), 170–71; Jerzy Kłoczowski and Lidia Müllerowa, "W dwudziestym stuleciu (1918–1980)," in *Zarys dziejów Kościoła katolickiego w Polsce,* by Jerzy Kłoczowski, Lidia Müllerowa, and Jan Skarbek (Kraków: Znak, 1986), 298; Andrej Chojnowski, "The Controversy over Former Uniate Property in Interwar Poland," *Nationalities Papers* 16, no. 2 (1988): 177–90.

14. Louis J. Gallagher, *Edmund A. Walsh, S.J.: A Biography* (New York: Benziger Brothers, 1962), 58; Francis McCullagh, *The Bolshevik Persecution of Christianity* (New York: E. P. Dutton, 1924), 111; Hansjakob Stehle, *Eastern Politics of the Vatican, 1917–1979* (Athens: Ohio University Press, 1981), 46–47; Francesco Tommasini, *La risurrezione della Polonia* (Milan: Fratelli Treves, 1925), 150–51; Zatko, *Descent,* 125, 169; James J. Zatko, "The Letters of Archbishop Lauri, Apostolic Nuncio in Warsaw, to Monsignor Constantine Budkiewicz of St. Catherine's, St. Petersburg, 1922–1923," *Polish Review* 4, nos. 1–2 (1959): 127–31; Gibson to Hughes, March 29 and April 5, 1923, Hugh Gibson Papers, HIA.

15. Dennis J. Dunn, *The Catholic Church and Russia: Popes, Patriarchs, Tsars, and Commissars* (Burlington, Vt.: Ashgate, 2004), 74–82.

16. McCullagh, *Bolshevik Persecution,* 308.

17. M. Cappuyns, "Dom Lambert Beauduin (1873–1960), quelques documents et souvenirs,"*Revue d'histoire ecclésiastique* 61, no. 2 (1966): 441. The d'Herbigny story is spicy enough to have inspired a roman à clef, John Gallahue, *The Jesuit* (New York: Stein and Day, 1973). Whatever its merit as fiction, the book has no value as history.

18. Skrzyński to Zamoyski, February 2, 1924, Ministerstwo Wyznań Religijnych i Oświecenia Publicznego (MWRiOP), no. 416, Archiwum Akt Nowych (AAN), Warsaw; Tretjakewitsch, *Bishop Michel d'Herbigny,* 14–128; Cappuyns, "Dom Lambert Beauduin," 442–43; Alexey Yudin, "The Union of Brest and Russia in the Beginning of the Twentieth Century: Metropolitan Andrej Šeptyc'kyi and the Russian Pro-Union Movement," in *Four Hundred Years Union of Brest (1596–1996): A Critical Re-evaluation,* ed. Bert Groen and Wil von den Bercken (Leuven: Peeters, 1998), 158–59.

19. Walter J. Ciszek and Daniel L. Flaherty, *With God in Russia* (New York: McGraw-Hill, 1964), 11–12; Ludwik Grzebień, ed., *Encyklopedia wiedzy o jezuitach na ziemiach Polski i Litwy, 1564–1995* (Kraków: Wydawnictwo WAM, 1996), 6; Tretjakewitsch, *Bishop Michel d'Herbigny*, 211–15.

20. Grzebień, *Encyklopedia wiedzy*, 470; Mgr. Valérien Meysztowicz, *L'Église Catholique en Pologne entre les deux guerres (1919–1939)* (Vatican City: n.p., 1944), 68–70.

21. McCullagh, *Bolshevik Persecution*, 319.

22. Governor of Lublin to Bolesław Miklaszewski, August 31, 1924, AAN-MWRiOP, no. 416.

23. Skrzyński to Zamoyski, February 2, 1924, AAN-MWRiOP, no. 416.

24. In AAN-MWRiOP, no. 416: MSZ to Miklaszewski, December 22, 1923, and internal memorandum of MWRiOP to Miklaszewski, November 12, 1924.

25. Report of meeting between Grabski and Borgongini-Duca, October 4, 1924, Ambasada R.P. przy Watykanie A.44.122/1, Instytut Historyczny im. Generała Sikorskiego, London (IHGS). Also Jerzy Wisłocki, *Konkordat polski z 1925 roku* (Poznań: UAM, 1977), 138.

26. Stehle, *Eastern Politics*, 80–102.

27. Tretjakewitsch, *Bishop Michel d'Herbigny*, 230–31; Constantin Simon, *Russicum: Witnesses of the Struggle for Christian Unity in Eastern Europe*, vol. 2, *The First Years, 1929–1939* (Rome: Opere Religiose Russe, 2002), 54–55.

28. Zbigniew Adamowicz and Alicja Wójcik, "Ludność Polski według wyznań," in *Religia i Kościół rzymskokatolicki w polskiej myśli politycznej, 1919–1993*, ed. Jan Jachymek (Lublin: Wydawnictwo Uniwersytetu Marii Curie-Skłodowskiej, 1995), 20; Tretjakewitsch, *Bishop Michel d'Herbigny*, 211–15; *Times* (London), September 14, 1927.

29. *Times* (London), August 4, 1928.

30. Tretjakewitsch, *Bishop Michel d'Herbigny*, 211–15; Serge Keleher, "Trapped between Two Churches: Orthodox and Greek Catholics in Eastern Poland," *Religion, State and Society* 23, no. 4 (1995): 369.

31. *Times* (London), February 26, 1930; Tretjakewitsch, *Bishop Michel d'Herbigny*, 263.

32. Protocol of Papal Commission for implementation of concordat, December 3, 1926, Prezydium Rady Ministrów 97–2, AAN; MSZ memorandum for Zaleski on relations with Holy See, December 1929, Ministerstwo Spraw Zagranycznych (MSZ), Ref. Wyznań, no. 2859, AAN; memorandum of [Stetson?] conversation with Paciorkowski and Suchenek of Polish Ministry of Interior, November 10, 1928, 860c.404/29, State Department Decimal File, RG 59, National Archives, Washington, D.C. (SDNA).

33. Krzysztof Krasowski, "Między Warszawą a Watykanem: Episkopat Polski wobec rządu i Stolicy Apostolskiej, 1918–1939," in *Szkice z dziejów papiestwa*, ed. Irena Koberdowa and Janusz Tazbir (Warsaw: Książka i Wiedza, 1989), 361; Konrad

Sadkowski, "The Roman Catholic Clergy, the Byzantine Slavonic Rite and Polish National Identity: The Case of Grabowiec, 1931–1934," *Religion, State and Society* 28, no. 2 (2000): 175–84.

34. Pius XI to Polish episcopate, November 1928, Acta Hlondiana, vol. 5, pt. 1, 6, Archiwum Archidiecezjalne w Poznaniu.

35. Dom M. Cappuyns, O.S.B., "Dom Lambert Beauduin (1873–1960), quelques documents et souvenirs,"*Revue d'histoire ecclésiastique* 61, nos. 3–4 (1966): 771; Ciszek, *With God,* 6–7; Simon, *Russicum,* 56–57, 90; Stehle, *Eastern Politics,* 128–42.

36. Czerwiński to Skrzyński, May 4, 1930, IHGS A.44.122/4; Sokołowski to Zaleski, August 5, 1930, MSZ, Ref. Wyznań, no. 2859, AAN.

37. Note in the matter of the Commissio pro "Russia," February 15, 1938, AAN-MWRiOP, no. 416. Also Walerian Meysztowicz, *Gawędy o czasach i ludziach* (London: Polska Fundacja Kulturalna, 1983), 287.

38. Janikowski to Zaleski, August 4, 1930, IHGS A.44.122/4.

39. Komarnicki to Zaleski, July 28, 1930, MSZ, Ref. Wyznań, no. 2859, AAN.

40. In MSZ, Ref. Wyznań, no. 2859: Janikowski to Zaleski, January 15, 1930, and Janikowski note of conversation with Marmaggi, June 4, 1930.

41. Skrzyński to Zaleski, March 10, 1931, IHGS A.44.122/6. In the same collection, also Janikowski to Zaleski, July 14, 1930, A.44.122/4.

42. Skrzyński to Zaleski, November 24, 1930, IHGS A.44.122/5. Also Skrzyński to MSZ, December [1930], Poland-Ambasada (Catholic Church), HIA; extract from note for the foreign minister, 1931, AAN-MWRiOP, no. 416.

43. After the Second World War, Bishop Charnets'kyi spent more than a decade as a prisoner in the Soviet Gulag and died in 1959, three years after his release. Pope John Paul II beatified him in 2001.

44. Skrzyński note of conversation with Sopuch, January 22, 1931, IHGS A.44.122/6; Tretjakewitsch, *Bishop Michel d'Herbigny,* 264–67.

45. Skrzyński to Zaleski, January 24, 1931, IHGS A.44.122/6.

46. In IHGS: Skrzyński to Zaleski, January 9, 1931, A.44.122/6, Skrzyński to MSZ, January 24, 1931, A.44.122/6, and Janikowski to Janusz Jędrzejewicz, September 21, 1931, A.44.122/7.

47. Skrzyński note of conversation with Sopuch, January 22, 1931, IHGS A.44.122/6; Tretjakewitsch, *Bishop Michel d'Herbigny,* 264–67.

48. Jędrzejewicz statement in Senate, March 1, 1932, AAN-MWRiOP, no. 416; Flack to Stimson, April 12, 1932, SDNA 860c.404/47.

49. Skrzyński to Zaleski, March 15, 1932, IHGS A.44.122/8; *Tablet,* June 4, 1932; Tretjakewitsch, *Bishop Michel d'Herbigny,* 267–68; Wilk, *Episkopat,* 178–83.

50. Krasowski, "Między Warszawą a Watykanem," 362; *Tablet,* September 24, 1932.

51. Pius XI to Hlond and Kakowski, January 6, 1933, Archiwum Prymasów Polski (APP), Archiwum Archidiecezjalne w Gnieźnie, Gniezno; *Tablet*, October 22, 1932.

52. Skrzyński to Zaleski, October 13, 1932, IHGS A.44.122/9. In the same collection, also Skrzyński to Beck, November 22, 1932.

53. Włodzimierz Piątkiewicz, *Prawda o Albertynie* (Kraków: Nakład Wydawniczy Księży Jezuitów, 1932).

54. Henryk Ignacy Łubieński, *Droga na wschód Rzymu* (Warsaw: By the author, 1932).

55. Kakowski statement, October 3, 1932, APP; Kakowski to Hlond, October 3, 1932, IHGS A.44.122/9.

56. In IHGS A.44.122/9: Skrzyński to Zaleski, October 13, 1932, and Skrzyński to Beck, October 24, 1932.

57. France, Ministère des Affaires Étrangères, *Bulletin périodique de la presse polonaise* (BPPP), no. 227; Sheldon Crosby to Stimson, October 14, 1932, SDNA 860c.404/50.

58. MSZ to Polish Embassy, Berlin, December 19, 1932, Ambasada RP w Berlinie, no. 1558, AAN.

59. Tretjakewitsch, *Bishop Michel d'Herbigny*, 275–76.

60. BPPP, no. 229. Also Paul Lesourd, *Entre Rome et Moscou, le Jésuite clandestine, Mgr Michel d'Herbigny* (Paris: Lethielleux, 1976), 159–61; Stehle, *Eastern Politics*, 142–43.

61. Skrzyński to Beck, February 9, 1933, IHGS A.44.122/10.

62. Stehle, *Eastern Politics*, 142–77. Meysztowicz, *Gawędy*, 288, and David Alvarez, *Spies in the Vatican: Espionage and Intrigue from Napoleon to the Holocaust* (Lawrence: University Press of Kansas, 2002), 149–51, contend that Deubner was a Soviet agent; Tretjakewitsch, *Bishop Michel d'Herbigny*, 275–76, concludes otherwise.

63. In IHGS A.44.122/10: Polish Legation, Moscow, to MSZ, January 27, 1933, and Skrzyński to Beck, February 9, 1933.

64. Tretjakewitsch, *Bishop Michel d'Herbigny*, 275–76; Antoine Wenger, *Rome et Moscou, 1900–1950* (Paris: Brouwer, 1987), 441–45.

65. Tretjakewitsch, *Bishop Michel d'Herbigny*, 65–66, 218, 237–38; Wenger, *Rome et Moscou*, 445–46.

66. Janikowski to Zaleski, July 14, 1930, IHGS A.44.122/4.

67. Stehle, *Eastern Politics*, 102; Lesourd, *Entre Rome et Moscou*, 237.

68. Grzebień, *Encyklopedia wiedzy*, 6.

69. Polish legation, Moscow, to MSZ, January 27, 1933, IHGS A.44.122/10.

70. Simon, *Russicum*, 68–69.

71. Lesourd, *Entre Rome et Moscou*, 149; Krasowski, "Między Warszawą a Watykanem," 361–62.

72. Casula, *Domenico Tardini,* 111–13; Wenger, *Rome et Moscou,* 454–57; Tretjakewitsch, *Bishop Michel d'Herbigny,* 279–81.

73. Alvarez, *Spies in the Vatican,* 149; Lesourd, *Entre Rome et Moscou,* 168–69, 173–74; Stehle, *Eastern Politics,* 163–64.

74. Cappuyns, "Dom Lambert Beauduin," 792; Casula, *Domenico Tardini,* 111–12; Thomas E. Hachey, ed., *Anglo-Vatican Relations, 1914–1939: Confidential Annual Reports of the British Ministers to the Holy See* (Boston: G. K. Hall, 1972), 280, 319; Lesourd, *Entre Rome et Moscou,* 161; Wenger, *Rome et Moscou,* 452.

75. Alvarez, *Spies in the Vatican,* 142.

76. Ciszek, *With God,* 10–11.

77. In IHGS: Janikowski to Beck, December 23, 1933, A.44.122/11, and Skrzyński to Beck, February 1, 1934, A.44.122/12; Krasowski, "Między Warszawą a Watykanem," 362–63.

78. In ASV, Affari Ecclesiastici Straordinari: Polonia: "Istruzioni della S. Congregazione Orientale," [1936–37], and Secretariat of State instructions for Cortesi, May 5, 1937.

79. Tytus Komarnicki and Józef Zarański, eds., *Diariusz i teki Jana Szembeka (1935–1945)* (Szembek) (London: Polish Research Centre, 1964), 1:195.

80. MSZ to Janikowski, November 21, 1938, IHGS A.44.252/1.

81. Text of agreement between Poland and Holy See, June 20, 1938, IHGS A.44.122/17; *Tablet,* August 6, 1938.

82. Szembek, 4:224, 273–74.

83. A. J. Drexel Biddle to Cordell Hull, May 25, 1938, SDNA 860c.404/64.

84. BPPP, no. 270. Also *Tablet,* September 10, 1938, October 1, 1938, and April 22, 1939.

85. Szembek, 4:327–28, 329–31.

86. In IHGS A.44.250/1: Janikowski to Beck, July 2, 1938, and note of Arciszewski conversation with Cortesi, August 4, 1938; Papée to Beck, AAN-MWRiOP, no. 435; Szembek, 4:498–500.

87. Szembek, 4:497.

88. Ibid., 4:495. Also Józef Beck, *Final Report* (New York: Robert Speller and Sons, 1957), 128–29.

89. Szembek, 4:501–2; Janikowski to Beck, March 14, 1939, IHGS A.44.53/1.

90. Szembek, 4:614–15; Papée to Beck, July 27, 1939, AAN-MWRiOP, no. 416.

91. Stanisław (Cat) Mackiewicz, *Historja Polski od 11 listopada 1918 r. do 17 września 1939 r.* (London: M. I. Kolin, 1941), 312–13.

Chapter 8

1. Adam Stefan Sapieha, "Pro memoria: Dlaczego zgodziłem sié wprowadzić do katedry na Wawelu Marszałka Piłsudskiego," May 19, 1939, in *Księga*

Sapieżyńska, ed. Jerzy Wolny (Kraków: Polskie Towarzystwo Teologiczne, 1986), 2:139–40. Accounts of Piłsudski's last moments varied. At the time, Sapieha received his information from the priest who arrived at the deathbed at the request of the Piłsudski family to administer last rites and testified that the dying man received the sacrament willingly and in a state of consciousness. Fr. Wacław Korniłowicz to Sapieha, May 16, 1935, ibid., 141. In essentials, this version is confirmed in Stefan Cardinal Wyszyński to Jan Gaździcki, June 6, 1977, in *Zeszyty historyczne* 121 (1997): 100–101, Wacław Jędrzejewicz, *Józef Piłsudski, 1867–1935: Życiorys* (London: Polska Fundacja Kulturalna, 1993), 278, and Wacław Jędrzejewicz, ed., *Kronika życia Józefa Piłsudskiego* (London: Polska Fundacja Kulturalna, 1989), 3:87. On the other hand, Archbishop Teodorowicz claimed to have knowledgeable sources who described this as a highly sanitized report of the circumstances of the marshal's death, Teodorowicz to Hlond, June 19, 1935, Acta Hlondiana, vol. 5, pt. 10, 238–39, Archiwum Archidiecezjalne w Poznaniu. Of course, it may be safely assumed that as regards the person of Piłsudski, Teodorowicz would make the worst of whatever his sources had to say.

2. Tytus Komarnicki and Józef Zarański, eds., *Diariusz i teki Jana Szembeka (1935–1945)* (Szembek) (London: Polish Research Centre, 1964), 1:293.

3. In Cardinal Sapieha Papers, Archiwum Kurii Metropolitalnej, Kraków: Piłsudski to Sapieha, April 7 and 19, 1927, and Sapieha to Professor Kallenbach, April 24, 1927; Sapieha, "Pro memoria," 2:139–40.

4. Jędrzejewicz, *Kronika życia,* 2:460.

5. Sapieha, "Pro memoria," 2:139–40; Wincenty Witos, *Moje wspomnienia* (Paris: Instytut Literacki, 1965), 3:397–98.

6. Hlond statement on death of Piłsudski, May 15, 1935, in *Kościół w czasie wojny polsko-bolszewickiej, 1919–1920,* ed. Marian Marek Drozdowski and Andrzej Serafin (Warsaw: Polska Akademia Nauk, 1995), 131; *Times* (London), May 17, 1935.

7. Witos, *Wspomnienia,* 3:397–98; Teodorowicz to Hlond, June 19, 1935, Acta Hlondiana, vol. 5, pt. 10, 238–39.

8. Skrzyński to Beck, July 3, 1935, Poland—Ambasada (Catholic Church), no. 31, Hoover Institution Archives, Stanford, Calif. (HIA). Also Count Bogdan Hutten-Czapski to Hlond, May 17, 1935, Acta Hlondiana, vol. 5, pt. 1, 261; Walerian Meysztowicz, *Gawędy o czasach i ludziach* (London: Polska Fundacja Kulturalna, 1983), 169.

9. Secretariat of State instructions for Cortesi, May 5, 1937, Affari Ecclesiastici Straordinari: Polonia, Archivio Segreto Vaticano, Vatican City (ASV).

10. *Times* (London), May 17, 1935.

11. Acta Hlondiana, vol. 5, pt. 10, 238–39.

12. Anna Cienciała, ed., *Polska polityka zagraniczna w latach 1926–1939: Na podstawie tekstów Józefa Becka* (Paris: Instytut Literacki, 1990), 185–86.

13. Skrzyński to Beck, March 3, 1936, Ambasada RP przy Watykanie A.44.122/15, Instytut Historyczny im. Generała Sikorskiego, London (IHGS);

François Charles-Roux, *Huit ans au Vatican, 1932–1940* (Paris: Flammarion, 1947), 174.

14. Krzysztof Krasowski, "Między Warszawą a Watykanem: Episkopat Polski wobec rządu i Stolicy Apostolskiej, 1918–1939," in *Szkice z dziejów papiestwa*, ed. Irena Koberdowa and Janusz Tazbir (Warsaw: Książka i Wiedza, 1989), 353.

15. In Archiwum Akt Nowych, Warsaw (AAN), Minsterstwo Spraw Zagranicznych (AAN-MSZ): Ref. Wyznań, dossiers on Catholic clergy, no. 2853, and Bp. Łosiński, no. 2854, at time of Piłsudski's death and funeral, 1935; Beck to Skrzyński, May 28, 1935, and Skrzyński to Beck, June 8, 1935, IHGS A.44.249/1; Adam Ludwik Szafrański, "Augustyn Łosiński, Biskup Kielecki (1910–1937) w świetle listów pasterskich, opinii i faktów," *Nasza przeszłość* 59 (1983): 215–40.

16. Szembek, 1:325–27; record of Beck's meeting with Marmaggi, July 30, 1935, IHGS A.44.249/1.

17. In IHGS A.44.249/1: Skrzyński to Beck, July 6 and September 14, 1935, Janikowski to Beck, July 25 and August 12, 1935, [Skrzyński?] to Beck, October 11, 1935; Skrzyński to Beck, July 3, 1935, Ambasada RP przy Watykanie, no. 31, HIA.

18. Szembek, 2:34–115 passim; Borkowski note of conversation with Marmaggi, March 11, 1936, IHGS A.44.122/15.

19. Borkowski note of conversation with Marmaggi, March 5, 1936, IHGS A.44.122/15.

20. Skrzyński to Beck, March 24, 1936, IHGS A.44.122/15.

21. Andrzej Micewski, *Roman Dmowski* (Warsaw: Verum, 1971), 387–94.

22. Szembek, 2:36.

23. France, Ministère des Affaires Étrangères, *Bulletin périodique de la presse polonaise* (BPPP), no. 259.

24. *New York Times*, February 12, 1937.

25. *Tablet*, March 6, 1937.

26. Szembek, 4:505.

27. MSZ memorandum for Mościcki on Polish-Vatican relations, May 18, 1937, AAN-MSZ, Ref. Wyznań, no. 2845; *Tablet*, March 6, 1937.

28. Skrzyński to Beck, April 1, 1937, IHGS A.44.122/16; Meysztowicz, *Gawędy*, 320. Skrzyński praised Cortesi's abilities, but a year later, Cardinal Hlond expressed his low estimate of the effectiveness of the nuncio and his staff in Warsaw. [Janikowski?] to Beck, July 8, 1938, IHGS A.44.122/17.

29. Secretariat of State instructions for Cortesi, May 5, 1937, ASV, Affari Ecclesiastici Straordinari: Polonia.

30. Szembek, 3:102–3.

31. *Tablet*, May 22, 1937.

32. Sapieha to Gen. Bolesław Wieniawa-Długoszowski, June 30 and November 3, 1935, Sapieha Papers; Jerzy Wolny, "Konflikt wawelski," in Wolny, *Księga*, 2:120–21; Meysztowicz, *Gawędy*, 308.

33. In AAN, Naczelny Komitet Uczczenia Pamięci Marszałka Józefa Piłsudskiego (NKUPMJP), no. 14, Kraków Provincial Governor Gnoiński to committee, March 11, 1937, committee to Gnoiński, April 10, 1937, statement of committee, June 25, 1937, protocol of committee meeting, July 4, 1937; Sapieha *Pro memoria* on Wawel matter, fall 1937, in Wolny, *Księga,* 2:74–79.

34. In AAN-NKUPMJP, no. 14: Sapieha to committee, June 17, 1937, protocol of committee meeting, June 19, 1937, and Sapieha to committee, June 20, 1937; Mościcki to Sapieha, and Sapieha's reply, June 22, 1937, Sapieha Papers.

35. Szyszko-Bohusz to Sapieha, June 20, 1937, Sapieha Papers.

36. Cortesi to Sapieha, June 23, 1937, in Wolny, *Księga,* 2:147–49.

37. Biddle to Hull, July 26, 1937, 860c.404/56, State Department Decimal File, RG 59, National Archives, Washington, D.C. (SDNA); *New York Times,* June 24, 1937.

38. Paweł Żółtowski, "Wspomnienia o kardynale Adamie Stefanie Sapieże z okazji 60-lecia ingresu na krakowską stolicę biskupią," *Nasza przeszłość* 38 (1972): 235.

39. *Times* (London), June 25 and 26, 1937. See also BPPP, no. 262.

40. Sapieha to Hlond, June 25, 1937, in Wolny, *Księga,* 2:154–55.

41. Sapieha to committee, June 17, 1937, AAN-NKUPMJP, no. 14; *New York Times,* June 26, 1937. Also *Times* (London), June 28, 1937.

42. *New York Times,* June 25, 26, and 27, 1937; *Tablet,* July 3, 1937; Adam Vetulani, "Arcypasterz krakowski na przełomie epok, Adam Stefan Sapieha w latach 1912–1939," in *Kościół w II Rzeczypospolitej,* ed. Zygmunt Zieliński and Stanisław Wilk (Lublin: Katolicki Uniwersytet Lubelski, 1980), 122.

43. Meysztowicz, *Gawędy,* 308.

44. Ibid., 332.

45. *Tablet,* July 3 and 10, 1937; J. Pietrzak, "Czy kardynał August Hlond był zwolennikiem sanacji?" in Zieliński and Wilk, *Kościół,* 92.

46. Janikowski to Beck, June 28 and 29, 1937, IHGS A.44.122/16.

47. Janikowski to Beck, June 30, 1937, AAN-MSZ, Ref. Wyznań, no. 2857. Also Thomas E. Hachey, ed., *Anglo-Vatican Relations, 1914–1939: Confidential Annual Reports of the British Ministers to the Holy See* (Boston: G. K. Hall, 1972), 381–82.

48. Borkowski, note of conversation with Cortesi, June 24, 1937, AAN-MSZ, Ref. Wyznań, no. 2857.

49. Cortesi to Sapieha, June 28, 1937, in Wolny, *Księga,* 2:155–56.

50. *New York Times,* July 1, 137; Vetulani, "Arcypasterz krakowski," 122.

51. Meysztowicz, *Gawędy,* 308–9.

52. Szembek to Polish legation, Rio de Janeiro, [ca. June 24, 1937], AAN-MSZ, Ref. Wyznań, no. 2857.

53. Biddle to Hull, July 26, 1937, SDNA 860c.404/56. Also Cienciała, *Józefa Becka,* 184–85; *Tablet,* July 10, 1937; *Times* (London), July 19, 1937.

54. In IHGS A.44.122/16: Cortesi to Beck, and Beck's reply, August 25, 1937, Romer, note of meeting between Cortesi and Mościcki, September 23, 1937; Cortesi to Beck, August 25, 1937, in Szembek, 3:318; Cortesi to Bp. Stanisław Rospond, July 3, 1937, in Wolny, *Księga,* 2:157–60; Cienciała, *Józefa Becka,* 187–88.

55. Sapieha to Mościcki, July 6, 1937, IHGS A.44.122/16. See as well Hlond to Cortesi, July 5, 1937, Archiwum Prymasów Polski (APP), Archiwum Archidiecezjalne w Gnieźnie, Gniezno; Cortesi to Hlond, July 7, 1937, Acta Hlondiana, vol. 5, pt. 10, 219–20; Mościcki to Sapieha, [July 1937], Sapieha Papers.

56. *Times* (London), July 16, 1937. Also Sapieha to Mościcki, July 11, 1937, Sapieha Papers; Janikowski to Beck, July 24, 1937, IHGS A.44.122/16.

57. Poland, Sejm, *Sprawozdanie stenograficzne z posiedzenia Sejmu Rzeczypospolitej,* July 20, 1937. In addition, *New York Times,* July 21, 1937.

58. Sapieha *Pro memoria* on Wawel matter, fall 1937, in Wolny, *Księga,* 2:174–79.

59. Sapieha to Cortesi, and Cortesi's reply, July 17, 1937, Sapieha Papers.

60. Janikowski to Beck, May 2, 1938, IHGS A.44.122/17.

61. Żółtowski, "Wspomnienia," 237.

62. Biddle to Hull, July 26, 1937, SDNA 860c.404/56

63. Antony Polonsky, *Politics in Independent Poland, 1921–1939: The Crisis of Constitutional Government* (Oxford: Oxford University Press, 1972), 428. For similar examples, Wiesław Mysłek, *Kościół katolicki w Polsce w latach 1918–1939: Zarys historyczny* (Warsaw: Książka i Wiedza, 1966), 580; Żółtowski, "Wspomnienia," 234–35.

64. Cortesi to Pacelli, January 7, 1938, ASV, Affari Ecclesiastici Straordinari: Polonia.

65. Bishop Kaczmarek is best remembered as the victim of a notable Stalinist show trial at the high point of the persecution of the Church in Communist Poland.

66. Szymon Rudnicki, "Nacjonalizm i religia," *Przegląd historyczny* 78, no. 1 (1987): 97–100; *Tablet,* February 26, 1938.

67. Hlond to Sapieha, June 27, 1939, Acta Hlondiana, vol. 4. Also Andrzej Micewski, *Z geografii politycznej II Rzeczypospolitej* (Warsaw: Więż, 1964), 245.

68. Szembek, 4:492.

69. Jan Gawroński, *Moja misja w Wiedniu, 1932–1938* (Warsaw: Państwowe Wydawnictwo Naukowe, 1965), 454–55.

70. Stanisław Sierpowski, *Stosunki polsko-włoskie w latach 1918–1940* (Warsaw: Państwowe Wydawnictwo Naukowe, 1975), 520.

71. Meysztowicz, *Gawędy,* 333–34; Sierpowski, *Stosunki,* 524–26; Szembek, 4:106, 121–25, 130–31; Alfred Wysocki, *Tajemnice dyplomatycznego sejfu* (Warsaw: Książka i Wiedza, 1988), 565–66, 568–72.

72. Charles-Roux, *Huit ans,* 174; Szembek, 4:280–81, 406, 466–67.

73. Janikowski to Beck, December 1, 1938, IHGS A.44.122/18.

74. Janikowski to Beck, December 29, 1938, IHGS A.44.122/18.

75. Roman Wapiński, *Roman Dmowski* (Lublin: Wydawnictwo Lubelskie, 1988), 380.

76. Sapieha to Pius XI, February 2, 1939, and Cortesi to Maglione, May 16, 1939, in Wolny, *Księga*, 2:391–92; John Paul II, *Rise, Let Us Be on Our Way* (New York: Warner, 2004), 133.

Chapter 9

1. Dale Ahlquist, *G. K. Chesterton: The Apostle of Common Sense* (San Francisco: Ignatius, 2003), 174.

2. *Summi pontificatus*, 23:106, October 20, 1939.

3. Bohdan Cywiński, *Ogniem próbowane—I: Korzenie tożsamości* (Rome: Papieski Instytut Studiów Kościelnych, 1982), 288; Jerzy Kłoczowski, *A History of Polish Christianity* (Cambridge: Cambridge University Press, 2000), 303; Bohdan Cywiński, "Spór o Piusa XII," *Rzeczpospolita*, March 17, 2001.

4. To my knowledge, the term first appears in Joseph Bottum, "The End of the Pius Wars," *First Things* 142 (April 2004): 18–24.

5. François Charles-Roux, *Huit ans au Vatican, 1932–1940* (Paris: Flammarion, 1947), 259–60.

6. Tytus Komarnicki and Józef Zarański, eds., *Diariusz i teki Jana Szembeka (1935–1945)* (Szembek) (London: Polish Research Centre, 1964), 4:506–7.

7. Owen Chadwick, *Britain and the Vatican during the Second World War* (Cambridge: Cambridge University Press, 1986), 46–47; Szembek, 4:517.

8. Oscar Halecki and James F. Murray Jr., *Pius XII: Eugenio Pacelli, Pope of Peace* (New York: Farrar, Straus, Young, 1951), 138; Ronald J. Rychlak, *Hitler, the War, and the Pope* (Columbus, Miss.: Genesis, 2000), 107, 110.

9. In Archiwum Akt Nowych, Warsaw (AAN), Minsterstwo Spraw Zagranicznych (AAN-MSZ): Gabinet Ministra, no. 52, and Skrzyński to Beck, February 10 and March 11, 1933; Skrzyński to Beck, February 27 and April 9, 1933, in *Watykan a stosunki polsko-niemieckie w latach 1918–1939*, ed. Jarosław Jurkiewicz (Warsaw: Książka i Wiedza, 1960), 48–49, 61–65; Anthony Rhodes, *The Vatican in the Age of the Dictators, 1922–1945* (New York: Holt, Rinehart and Winston, 1973), 178; Rychlak, *Hitler*, 58.

10. Note of conversation with Marmaggi, December 27, 1933, AAN-MSZ, Gabinet Ministra, no. 52; in Ambasada RP przy Watykanie A.44.122, Instytut Historyczny im. Generała Sikorskiego, London (IHGS) [Skrzyński?] to Beck, November 3, 1933, #11, Skrzyński to Beck, February 10 and September 20, 1934, # 12–13.

11. In AAN-MSZ, Ref. Wyznań: Skrzyński to Beck, January 5 and April 5, 1935, no. 2836, and April 8, 1935, no. 2785; Szembek, 1:302; Charles-Roux, *Huit ans,* 105–6.

12. Skrzyński to Beck, May 9, 1936, AAN-MSZ, Ref. Wyznań, no. 2785; Skrzyński to Beck, June 24, 1936, IHGS A.44.122/15; in Jurkiewicz, *Watykan a stosunki:* fragment of letter to "Władysław," April 1, 1936, Skrzyński to Beck, May 10, 1936, Janikowski to Beck, September 28, 1936, and Skrzyński to Beck, October 3, 1936, 66–74, 80–86; Rychlak, *Hitler,* 76; Szembek, 2:23–24, 209.

13. Tadeusz Jackowski to Beck, September 16, 1936, in Jurkiewicz, *Watykan a stosunki,* 78–79; *Tablet,* December 19, 1936, 871, January 9, 1937, 48–49, and February 19, 1938, 237.

14. Charles R. Gallagher, "Personal, Private Views," *America,* September 1, 2003, 8–10; Halecki and Murray, *Pius XII,* 139–41; Walerian Meysztowicz, *Gawędy o czasach i ludziach* (London: Polska Fundacja Kulturalna, 1983), 274; *National Catholic Register,* August 5–11, 2001, September 14–20, 2003, and October 5–11, 2003; Rychlak, *Hitler,* 93, 97.

15. In IHGS A.44.115: Janikowski to Beck, September 29 and December 28, 1938, #1, and [Janikowski?] to Beck, June 28, 1939, #2. Tardini served as Cardinal Secretary of State during the pontificate of John XXIII.

16. Chadwick, *Britain and the Vatican,* 53–55; Szembek, 4:519.

17. Chadwick, *Britain and the Vatican,* 46–47; Halecki and Murray, *Pius XII,* 141; William M. Harrigan, "Pius XII's Efforts to Effect a Détente in German-Vatican Relations," *Catholic Historical Review* 49, no. 2 (1963): 179–82; Peter C. Kent, "A Tale of Two Popes: Pius XI, Pius XII and the Rome-Berlin Axis," *Journal of Contemporary History* 23, no. 4 (1988): 589–608.

18. Szembek, 4:566; in IHGS: Zubrzycki to MSZ, March 31, 1939, A.44.53/1, and Janikowski to Beck, May 4, 1939, A.44.115/1; Halecki and Murray, *Pius XII,* 95.

19. Szembek, 4:561–62; Szembek, note of conversation with Cortesi, April 17, 1939, IHGS A.44.122/19. In his memoir, *As I Recall It* (Washington, D.C.: Williams and Heintz, 1957), 241–42, Charles Dewey, the onetime American financial adviser to Poland, claimed to have undertaken a secret mission to Poland in early summer, with the knowledge and blessing of his home archdiocese in Chicago and the Vatican, in a fruitless attempt to convince Warsaw to accept changes in the status of Danzig and the Corridor in exchange for a package of compensations. Perhaps. Dewey had earned a reputation for exaggerating his own exploits, and I have found no reference to such a journey in any archival collections or in the Charles Dewey Papers at the Chicago Historical Society.

20. Maglione to nuncios of Paris, London, and Warsaw, and apostolic delegate to London, May 3, 1939, in *Actes et documents du Saint Siège relatifs à la seconde guerre mondiale,* vol. 1, *Le Saint Siège et la guerre en Europe, mars 1939–août 1940,* ed. Pierre Blet, Angelo Martini, and Burkhart Schneider (ADSS) (Vatican City: Li-

breria Editrice Vaticana, 1965), #19, 20; Osborne to Halifax, May 4, 1939, in Great Britain, Foreign Office, Documents on British Foreign Policy, 1919–1939, ser. 3 (DBFP), 5:411. In his *How War Came: The Immediate Origins of the Second World War* (New York: Pantheon, 1989), Donald Cameron Watt dismisses the Vatican peace initiative of the spring in a chapter entitled "The Amateurs Attempt to Avert a War." One may take his implied point but still ask if the professionals handled the situation any better.

21. Pietro Tacchi Venturi, S.J., to Maglione, May 2, 1939, ADSS #18, 118–19; Charles-Roux, *Huit ans,* 315–17.

22. In IHGS: Beck note of conferences with British ambassador and Nuncio Cortesi, April 8–9, 1939, A.44.122/19, Beck to Polish Embassy, Vatican, May 10, 1939, and Janikowski to MSZ, May 11, 1939, A.44.53/1; in ADSS, Polish Embassy to Maglione, May 9, 1939, #34, 135–36, and Cortesi to Maglione, May 10, 1939, #37, 139; Kennard to Halifax, May 9, 1939, DBFP, 5:475–76.

23. In United States, Department of State, *Foreign Relations of the United States,* 1939: Bullitt to Hull, May 6, 1939, Biddle to Hull, May 8, 1939, and Bullitt to Hull, May 9, 1939, 1:179–84; Halifax to Osborne, May 5, 1939, DBFP, 5:435–36.

24. In ADSS: Abp. Cesare Orsenigo to Maglione, May 6, 1939, #29, 129–32, Maglione diplomatic circular, May 10, 1939, #38, 139–40; German record of meeting between Hitler and Orsenigo, May 10, 1939, Germany, Auswärtiges Amt, *Akten zur deutschen auswärtigen Politik, 1918–1945,* ser. D, 6:352–54; Osborne to Halifax, May 10, 1939, DBFP, 5:498–99; Szembek, 4:598.

25. In ADSS: Orsenigo to Maglione, May 17, 1939, #47, 150–53, Orsenigo to Maglione, June 23, 1939, #70, 185–86, note of Tardini, July 4, 1939, #83, 197, Abp. Valerio Valeri to Maglione, July 4, 1939, #84, 198–200, note of Maglione, July 7, 1939, #85, 200–201, Osborne to Maglione, July 9, 1939, #87, 201–4, and Maglione to Osborne, July 15, 1939, #90, 209–12; Osborne to Halifax, May 29, 1939, DBFP, 5:718–19.

26. Janikowski to Beck, June 1 and July 12, 1939, IHGS A.44.115/2.

27. In ADSS: Maglione note, May 29, 1939, #53, 160–61, Notes of Tardini, June 6–7, 1939, #57, 170–71, and Borgongini Duca to Maglione, June 14, 1939, #62, 177; Georges Roche and Philippe Saint Germain, *Pie XII devant l'histoire* (Paris: Robert Laffont, 1972), 137.

28. In ADSS: Maglione to Cortesi, June 16, 1939, #64, 178, and Cortesi to Maglione, June 22, 1939, #69, 184.

29. In ADSS: Maglione to Orsenigo, June 28, 1939, #77, 193, Maglione to Cortesi, June 30, 1939, #78, 193, Maglione to Orsenigo, July 1, 1939, #80, 194–95, Borgongini Duca to Maglione, July 1, 1939, #81, 195–96, and Maglione to Pacini, July 22, 1939, #92, 212–13; Charles-Roux, *Huit ans,* 322.

30. [Janikowski?] to Beck, June 28, 1939, IHGS A.44.115/2; P. Loraine to Halifax, July 7, 1939, DBFP, 6:293–94; Szembek, 4:634, 649; Chadwick, *Britain and the Vatican,* 71, 77–78.

31. Szembek, 4:615; Charles-Roux, *Huit ans,* 340.

32. Papée to Beck, August 2 and August 3, 1939, IHGS A.44.122/19; Szembek, 4:683.

33. In ADSS: Cortesi to Maglione, August 14, 1939, #94, 213, Maglione to Cortesi, August 15, 1939, #95, 214, note of Maglione, August 16, 1939, #96, 214–15, and Cortesi to Maglione, August 18, 1939, #102, 220.

34. Osborne to Halifax, August 12, 1939, DBFP, 6:674–75.

35. Bonifacio Pignotti to Ciano, August 18, 1939, in Italy, Ministero degli Affari Esteri, *I documenti diplomatici italiani* (IDDI), ser. 8, 13:55–56; Pius XII to Venetian pilgrims, August 19, 1939, ADSS, # 105, 222–24.

36. Charles-Roux to Tardini, August 20, 1939, ADSS, #106, 224–25.

37. Papée to Tardini, August 22, 1939, ADSS, #109, 227.

38. Charles-Roux, *Huit ans,* 328.

39. Papée to MSZ, August 24, 1939, IHGS A.44.53/1; Osborne to Tardini, August 22 and August 23, 1939, ADSS, #110–11, 228–30; in DBFP, Halifax to Osborne, August 22, 1939, 7:117–18, and Osborne to Halifax, August 24, 1939, 7:182–83.

40. Radio message of Pius XII, August 24, 1939, ADSS, #113, 230–38.

41. Meysztowicz, *Gawędy,* 275.

42. Papée to Beck, August 30, 1939, IHGS A.44.122/19.

43. In ADSS: note of Tardini, August 26, 1939, #131, 249, and notes of Montini and Tardini, August 28, 1939, #144, 256.

44. Józef Beck, *Final Report* (New York: Robert Speller and Sons, 1957), 202.

45. For example, Stanisław Sierpowski, *Stosunki polsko-włoskie w latach 1918–1940* (Warsaw: Państwowe Wydawnictwo Naukowe, 1975), 619.

46. Tadeusz Wyrwa, "Watykan a rząd polski w Angers," *Zeszyty historyczne* 72 (1985): 182.

47. Pignotti to Tardini, August 25, 1939, IDDI, 13:174.

48. Tardini to Maglione, August 30, 1939, ADSS, #152, 262–63.

49. Maglione to Cortesi, August 30, 1939, ADSS, #153, 263–64.

50. Rhodes, *Vatican,* 238.

51. In ADSS: Cortesi to Maglione, Maglione to Cortesi, and Maglione to Cortesi, August 31, 1939, #165–67, 274–75.

52. In ADSS: Message of Pius XII, August 31, 1939, #160, 271, Cortesi to Maglione, August 31, 1939, #170, 276; Szembek, 4:704–5.

53. In *Records and Documents of the Holy See Relating to the Second World War,* vol. 1, *The Holy See and the War in Europe, March 1939–August 1940,* ed. Pierre Blet, Angelo Martini, and Burkhart Schneider (RDHS) (Washington, D.C.: Corpus Books, 1968): Cortesi to Maglione, September 3, 1939, #181, 267; Beck, *Final Report,* 201–2; Charles-Roux, *Huit ans,* 332–33; Halecki and Murray, *Pius XII,* 114–17. The Vatican made no attempt to gloss over the fact that it regarded Beck's behavior as unhelpful and offensive, Secretariat of State to British Legation,

November 13, 1939, and Tardini to Osborne, November 16, 1939, RDHS, #218–19, 309–12.

54. Wojciech Necel, ed., *Z notatnika Kardynała Augusta Hlonda* (Poznań: Hlondianum, 1995), 108–9.

55. Halecki and Murray, *Pius XII*, 117.

56. Notes of Maglione, September 1, 1939, ADSS, #171, 277.

57. In IHGS: Papée to MSZ, September 2, 1939, A.44.53/1, and Papée to Beck, September 4, 1939, A.44.122/20.

58. Papée to MSZ, September 6, 1939, IHGS A.44.53/1; Charles-Roux to Maglione, September 11, 1939, RDHS, #198, 281; Meysztowicz, *Gawędy*, 288–89.

59. David Alvarez, "The Vatican and the Fall of Poland," in *The Opening of the Second World War*, ed. David Winegate Pike (New York: Peter Lang, 1991), 92; Paul Duclos, *Le Vatican et la seconde guerre mondiale* (Paris: A. Pedone, 1955), 54; Camille M. Cianfarra, *The Vatican and the War* (New York: Dutton, 1944), 191–92; Harold H. Tittmann Jr., *Inside the Vatican of Pius XII: The Memoirs of an American Diplomat during World War II* (New York: Image, 2004), 110–12; Valeri to Maglione, September 29, 1939, RDHS, #212, 294–95.

60. In ADSS: notes of Pope Pius XII, September 13, 1939, #200, 283–84, and Pius XII to Belgian ambassador, September 14, 1939, #202, 284–87.

61. Necel, *Z notatnika Kardynała*, 110–18; Cortesi to Maglione, and Tardini to Cortesi, September 5, 1939, RDHS, #189–90, 274–75; Philip V. Cannistraro, Edward D. Wynot Jr. and Theodore P. Kovaleff, eds., *Poland and the Coming of the Second World War: The Diplomatic Papers of A. J. Drexel Biddle, Jr., United States Ambassador to Poland, 1937–1939* (Columbus: Ohio State University, 1976), 137–38; Stanisław Kosiński, "August Hlond," in *Na stolicy prymasowskiej w Gnieźnie i w Poznaniu: Szkice o prymasach Polski w okresie niewoli narodowej i w II Rzeczypospolitej*, ed. Feliks Lenort (Poznań: Księgarnia Św. Wojciecha, 1982), 356; Andrzej Micewski, *Z geografii politycznej II Rzeczypospolitej* (Warsaw: Więź, 1964), 306; Chadwick, *Britain and the Vatican*, 80.

62. Anna Cienciała, ed., *Polska polityka zagraniczna w latach 1926–1939: Na podstawie tekstów Józefa Becka* (Paris: Instytut Literacki, 1990), 285; Cortesi to Maglione, September 17, 1939, RDHS, #204, 289.

63. Kosiński, "August Hlond," 355–56; Carlo Falconi, *The Silence of Pius XII* (Boston: Little, Brown and Co., 1970), 133; Tadeusz Żychiewicz, "Prymas Polski August kardynał Hlond w setną rocznicę urodzin," *Tygodnik powszechny*, July 26, 1981; Jean Chélini, *L'Église sous Pie XII: La tourmente (1939–1945)* (Paris: Fayard, 1983), 132.

64. Charles-Roux, *Huit ans*, 343; Duclos, *Le Vatican*, 53.

65. Cianfarra, *Vatican and the War*, 190–91; *Tablet*, September 30, 1939. The English Catholic writer Evelyn Waugh noted in his journal entry for September 25: "Russian conquests in Poland . . . [are] a more terrible fate for the allies we are

pledged to defend than conquest by Germany." Michael Davie, ed., *The Diaries of Evelyn Waugh* (London: Weidenfeld and Nicolson, 1976), 443.

66. Chélini, *L'Église sous Pie XII,* 132; Falconi, *Silence,* 142, 400; Tadeusz Wyrwa, "Kościół i państwo w pierwszym dzisięcioleciu PRL," *Zeszyty historyczne* 82 (1987): 60.

67. Necel, *Z notatnika Kardynała,* 119–20; Charles-Roux, *Huit ans,* 344.

68. Necel, *Z notatnika Kardynała,* 120.

69. Kard. August Hlond, *Na straży sumienia narodu* (Ramsey, N.J.: Don Bosco, 1951), 256–59; Charles-Roux, *Huit ans,* 345; Chadwick, *Britain and the Vatican,* 80–81.

70. Philippe Chenaux, *Pie XII: Diplomate et pasteur* (Paris: Cerf, 2003), 238.

71. Meysztowicz, *Gawędy,* 276. Compare Papée's report to MSZ, September 30, 1939, IHGS A.44.53/1, with his later account in Kazimierz Papée, *Pius XII a Polska, 1939–1949: Przemówienia, listy, komentarze* (Rome: Studium, 1954), 13–17.

72. Chadwick, *Britain and the Vatican,* 81–82; Papée to MSZ, October 6, 1939, IHGS A.44.122/20.

73. Chenaux, *Pie XII,* 238–39; Alessandro Duce, *Pio XII e la Polonia* (Rome: Studium, 1997), 96; Thomas E. Hachey, ed., *Anglo-Vatican Relations, 1914–1939: Confidential Annual Reports of the British Ministers to the Holy See* (Boston: G. K. Hall, 1972), 400–401.

74. Chadwick, *Britain and the Vatican,* 82; Alvarez, "The Vatican and the Fall of Poland," 93; Tittmann, *Inside the Vatican,* 110–12; Cywiński, "Spór."

75. Walter J. Ciszek and Daniel Flaherty, *He Leadeth Me* (Garden City, N.Y.: Doubleday, 1973), 17–18.

76. Carlo Felice Casula, *Domenico Tardini (1888–1961): L'Azione della Santa Sede nella crisi fra le due guerre* (Rome: Studium, 1988), 165–66.

77. Tittmann, *Inside the Vatican,* 110–12.

78. Necel, *Z notatnika Kardynała,* 120–21; Pope John Paul II, *Autobiografia* (Kraków: Wydawnictwo Literackie, 2005), 35.

79. Necel, *Z notatnika Kardynała,* 120.

80. Chenaux, *Pie XII,* 238.

81. Chadwick, *Britain and the Vatican,* 84–85; Papée to foreign minister, October 30, 1939, IHGS A.44.117/2.

82. [Papée?] to foreign minister, November 2, 1939, IHGS A.44.122/20.

83. *America,* October 28, 1939, 64.

84. See chapter 2 of Michael Phayer, *Pius XII, the Holocaust, and the Cold War* (Bloomington: Indiana University Press, 2008).

85. Notably George Weigel, *The Final Revolution: The Resistance Church and the Collapse of Communism* (New York: Oxford University Press, 1992).

86. Martin Conway, *Catholic Politics in Europe, 1918–1945* (London: Routledge, 1997), 2–4.

87. Tom Buchanan and Martin Conway, eds., *Political Catholicism in Europe, 1918–1965* (Oxford: Oxford University Press, 1996), 8, 19.

88. Kłoczowski, *Polish Christianity,* 296–97; Jerzy Kłoczowski and Lidia Müllerowa, "W dwudziestym stuleciu (1918–1980)," in *Zarys dziejów Kościoła katolickiego w Polsce,* by Jerzy Kłoczowski, Lidia Müllerowa, and Jan Skarbek (Kraków: Znak, 1986), 338–39; Jerzy Kłoczowski, "O polskim Kościoła ostatniego wieku," *Rzeczpospolita,* September 28, 1999.

Bibliography

The bibliography that follows includes all sources, original and published, that have been used in preparation of this book and cited in the notes. However, on its own the listing may not provide readers with all the information they may wish. For that reason, a brief prefatory essay may serve two helpful purposes. First, it aims to give a fuller description of the archival materials that make up the backbone of this study. Second, it hopes to sketch a serviceable if necessarily incomplete guide to the basic published literature in the two fields brought together in the monograph: the history of Poland in the first half of the twentieth century, and that of the Catholic Church in the same period. Some readers may come from one of these areas of interest without being fully acquainted with the other. Mainly for their benefit, I will suggest a selection of titles that can supply valuable relevant background information, primarily those in English, and emphasizing the general, rather than the more specialized, works that appear most frequently in the notes. Entries in Polish are identified by their equivalents in English as well; for those in other languages, the assumption is that the original will do.

Archival Sources

This book is based largely on evidence gathered from unpublished Polish governmental and ecclesiastical documents residing in archives located in Poland or scattered to other lands by war and emigration. The Archiwum Akt Nowych (Archive of New Documents) in Warsaw holds the records of the two departments of the interwar Polish state that had most to do with the Catholic Church at home and abroad: the Ministerstwo Spraw Zagranicznych (Ministry of Foreign Affairs) and the Ministerstwo Wyznań Religijnych i Oświecenia Publicznego (Ministry of Religious Bodies and Public Education). The papers of the Polish Embassy to the Holy See are found within the collections of the Instytut Historyczny im. Generała Sikorskiego (General Sikorski Historical Institute) in London, the base of the Polish Government in Exile. A microfilm copy of this same file, though difficult to read for technical reasons, may be examined at the Hoover Institution Archives, Stanford, California.

There is no centralized archive of official documents of the Catholic Church in Poland, or of the papers of its leaders. Instead, each diocese is responsible for maintaining its own historical records and organizing them for the use of researchers.

In some cases, much was lost in the massive destruction of World War II. Maria Dębowska, ed., *Archiwa Kościoła katolickiego w Polsce: Informator* (Catholic Church Archives in Poland: A Guide) (Kielce: Jedność, 2002) provides a thorough directory of these repositories. In the Archdiocesan Archiwum Kurii Metropolitalnej (Archive of the Metropolitan Curia) of Kraków, the extensive papers of Cardinal Sapieha are essential. So is the Archive of the Primates of Poland at the Archiwum Archidiecezjalne w Gnieźnie (Archdiocesan Archive in Gniezno). The Archiwum Archidiecezjalne w Poznaniu (Archdiocesan Archive in Poznań) possesses the Acta Hlondiana, featuring the correspondence of Cardinal Hlond. The main attraction of the Archiwum Archidiecezjalne Warszawskie (Archdiocesan Archive of Warsaw) is the instructive typescript memoir of Cardinal Kakowski, "Z niewoli do niepodległości" (From Bondage to Independence).

Of course, the indispensable resource for the policies of the papacy is the Archivio Segreto Vaticano, Vatican City. An aura of mystery surrounds this "Secret Archive," deriving both from its deceptively forbidding name and from the widespread suspicion that its main function is to hide from public view unflattering truths about the history of the Church. In fact, it is an archive like any other, no more restrictive than most—though none can match the combination of the vastness and antiquity of its holdings and the splendor of its setting within the Apostolic Palace. Owen Chadwick, *Catholicism and History: The Opening of the Vatican Archives* (Cambridge: Cambridge University Press, 1978), is a fascinating account of the transformation of the Archive from the confidential historical memory of the popes into a treasure house for historians. In 2006, Pope Benedict XVI, responding to intense curiosity about the role of the Holy See in the run-up to the Second World War, declared the files of the Secret Archive dating from the pontificate of Pius XI (1922–39) open to access for the first time. In the collections of the Secretariat of State, important documents touching on Poland usually made their way into the records of the Congregation of Extraordinary Church Affairs. By comparison, the papers of the Papal Nunciature in Warsaw tend to deal with routine matters. The Archivio Segreto holds the very interesting personal archive from the era of Benedict XV, already available to researchers before 2006, of Achille Ratti, the future Pius XI, as nuncio to Poland from 1918 to 1921, a revealing mixture of private and official correspondence.

Published Materials

There is no better introduction to twentieth-century Polish history in English than the stylish and authoritative M. B. Biskupski, *The History of Poland* (Westport, Conn.: Greenwood, 2000). The justly praised standard survey by Norman Davies, *God's Playground: A History of Poland* (New York: Columbia University Press), makes a point of emphasizing the importance of Catholicism in national tradition. On the interwar Second Republic, Antony Polonsky, *Politics in Independent Poland, 1921–1939: The Crisis of Constitutional Government* (Oxford: Oxford University Press, 1972), holds up well, although neither religion nor foreign policy is its main interest. For the latter, Piotr S. Wandycz, *Polish Diplomacy, 1914–1945: Aims and Achievements* (London: Orbis, 1988), provides a masterly introduction.

The leading overviews of the Catholic Church in the modern era are Henri Daniel-Rops, *A Fight for God, 1870–1939* (London: J. M. Dent and Sons, 1966); Hubert Jedin et al., eds., *History of the Church*, vol. 10, *The Church in the Modern Age* (New York: Crossroad, 1981); and Jean-Marie Mayeur, ed., *Histoire du Christianisme des origines à nos jours*, vol. 12, *Guerres mondiales et totalitarismes (1914–1958)* (Paris: Desclée-Fayard, 1990). For the broad sweep of Catholicism in Poland through the centuries, Jerzy Kłoczowski, *A History of Polish Christianity* (Cambridge: Cambridge University Press, 2000), is unmatched. Brian Porter, "The Catholic Nation: Religion, Identity, and the Narratives of Polish History," *Slavic and East European Journal* 45, no. 2 (2001): 289–99, offers a brief but stimulating reflection on an important theme.

Several useful works focus on various aspects of the history of Catholicism during the interwar years related to the subject of this book. On the Church in Poland, see Bohdan Cywiński, *Ogniem próbowane—I: Korzenie tożsamości* (Tried by Fire: The Roots of Identity) (Rome: Papieski Instytut Studiów Kościelnych, 1982); Mgr. Valérien Meysztowicz, *L'Église Catholique en Pologne entre les deux guerres (1919–1939)* (Vatican City: n.p., 1944); and Zygmunt Zieliński and Stanisław Wilk, eds., *Kościół w II Rzeczypospolitej* (The Church in the Second Republic) (Lublin: Katolicki Uniwersytet Lubelski, 1980). The policies of the Holy See are covered in J. Derek Holmes, *The Papacy in the Modern World, 1914–1978* (London: Burns and Oates, 1981), and Anthony Rhodes, *The Vatican in the Age of the Dictators, 1922–1945* (New York: Holt, Rinehart and Winston, 1973). For the political thrust of Catholicism in Poland and elsewhere on the continent, consult Martin Conway, *Catholic Politics in Europe, 1918–1945* (London: Routledge, 1997).

Studies of Catholicism and the Church in interwar Polish public affairs in English are still scant. My own articles are listed in the bibliography, and have been incorporated here and there within this volume. Edward D. Wynot Jr., "The Catholic Church and the Polish State, 1935–1939," *Journal of Church and State* 15, no. 2 (1973): 223–40, deals with the phase after the death of Piłsudski.

There is an abundance of published primary sources on the Ratti mission to Poland, though all in languages other than English. Stanisław Wilk, ed., *Achilles Ratti (1918–1921)*, Acta Nuntiaturae Polonae 57 (Rome: Institutum Historicum Polonicum, 1995–96), reproduces papers from his Warsaw nunciature. Terzo Natalini, ed., *I diari del cardinale Ermenegildo Pellegrinetti, 1916–1922* (Vatican City: Archivio Segreto Vaticano, 1994), is the diary of Ratti's *chargé*, who recorded his candid observations on the difficulties they encountered. Primarily a guide to the Ratti collection in the Vatican Archive, Ottavio Cavalleri, ed., *L'Archivio di Mons. Achille Ratti, visitatore apostolico e nunzio a Varsavia (1918–1921): Inventario* (Vatican City: Archivio Segreto Vaticano, 1990), is made more valuable by the inclusion of Pellegrinetti's "final report" on the future pope's Polish sojourn.

Three Polish entries shed light on significant aspects of the role of the Church in the Second Republic. Stanisław Grabski, *Pamiętniki* (Memoirs), 2 vols. (Warsaw: Czytelnik, 1989), includes the reminscences of the Polish negotiator of the concordat of 1925. The polemic of Roman Dmowski, *Kościół, Naród, i Państwo* (Church, Nation, and State) (Chicago: Instytut Romana Dmowskiego, 1985), exerted considerable influence in Poland upon its original publication in 1927. Jerzy Wolny, ed., *Księga Sapieżynska* (The Book of Sapieha), 2 vols. (Kraków: Polskie Towarzystwo Teologiczne, 1986), a compilation of essays and documents relating to Archbishop Adam Sapieha, covers a broader range of subjects than the title might suggest.

For Jewish issues, see Ezra Mendelsohn, *The Jews of East Central Europe between the World Wars* (Bloomington: Indiana University Press, 1983), and Antony Polonsky, Ezra Mendelsohn, and Jerzy Tomaszewski, eds., *Jews in Independent Poland, 1918–1939* (Oxford: Littman Library of Jewish Civilization, 2004). Ronald Modras, *The Catholic Church and Antisemitism: Poland, 1933–1939* (Langhorne, Penn.: Harwood, 1994), has much to say of Polish Catholic attitudes toward Jews, most of it unpleasant.

The territories and peoples of the eastern kresy of interwar Poland are treated in Timothy Snyder, *The Reconstruction of Nations: Poland, Ukraine, Lithuania, Belarus, 1569–1999* (New Haven, Conn.: Yale University Press, 2003), and Bohdan Budurowycz, "Poland and the Ukrainian Problem, 1921–1939," *Canadian Slavonic Papers* 25, no. 4 (1983): 473–500. On the Greek Catholic Metropolitan Sheptyts'kyi, consult Paul R. Magocsi, ed., *Morality and Reality: The Life and Times of Andrei Sheptyts'kyi* (Edmonton: Canadian Institute of Ukrainian Studies, 1989), and Andrzej Zięba, ed., *Metropolita Andrzej Szeptycki* (Metropolitan Andrei Sheptyts'kyi) (Kraków: Polska Akademia Umiejętności, 1994). Jerzy Matulewicz, *Pisma wybrane* (Selected Writings) (Warsaw: Wydawnictwo Księży Marianów, 1988), includes the journals of the embattled bishop of Vilna.

The hard lot of Catholicism in the Soviet Union in the days of Lenin and Stalin is described in Dennis J. Dunn, *The Catholic Church and Russia: Popes, Patriarchs, Tsars and Commissars* (Burlington, Vt.: Ashgate, 2004), and James J. Zatko, *Descent into Darkness: The Destruction of the Roman Catholic Church in Russia, 1917–1923* (Notre Dame: University of Notre Dame Press, 1965). For the Holy See and Russia, and the spectacular failure of the conversion drive spearheaded by Bishop d'Herbigny, see Hansjakob Stehle, *Eastern Politics of the Vatican, 1917–1979* (Athens: Ohio University Press, 1981).

By far the best published source for the reaction of Pius XII to the outbreak of World War II is Pierre Blet, Angelo Martini, and Burkhart Schneider, eds., *Records and Documents of the Holy See Relating to the Second World War*, vol. 1, *The Holy See and the War in Europe, March 1939–August 1940* (Washington, D.C.: Corpus Books, 1968), the translated version of the initial volume within the massive series of documents released by the Vatican three years earlier in response to the controversies aroused by Rolf Hochhuth's play *The Deputy.* Readers will also profit from Owen Chadwick, *Britain and the Vatican during the Second World War* (Cambridge: Cambridge University Press, 1986), and the essay of David Alvarez, "The Vatican and the Fall of Poland," in *The Opening of the Second World War*, ed. David Wingeate Pike (New York: Peter Lang, 1991), 91–94. In other languages, François Charles-Roux, *Huit ans au Vatican, 1932–1940* (Paris: Flammarion, 1947), and Wojciech Necel, ed., *Z notatnika Kardynała Augusta Hlonda* (From the Notebook of Cardinal August Hlond) (Poznań: Hlondianum, 1995), are useful.

Archival Collections

Archivio Segreto Vaticano, Vatican City

Archive of Mons. Achille Ratti, 1918–1921
Segretaria di Stato, Affari Ecclesiastici Straordinari: Polonia
Segretaria di Stato, Affari Ecclesiastici Straordinari: Russia
Segretaria di Stato, Rapp. Pontifice: Polonia

Archiwum Akt Nowych, Warsaw

Ambasada RP w Berlinie
Ambasada RP w Londynie
Ambasada RP w Paryżu
Franciszek Potocki Papers
J. i A. Piłsudskich Papers
Ministerstwo Spraw Zagranicznych
Ministerstwo Wyznań Religijnych i Oświecenia Publicznego
Naczelny Komitet Uczczenia Pamięci Marszałka Piłsudskiego
Prezydium Rady Ministrów

Archiwum Archidiecezjalne w Gnieźnie, Gniezno

Archiwum Prymasów Polski

Archiwum Archidiecezjalne w Poznaniu, Poznań

Acta Hlondiana

Archiwum Archidiecezjalne Warszawskie, Warsaw

Kard. Aleksander Kakowski, "Z niewoli do niepodległości" (typescript memoir)

Archiwum Kurii Metropolitalnej, Kraków

Cardinal Sapieha Papers

Hoover Institution Archives, Stanford, Calif.

Hugh S. Gibson Papers
Poland, Ambasada (Catholic Church) (microfilm)

Instytut Historyczny im. Generała Sikorskiego, London

Ambasada R.P. przy Watykanie

Joseph Pilsudski Institute of America, New York

Ambasada R.P. w Londynie

National Archives, Washington, D.C.

State Department Decimal File, RG 59

Yale University Library, New Haven, Conn.

Archiwum Adiutantury Generalnej Naczelnego Dowództwa (Archiwum Belwederskie) (microfilm)

Published Documents

Blet, Pierre, Angelo Martini, and Burkhart Schneider, eds. *Actes et documents du Saint Siège relatifs à la seconde guerre mondiale.* Vol. 1, *Le Saint Siège et la guerre en Europe, mars 1939–août 1940.* Vatican City: Libreria Editrice Vaticana, 1965.

———, eds. *Records and Documents of the Holy See Relating to the Second World War.* Vol. 1, *The Holy See and the War in Europe, March 1939–August 1940.* Washington, D.C.: Corpus Books, 1968.

Cannistraro, Philip V., Edward D. Wynot Jr., and Theodore P. Kovaleff, eds. *Poland and the Coming of the Second World War: The Diplomatic Papers of A. J. Drexel Biddle, Jr., United States Ambassador to Poland, 1937–1939.* Columbus: Ohio State University, 1976.

Cappuyns, M., "Dom Lambert Beauduin (1873–1960), quelques documents et souvenirs." *Revue d'histoire ecclésiastique* 61, no. 2 (1966): 424–54; nos. 3–4 (1966): 761–807.

Cavalleri, Ottavio, ed. *L'Archivio di Mons. Achille Ratti, visitatore apostolico e Nunzio a Varsavia (1918–1921).* Vatican City: Archivio SegretoVaticano, 1990.

Drozdowski, Marian Marek, and Andrzej Serafin, eds. *Kościół w czasie wojny polsko-bolszewickiej, 1919–1920.* Warsaw: Polska Akademia Nauk, 1995.

Germany, Auswärtiges Amt. Akten zur deutschen auswärtigen Politik, 1918–1945.

Great Britain, Foreign Office. Documents on British Foreign Policy.

Hachey, Thomas E., ed. *Anglo-Vatican Relations, 1914–1939: Confidential Annual Reports of the British Ministers to the Holy See.* Boston: G. K. Hall, 1972.

Italy, Ministero degli Affari Esteri. I Documenti diplomatici italiani.

Janowska, Halina, ed. *Archiwum polityczne Ignacego Paderewskiego.* 4 vols. Wrocław: Zakład Narodowy im. Ossolińskich, 1973–74.

Jurkiewicz, Jarosław, ed. *Watykan a stosunki polsko-niemieckie w latach 1918–1939.* Warsaw: Książka i Wiedza, 1960.

Liebmann, Max, ed. "Les conclaves de Benoît XV et de Pie XI, notes du cardinal Piffl." *La revue nouvelle* 38, nos. 7–8 (1963): 34–52.

Papée, Kazimierz. *Pius XII a Polska, 1939–1949: Przemówienia, listy, komentarze.* Rome: Studium, 1954.

Sierpowski, Stanisław. "Nieznane listy nuncjusza apostolskiego w Polsce—Achillesa Rattiego z lat 1920–1921." *Życie i myśl* 39, nos. 1–2 (1991): 48–56.

United States, Department of State. Foreign Relations of the United States.

Wilk, Stanisław, ed. *Achilles Ratti.* Acta Nuntiaturae Polonae 57. Rome: Institutum Historicum Polonicum, 1995–96.

Zatko, James J. "The Letters of Archbishop Lauri, Apostolic Nuncio in Warsaw, to Monsignor Constantine Budkiewicz of St. Catherine's, St. Petersburg, 1922–1923." *Polish Review* 4, nos. 1–2 (1959): 127–31.

Governmental Publications

France, Ministère des Affaires Étrangères. *Bulletin périodique de la presse polonaise.*

Poland, Sejm. *Sprawozdanie stenograficzne z posiedzenia Sejmu Rzeczypospolitej.*

Press

America

Commonweal

First Things

Gazeta świąteczna (Warsaw)

Gazeta warszawska (Warsaw)

Kurjer lwowski (Lwów)
Le messager polonais (Warsaw)
National Catholic Register
New York Times
L'Osservatore romano
Przegląd wieczorny (Warsaw)
Rzeczpospolita (Warsaw)
Tablet
Times (London)
Tygodnik powszechny

Diaries and Memoirs

Baranowski, Władysław. *Rozmowy z Piłsudskim, 1916–1931.* Warsaw: Zebra, 1990.

Beck, Józef. *Final Report.* New York: Robert Speller and Sons, 1957.

Charles-Roux, François. *Huit ans au Vatican, 1932–1940.* Paris: Flammarion, 1947.

Chesterton, G. K. *The Autobiography of G. K. Chesterton.* San Francisco: Ignatius, 1986.

Cienciała, Anna M., ed. *Polska polityka zagraniczna w latach 1926–1939: Na podstawie tekstów Józefa Becka.* Paris: Instytut Literacki, 1990.

Ciszek, Walter J., and Daniel Flaherty. *He Leadeth Me.* Garden City, N.Y.: Doubleday, 1973.

———. *With God in Russia.* New York: McGraw-Hill, 1964.

Confalonieri, Carlo. *Pio XI vista da vicino.* Turin: Editrice S.A.I.E., 1957.

Davie, Michael, ed. *The Diaries of Evelyn Waugh.* London: Weidenfeld and Nicolson, 1976.

Dewey, Charles S. *As I Recall It.* Washington, D.C.: Williams and Heintz, 1957.

Dmowski, Roman. *Polityka polska i odbudowanie państwa.* Warsaw: Perzyński, Niklewicz, 1925.

Dzierzbicki, Stanisław. *Pamiętnik z lat wojny, 1915–1918.* Warsaw: Państwowy Instytut Wydawniczy, 1983.

Gawroński, Jan. *Moja misja w Wiedniu, 1932–1938.* Warsaw: Państwowe Wydawnictwo Naukowe, 1965.

Grabski, Stanisław. *Pamiętniki.* 2 vols. Warsaw: Czytelnik, 1989.

Grabski, Władysław. *Dwa lata pracy u podstaw państwowości naszej (1924–1925).* Warsaw: Hoesick, 1927.

Hutten-Czapski, Bogdan. *Sześćdziesiąt lat życia politycznego i towarzyskiego.* 2 vols. Warsaw: Hoesick, 1936.

Jędrzejewicz, Wacław. *Wspomnienia.* Wrocław: Ossolineum, 1993.

John Paul II. *Autobiografia.* Kraków: Wydawnictwo Literackie, 2005.

———. *Rise, Let Us Be on Our Way.* New York: Warner, 2004.

Komarnicki, Tytus, and Józef Zarański, eds. *Diariusz i teki Jana Szembeka (1935–1945).* 4 vols. London: Polish Research Centre, 1964.

Laroche, Jules. *La Pologne de Pilsudski: Souvenirs d'une ambasade, 1926–1935.* Paris: Flammarion, 1953.

Matulewicz, Jerzy. *Pisma wybrane.* Warsaw: Wydawnictwo Księży Marianów, 1988.

Meysztowicz, Walerian. *Gawędy o czasach i ludziach.* London: Polska Fundacja Kulturalna, 1983.

Natalini, Terzo, ed. *I diari del cardinale Ermenegildo Pellegrinetti, 1916–1922.* Vatican City: Archivio Segreto Vaticano, 1994.

Necel, Wojciech, ed. *Z notatnika Kardynała Augusta Hlonda.* Poznań: Hlondianum, 1995.

Piłsudska, Aleksandra. *Wspomnienia.* Warsaw: Novum, 1989.

Rataj, Maciej. *Pamiętniki.* Warsaw: Ludowa Spółdzielnia Wydawnicza, 1965.

Stone, Daniel, ed. *The Polish Memoirs of William John Rose.* Toronto: University of Toronto, 1975.

Tittmann, Harold H., Jr. *Inside the Vatican of Pius XII: The Memoirs of an American Diplomat during World War II.* New York: Image, 2004.

Witos, Wincenty. *Moje wspomnienia.* 3 vols. Paris: Instytut Literacki, 1964–65.

Wysocki, Alfred. *Tajemnice dyplomatycznego sejfu.* Warsaw: Książka i Wiedza, 1988.

Contemporary Works

Abraham, Władysław, Michał Rostworowski, Stanisław Kutrzeba, Stanisław Estreicher, Władysław Leopold Jawerski, Stanisław Wróblewski, Fryderyk Zell, and Tadeusz Dwernicki, eds. *Nasza konstytucja.* Kraków: By the author, 1922.

Barycka, Janina. *Stosunek kleru do Państwa i oświaty.* Warsaw: Nasza Księgarnia, 1934.

Bednorz, Fr. Herbert. *Le concordat de Pologne de 1925.* Paris: Domat-Montchrestien, 1938.

Belloc, Hilaire. *Essays of a Catholic.* Freeport, N.Y.: Books for Libraries, 1967.

———. *Places.* London: Cassell and Co., 1942.

———. *Return to the Baltic.* London: Constable and Co., 1938.

Boy-Żeleński, Tadeusz. *Nasi okupanci.* Warsaw: Bibljoteka Boya, 1932.

Chesterton, G. K. *The End of the Armistice.* London: Sheed and Ward, 1940.

———. *Generally Speaking.* Freeport, NY: Books for Libraries, 1968.

Clipper, Lawrence J., ed. *The Collected Works of G. K. Chesterton.* Vol. 34, *The Illustrated London News, 1926–1928.* San Francisco: Ignatius, 1986.

Dmowski, Roman. *Kościół, Naród i Państwo.* Chicago: Instytut Romana Dmowskiego, 1985.
G. M. "Poland and Christendom." *Month,* December 1931, 544–47.
Gerstmann, Adam, ed. *Konkordat Polski ze Stolicą Apostolską.* Lwów: Bibljoteka Religijna, 1925.
Goodhart, Arthur L. *Poland and the Minority Races.* New York: Brentano's, 1920.
Hlond, Kard. August. *Na straży sumienia narodu.* Ramsey, N.J.: Don Bosco, 1951.
Jaworski, Władysław Leopold. "Kościół Rzymsko-Katolicki a Konstytucja polska." *Ruch prawniczy* 2, no. 1 (1922): 1–8.
Loiseau, Charles. "La politique du Saint-Siège en Europe centrale (1919–1936)—II." *Le monde slave* 14, no. 1 (1937): 98–121.
———. "The Vatican and the New States of Central Europe." *Living Age,* November 8, 1919, 321–27.
Łubieński, Henryk Ignacy. *Droga na wschód Rzymu.* Warsaw: By the author, 1932.
McCullagh, Francis. *The Bolshevik Persecution of Christianity.* New York: E. P. Dutton, 1924.
Mackiewicz, Stanisław (Cat). *Historja Polski od 11 listopada 1918 r. do 17 września 1939 r.* London: M. I. Kolin, 1941.
Morgan, Thomas B. *A Reporter at the Papal Court: A Narrative of the Reign of Pope Pius XI.* New York: Longmans, Green and Co., 1937.
Murray, John. "St. Andrew Bobola and Poland." *Month,* July 1938, 23–29.
Piątkiewicz, Włodzimierz. *Prawda o Albertynie.* Kraków: Nakład Wydawniczy Księży Jezuitów, 1932.
Piotrowicz, Wiktor. *Z zagadnień wyznaniowych w Polsce.* Vilna: Lux, 1929.
Speaight, Robert, ed. *Letters from Hilaire Belloc.* London: Hollis and Carter, 1958.
Teeling, William. *Pope Pius XI and World Affairs.* New York: Frederick A. Stokes, 1937.
Tommasini, Francesco. *La risurrezione della Polonia.* Milan: Fratelli Treves, 1925.
Vistalli, Francesco. *Benedetto XV.* Rome: Tipografia Poliglotta Vaticana, 1928.
Williamson, Benedict. *The Story of Pope Pius XI.* New York: P. J. Kennedy and Sons, 1931.

Secondary Works

Ahlquist, Dale. *G. K. Chesterton: The Apostle of Common Sense.* San Francisco: Ignatius, 2003.
Ajnenkiel, Andrzej. *Od rządów ludowych do przewrotu majowego: Zarys dziejów politycznych Polski, 1918–1926.* Warsaw: Wiedza Powszechna, 1978.
Allitt, Patrick. *Catholic Converts: British and American Intellectuals Turn to Rome.* Ithaca, N.Y.: Cornell University Press, 1997.

Alvarez, David. *Spies in the Vatican: Espionage and Intrigue from Napoleon to the Holocaust.* Lawrence: University Press of Kansas, 2002.

Anderson, Robin. *Between Two Wars: The Story of Pope Pius XI (Achille Ratti), 1922–1939.* Chicago: Franciscan Herald Press, 1977.

Aveling, J. C. H. *The Jesuits.* London: Blond and Briggs, 1981.

Bańka, Józef. "Dekret ks. kard. Adolfa Bertrama z 21 XI 1920 roku a ks. Achilles Ratti, późniejszy Papież Pius XI." *Nasza przeszłość* 36 (1971): 287–306.

Blobaum, Robert, ed. *Antisemitism and Its Opponents in Modern Poland.* Ithaca, N.Y.: Cornell University Press, 2005.

———. "The Politics of Antisemitism in *Fin-de-Siècle* Warsaw." *Journal of Modern History* 73, no. 2 (2001): 275–306.

Bozowski, Bronisław. "Ks. Kardynał Aleksander Kakowski." *Więż* 5 (May 1973): 99–113.

Braun, Jerzy, ed. *Poland in Christian Civilization.* London: Veritas, 1985.

Browne-Olf, Lillian. *Their Name Is Pius: Portraits of Five Great Modern Popes.* Milwaukee, Wisc.: Bruce, 1941.

Buchanan, Tom, and Martin Conway, eds. *Political Catholicism in Europe, 1918–1965.* Oxford: Oxford University Press, 1996.

Castellan, Georges. *Dieu garde la Pologne! Histoire du catholicisme polonais, 1795–1980.* Paris: Robert Laffont, 1981.

Casula, Carlo Felice. *Domenico Tardini (1888–1961): L'Azione della Santa Sede nella crisi fra le due guerre.* Rome: Studium, 1988.

Chadwick, Owen. *Britain and the Vatican during the Second World War.* Cambridge: Cambridge University Press, 1986.

Chajn, Leon. *Polskie wolnomularstwo, 1920–1938.* Warsaw: Czytelnik, 1984.

Chélini, Jean. *L'Église sous Pie XII: La tourmente (1939–1945).* Paris: Fayard, 1983.

Chenaux, Philippe. *Pie XII: Diplomate et pasteur.* Paris: Cerf, 2003.

Chojnowski, Andrej. "The Controversy over Former Uniate Property in Interwar Poland." *Nationalities Papers* 16, no. 2 (1988): 177–90.

Cianfarra, Camille M. *The Vatican and the War.* New York: Dutton, 1944.

Colombo, Carlo, ed. *Pio XI nel trentesimo della morte (1939–1969), raccolta di studi e di memorie.* Milan: Ufficio Studi Arcivescovile, 1969.

Conway, Martin. *Catholic Politics in Europe, 1918–1945.* London: Routledge, 1997.

Coppa, Frank J. "The Contemporary Papacy from Paul VI to Benedict XVI: A Bibliographical Essay." *Catholic Historical Review* 92, no. 4 (2006): 597–608.

———, ed. *Controversial Concordats: The Vatican's Relations with Napoleon, Mussolini and Hitler.* Washington, D.C.: Catholic University of America Press, 1999.

———. "The Hidden Encyclical of Pius XI against Racism and Anti-Semitism Uncovered—Once Again." *Catholic Historical Review* 84, no. 1 (1998): 63–72.

Coren, Michael. *Gilbert: The Man Who Was G. K. Chesterton.* New York: Paragon, 1990.

Corrin, Jay P. *G. K. Chesterton and Hilaire Belloc: The Battle against Modernity.* Athens: Ohio University Press, 1981.

Cywiński, Bohdan. *Ogniem próbowane—I: korzenie tożsamości.* Rome: Papieski Instytut Studiów Kościelnych, 1982.

Daniel-Rops, Henri. *A Fight for God, 1870–1939.* London: J. M. Dent and Sons, 1966.

Dewar, Diana. *Saint of Auschwitz: The Story of Maximilian Kolbe.* San Francisco: Harper and Row, 1982.

Duce, Alessandro. *Pio XII e la Polonia.* Rome: Studium, 1997.

Duclos, Paul. *Le Vatican et la seconde guerre mondiale.* Paris: A. Pedone, 1955.

Dunn, Dennis J. *The Catholic Church and Russia: Popes, Patriarchs, Tsars and Commissars.* Burlington, Vt.: Ashgate, 2004.

Falconi, Carlo. *The Popes in the Twentieth Century: From Pius X to John XXIII.* Boston: Little, Brown, 1967.

———. *The Silence of Pius XII.* Boston: Little, Brown, 1970.

Friszke, Andrzej. *O kształt niepodległej.* Warsaw: Więź, 1989.

Gallagher, Louis Jr. *Edmund A. Walsh, S.J.: A Biography.* New York: Benziger Brothers, 1962.

Gallahue, John. *The Jesuit.* New York: Stein and Day, 1973.

Groen, Bert, and Wil van den Bercken, eds. *Four Hundred Years Union of Brest (1596–1996): A Critical Re-evaluation.* Leuven: Peeters, 1998.

Grott, Bogumił. *Nacjonalizm i religia: Proces zespalania nacjonalizmu z katolicyzmem w jedną całość ideową w myśli Narodowej Demokracji, 1926–1939.* Kraków: Uniwersytet Jagielloński, 1984.

Grzebień, Ludwik. *Encyklopedia wiedzy o jezuitach na ziemiach Polski i Litwy, 1564–1995.* Kraków: Wydawnictwo WAM, 1996.

Halecki, Oscar, and James F. Murray Jr. *Pius XII: Eugenio Pacelli, Pope of Peace.* New York: Farrar, Straus and Young, 1954.

Harrigan, William M. "Pius XII's Efforts to Effect a Détente in German-Vatican Relations." *Catholic Historical Review* 49, no. 2 (1963): 173–91.

Hass, Ludwik. *Masoneria polska XX wieku: Losy, loże, ludzie.* Warsaw: Polczek, 1993.

Hayward, Fernand. *Un pape méconnu, Benoît XV.* Tournai: Casterman, 1955.

Hecht, Robert A. *An Unordinary Man: A Life of Father John LaFarge, S.J.* Lanham, Md.: Scarecrow, 1996.

Herling, Marta, ed. *"Polonia Restituta": L'Italia e la ricostruzione della Polonia, 1918–1921.* Milan: Centro di Studi sull'Europa Orientale, 1992.

Heydenkorn, Benedykt. "Polityczna działalność Metropolity Szeptyckiego." *Zeszyty historyczne* 72 (1985): 99–114.

Holmes, J. Derek. *The Papacy in the Modern World, 1914–1978.* London: Burns and Oates, 1981.

Jachymek, Jan, ed. *Religia i Kościół rzymskokatolicki w polskiej myśli politycznej, 1919–1933*. Lublin: Wydawnictwo Uniwersytetu Marii Curie-Skłodowskiej, 1995.

Jedin, Hubert, John Dolan, Konrad Repgen, and Gabriel Adriányi, eds. *History of the Church*. Vol. 10, *The Church in the Modern Age*. New York: Crossroad, 1981.

Jędrzejewicz, Wacław. *Józef Piłsudski, 1867–1935: Życiorys*. London: Polska Fundacja Kulturalna, 1993.

———, ed. *Kronika życia Józefa Piłsudskiego*. 3 vols. London: Polska Fundacja Kulturalna, 1977–89.

Kaiser, Wolfram, and Helmut Wohnout, eds. *Political Catholicism in Europe, 1918–1945*. London: Routledge, 2004.

Keleher, Serge. "Trapped between Two Churches: Orthodox and Greek Catholics in Eastern Poland." *Religion, State and Society* 23, no. 4 (1995): 365–72.

Kent, Peter C. "A Tale of Two Popes: Pius XI, Pius XII and the Rome-Berlin Axis." *Journal of Contemporary History* 23, no. 4 (1988): 589–608.

Kłoczowski, Jerzy. *Dzieje chrześcijaństwa polskiego*. Paris: Éditions du Dialogue, 1991.

———. *A History of Polish Christianity*. Cambridge: Cambridge University Press, 2000.

Kłoczowski, Jerzy, Lidia Müllerowa, and Jan Skarbek. *Zarys dziejów Kościoła katolickiego w Polsce*. Kraków: Znak, 1986.

Koberdowa, Irena, and Janusz Tazbir, eds. *Szkice z dziejów papiestwa*. Warsaw: Książka i Wiedza, 1989.

Korolevskij, Cyrille. *Métropolite André Szeptyckyj, 1865–1944*. Rome: Ukrainian Theological Society, 1964.

Krasowski, Krzysztof. *Episkopat katolicki w II Rzeczypospolitej*. Warsaw: Redakcja Naukowa, 1992.

Krzywobłocka, Bożena. *Chadecja, 1918–1937*. Warsaw: Książka i Wiedza, 1974.

Lenort, Feliks, ed. *Na stolicy prymasowskiej w Gnieźnie i w Poznaniu: Szkice o prymasach Polski w okresie niewoli narodowej i w II Rzeczypospolitej*. Poznań: Księgarnia Św. Wojciecha, 1982.

Lesourd, Paul. *Entre Rome et Moscou, le Jésuite clandestin, Mgr Michel d'Herbigny*. Paris: Lethielleux, 1976.

Magocsi, Paul R., ed. *Morality and Reality: The Life and Times of Andrei Sheptyts'kyi*. Edmonton: Canadian Institute of Ukrainian Studies, 1989.

Makowski, Bronisław. *Litwini w Polsce, 1920–1939*. Warsaw: Państwowe Wydawnictwo Naukowe, 1986.

Malej, Witold. "Kardynał Aleksander Kakowski w świetle własnych wspomnień." *Nasza przeszłość* 8 (1958): 243–79.

Mayeur, Jean-Marie, ed. *Histoire du Christianisme des origines à nos jours*. Vol. 12, *Guerres mondiales et totalitarismes (1914–1958)*. Paris: Desclée-Fayard, 1990.

Mendelsohn, Ezra. *The Jews of East Central Europe between the World Wars.* Bloomington: Indiana University Press, 1983.
Meysztowicz, Valérien. *L'Église Catholique en Pologne entre les deux guerres (1919–1939).* Vatican City: n.p., 1944.
Micewski, Andrzej. *Roman Dmowski.* Warsaw: Verum, 1971.
———. *Z geografii politycznej II Rzeczypospolitej.* Warsaw: Więż, 1964.
Michnik, Adam. *The Church and the Left.* Chicago: University of Chicago Press, 1993.
———. *Letters from Prison and Other Essays.* Berkeley and Los Angeles: University of California Press, 1985.
Mistewicz, Teodor. "Stosunek Romana Dmowskiego do religii i Kościoła." *Studia historyczne* 32, no. 1 (1989): 57–72.
Modras, Ronald. *The Catholic Church and Antisemitism: Poland, 1933–1939.* Langhorne, Penn.: Harwood, 1994.
Morozzo della Rocca, Roberto. *Le nazioni non muoiono: Russia rivoluzionaria, Polonia indipendente, e Santa Sede.* Bologna: Il Mulino, 1992.
Mourin, Maxime. *Le Vatican et l'URSS.* Paris: Payot, 1965.
Mysłek, Wiesław. *Kościół katolicki w Polsce w latach 1918–1939: Zarys historyczny.* Warsaw: Książka i Wiedza, 1966.
Pajewski, Janusz. *Odbudowa państwa polskiego, 1914–1918.* Warsaw: Państwowe Wydawnictwo Naukowe, 1978.
Pałyga, Edward J. *Polsko-watykańskie stosunki dyplomatyczne: Od zarania II Rzeczypospolitej do pontyfikatu papieża-Polaka.* Warsaw: Instytut Wydawniczy Związków Zawodowych, 1988.
Papierzyńska-Turek, Mirosława. *Sprawa ukraińska w Drugiej Rzeczypospolitej, 1922–1926.* Kraków: Wydawnictwo Literackie, 1979.
Passelecq, Georges, and Bernard Suchecky. *L'Encyclique cachée de Pie XI.* Paris: Découverte, 1995.
Pease, Neal. "God's Patriot: Jerzy Matulewicz as Bishop of Vilna, 1918–1925." *East Central Europe/L'Europe du Centre-Est* 18, no. 1 (1991): 69–79.
———. "Poland and the Holy See, 1918–1939." *Slavic Review* 50, no. 3 (1991): 521–30.
———. "The Polish Test: Roman Catholic Views of 20th Century Polish History." *Religion in Communist Lands* 18, no. 3 (1990): 253–61.
———. "The 'Unpardonable Insult': The Wawel Incident of 1937 and Church-State Relations in Poland." *Catholic Historical Review* 77, no. 3 (1991): 422–36.
Perejda, George J. *Apostle of Church Unity: Metropolitan Andrew Sheptytsky.* Winnipeg: Redeemer's Voice, 1960.
Peters, Walter H. *The Life of Benedict XV.* Milwaukee, Wisc.: Bruce, 1959.
Phayer, Michael. *Pius XII, the Holocaust, and the Cold War.* Bloomington: Indiana University Press, 2008.

Pike, David Wingeate, ed. *The Opening of the Second World War.* New York: Peter Lang, 1991.

Polonsky, Antony. *Politics in Independent Poland, 1921–1939: The Crisis of Constitutional Government.* Oxford: Oxford University Press, 1972.

Porter, Brian. "The Catholic Nation: Religion, Identity, and the Narratives of Polish History." *Slavic and East European Journal* 45, no. 2 (2001): 289–99.

———. *When Nationalism Began to Hate: Imagining Modern Politics in Nineteenth Century Poland.* New York: Oxford University Press, 2000.

Prus, Edward. *Władyka świętojurski, rzecz o arcybiskupie Andrzeju Szeptyckim (1865–1944).* Warsaw: Instytut Wydawniczy Związków Zawodowych, 1985.

Rędziński, Kazimierz. "Watykańscy komisarze a plebiscyt górnośląski." *Człowiek i światopogląd* 7–8 (1985): 53–66, 77–90.

Rhodes, Anthony. *The Vatican in the Age of the Dictators, 1922–1945.* New York: Holt, Rinehart and Winston, 1973.

Roche, Georges, and Philippe Saint Germain. *Pie XII devant l'histoire.* Paris: Robert Laffont, 1972.

Rossini, Giuseppe, ed. *Benedetto XV, i cattolici e la prima guerra mondiale.* Rome: Edizioni 5 Lune, 1963.

Rudnicki, Szymon. "Nacjonalizm i religia." *Przegląd historyczny* 78, no. 1 (1987): 93–100.

———. *Obóz Narodowo-Radykalny: Geneza i działalność.* Warsaw: Czytelnik, 1985.

Rychlak, Ronald J. *Hitler, the War, and the Pope.* Columbus, Miss.: Genesis, 2000.

Sadkowski, Konrad. "The Roman Catholic Clergy, the Byzantine Slavonic Rite and Polish National Identity: The Case of Grabowiec, 1931–34." *Religion, State and Society* 28, no. 2 (2000): 175–84.

Siemaszko, Z. S. "Biskup wileński (1918–1925) Matulewicz na tle ówczesnych stosunków polsko-litewsko-białoruskich." *Zeszyty historyczne* 84 (1988): 3–29.

Sierpowski, Stanisław. *Stosunki polsko-włoskie w latach 1918–1940.* Warsaw: Państwowe Wydawnictwo Naukowe, 1975.

Simon, Constantin. *Russicum: Pioneers and Witnesses of the Struggle for Christian Unity in Eastern Europe.* Vol. 2, *The First Years, 1929–1939.* Rome: Opere Religiose Russe, 2002.

Snyder, Timothy. *The Reconstruction of Nations: Poland, Ukraine, Lithuania, Belarus, 1569–1999.* New Haven, Conn.: Yale University Press, 2003.

Speaight, Robert. *The Life of Hilaire Belloc.* New York: Farrar, Straus and Cudahy, 1957.

Stehle, Hansjakob. *Eastern Politics of the Vatican, 1917–1979.* Athens: Ohio University Press, 1981.

Stehlin, Stewart A. *Weimar and the Vatican, 1919–1933: German-Vatican Diplomatic Relations in the Interwar Years.* Princeton, N.J.: Princeton University Press, 1983.

Steinlauf, Michael C., and Antony Polonsky, eds. *Jewish Popular Culture and Its Afterlife.* Polin: Studies in Polish Jewry 16. Oxford: Littman Library of Jewish Civilization, 2003.

Stępień, Stanisław, ed. *Kardynał Adam Stefan Sapieha.* Przemyśl: Południowo-Wschodni Instytut Naukowy w Przemyślu, 1995.

Szafrański, Adam Ludwik. "Augustyn Łosiński Biskup Kielecki (1910–1937) w świetle listów pasterskich, opinii i faktów." *Nasza przeszłość* 59 (1983): 215–40.

Szczudłowski, Piotr. "Polityczna działalność abpa Józefa Teofila Teodorowicz w okresie II Rzeczypospolitej." *Nasza przeszłość* 81 (1994): 115–61.

Świętek, Ryszard. "Les contacts entre la franc-maçonnerie polonaise et française (visite de Józef Piłsudski en France en 1921)." *Acta Poloniae historica* 54 (1986): 167–85.

Terej, Jerzy Janusz. *Rzeczywistość i polityka: Ze studiów nad dziejami najnowszymi Narodowej Demokracji.* Warsaw: Książka i Wiedza, 1971.

Tomaszewski, Jerzy, ed. *Najnowsze dzieje żydów w Polsce w zarysie (do 1950 roku).* Warsaw: Państwowe Wydawnictwo Naukowe, 1993.

Torzecki, Ryszard. "Z problematyki stosunków polsko-ukraińskich." *Dzieje najnowsze* 17, no. 2 (1985): 151–66.

Tretjakewitsch, Léon. *Bishop Michel d'Herbigny SJ and Russia: A Pre-ecumenical Approach to Christian Unity.* Würzburg: Augustinus Verlag, 1990.

Urban, Wincenty. *Ostatni etap dziejów Kościoła w Polsce przed nowym tysiącleciem, 1815–1965.* Rome: Hosianum, 1966.

Wapiński, Roman. *Roman Dmowski.* Lublin: Wydawnictwo Lubelskie, 1988.

Ward, Maisie. *Gilbert Keith Chesterton.* New York: Sheed and Ward, 1943.

Watt, David Cameron. *How War Came: The Immediate Origins of the Second World War, 1938–1939.* New York: Pantheon, 1989.

Weigel, George. *The Final Revolution: The Resistance Church and the Collapse of Communism.* New York: Oxford University Press, 1992.

Wenger, Antoine. *Rome et Moscou, 1900–1950.* Paris: Brouwer, 1987.

Wilk, Stanisław. *Episkopat Kościoła katolickiego w Polsce w latach 1918–1939.* Warsaw: Wydawnictwo Salezjańskie, 1992.

Wisłocki, Jerzy. *Konkordat polski z 1925 roku.* Poznań: UAM, 1977.

Wolny, Jerzy, ed. *Księga Sapieżyńska.* 2 vols. Kraków: Polskie Towarzystwo Teologiczne, 1986.

Wynot, Edward D., Jr. "Prisoner of History: The Eastern Orthodox Church in Poland in the Twentieth Century." *Journal of Church and State* 39, no. 2 (1997): 319–38.

Wyrwa, Tadeusz. "Kościół i państwo w pierwszym dziesięcioleciu PRL." *Zeszyty historyczne* 82 (1987): 59–85.

———. "Watykan a rząd polski w Angers." *Zeszyty historyczne* 72 (1985): 182–96.

Zatko, James J. *Descent into Darkness: The Destruction of the Roman Catholic Church in Russia, 1917–1923.* Notre Dame: University of Notre Dame Press, 1965.

Zieliński, Zygmunt, and Stanisław Wilk, eds. *Kościół w II Rzeczypospolitej.* Lublin: Katolicki Uniwersytet Lubelski, 1980.

Zięba, Andrzej, ed. *Metropolita Andrzej Szeptycki.* Kraków: Polska Akademia Umiejętności, 1994.

———. "Metropolita Andrzej Szeptycki." *Kwartalnik historyczny* 92, no. 4 (1985): 885–900.

Żółtowski, Paweł. "Wspomnienia o kardynale Adamie Stefanie Sapieże z okazji 60-lecia ingresu na krakowską stolicą biskupią." *Nasza przeszłość* 38 (1972): 215–49.

Index